Twelve African Writers

Gerald Moore was born in London and educated at Dauntsey's School and Cambridge. Early in 1953 he went out to Nigeria to join the Department of Extra-Mural Studies at Ibadan. Since then, he has spent some seventeen years teaching in various parts of Africa, and in Hong Kong. From 1966 to 1976 he was at Sussex University where, as Reader in English in the School of African and Asian Studies, he pioneered the study of Third World literatures as part of an integrated undergraduate programme. In 1976, Gerald Moore returned to Nigeria as Visiting Professor at the University of Ife and then spent three years at the newly-founded University of Port Harcourt. He is now Professor of English in the University of Jos.

Professor Moore began publishing criticism of African literature as long ago as 1957, when he contributed to the first number of the journal *Black Orpheus*. He also featured in the first number of *Transition*, when it appeared in Kampala in 1961. His first book, *Seven African Writers*, appeared in 1962 and was quickly followed by the popular anthology *Modern Poetry from Africa*. In 1969 he published *The Chosen Tongue*, a thematic study of Anglophone literature in Africa and the Caribbean. His full-length study, *Wole Soyinka*, was published in 1971 and revised in 1978. Apart from critical and editorial work, Professor Moore has also published translations of poetry by Tchicaya U Tam'si and J-B. Tati-Loutard, and of two major novels by Mongo Beti, *The Poor Christ of Bomba* (1971) and *Remember Ruben* (1980).

Hutchinson University Library for Africa

General Editors: Michael Crowder and Paul Richards

The Development of African Drama
Michael Etherton

The Development Process: A Spatial Perspective
Akin Mabogunje

Forced Migration: The Impact of the Export Slave Trade on African Societies
Edited by J. E. Inikori

A Handbook of Adult Education for West Africa
Edited by Lalage Bown and S. H. Olu Tomori

A History of Africa
J. D. Fage

Indigenization of African Economies
Edited by Adebayo Adedeji

Peasants and Proletarians: The Struggles of Third World Workers
Edited by Robin Cohen, Peter C. W. Gutkind and Phyllis Brazier

Rural Development: Theories of Peasant Economy and Agrarian Change
Edited by John Harriss

Rural Settlement and Land Use
Michael Chisholm

Studies in Nigerian Administration
Edited by D. J. Murray

Technology, Tradition and the State in Africa
Jack Goody

Twelve African Writers
Gerald Moore

West Africa Under Colonial Rule
Michael Crowder

West African Resistance: The Military Response to Colonial Occupation
Edited by Michael Crowder

in association with the International African Institute

Islam in Tropical Africa
Edited by I. M. Lewis

The Drums of Affliction: A Study of Religious Processes among the Ndembu of Zambia
V. W. Turner

In association with Zed Press

African Women
Christine Obbo

Twelve African Writers

Gerald Moore

Hutchinson University Library for Africa

London Melbourne Sydney Auckland

HUTCHINSON UNIVERSITY LIBRARY FOR AFRICA

Hutchinson & Co. (Publishers) Ltd

An imprint of the Hutchinson Publishing Group

17-21 Conway Street, London W1P 6JD

Hutchinson Group (Australia) Pty Ltd
30-32 Cremorne Street, Richmond South, Victoria 3121
PO Box 151, Broadway, New South Wales 2007

Hutchinson Group (NZ) Ltd
32-34 View Road, PO Box 40-086, Glenfield, Auckland 10

First published in 1980
Reprinted 1983

Set in Monotype Times New Roman

Printed in Great Britain by The Anchor Press Ltd
and bound by Wm Brendon & Son Ltd
both of Tiptree, Essex

British Library Cataloguing in Publication Data

Moore, Gerald, *b. 1924*
  Twelve African writers.
  1. African literature — History and criticism
  I. Title
  809'.896   PL8010

ISBN 0 09 141850 X cased
     0 09 141851 8 paper

Contents

Introduction   7

1   Léopold Sédar Senghor: **Assimilation or Negritude**   17

2   Ezekiel Mphahlele: **The Urban Outcast**   41

3   Sembène Ousmane: **The Primacy of Change**   69

4   Camara Laye: **The Aesthetic Vision**   85

5   Alex La Guma: **Through Suffering to Resistance**   105

6   Chinua Achebe: **Unless Tomorrow**   123

7   Tchicaya U Tam'si: **The Uprooted Tree**   147

8   Okot p'Bitek: **The Horn of the Grasslands**   171

9   Mongo Beti: **From Satire to Epic**   193

10 Wole Soyinka: **Across the Primeval Gulf**   217

11 Kofi Awoonor: **The Neglected Gods**   237

12 Ngugi wa Thiong'o: **Towards Uhuru**   263

References   289

Bibliography   301

Suggested further reading   313

Acknowledgements   317

Index   319

And it is the same breath, liquid, without acolyte,
like invisible mushrooms on stone surfaces.

And at this chaste instant of delineated anguish,
the same voice, importunate, aglow with the goddess –

unquenchable, yellow, darkening homeward
like a cry of wolf above crumbling houses –

Christopher Okigbo, 'Distances VI'

Introduction

This book started out as a revision and expansion of my *Seven African Writers*, first published in 1962. At that time, the concept of African literature was for many readers a new one. There was a general failure to connect literary activity which expressed itself in writing, with the immense riches of African oral culture. And this failure of connection could be found as often among Africans – owing to the peculiar nature of colonial education – as among Europeans. Much of the exaggerated surprise which greeted the flood of African novels and poems published in the years from 1956 onwards would have been avoided if critics had paused to reflect that their authors were not starting from scratch, even if the activity of writing, or of writing in a foreign language, was relatively new. Writing is in any case only the record of a work of literature, not the work of art itself. The researches of Albert Lord and others have made it clear that the *Iliad* and the *Odyssey*, those twin pillars of classical Western culture, were works of oral art until some scribe (probably not 'Homer' himself) had the happy idea of recording them in writing. The problems of establishing a vital connection between a rich and ancient oral tradition, expressed in languages which have special tonic and sonic qualities of their own, and the activity of writing for the page in the new languages of colonialism, are complex and daunting enough. But this does not warrant the assumption that the first generation of African writers were doing something intrinsically new. Rather, they were performing a function as ancient as African cultures themselves, but for a new market and under new conditions.

To establish this connection was only one of the tasks facing the critic. In 1962, even pioneer works like the early novels of Camara Laye, Ferdinand Oyono, Mongo Beti and Chinua Achebe were only a few years old, and were still little known in Africa itself. The names of Wole Soyinka, Christopher Okigbo or J. P. Clark were familiar only to a small circle of friends and admirers in Lagos or Ibadan. Another task before the critic was therefore one of introduction, rather than of the sort of critical comparison and analysis which requires of the reader at least a measure of familiarity with the works themselves.

Thus it quickly became apparent that what was needed nearly twenty years later was a largely new book, with different standards of selection, presentation and approach; not a work which could usefully be conceived of as a revision of one which had served its purpose in its different day. It was not just that most of the seven original writers had since greatly extended their output and their reputations. It was not even just that many new names had risen on the horizon and demanded admission. Most important were the changes in Africa itself, and in the perception and role of literature within the continent. It was no longer a question, if it ever was, of announcing a new dawn, or of persuading the reader of the existence of what was being examined. The intervening years had produced a rich crop not only of writers but of critics, theses, conference papers and teachers' notes. African literature had, in that sense, arrived. But there was still a sad parochialism about much of this activity; a tendency to laud one's local favourite as 'the greatest', without really knowing what or whom one was comparing him with.

The whole field of African literary activity is, of course, too broad to be surveyed critically by any one writer, though valiant efforts have been made by the late Janheinz Jahn, Kofi Awoonor and Ronald Dathorne, amongst others. The volume of work published in African languages now greatly exceeds that in any one of the stranger languages which have also taken root there; the latter is formidable enough, particularly in the cases of French, English and Portuguese. But the amount of work recently done in the recording and study of oral literature, stretching from epic to epigram, also demanded its meed of attention. What is pleaded for is not such a superhuman overview, but a bit more willingness to break new ground; to step beyond what have already become the 'safe' writers and risk a few comparisons which are not backed by precedent and received opinion. I would have liked to go much further in this direction had space permitted, and to have drawn attention to such new writers as Nuruddin Farah of Somalia, who is rapidly developing into an outstanding novelist; to the exciting new dramatists of Tanzania and Nigeria, such as Ebrahim Hussein, Kole Omotoso or Femi Osofisan; to the many new poets who have so greatly extended the scope of the art in Africa, especially in the urban South. But, where so many established names had to be excluded, it was difficult to justify the devotion of a whole chapter apiece to writers who are still relatively little known outside their own countries and whose work has not yet had time to display a pattern of development.

It is time, now, to state what criteria have been followed in arriving at the final selection. These may be summarized as: a representative spread between West, Central, South and East Africa; a balance between Francophone and Anglophone writers; a balance between works of poetry, fiction and drama; and an avoidance of writers who have offered us only a single work, however brilliant. In this last category one thinks of works which are themselves of major importance, such as Cheikh Hamidou Kane's *L'Aventure Ambiguë* (1962), Malick Fall's *La Plaie* (1967) and Ahmadou Kourouma's *Les Soleils des Indépendances* (1968). To have included these would have been to write a different kind of book; one which discussed individual works of distinction, rather than one attempting the situation and exploration of writers in terms of their whole output and the pattern of their development.

Every writer included here has been publishing for at least fifteen years and has shown an ability not only to write well, but to change and grow. This is certainly not to say, however, that there are no other African writers who would meet these criteria. The choice of who to put in and who to leave out has been difficult, and in the last resort there is bound to be a subjective element in such decisions. I am well aware that another critic, using these same criteria, might have come up with an entirely different list. My own must be judged on the extent of what it manages to say about the state of the literary art in Africa today.

One other consideration has been a desire to maintain some degree of continuity with *Seven African Writers*, even though what has emerged is substantially a new work. Not to have done this would have implied that there was nothing further to be said about any of the original seven. After some reflection, however, I did decide to omit two of them in favour of writers who have risen to prominence in the intervening years. David Diop was already dead when *Seven African Writers* was conceived, but his brilliant promise and ardent revolutionary fervour pleaded then for his admission in a work where the individual chapters were in any case much shorter than the present ones. In the years since his death, no further manuscripts have come to light which would add to the slim volume of poems,

Coups de Pilon (1957), on which his fame rests. The years since 1957 have, however, seen the unfolding of the entire poetic and dramatic *œuvre* of Tchicaya U Tam'si, and his claims to a place were clearly stronger. So far as Amos Tutuola is concerned, he has published a few, generally rather slight works since 1962; but I remain of the opinion that his best book, and certainly his most famous, is still *The Palm-Wine Drinkard* (1952), closely followed by *My Life in the Bush of Ghosts* (1954). To have included him again, therefore, could certainly not have been justified in terms of what he has achieved since, nor (as in the case of Senghor) in terms of his continuing influence and controversial status. That place had finally to go to a writer of the stature and topicality of Wole Soyinka.

As for the seven new names, I hope the chapters on each will sufficiently justify their selection. Probably the most difficult choice here was between Kofi Awoonor and Ayi Kwei Armah. The latter is the more controversial writer and the one whose fame has been more quickly gained. Awoonor was finally preferred because his work has been insufficiently examined as a whole. There is an enriching unity between his concerns as a poet, novelist, translator and critic which Chapter 11 attempts to explore. As another writer working in constant relationship with a specific literary tradition (the Ewe), his work offers comparison both with that tradition and with the parallel development of Okot p'Bitek, whose work is likewise a continuation and development of the poetic and musical context in which he grew up.

Nigeria presented choices less strict but no less drastic. It would have been possible to devote the entire book to Nigerian writers without stepping beyond established names. Accomplished novelists like Elechi Amadi have claims no less strong than Nigeria's poets and dramatists. Yet, as it is, Nigeria and Senegal claim a third of the whole book between them. Choice had therefore to be based on the balance of the work as a whole, not simply on intrinsic merit.

But why twelve names in all, clearly a severe restriction when the book claims a continental dimension? The answer is that I preferred longish chapters which could begin to demonstrate both the overall achievement and the development of the writers chosen. Twelve such chapters amount to a book which is substantial, but I hope not unwieldy. The past two decades have seen a proliferation of anno- tated anthologies, of critical collections by several hands (usually the product of conferences) and of works purporting to discuss the African novel or African literature as a whole. There have also been special studies devoted to single writers, such as Achebe, Ngugi, Okot, Beti, Soyinka and Senghor. The present work is intended to fall somewhere between, since it offers scope both for the critical appraisal of individual writers and for comparativity. Ideally, North and North-east Africa could have been included in this comparison, since there is more basis for it than is always recognized by campaigners for an exclusively black perspective. But this, like many other intrinsically desirable exercises, had to be left till another occasion.

In recent years there has been much debate about the critical standards which are appropriate to the discussion of African literature. One school of thought maintains that nothing written in a European language can be African anyway, which does not help us farther forward. Those who accept the validity of a modern literature written in those languages may still differ drastically about how it should be criticized. At one extreme we have critics like Eustace Palmer,[1]* who maintain that there are no other available standards than those developed in literary practice elsewhere. At the other we have those like Stanley Macebuh[2] and Isidore Okpewho,[3] who maintain that it is imperative to formulate a 'black aesthetic' (presumably for all the arts), to which any acceptable critical practice must refer. Somewhere in between comes Charles Larson,[4] who begins by recognizing unique qualities in African fiction but ends up by congratulating it on its imminent emergence into 'universality'. Thus Larson manages to recognize special qualities in African literature, but to give the impression that these are relics or traces of immaturity which must be shed during Africa's march to join something called 'Universal Literature'. But if we ask who occupies this literary Hall of Fame, we shall surely end up with writers as immitigably Russian as Dostoevsky; as immitigably American as Melville; or as immitigably French as Flaubert. In other words, the true road to universal status in literature – if such a phenomenon indeed exists – is not through the abandonment of one's cultural or national identity, but through the most intense and searching realization of it.

My own view is that the debate is not really about 'standards' at all, but about methodology. African criticism has its own formalists, its own structuralists and its own Marxists, all equally convinced of the validity of their chosen methods. But the more sophisti-

*References to each chapter appear in a section beginning on page 289.

cated modern Marxist critics, like Brecht, Macherey and Eagleton, have argued that all these methodologies, scrupulously applied, have a certain value, since all ask questions of the text which are not posed by the others. I accept this proposition, whilst agreeing also with the more basic Marxist proposition that a work of art is not and cannot ever be free from the conditioning imposed by history, class and market conditions. The type of 'pure' formalism which denies this appears to me merely silly; and I don't believe it can have anything to contribute to our understanding of African literature. The societies in which that literature has grown have never conceived of the artwork as having some sort of innate justification or reason to exist, irrespective of demand. The artist is a producer like any other; he cannot persist in carving masks when all the demand is for table-tops. To accept this is not to accept determinism, to strip the artist of all individuality and creative vision. We shall judge him by what he makes of the conditions of his time and place in the continuum of history, but we shall not ignore these conditions. As I hope the following pages will show, the development of the African artist's work has often been simply the development of this kind of historical awareness in himself.

Form, structure and ideology will therefore each be exposed or discussed where this seems likely to illuminate the work concerned. It is as absurd to start away from the political tendency of a book, pretending that it isn't or shouldn't be there, as to ignore its form or structure in favour of sternly questioning whether that tendency is 'correct' or not. In his search for significant order and his failure to find it in the flux of modern life, the artist can appear reactionary. This could be said with equal justice of writers as diverse as Yeats, Eliot, Faulkner or Golding, but we have not said enough about them when we have said only this. In *Formalism and Marxism*,[5] Tony Bennett has recently argued that the search for a Marxist aesthetic cannot be fruitful without some creative dialogue with formalist criticism. The work of Louis Althusser[6] and his followers has made such a dialogue possible and we see its fruits in works such as Macherey's *Theory of Literary Production*[7] and Eagleton's *Criticism and Ideology*.[8] So far as the aesthetics of a work are concerned, formalism still has much to tell us, just as structuralism has something to tell us about its language.

It may be necessary also to say something about terminology. The vexed word 'realism' has caused as much ambiguity in the criticism of African literature as it has elsewhere. Senghor first startles us a

little by espousing Frobenius's definition of realism as being something absolutely opposed to fact and reason:

We let ourselves be seduced by the glowing theories of Frobenius, according to which the Negro soul and the German soul are sisters. Were they
not . . . daughters of the 'Ethiopian culture', which meant 'surrender to a
paideumatic essence',* emotional capacity, and a sense of reality, while the
'Hamitic culture', with which Western rationalism is related, expressed the
desire for domination, the gift of invention and the sense of fact? . . .
Following his agitation, we stood up against the order and values of the
West, especially against its reason.[9]

The word 'seduced' here is perhaps more apt than its author
realizes, for Senghor allows himself to ignore the curious juggling
with science and history by which Frobenius divided African cultures into two antipathetic halves, which corresponded exactly to the
sort of opposition he wanted to create between German (Aryan?) ir-
rationalism and Gallic reason. Setting aside the proto-Fascist flavour
of this particular Frobenius theory, it also flies in the face of Senghor's
attempts elsewhere to establish the unity of black African cultures.
Frobenius seems rather to be arguing for the unity of 'Ethiopian'
and German cultures. It scarcely serves Senghor's general purposes
to make distinctions of this kind, within either European or African
civilizations.

According to this theory, then, realism has nothing to do with the
appearances of life and events, nor with rational causality; it is
concerned only with penetrating beneath appearance to the 'soul' or
'essence' of all phenomena. This bears a curious resemblance to what
is elsewhere called 'idealism', but African critics seem to be united
in their detestation of that word as being too 'Platonic' or 'Western'.

In his search for 'the aesthetics of old African art' Okpewho does,
however, refine considerably upon the sense of the word 'reality',
and thereby helps us to understand what Senghor may also have
meant by it. He argues that the African artist approached reality on
two different levels. There was the surface reality reflected in the
portrait sculpture of Ife, Benin and the Baluba (decorated spoons,
bowls, stools, etc.) among others. But, he goes on to say,

. . . the artist has a further level of realism for what has been called the
'spirit-regarding order'. Art critics have repeatedly called this style of art
'abstract', and that quite erroneously . . . The distinction is worth emphas-
izing, because abstraction properly belongs to an age or culture which has

Paideuma may be translated as 'the soul of a culture'.

lost all touch with the real and the concrete – an age, as it were, of 'disbelief'. But these horrendous shapes that feature both in the folklore and the visual arts are as *real* as the forests and the sequestered shrines that they inhabit.[10]

At first, this may seem to help us forward quite a bit. As a key to traditional African aesthetics it may well have its value. Okpewho's 'reality' would also embrace equally the Lagos slums of Ekwensi and the forest phantasmagoria of Tutuola or Fagunwa, which are as 'real' to their authors as the price of a room in Surulere is to Ekwensi's city-dwellers. More sober reflection, however, will show us all kinds of objections to this double-barrelled use of the term 'realism'. To begin with, the brass heads of Ife (and many of the terracottas) have been far more accurately described as 'idealized naturalism', than as portraiture. They convince us, like much of Greek sculpture, as representing the ideal of beauty in an Ife prince or princess, rather than the perhaps disappointing reality of an individual royal model. The heads are too long, too regular in proportion, too lofty and remote in expression, to suggest actual portraiture. In traditional African cultures, such as ancient Ife, realism did perhaps embrace both this kind of idealized portraiture, and the freer depiction of gods, spirits, etc., in masks and images. But one suspects that realism in the sense that the novel has given it (the sense accepted by Ekwensi, or Beti, or Sembène Ousmane, or Achebe) would have meant little to that society. The sweeping changes both in physical environment and derived value systems which characterize modern Africa, make it rather dubious to derive an aesthetic for the modern novel, for instance, from speculations about what the ancestors may have conceived as 'realism'. For most of the producers and the consumers of the African novel are far removed (further than perhaps they would like to admit) from the world which created the great masks and images of a relatively enclosed, spirit-regarding society. To use the word 'realism' in Okpewho's two senses would be to use it to include everything, which robs it of value as a critical term. In the following pages, therefore, the word will be used in its more conventional sense, as having something to do with the immediate appearances, rather than the unseen spiritual essences, of daily life. Used in that way, its meaning is close to that of naturalism; it is *representational*, although there can of course be deeper levels of realism, where the artist's insight compels us to accept the justice of what he observes, but we have missed.

Since writing the above I have read Kole Omotoso's monograph

The Form of the African Novel (Ibadan, Fagbamigbe Publishers, 1979) in which he suggests employing the term Marvellous Realism to describe those works which are penetrated with a sense of a spirit – regarding reality, rather than a materialist one. The term was first applied to certain works of Caribbean and Latin American literature by the late Alejo Carpenter, for exactly the same reasons as might justify its application to works such as Laye's *le Regard du Roi,* Tutuola's *Palm-Wine Drinkard,* Okara's *The Voice,* or Soyinka's *The Interpreters,* among many others. Realism in the conventional sense could then be applied to writers like Beti, Oyono, Ekwensi, Sembène or Ngugi.

Nor do I think it useful to dismiss the word 'abstract' as the concern only of those who 'have lost all touch with the real and the concrete'. Who are these, one is compelled to ask? Most critics will agree that there is an element of abstraction in all attempts to simplify or reinterpret form. The artist abstracts from the phenomena before him those elements of structure which seem to him important. The approach of the Baoule or Igbo artist to the human face or body does not differ essentially in this respect from Henry Moore's way with a 'Reclining Woman', or Georges Braque's with a stack of fruit, which were in any case partly inspired by the formal elements of West African sculpture. To ignore these parallels and connections is to claim altogether too much exclusiveness for the arts of Africa. The search for peculiar and immutable African values is not assisted by a refusal to admit (even on the part of some self-styled Marxists) that great changes in material conditions are bound to produce ideological and cultural changes also. No wonder heads of state prefer the sort of 'African culture' which is presented at festivals and international jamborees. Fiction, film, drama and popular song which develop from contemporary struggle are less sure of a good reception there. The critic must be careful that, in his search for a black aesthetic, he does not lend respectability to this exclusive attitude. A more scrupulous and informed criticism will serve the purpose of showing what real cultural differences survive and persist through the hurricane of change which afflicts us all.

All translations are by the author, unless otherwise indicated in the references.

Léopold Sédar Senghor

Born in Joal, Senegal, in 1906 of Serere stock, his father being a groundnut merchant and Catholic convert. Took the *baccalauréat* in Dakar and went to France in 1928, where he completed the *agrégé* and began teaching in French secondary schools. Began writing poetry and criticism in the 1930s, but published his first volume, *Chants d'Ombre*, in 1945. This was followed in 1948 by *Hosties Noires* and his anthology of black poetry, with an influential preface by Jean-Paul Sartre. Entered politics in 1948 and soon dominated Senegalese affairs, leading the country to independence in 1960, since when he has remained President of the Republic. Senghor's collected poems were published in 1973 and an important collection of essays, *Liberté 1*, in 1964.

1   Assimilation or Negritude

Léopold Sédar Senghor, whose name booms like a line of his own sonorous verse, is many things to many men. The points at which his mind or his life touch those of others are exceptionally various; as must be the case with any man who claims equal eminence as poet, scholar, and statesman. Among African presidents, Senghor shares this distinction with Agostinho Neto of Angola, a man for whom he had little political sympathy, and it must be said of both men that the policies they pursued in power are very much those we would expect from their poetry. Senghor's preoccupation with acknowledging an equal heritage from Africa and from Europe, the constant search in his poetry for the keynote of reconciliation, are the marks also of his astute but accommodating foreign policy, of his almost limitless collaboration with France. And his poetic claim to representative status, as the champion of his people, is matched by the skill with which he has dominated Senegalese political life for over twenty years. The revolutionary fire and passionate aspiration of Neto's poetry, by contrast, should also prepare us for the very different kind of struggle the Angolan people have had to undergo, and the very different political leadership they have enjoyed. It would be equally false to say of either man: 'What a pity he is a politician! It interferes with my enjoyment of him just as a poet!' For poet and politician are so deeply wedded in both of them that this sort of juxtaposition is just not possible, even if it were desirable. Both wrote like men who confidently expected to play a leading part in the affairs of their countries. It is even possible that Africa would have little time for a prominent poet who did not have such expectations.

This representative note is struck very early in Senghor's work, in these lines from 'The Return of the Prodigal Son':

Tomorrow I take the way of Europe,
    way of the ambassador
In longing for my black country.[1]

Exile, then, is seen neither as escapism nor as the search for a purely personal advantage, but as a duty and a sacrifice. It is no accident that Senghor is a Senegalese, for his career embodies the Senegalese dilemma. Alone among the West African colonies, Senegal was largely occupied by colonial troops over a hundred years ago, and subsequently became the springboard for the French conquest of the western Sudan. Under Governor Faidherbe a large area of modern Senegal was brought under direct French rule by 1865, at a time when European penetration elsewhere along the coast was a matter of scattered forts and trading stations, or such narrow coastal strips as the Lagos, Gold Coast and Sierra Leone colonies. The process of political assimilation was embarked on with the revolution of 1848, when all Africans or mulattos born in the coastal 'communes' of St Louis and Gorée were accorded French citizenship and voting rights (they sent their first mulatto Deputy to Paris that same year). After an interlude of suspension during the Second Empire, these rights were restored and the communes of Dakar and Rufisque added in the 1880s. The same period saw the establishment of a General Council for the colony, with a large proportion of black or mulatto members, and of municipal councils for Dakar and St Louis. By 1914, the four communes were able to send their first black Deputy, Blaise Diagne, to Paris, and thereafter Senegal always had black representation in the French Chamber of Deputies.

These exceptional rights, which naturally came under attack from time to time both in France and among the whites in Senegal, were jealously guarded by the 'originaires' (native-born) citizens of the communes, and the most effective way of defending them was to insists on one's *political* Frenchness, whilst preserving one's right to be a Muslim or to follow other local practices. This helps to explain how one could have Blaise Diagne telling the shocked Third Pan-African Congress in Paris in 1921, 'We French natives wish to remain French, since France has given us every liberty.'

While Diagne was expressing these sentiments, the rest of Senegal and of France's vast West and Equatorial Africa was languishing under a harsh system of administration known as the *indigénat*, coupled with forced labour and occasional drives for military conscription. The logical consequence of assimilation would have been the gradual extension of French citizenship to more and more of its inhabitants, whose number would finally exceed those of France itself, with all that this implied for political and social life there. For these reasons, as well as for an increasing belief that

Africans did, after all, have distinctive cultures and institutions of their own, the policy of political assimilation was never vigorously extended beyond the four communes. French citizenship by naturalization, however, was increasingly offered to the new Western-educated elite, both in Senegal and, later, in the other colonies. Consequently, the number of French citizens in Senegal reached 78,000 in 1936, whilst there were some 2000 elsewhere in French Africa. The object was to create a *cadre* of citizens who would be more attached to the privileges which linked them with France than to indigenous aspirations. Bernard Dadié's novel *Climbié*[2] gives a remarkably clear and frank account of this process, as applied to a tiny vanguard of students in the Ivory Coast. Senegal also had its part to play here, as most of this new elite had to go there in order to study in its *lycées* (secondary schools) or at the École William Ponty in Dakar. All higher educational and political aspirations were channelled towards Paris, since it was there alone that one could qualify for the professions, take a degree or sit as a Deputy representing one's territory. The alternative policy of 'association', which developed increasingly after 1910, was thus a means of limiting access to French citizenship rights, not an invitation to the development of nationalistic aspirations. As late as the Brazzaville Conference of 1944, all idea of eventual independence for the African colonies, at however remote a date, was categorically ruled out. What was extended to the other colonies was the right to send Deputies to Paris and to participate in French political life. It was the *loi cadre* of 1956 which finally paved the way towards effective political action by extending the franchise for the various national assemblies. Higher educational devolution began in the following year with the formation of the University of Dakar.

Assimilationist politics thus survived in the idea of centring all political aspirations upon Paris, even when the idea of extending French citizenship was played down. But assimilation also had concomitant educational and cultural effects which were more pervasive and long-lasting than the vagaries of colonial policy. There was no attempt to devise a system of education adapted to African cultures or aspirations, since the fortunate *évolué* ('evolved person') would sit side by side with French children in the local *lycée*, enjoying exactly the same syllabus. Naturally enough, this was designed to make the child think of itself as French, to admire the colonizing heroes of France (from Napoleon to Faidherbe and Lyautey), and to regard the heroes of African resistance to conquest, such as

Al-Hadj Umar and Samory, as so many misguided brigands who impeded the flow of French benevolence and civilization. Likewise, little attempt was made to encourage the study and practice of the extensive African languages of the Western Sudan, such as Manding, Wolof and Fula; education was synonymous with fluency in French.

All colonial systems are, of course, assimilationist to a certain degree, since colonial rule over others must justify itself conceptually as the rule of the better over the worse. It is the degree rather than the fact of assimilation which was so pronounced in French Africa, and which has left its mark to this day in the ambivalence of so much Francophone African policy. The stationing of French troops and aircraft in many of these countries (including Senegal) nearly twenty years after independence; the openly interventionist role of these troops in other parts of Africa, the steadfast refusal to condemn such intervention in the UN, the OAU or elsewhere; the fondness for 'dialogue' with South Africa and secret exchanges within Pretoria; the big increase in the white population of many of these countries since 1960; all these are some of the continuing effects of assimilation, and establish that it was far from a failure. Its original aim of tying the African territories perpetually to France by specific political arrangement was not fulfilled, but the demonstrations of grief by African leaders over the coffin of their 'father' General de Gaulle are the stuff of more durable links than any specific political arrangements.

The reader will forgive this excursion into Senegalese history, because without it the formation of Senghor and other intellectuals of the older generation, such as Lamine Guèye and Alioune Diop, is difficult to understand. The insistence upon African values was not seen by that generation as involving a rejection of what France had contributed to Senegalese tradition. The fusion of French and Senegalese notions of excellence helps to explain Senghor's dominance of the political scene for thirty years. He combines the eminence of the *griot* (the master of speech and of indigenous poetic tradition) with that of the scholar who has won respect elsewhere and has carried that respect back with him to his native land. When Senghor writes of himself, 'Je suis le Dyali' (I am the *griot*), he is not boasting, but stating a revealing truth about his peculiar position, for the traditional *griot* was also noted often for his political shrewdness and experience. It was partly Senghor's prestige as a kind of modern *griot* which enabled him to build a political position based on support from the rural masses rather than the urban elites who had formerly dominated Senegalese politics. His general allegiance to France did not prevent him from fighting a long campaign against French balkanization of the former West African Federation in the years 1956 to 1960. These are some of the paradoxes which characterize both Senegalese politics and Senghor's own career.

As both a beneficiary and a victim of the assimilationist educational system, Senghor felt its effects from the age of seven, or perhaps earlier, through the influence of an already *assimilé* father, a Catholic in a predominantly Moslem society, and a prosperous trader in a land of widespread poverty. The intention and the effect of the system was to distance the child step-by-step from his own culture and values, exposing him at the same time to the very real seductive power of French civilization, ranging from the tangible delights of red wine (a specially favoured import), good bread and *charcuterie* to the more rarefied ones of Voltaire's prose or Rousseau's libertarian sentiments. This alienation from oneself, coupled with the prolonged exile in France then necessary to any higher education, called forth the counter-assertion of negritude, but it was a counter-assertion made very much in the intellectual terms, as well as in the language of the conqueror. The ambivalence of Francophone African policies is one which lies also at the heart of negritude itself. Senghor is not only the leading theoretician of negritude, of the black personality and its unique qualities, but also one of the leading practitioners of those black policies which often tie Dakar, Abijan and Libreville so intimately to France that they sometimes seem only a Métro ride from Paris, rather than so many thousands of miles on the map.

To recognize this ambivalence is not to belittle Senghor as a poet, but to prepare ourselves for an understanding of the conflicting materials out of which his poetry and his life have been built. It's more than fifty years since the young Senghor arrived in France; more than forty since his first poems and critical essays began to appear. His work contains within itself much of the tension, anguish, hope and striving which characterized Senegalese and African experience during those same years.

Senghor was one of the first Africans to pursue a French academic education to a high level, and the first to complete his *agrégé*, the state qualification for teaching in senior schools. He was born in 1906 in the little coastal port of Joal, where his father was a ground-nut dealer. Joal dates back to the arrival of the Portuguese navigators on this coast in the mid fifteenth century, and Senghor has written charmingly of it in one of his earlier poems:

I remember the funeral feasts steaming with the blood of fatted herds
The noise of quarrels, the rhapsodies of the priests.
I remember the pagan voices chanting the *Tantum Ergo*
And the processions and palms and triumphal arches.
I remember the dance of the nubile girls
The chorus of wrestlers – oh! the final dance of the young men, chests
Inclined, and the shrill love-cry of the women – *Kor Siga!*[3]

In his boyhood he moved among the Serere farmers and fishermen of the district, listening to the tales of the poets and the old women about the ancient Africa which preceded the French conquest, the Africa of 'proud warriors on ancestral savannahs' (David Diop). This was a period of his life which was to achieve great significance in retrospect, a period which he is constantly opposing to the velleities of 'assimilation', using it as a kind of touchstone of original virtue and sincerity; it is his 'kingdom of childhood'. Dominant in in the memory of those years is the figure of his maternal uncle Tokô'Waly, who was his principal instructor in the traditional culture of the savannahs:

You, Tokô'Waly, you hear the inaudible
And you explain to me the signs spoken by the Ancestors in the marine
      serenity of the constellations
The Bull the Scorpion the Leopard, the Elephant the familiar fishes
And the Milky Way of the Spirits by the celestial strand which never ends.[4]

But from the age of seven Senghor began an intensive study of the French language. After some years spent in preparation for the priesthood, his outstanding promise took him to the Lycée van Vollenhoven in Dakar, which he left at the age of 22. In 1928 he sailed for France to continue his studies at the Lycée Louis-le-Grand and the Sorbonne in Paris. Here he was soon joined by Aimé Césaire, seven years his junior, and the two men began the long series of conversations and experiments which, as they saw it, prepared them for the task of 'giving a tongue to the black races'. Another acquaintance of this period was Léon Damas of French Guiana. None of these three men began to publish until the late 1930s; they had first to master the strange status of the 'assimilated' man living in a society to which he does not belong. We discover from Senghor, as later from Camara Laye, that the overwhelming impression of the star pupil from French Africa who won his way to Paris was one of isolation. Only in this new context did he discover the fallacy that had underlain his whole education: he was not and could never be a Frenchman. He had therefore to settle down and rediscover what it was to be an African. To this task he was able to bring all the intellectual curiosity, the mastery of language and the knowledge of literature which were the abiding and noble parts of the education he had been given. The supreme irony of 'assimilation' is that it has inadvertently contributed more than anything else to this process – the rediscovery of Africa.

The search for 'Africanity' can take a form as simple as Senghor's poem 'Totem':

I must hide him in my innermost veins
The Ancestors whose stormy hide is shot with thunder and lightning
My animal protector, I must hide him
That I may not break the barriers of scandal.
He is my faithful blood which demands fidelity
Protecting my naked pride against
Myself and the scorn of luckier races.[5]

It can also assume the length and complexity of Césaire's *Cahier* or Damas's *Black Label*. The style which Senghor made for himself actually owes little to the scornful whiplash of Césaire's poetry, or to the staccato lines and typographical tricks of Damas, inspired partly by the latter's reading of American poetry. But Césaire undoubtedly exercised a powerful and liberating influence on Senghor through his intellect and personality, an influence which Senghor has generously acknowledged in his memorable 'Letter to a Poet':

To you beloved Brother and friend, my abrupt and brotherly salute!
From the black-backed gulls, the canoers of the deep seas I have tasted
    your news
Mingled with spices, with the odorous sounds of Rivieras of the South and
    the Islands. . . .

Your music charms me across the years, under the cinders of your eyelids
That glowing warmth towards which we stretched our hearts and hands of
    yesterday!
Have you forgotten your special honour, which is to sing
Of Ancestors, Princes and Gods, not of flowers or dewdrops? . . .

In the dark pits of my memory, I touch
Your face, where I drink waters that assuage my long regret.
You recline royally, leaning upon the cushion of a bright Hill,
Your body presses the earth which the tom-toms
Scarcely shake, your song fills the watery plains and your verse breathes
    like the night and the distant sea.

You sing the Ancestors and the true Princes
You break a star from the sky
Just for cross-rhythm; and the poor throw at your naked feet
The rough mats of their year's earnings
And the women their amber hearts and the dance of their torn souls.
My friend, my friend you are coming!
I will await you – the harbour master knows – there under the lemon trees.
You will come to the feast of our expectation! When the soft light of sunset
    falls over the roofs
And the athletes display their youth, decked like fiancés, you will be here.[6]

Curiously, despite the passionate warmth of this poem, Senghor casts Césaire very much in his own image; for it is the African poet who more habitually sings of 'Ancestors, Princes and Gods' and whose verse 'breathes like the night'. Césaire is far more the poet of blazing tropical noon, of volcanic menace and the dry crack of the tornado.

Perhaps the rhetorical and dramatic tradition of French verse then offered more scope to African poetic gifts than the somewhat quieter and more introspective English tradition. Or perhaps English poetry was not in a condition just at this time to assist writers who felt they had something big and urgent to say. Whatever the explanation, the body of excellent black poetry in French, whether African or Afro-Caribbean, far exceeded that in English. By 1958 there were still no Anglophone poets in Africa or the West Indies whom one could think of putting in the class of Paul Niger and Guy Tirolien of Guadaloupe, Léon Damas of Guiana, Aimé Césaire of Martinique, Jacques Roumain or Roussan Camille of Haiti, Senghor and David Diop of Senegal. Nor had any of the English-speaking poets attained the position in literary circles that these writers enjoyed. This divorce between the literary and public worlds has largely remained a characteristic of independent Anglophone Africa, just as countries like Angola, Cameroun, Congo and Senegal have continued to give high honour and public office to many of their writers.

Senghor, then, was able to find his literary bearings in company with other black poets – though none of them was African – who shared some of his preoccupations. With Césaire he began to develop the new literary programme of negritude, which demanded of its poets a strong verbal rhythm, a wealth of African allusions and a general exaltation of 'the African personality'. The true past of the black man must be rediscovered beneath the layers of colonial history, his culture vindicated, and his future prepared. Senghor alone, however, insisted upon the musical aspect of rhythm, even demanding that his poetry should be recited to the accompaniment of African instruments. Almost at once we find him creating, through the use of the long line, that rolling, deep-breathed sound which distinguishes all his verse. To give a true idea of this quality it is necessary to quote him in French. Here is the opening of his poem 'Nuit de Sine' (Night of Sine):

Femme, pose sur mon front tes mains balsamiques, tes mains douces plus
    que fourrure.
Là-haut les palmes balancées qui bruissent dans la haute brise nocturne
A peine. Pas même la chanson de nourrice.
Qu'il nous berce, le silence rythmé.
Écoutons son chant, écoutons battre notre sang sombre, écoutons
Battre le pouls profond de l'Afrique dans la brume des villages perdus.[7]

[Woman, rest on my brow your balsam hands, your hands gentler than fur.
The tall palm trees swinging in the night wind
Hardly rustle. Not even cradle songs.
The rhythmic silence rocks us.
Listen to its song, listen to the beating of our dark blood, listen
To the beating of the dark pulse of Africa in the mist of lost villages.]

The English is lighter, more staccato. The full bass of 'écoutons battre notre sang sombre' cannot be struck even in the best translation, though Senghor always reads well in English because the flow of his imagery is not lost.

All the poems quoted so far are from *Chants d'Ombre* (Songs of Shadow), Senghor's first book, published in 1945. Many of the poems in this collection, however, must have been written during the late 1930s, and their publication was held up by the war. There is no flavour of the apprentice about this work; Senghor's distinctive music moves all through it and his mastery of French is already absolute. There has been much controversy about the sources of inspiration for the long, unrhymed and irregular lines which are essential to the peculiar effect of his poetry. On the one extreme, Reed and Wake assert in their introduction to *Senghor: Prose and Poetry*:

His poetry, though it draws on traditional themes at times and even traditional African modes of expression, is essentially French poetry in a particular tradition. Paul Claudel is perhaps the greatest poet in this tradition of free-verse writing which makes use of the long copious line or *verset*, is fond of elemental imagery, unafraid of rhetoric, repetition and direct effects with heavily evocative words.[8]

On the other side, the late Janheinz Jahn argued in his *History of Neo-African Literature* that these 'traditional African modes of expression' (admitted by Reed and Wake, and somewhat at odds with their thesis) are precisely what predominates in Senghor's poetry. The parallelism of his praise poems, the constant address to the person or object praised, the imagery which continually evokes the history and heroic legends of Senegal, are all features derived from the *griot* traditions of the region, rather than from anything in French poetry. Jahn even goes so far as to say that the rhythm of Senghor's verse is derived from that of Serere praise poetry, and somehow survives the transition from its original language to one of totally different characteristics. Abiola Irele, whose book gives the best available account of Senghor's prosody, has also given the best summary of his practice:

He has forged a personal style by the integration of the formal structure of French poetry, and the intrinsic qualities of the French language itself, with elements borrowed from the oral poetry of his native land, rendering more adequately his individual feeling for the African universe he explores.[9]

It is best to stick to what is certain. The qualities attributed to the praise poems by Jahn are undeniably present there, and are certainly common qualities in the *griot* tradition. But it must be remembered that Senghor's higher studies in Senegal and Paris, ranging from 1922 to 1935, were entirely confined to French and Classical languages and literatures. It would be surprising if he had escaped the influence of Claudel, one of the dominant poets of the epoch and a kind of literary saint to those who shared his deep Catholic piety. Certainly, Claudel's *verset* must have shown him how French verse could be liberated from the classical tradition, with its strict rules of rhyme and number, and made to produce an entirely different, more flexible music. To illustrate what the argument is about, we might look at the opening lines of Claudel's 'Ballade' and then at those of Senghor's 'Chant de Printemps'. First the Claudel:

Les négociateurs de Tyr et ceux-là qui vont à leurs affaires aujourd'hui
    sur l'eau dans les grandes imaginations mécaniques,
Ceux que le mouchoir par les ailes de cette mouette encore accompagne
    quand le bras qui l'agitait a disparu,

Ceux à qui leur vigne et leur champ ne suffisait pas, mais Monsieur avait
   son idée personele sur l'Amérıque,
Ceux qui sont partis par toujours et qui n'arriveront pas encore. . . .[10]

[The Tyrian merchants and those who go on business today over the water
   in great mechanical imaginings,
Those whom the handkerchief still accompanies through the wings of this
   seagull when the arm that waved it has disappeared,
Those for whom their vine and their field were not sufficient, but the
   gentleman had his own ideas about America,
Those who have gone for ever and will never arrive either. . . .]

Now the Senghor:

Des chants d'oiseaux montent lavés dans le ciel primitif
L'odeur verte de l'herbe monte, Avril!
J'entends le souffle de l'aurore émouvant les nuages blancs de mes rideaux
J'entends la chanson du soleil sur mes volets mélodieux
Je sens comme une haleine et le souvenir de Naëtt sur ma nuque nue qui
   s'émeut
Et mon sang complice malgré moi chuchote dans mes veines.
C'est toi mon amie – ô! Écoute les souffles dans l'avril d'un autre contin-
   ent
Oh! Écoute quand glissent glacées d'azur les ailes des hirondelles migratrices
Écoute le bruissement blanc et noir des cigognes a l'extrème de leurs voiles
   deployées
Écoute le message du printemps d'un autre âge d'un autre continent
Écoute le message de l'Afrique lointaine et le chant de ton sang!
J'écoute la sève d'Avril qui dans tes veines chante.[11]

[The song of the birds rises all washed into the pristine sky
The green smell of the grass rises, April!
I hear the breath of dawn blowing the white clouds of my curtains
I hear the song of the sun melodious on my shutters
I feel something like a breath and the memory of Naëtt on my naked neck
   which trembles
And my accomplice blood whispers in my veins despite me.
It is you my love – Oh! Listen to the gusts already warm in the April of
   another continent
Oh! Listen when the wings of migrating swallows glide frozen with blue-
   ness
Listen to the rustling white and black of the storks at the extremity of their
   outstretched wings
Listen to the springtime message of another age another continent
Listen to the message of distant Africa and the song of your blood!
I hear the sap of April chanting in your veins.]

It is scarcely necessary to note the parallelism of this poem or the unrelating ardour of its address, but the structure of this opening stanza is interesting for other features also. We may note that lines 3–6 celebrate the poet's own sensations of spring as he lies abed in Paris, whereas lines 7–11 celebrate the sensations of the distant girl Naëtt in the hot grip of an African spring. The transition from him to her is made in line 7, where he identifies the tingling in his blood with her memory, and is reinforced in the next line by the image of the migratory birds whose wings are 'frozen' by the intense azure of a tropical sky. In line 12 the transition is made back to the poet, but it is made in such a way as to unite the two worlds of the poem in a single image. The parallelism in fusing the world of Africa and infancy with that of responsibility and exile is a constant feature of Senghor's poetry right down to *Éthiopiques* (1956), though it is not always accomplished with the same brilliance and energy as it is here.

Turning from the Senghor to the Claudel, we note that the latter's poetry is much busier; each line says a great deal and says it rather fast, compared with the slow musical roll of the African poet, who is passionate without being hurried. Senghor seems to attach more importance to the purely musical qualities of his verse, making more use of alliteration, assonance and repetition. Claudel's poise is ironic and somewhat patrician, whereas Senghor's is sensuous and eager. In a word, whatever the formal resemblances, the content and character of the two poems are as different as they could be.

In *Chants d'Ombre* Senghor had already asserted not only his personal music but the major preoccupations which haunt his verse to this day. Chief among these is his insistence on communion with the dead, with the ancestors and defeated princes of his people, from whom his own education sought to isolate him. How far this is a poetic attitude, how far a deep conviction, it is impossible to say. Senghor, in any case, has expressed unforgettably the classical African view of the dead as the principal force controlling the living, benevolent but watchful. In a poem like 'In Memoriam', he invokes the dead from his lonely exile in Paris, seeking to draw strength from their company and example:

It is Sunday.
I fear the crowd of my brothers with stony faces.
From my tower of glass filled with pain, the nagging Ancestors
I gaze at roofs and hills in the fog
In the silence – the chimneys are grave and bare.

At their feet sleep my dead, all my dreams are dust
All my dreams, the liberal blood spills all along the streets, mixing with the
    blood of the butcheries.
And now, from this observatory as from a suburb
I watch my dreams float vaguely through the streets, lie at the hills' feet
Like the guides of my race on the banks of Gambia or Saloum,
Now of the Seine, at the feet of these hills.[12]

Here the dead serve as a bridge between Senghor and everything
which his education has turned him away from. By mingling the
names of the Seine, the river of Paris, with those of his homeland
(Sine, Gambia, Saloum) he stresses the universality of their presence.
Looking out from his attic window, he suddenly sees the blood of the
French conquest filling the narrow streets; but he sees also the
presence which can reconcile him with his strange white brothers. It
is to the dead, or in other poems, to his mother, that he seeks to
justify his present life, his present interests, his apparent immersion
in the affairs of a Parisian savant:

Be Blessed, Mother!
I will not send the East Wind over these sacred images as over the sands of
    the road.
You do not hear me when I hear you, like an anxious mother who forgets
    to push Button A
But I will not efface the footprints of my father or of my father's fathers in
    this head open to all the winds and plunders of the North.
Mother, in this study lined with Latin and Greek, breathe the fumes of the
    evening victims of my heart.
May the protecting spirits save my blood from slackening like that of the
    assimilated and the civilized!

Though I come late, I stand upright before the Ancestors and offer one
    chicken without stain, so that before the milk and millet beer
May spurt upon me and my fleshy lips the warm salt blood of a bull in the
    prime of his life, in the splendour of his fatness![13]

This, then, is 'negritude upright'. With this key Senghor has un-
locked his lips and sent forth a river of rich sombre melody. Yet
as we read on into his second volume, *Hosties Noires* (*Black Wafers*,
1945), we do begin to wonder how far Senghor's negritude can be
seen as embodying what Wole Soyinka has called a genuine 'self-
apprehension', an untrammelled apprehension of himself as an
African.[14] Sometimes it seems to contain a suspiciously large element
of apprehension in terms of the Other. It must be remembered that
Senghor's early years in Paris coincided with those in which many

white scholars, such as Maurice Delafosse, Georges Balandier and Marcel Griaule, were saying the same sort of things about black personality and civilization that Senghor was saying. Even Catholic racist writers like Charles Maurras were at least in agreement about the profound differences between white and black cultures, even if they went on to rationalize from this a hierarchy of values with France at the top. But the whole tendency of Senghor's mind is towards synthesis rather than separation. Having established the unique qualities of African cultures, his desire is not to hold them in isolation, but to pool them in what he calls 'The Civilization of the Universal'. This notion, derived in part from the biologist Teilharde de Chardin, regards human cultures as organic and evolutionary, with a tendency to combine themselves into new wholes.

It seems that Senghor's construct of 'La Civilization Négro-Africaine' (Black African Civilization), a construct made up essentially in exile, is built not only out of materials remembered from his childhood, but out of his reactions to such writers as those just mentioned. It is partly an argument with Europe, rather than a free, spontaneous expression; and perhaps this is inevitable, because Senghor's public life in these years was frequently one of argument. As a professor of French language and literature in the *lycées* of Tours and Paris, a position which he occupied from 1935 to 1940, the poet must have felt the continual need to assert his difference if he were not to sink entirely into the imposed role of a Black Frenchman. Such an assertion, though humorously made, can be found in the poem, 'Que M'accompagne Koras et Balafong' ('Let Koras and Balafong Accompany Me'), written during those years:

My lambs, you my affection with those eyes which will never see my age
I was not always a shepherd of blond heads on the arid plain of your books
Not always a good public servant, deferent to his superiors
Good colleague polite elegant – and the gauntlets? – smiling laughing
　　rarely
Old France old University, the whole rosary told over,
My childhood, my lambs, is old as the world and I am young as the
　　eternally young dawn of the world.
The poetesses of the shrine nourished me
The griots of the King sang to me the true legend of my race to the sound
　　of lofty koras.[16]

But in *Hosties Noires* the poet's position has become still more ambivalent than that of the black shepherd of blond heads, for if Senghor was not obliged to remain in France after his graduation (he had not yet entered parliamentary politics), he carried his allegiance to the French part of his heritage still further by taking French citizenship and by volunteering to fight a war which many black intellectuals regarded as an irrelevance, except in so far as it might indirectly further African liberation. Just how irrelevant the immediate struggle was to that liberation was brutally illustrated on VE Day, 15 May 1945, when French planes and machine-guns decimated a hostile Algerian demonstration in the streets of Setif – a demonstration sparked off by all the heady talk of freedom and justice which then filled the air. This was only a prelude to the eight-year colonial wars in Indo-China (1946–54) and Algeria (1954– 62).

Senghor, who swiftly found himself a prisoner-of-war in German hands, could only mourn the thousands of Senegalese riflemen who fell on the battlefields of Europe, as others were later to fall in Indo-China and Algeria, fighting in what was now quite clearly the imperial interest of France. But, despite the warmth and compassion of these poems, perhaps he might have done better to tell the soldiers, as Léon Damas had already done, to 'go and invade Senegal!'[16]

It is these anomalies which make much of the more public, less personal poetry of *Hosties Noires* difficult to read, and which culminate in the last stanzas of the closing poem, 'Prayer for Peace'. After enumerating some of the worst colonial excesses of France and Europe, Senghor cries:

Ah! Lord, free my memory from this
    France which is not France, this mask
    of pettiness and hate on the face of France
This mask of pettiness and hate for which I have
    nothing but hate – but I am
    allowed to hate Evil
For I have a great weakness for France.
Bless this strangled people who twice knew
    how to free their hands and dared
    proclaim the advent of the poor to royalty
Who made the slaves of the day into men
    free equal fraternal
Bless this people who have brought me Your
    Good News, Lord, and opened my
    heavy eyelids to the light of faith.
They have opened my heart to knowledge of the
    world, showing me the rainbow in the new faces of my brothers.[17]

No, however we may strive to explain such lines historically, they cannot but jar upon the contemporary ear. Here, as elsewhere in *Hosties Noires*, Senghor's perpetual search for reconciliation has betrayed him; he appears before us with a paper dagger and an ingratiating smile. It is assimilation rather than negritude which triumphs in such writing.

His poetry is often at its best when he abandons the search for reconciliation and is content to register a single emotion without too much care for the consequences. The love poems of *Chants pour Naëtt* (Songs for Naëtt) (1949) have this quality of abandon and seem to derive a lot of their rhythmic energy from it. Senghor's verse here moves faster than usual and his imagery glows with an extraordinary warmth:

I will pronounce your name Naëtt, I will declaim you, Naëtt!
Naëtt, your name is mild like cinnamon, it is the fragrance in which the
   lemon grove sleeps,
Naëtt, your name is the sugared clarity of blooming coffee trees
And it resembles the Savannah, that blossoms forth under the masculine
   ardour of the midday sun.
Name of dew, fresher than shadow of tamarind,
Fresher even than the short dusk, when the heat of day is silenced.
Naëtt, that is the dry tornado, the hard clap of lightning,
Naëtt, coin of gold, shining coal, you my night, my sun!
I am your hero, and now I have become your sorcerer, in order to pro-
   nounce your names.
Princess of Elissa, banished from Futa on the fateful day.[18]

A different but equal satisfaction can be found in a poem like 'New York' from *Ethiopiques* (1956). This achieves a completely acceptable stance of negritude by its sincere and illuminating opposition of downtown Manhattan and Harlem. The structure of this poem is extremely successful, with its explosive opening, its gradual mounting sense of dry sterility, its sudden transition to the refreshing warmth and smell of Harlem, and the splendid broad gesture which ends it: For reasons of space, I will quote only a few lines from each of these movements:

NEW YORK

New York! At first I was confused by your beauty, by those great golden
   long-legged girls.
So shy at first before your blue metallic eyes, your frosted smile
So shy. And the anguish in the depths of sky-scraper streets

Lifting eyes hawkhooded to the sun's eclipse.
Sulphurous your light and livid the towers with heads that thunderbolt the
  sky
The sky-scrapers which defy the storms with muscles of steel and stone-
  glazed hide.
But two weeks on the bare sidewalks of Manhattan
 – At the end of the third week the fever seizes you with the pounce of a
  leopard
Two weeks without rivers or fields, all the birds of the air
Falling sudden and dead on the high ashes of flat roof-tops. . . .
Nights of insomnia oh nights of Manhattan! So agitated by flickering
  lights, while motor horns howl of empty hours
And while dark waters carry away hygienic loves, like rivers flooded with
  the corpses of children.

II

Harlem Harlem! Now I saw Harlem! A green breeze of corn springs up
  from the pavements ploughed by the naked feet of dancers
Bottoms waves of silk and sword blade breasts, water-lily ballets and
  fabulous masks.
At the feet of police horses roll the mangoes of love from low houses
And I saw along the sidewalks streams of white rum streams of black milk
  in the blue fog of cigars. . . .

III

New York! I say to you: New York let black blood flow into your blood
That it may rub the rust from your steel joints, like an oil of life
That it may give to your bridges the bend of buttocks and the suppleness
  of creepers. . . .

There are your rivers murmuring with scented crocodiles and mirage-eyed
  manatees. And no need to invent the Sirens.
But it is enough to open the eyes to the rainbow of April
And the ears, above all the ears, to God who out of the laugh of a saxo-
  phone created the heaven and the earth in six days.
And the seventh day he slept the great sleep of the negro.[19]

A similar strength and wholeness are achieved when Senghor turns
aside from his long love affair with France, from his obsession with
being 'Ambassador of the Black Peoples', and plunges himself into
communion with his childhood, with his native landscape, with the
broad night of the savannah, with all that he associates with his
ancestors. Here the poet has no need to justify or excuse anything.
He is serene, and this serenity fills his verses with its quiet music. In
such a mood Senghor's sincerity marks the page and he writes

unforgettably. The following lines are taken from *Ethiopiques*, a volume in which too much space is devoted to lamentations of exile – and now it is exile *from* Europe that the poet is lamenting, exile from all that is symbolized by 'the Princess de Belfort' (a synonym for his second wife, a Norman aristocrat). But in this extract of his poem, 'Pour Khalam' Senghor breaks free from all that, and redis-covers his purest vein of introspection:

I don't know when it was, I always confuse childhood with Eden
As I mix up Death and Life – a bridge of kindness joins them.

Now I was returning from Fa'oye, having drunk at the solemn tomb
As the Manatees drink at the fountain of Simal.
Now I was returning from Fa'oye, and horror was at its height
And it was the hour when we see the Spirits, when the light is transparent
And we must leave the pathways, to evade their brotherly and mortal clasp,
The soul of a village beat in the distance. Was it of the Living or the Dead?[20]

Notable also in *Ethiopiques* is the stronger drive of Senghor's rhythm, which now develops a shorter breath and a more regular fall. His poem 'L'Absente' yearns for the coming of spring to the dry savannah and equates it with the long-predicted arrival of the Queen of Saba ('The Absent') from the East. Perhaps this Ethiopian figure symbolizes for him the integration of his Christian faith and his African identity, just as the rape of Ethiopia in 1935–6 symbolizes the continued spoliation of the continent:

Puisque reverdissent nos jambes pour la dance de la moisson
Je sais qu'elle viendra la Très-Bonne-Nouvelle,
Au solstice de Juin comme dans l'an de la défaite et dans l'an de l'espoir.
La précèdent de longs mirages de dromadaires, graves des essences de sa
     beauté.
La voilà l'Ethiopienne, fauve comme l'or mur incorruptible comme
     l'or. . . .[21]

[Because our legs grow green for the harvest dance
I know that she is coming the Ever-Good-News,
At the June solstice as in the year of defeat and in the year of hope.
Preceded by long mirages of dromedaries, heavy with the essence of her
     beauty.
Behold the Ethiopian Queen, savage as ripe gold incorruptible as gold. . . .]

Here the more regular fall of the metre is countered by the forward rush of the poem. But turning from *Éthiopiques* to *Nocturnes* (1961), one is conscious of a certain slackening of energy. Nowhere is this more evident than in the poet's decision to republish the *Chants pour Naëtt*, originally issued in 1949 in honour of his black wife Ginette Eboué, and to suppress all mention of their original subject, Naëtt. The effect is to render the poems less compelling as the expression of a passionate lyrical urge.

Also, the five Elégies which follow the love-songs, and complete the volume, despite a sombre richness of sound, do occasionally collapse into unabashed nostalgia and escapism. 'The splendour of honours is like a Sahara', cries the poet in 'Elégie de Minuit' (Elegy of Midnight) and, after lamenting his inability to find rest either in his books or in sexual love, he pleads that he may be:

born again into the Kingdom of Childhood
    rustling with dreams
Let me be the shepherd to my shepherdess
    by the sea-flats of Dyilor where the Dead flourish. . . .[22]

The tendency of these poems is more and more in divergence from the tendency of his actual life-style, for the Presidential Palace in Dakar represents a more drastic exile from the Kingdom of Childhood than even his Parisian exile did. The poetry has become compensation for the time and energy his public life now consumes.

The composition of the Elégies coincides with the years 1957 to 1959, when Senghor was becoming almost entirely absorbed in affairs of state, and when he was fighting vainly to arrest the deliberate balkanization of West Africa by the French government by means of the *loi cadre*, which encouraged the growth of petty 'independent' territories, relying heavily on French military and financial support. His success in dominating Senegalese political life for twenty years has been marred by his failure to achieve a wider association with his neighbours, even if one doubts whether the achievement of a greater federation would significantly have altered the conservative and pro-French bent of his foreign policy.

These twenty years of power, though rich in policy statements and refinements of his theoretical position, have been thin in poetry. But what poet has not found public life to be the enemy of the muse? The harvest of those years, at any rate, is represented by the thirty short poems published with his collected volume in 1973, as 'Lettres de l'Hivernage'. The title can only be translated as 'Letters of the Rainy Season', since Senghor specifically tells us that, in his region, 'l'Hivernage' is not winter, but summer and the advent of autumn. He now addresses Africa, not as a poet, but as a statesman. Hence, the quieter, more domestic tone of these poems, which no longer carry the burden of the writer's hopes, ambitions and concerns. They do not merely express escapism, as happened occasionally with the Elégies, but they are an escape by their very nature from the incessant anxiety and activity of statesmanship:

'What are you doing? What are you talking about? Of whom?'
You ask again and again.
Nothing is more melodious than the hundred metres sprinter
Than those long arms and legs, like pistons of shiny olive.

Nothing is stronger than the nude bust, the harmonious triangle of Kaya-Magan
Shooting the charm of his lightning.

If I swim like a dolphin, erect the South Wind
It is for you I walk in the sand, like a dromedary

I am not the king of Ghana, nor the runner of the hundred metres.
Now you will write me no more 'What are you doing?' . . .

For I think of nothing, my eyes drink the blueness, rhythmically;
If not of you, like the black wild duck with white belly.[23]

Leaving aside that the final image is not very flattering, the contrast could hardly be greater between this quietist poetry and that of his maturity, in which the poet claimed the right to sing for his people, to be their *dyali* (griot).

Senghor once defended himself from the charge of exoticism in a somewhat mannered essay, 'As the Manatees go to Drink at the Source'. There he argued that he was writing primarily for an African audience, to whom such words as *kora, balafong, dyali* and *khalam* were familiar. If they were exotic to the French reader, that was not his concern. They were not in intention picturesque, but descriptive;

For all is sign and sense at the same time for the African Negro; each being, each thing; but also the matter, the form, the colour, the smell and gesture and rhythm and tone and timbre: the colour of the lappa, the shape of the kora, the design of the bride's sandals, the steps and gestures of the dancer, the mask and so on.[24]

Reading such passages, the suspicion grows that what Senghor is describing is the unifying faculty of the artist in man, not specifically in African man. The enemies of spontaneity and passion move amongst us all, and they do not always carry white masks. But Senghor's claim that he writes primarily for his people, although dismissed by Reed and Wake, has perhaps been validated by events. When he began writing in Paris over forty years ago, it is probable that his readership, beyond the immediate circle of his friends, was largely French. But with the spread of literacy in French over those same years, with the public readings which are a feature of his life in Dakar, with the ascent of Senghor himself to a position of international fame, it seems likely that his poetry is now and will for many years remain among the best known in Africa.

It is his achievement to have built a poetic career out of tensions which might have destroyed him: out of loneliness and alienation, the brilliant seductive charm of Paris, the deep strong pull of Africa, the disaster of war, the emerging hope of new nations bloodily crushed from Vietnam to Tananarivo, crushed more often than not by his conscripted fellow-countrymen, for whom he has written so eloquently in his poem 'Assassination':

The great song of your blood will vanquish machines and cannons
Your liquid speech, evasions and lies.
No hate in your soul void of hatred, no cunning in your soul void of cunning.
O black martyrs immortal race, let me speak the words of pardon.[25]

Those who come to Europe now as representatives of a free people, as members of a warm confident army of students or delegates, may well stick the label 'frenchified' across the works of this African who loves Paris, who has let the heritage of Europe flood his being, who has taken a French wife and embraced the Catholic faith. But if they wish to understand the dilemma of those who preceded them forty years ago, they may read of it in the work of this 'cultural mulatto', to use his own label. Their problems of identification will be different, perhaps easier. Senghor has left a monument to his which cannot be ignored. He has left it in those poems of reconciliation like 'Paris in the Snow', where reconciliation is stated and not merely pleaded for. He has left it in poems like 'New York' and 'Night of Sine' which move in a single direction to a point of discovery and repose. He has created a new music and expressed within it a new dilemma, a whole life.

To summarize Senghor's achievements as a poet is no easy task, since his creative work spans four decades, decades which have seen drastic and successive changes in the horizon of African possibilities.

It is well to remember that in the late 1930s, when Senghor's first poems were written, no one in any part of Africa was talking about total independence; the talk everywhere was of greater autonomy within a specific 'family of nations'. The radical of today builds, often unconsciously, upon the changes in sensibility which have preceded him. Whoever writes in English, French or Portuguese, with whatever originality or ingenuity, is forced to compromise to some extent with the language he selects (or, as Senghor once put it, is selected by). Even if he rejects that compromise, and writes in his own tongue, he cannot return imaginatively to a pristine Africa which stands outside the modern consciousness. In this connection, we might look at the words of another poet of a more recent generation, the late Christopher Okigbo:

I belong, integrally, to my own culture, to my own society, just as, I believe, I belong to societies other than my own. The truth is that the modern African is no longer a product of an entirely indigenous culture. The modern sensibility which the African poet is trying to express is by its very nature complex; and it has complex values, some of which are indigenous, some exotic, some traditional, some modern.[26]

This eminently sensible view will offend the cultural purists, but it may help us to understand why a poetry like Senghor's, which is consciously situated between African and Western cultures, is not necessarily weakened or invalidated thereby. What is true of Senghor is true equally of Senegal herself, and we can hardly demand of a poet that he be more authentic than the country which produced him and whose voice he aspires to be. Senghor is in that sense indisputably a national poet, one whose work is intimately involved with the re-emergence of Senegal as a nation and is familiar to every citizen who cares for literature. The criticisms of his work which we have registered must be measured against that kind of assessment.

Ezekiel Mphahlele

Born 1919 in the slums of Pretoria. After an impoverished childhood made his way to St Peter's School, Johannesburg, and the Kilnerton Institution. Began teaching and took his BA and MA externally from the University of South Africa. Left teaching in protest against the Bantu Education Act and worked for *Drum* Magazine. His first book of stories, *Man Must Live*, appeared in 1947. Ten years later he left South Africa for Nigeria and began twenty years of wandering exile, ending with his return to South Africa in 1978. His most famous book, the autobiography *Down Second Avenue*, appeared in 1959, whilst he was working in Nigeria. His first critical work, *The African Image*, followed in 1962.

2 The Urban Outcast

The advent of Ezekiel Mphahlele's first book, *Down Second Avenue* (1959), at the same moment that West African writing was beginning to assert itself, was a challenge to the understanding both of Western readers and of African readers themselves. There is hardly a single generalization which could be made about the predominantly peasant culture of West, East or Central Africa which would be equally applicable to the urban, industrialized Africa for which Mphahlele spoke. This Africa of vast segregated modern cities, mine-dumps, skyscrapers and jazz-clubs was as alien and remote to the Nigerian or Senegalese reader of that time as Dallas or Harlem might have been. But the challenge to South African understanding by the new West African writers was equally great, for there was an almost insuperable temptation for them to lump together the tropical cultures of Africa as 'backward' (and perhaps backward-looking), because of certain characteristics which they shared with the rural and tribal remnants of South Africa itself – remnants often dismissed as 'blanket-Africans' by the city-dweller.

In truth, the black man in urban South Africa had then more in common with the North American blacks than with his neighbours in tropical Africa. Like the black American, he inhabits a society which is dominated by whites in a far grimmer and more universal sense than any tropical colony has ever been. And this domination is expressed not merely in the colonial ritual and pantomime satirized during that same decade by Mongo Beti, Ferdinand Oyono and Chinua Achebe, but in every department of his daily life. His residence, his movements, his place and grade of work, his education, his sexual and family life are all subject to intense regulation, all governed by an alien mythology about the black man's place in the natural scheme of things. He cannot even walk down a street at certain hours without breaking the law. An outcast in his own country, he has to scrutinize every doorway, every bench, every counter, to make sure that he has segregated himself correctly. He is permanently on the run. Above all, since the whites, numbering a fifth of the population, own most of the land and all the cities, they are simply much more visible than in tropical Africa. There, even in colonial times, it was quite possible for a villager to pass his whole life without ever setting eyes on a European.

This very comparison is in fact made by Mphahlele in his first book of critical essays *The African Image*, where he discusses the concept of 'roots' and expresses his usual impatience with any attempt to seek these in some quality of unique 'Africanity':

How similar the American Negro's cultural predicament is to ours in South Africa and in other multi-racial communities! The needle that registers your response as a writer swings between protest and romantic writing, and then, when you are spiritually emancipated, the needle quivers around the central point – the meeting point between rejection and acceptance. Then you know both how excruciating and exciting it is to be the meeting point of two streams of consciousness and the paradoxes they pose. That is what makes our art. If there is any *negritude* in the black man's art in South Africa, it is because we *are* African. . . . Simply because we respond intensely to situations is no reason why we should think non-Africans are incapable of doing so, or that we are the only section of the human race who are full of passionate intensity.[1]

But more important in the cultural formation of the South African than the restrictions which frustrate him, is the direction of his aspirations. Partly as a result of his very exclusion, partly as a result of the far greater urbanization and industrialization of the South, and partly as a result of the impoverishment of the over-crowded 'Homelands', the black South African is oriented more and more towards a way of life which hysterically denies him admittance. A member of the most educated, Westernized and (patchily) prosperous black community in Africa, he asks only that he be accepted as such. No amount of official mystification about 'the Bantu' will induce him to look back to the tribe and the Bantustan as offering an adequate way of life. He is drawn irresistibly towards the cities, which need his labour but deny his civil existence. But in the cities he can exist only on sufferance and in circumstances which emphasize his helot status.

West African writers like Senghor and Camara Laye, brought up amid traditional cultures still rich and alive – though distanced from them by their own educational selection – could bend their energies to resisting the process of 'assimiliation' and to re-asserting their

African identity. French-style assimilation might, in the 1950s, have seemed a much more tempting bargain to the black man in Detroit or Pretoria. Although it is a process which rests ultimately on the arrogant assumption that the white metropolitan culture is the only one of any possible validity, it does at least accept the logic of that assumption by opening its doors to the selected African on terms of something like equality. Only when he strolls along the boulevards of Paris does the assimilated African become conscious of how much of himself he has lost in the process. The bright young man from the High Veld might have considered that loss worthwhile, or at any rate inevitable, and relished the enlarged possibilities of life, work and movement it brought him. But for him there were no boulevards; only the tram-lines of the Bantu Education Act, leading nowhere. For the same reason the black South African exile often finds it relatively easy to adjust to life in the cities of the West. Instead of presenting a completely alien world, they must often seem a bit like Cape Town without apartheid.

This is the supreme irony of the South African situation and the irony which, without specifically dwelling on it, Mphahlele makes manifest. His whole life has been an unrelenting struggle to achieve the way of life for which his urban upbringing and liberal education had prepared him. But to achieve that life, he had to become an exile. The logic of events drove him, through Nigeria, Paris, Kenya and Zambia to that urban black America whose similarity he had always recognized. But at the root of the dissatisfaction he felt for all these places lay a certain perverse nostalgia, and it must have been this very nostalgia which finally induced him to return to Vorster's South Africa.

In his autobiography, *Down Second Avenue*, Mphahlele looks back on his few years in the Bapedi Reserve of the northern Transvaal (nowadays the site of another Bantustan) with little but bitterness and fear:

I have never known why we – my brother, sister and I – were taken to the country when I was five. We went to live with our grandmother – paternal grandmother. My father and mother remained in Pretoria where they both worked, my father as a shop messenger in an outfitter's firm; mother as a domestic servant. I remember feeling quite lost during the first weeks in the little village of Maupaneng. My grandmother sat there under a small lemon tree next to the hut, as big as fate, as formidable as a mountain, stern as a mimosa tree. She was not the smiling type. When she tried, she succeeded in leering muddily. But then she was not the crying type either:

she gave her orders sharp and clear. Like the sound she made when she pounded on the millstone with a lump of iron to make it rough enough for grinding on. I do not remember ever being called gently by her. One of her two daughters was the spit of her; the other anaemic and fawning. But they seldom came home. They worked in Pretoria. When they were not working they had children, without being able to secure a man they could really call a husband. I haven't seen them or my grandmother for the past twenty years, although I know they are still alive.

Things stand out clearly in my mind from those years: my granny, the mountain at the foot of which the village clung like a leech, and the mountain darkness, so solid and dense. And my granny seemed to conspire with the mountain and the dark to frighten us.[2]

There is nothing here of Laye's poetic nostalgia, his elegy for a life full of its own innate beauty and significance. Mphahlele's writing here is more like the taste of blood on the tongue. The symbols of mountain, darkness and brooding woman – to which may be added the terrible Leshoana River with its frequent floodings and drownings – stand for an existence which remains to him both alien and threatening, for all that Mphahlele partakes of it from the age of five to that of thirteen. Yet Laye and Mphahlele are almost exact contemporaries, equally devoted to rendering for us the quality of their experience in the years of growing. What divides them is three thousand miles of Africa.

Quite as revealing as the contrast with Laye is a comparison with the somewhat idealized recollection of a spell in a tribal reserve offered by Peter Abrahams in his fine autobiography, *Tell Freedom* (1954). Abrahams writes as someone brought up in a coloured slum of Johannesburg, sharing his tribal vernacular (Afrikaans) with the dominant white group and his aspirations with the petit-bourgeoisie. He had no real means of access to or identification with the relatively integrated Bantu culture which he met in the reserve, and his very distance from it lent it a certain romantic glow. The same romantic glow persists in the presentation of Abrahams' African characters in a novel like *Wild Conquest*, and considerably weakens his achievement there. Behind the rather tapestry-like chiefs and warriors of that novel lie autobiographical passages like the following, in which Abrahams describes his brief childhood friendship with the Zulu boy Joseph:

I learnt to fight with sticks; to weave a green hat of young
willow wands and leaves; to catch frogs and tadpoles with my
hands; to set a trap for the *springhaas*; to make the sounds of

the river birds.
There was the hot sun to comfort us. . . .
There was the green grass to dry our bodies. . . .
There was the fine sand with which to fight. . . .
There were our giant grasshoppers to race. . . .
There were the locust swarms when the sky turned black and we
caught them by the hundreds. . . .
There was the rare taste of crisp, brown baked, salted locusts. . . .
There was the voice of the wind in the willows. . . .
There was the voice of the heaven in thunderstorms. . . .
There were the voices of two children in laughter, ours. . . .[3]

This kind of lyricism ignores the extent to which even the remotest
pagan existence in the wide bosom of South Africa is self-divided,
impoverished and dispossessed as surely as any other. Still more is
this true of the Christianized community in which Mphahlele moved,
with its harsh scorn and hatred for anything 'heathen' or genuinely
indigenous. So bigoted were his companions that, as if their own
poverty were not enough, they would not even step in a pagan
footprint, and kept the whole width of the Leshoana between themselves and any culture which could reasonably be called aboriginal.
Thus their own tribal brothers of a saner day had mysteriously
evolved into devils to be shunned, and to be loaded in their absence
with the accusations of every kind of dirtiness and depravity.

Life in Maupaneng was an almost daily round of whippings for
every petty transgression of the narrow bounds of duty imposed on
the children. It came therefore as something of an excitement and
relief when their mother appeared one day and announced that she
was taking them back to Pretoria to live with her. So the thirteen-
year-old Ezekiel and his younger brother and sister set off once more
for the city they had left in infancy.

The new dispensation did not last long. Their cruel and drunken
father, whose refusal to pay for the children's keep had led to their
recall in a desperate bid to confront him with his responsibilities,
became more and more violent towards their mother. One Sunday
morning he poured boiling food all over her and then struck her on
the head with the iron cooking pot. Their mother went to hospital
and their father to court, never to be seen again. Now Mphahlele's
mother had to return to full-time domestic work, and the children
were deposited with their other grandmother in the roaring slum of
Second Avenue, in the Marabastad location of Pretoria. This
grandmother and her daughter Dora made their living by brewing

illicit beer and taking in white people's washing. Also in the household were Dora's three brothers, her three children and a medicine man who provided herbal remedies and charms in return for free bed-space on the verandah. So every night found six adults and six children sleeping in the hot, confined house, most of them on the floor.

The next few years were punctuated with police raids. Mphahlele was not yet fifteen when he suffered his first assault from a white constable. He learnt the full humiliation of his position as he cycled about the city, collecting the dirty washing of hostile and moody white customers. But somehow, at the sacrifice of any real life with her own children, his mother managed to save enough to put him through primary school. Though he rose daily at four to do the domestic chores or the washing round, and the nights were orchestrated by retching customers and police whistles, he passed out in the first grade. So his mother strained an extra inch and sent him to St Peter's Secondary School in Johannesburg.

Mphahlele's fierce prose evokes all the strain of those years of adolescence. Both structure and style in *Down Second Avenue* show the attempt to enlarge the normal limits of autobiography, so that the book will be both a record of events, more or less chronological, in the author's life, *and* an immediate, impressionistic evocation of certain typical moods and moments which don't belong at any special place within it, but must be allowed to spill their fear and anguish over the book as a whole. These are evoked in the sections called Interludes, which contain some of Mphahlele's most angry and electric writing in the book. The search for immediacy has muted the common tendency for the writer (especially the exile) to see even the painful events of youth and childhood through a certain softening haze. In the Interludes we actually hear the steely clang of police boots in the yard, the thunder of hard knuckles on the door at dawn, the sirens, the cries and the sickening blows which authority rains upon the unprotected:

Saturday night. Darkness. Sounds of snoring from my uncle at the corner. Like the muted lowing of a cow. My younger brother doesn't stir beside me. Nor the youngest uncle the other side of him under the same blanket as we. I know the cold air coming through the hole in the flooring boards will whip us out of sleep as it plays upon bare flesh, else one's leg will rest on my neck and then I shall dream that some fiend is slitting my throat and I shall jump up with a scream. My sister also on the floor is kicking the legs of the table she's sleeping under. Grandmother and three of Aunt Dora's children are lying quiet on the old double bed. The only door and the only window are shut. . . . I can't sleep I can't get up to walk about in the yard because my bones are aching because I was cleaning the house and turning everything up and choking in the dust I was making. . . . Tins of beer dug into the floor behind the stack and the strong smell of fermenting malt and grey spots on the floor around the holes. No policeman will find it easily. Policeman? Saturday night. The men in uniform may even now be sniffing about in the yard. Far to the west end of Marabastad a police whistle, the barking of dogs – no it must be in Fourth Avenue because I can hear heavy-booted footsteps, it's sure to be a person running away from the law, the police cells, the court and the jail. Saturday night, and it's ten to ten. I can hear the big curfew bell at the police station peal ten to ten, ten to ten, ten to ten for the Black man to be out of the streets to be at home to be out of the policeman's reach. . . . The whistle is very near now and the hunted man must be in Second Avenue but the bell goes on pealing lustily and so Black man you must run, wherever you are, run.[4]

The effectiveness of this passage depends on the gradual extension of consciousness from the sleeping boy to the other sleepers, to the night beyond the walls and to those who suffer in it, whose suffering or danger obtrude so strongly into the consciousness of the boy as to make him appear fortunate in his discomfort and confinement. So the last words 'run, wherever you are, run', despite their general application to every black man in the South, acquire also a certain quality of contentment – for tonight, at least, Mphahlele himself doesn't have to do any running. The process is very like that achieved in J. P. Clark's celebrated poem 'Night Rain', though the comfort and familiarity finally achieved there are far beyond anything that *Second Avenue* can afford. The intermittent abandonment of punctuation probably doesn't contribute much to the effectiveness of the passage, which derives more from its overall structure. Writing without punctuation demands a control of texture and rhythm which few writers can sustain. It isn't something which can usefully be switched on and off again. And it is doubtful whether any subsequent essay in non-punctuation has rivalled the success of the first major example, the closing pages of *Ulysses*, where the technique genuinely sets us adrift in the current of Molly Bloom's warm and muddled hedonism.

Nevertheless, the Interludes do achieve their aim of breaking up the texture of the chronological narrative and preventing it from imposing any soporific, far-away-and-long-ago spell upon the reader. The narrative itself shows us that Mphahlele was sixteen before he succeeded in moving even a little away from a background which condemned most of his schoolfellows to messenger-type jobs for the rest of their lives. As a boarder at St Peter's, he first sampled an entirely different existence. There was great intellectual freedom in the school, good conditions of work, and a general expectation among the students that they would enter the professions as leaders of their people – leaders of a type then rendered obsolete by the banning of all overt political activity among Africans and the jailing or killing of all such men as Sobukwe, Mandela, Sisulu and Biko.

A contemporary hero was Peter Abrahams, already full of a precocious confidence which distanced him from the other boys, as someone who already knew where he was going. From Abrahams the young Mphahlele first heard of Marcus Garvey's Black Zionism and irredentism, a message entirely new to the other boys. Abrahams, too, was already writing at this time and distributing his poetry among his fellows, an example which was precious to Mphahlele because: 'here was a boy writing something like the collection of English poetry we were learning as a set book . . .'.

The elitism implicit in the existence of schools such as St Peter's was already becoming a painful anomaly even in the 1950s, for it aroused expectations of a liberal and open society in which advancement would depend on merit rather than pigmentation; but these were expectations which Jan Smuts's United Party had no more real intention of fulfilling than their Nationalist successors. From St Peter's, Mphahlele moved to an institution which could only strengthen these expectations, Adams College in Natal. Nothing in the syllabus there could prepare the teachers it trained to operate the obscurantist provisions of the Bantu Education Act, which now lay only a few years in the future. Although Adams lacked the intellectual freedom of St Peter's and was dominated by a somewhat narrow and repressive missionary atmosphere, it was nevertheless dedicated to the proposition that education in a single nation must be a single process. Even so, Mphahlele did not at once enter the teaching profession, but spent several years as a general clerical assistant to Dr Arthur Blaxall at a home for the blind. Blaxall, evidently the kindest and gentlest of men, was later tried and sentenced under one of the innumerable acts which bolster the power of the South African prison-state.

His teaching career began in 1945, a year which also saw the death of his mother from diabetes, his marriage, and the final dispersion of the Marabastad community by the total destruction of that township, in the interests of establishing the usual 'cordon sanitaire' around the white suburbs. But this career was abruptly cut short only a few years later, when Mphahlele was banned from teaching because of his vigorous opposition to the Bantu Education Act. Forbidden to earn his living by teaching anywhere in South Africa, he eked out a miserable existence as a messenger (variously known as 'John', 'Jim' and 'Kaffir') in several white firms. For a few months he taught in the then Basutoland Protectorate, and this experience was probably important in being his first contact with a part of Africa not totally dominated by white interests. Poor the Basuto might be among their cold mountains, but helots they were not. It was a period of intense self-communion for Mphahlele:

I went to Basutoland in search of something. What it was I didn't know. I stood one night a few yards away from the foot of a hill. You find solid, palpable darkness in Basutoland. I tried to rip the dark with the razor edge of my desire; but I found nothing to ease the heaviness of my soul. I scoured the sky with my eyes: in my fancy I raked the stars together, leaving a sieve in the velvet sky. Then I collected them and splashed the sky with them. Some of the stars were pulverized in transit and chalked the blue with a milky way. You know, it reminded me of the powder of an exhausted moth-killer. Still, I couldn't find it. . . . The autumn trees might tell me something, I thought. Brown and yellow leaves fluttered in the air, and fell with arrogant smugness on the ground. The trees themselves stood about like debauched men.[5]

In the same feverish mood, Mphahlele returned to South Africa for a last attempt at living in a society which had driven him into a corner of his own being. For a couple of years he worked on *Drum* Magazine as a reporter and literary editor, and there many of his own early stories were first printed. *Drum* was then in its most creative and militant phase, under the imaginative editorship of Anthony Sampson, and with such writers at its disposal as Lewis Nkosi, Can Themba, Harry Nxumalo, Bloke Modisane, Casey Motsisi and Todd Matshikiza. But Mphahlele took a strong dislike to the general character and tendency of the paper; his reasons make interesting reading now that these tendencies in *Drum* and its sister glossies have become so much stronger, under the twin pressures of political conformity and commercial advantage:

I had no illusions about my inability to become a journalist. My whole outlook resisted journalism; my attitude towards the white press; towards the double stream of newspaper policy in South Africa where there is a press for whites and a press for non-whites; towards *Drum*'s arbitrary standard of what the urban African wants to read: sex, crime and love stories. . . . It was to the credit of Anthony Sampson and even more of that daring reporter, the late Henry Nxumalo, that *Drum*'s annual exposure of social and political evils were the dynamic piece of journalism they deserved to be. . . . I tried to be happy in a job that interested me more than reporting – the editing of short stories. Even here I was supposed to let in the 'wet sentimental sexy stories and tough crime stories'. I tried to argue with the proprietor [Jim Bailey] whenever he interviewed me that *Drum* had plunged into a reading world that hadn't developed any definite magazine taste; that it should produce healthy material in an original style wherever possible and, in a sense, dictate what the public should read, without necessarily being snobbish or intellectual. He told me that it wasn't *Drum*'s mission.[6]

No one disputes that *Drum* could have done better with its opportunities, but it may be suspected that Mphahlele's prescription of 'healthy material' is that of the schoolmaster rather than that of an editor of what aspired to be a popular magazine, and owed whatever influence it had precisely to its popularity. On the other hand, he was certainly right in arguing that its readers' tastes were still relatively unformed, and needn't be packaged into tabloid form merely for the convenience of those who couldn't be bothered to seek a fresh formula. Again, his regret at the segregation of South Africa's press is probably very much the regret of someone brought up in the old liberal hopes which finally exploded at Sharpeville. If real press freedom were restored to all of South Africa, it is highly unlikely that a newspaper could be devised of broad enough appeal to sell equally well to both black and white readers. Neither race any longer wishes to read much about the daily doings of the other. A specialized political, intellectual or literary journal, such as the *Classic*, is another matter, and can establish a genuine national following among those few for whom it is written.

Despite the frustrations of these last years in South Africa, Mphahlele managed to complete both BA and MA degrees externally with the University of South Africa. But still he couldn't teach. The links that had bound him to South Africa weakened with the death of his mother and that of Rebone, the wild girl he had loved all through his youth, and whose father had been hanged for killing a white policeman who obscenely insulted him in his own home. Mphahlele was now faced with the dilemma which obsesses every decent South African, the dilemma of which Bloke Modisane wrote so well in his article 'Why I Ran Away'.[7] Should he stay on and fight, and perhaps be destroyed inwardly by his own bitterness? Or go into exile, live and breathe among free men, but perhaps lose himself in another way? The time had come when he could no longer hesitate before this choice. In 1957 he left for Nigeria, where he was to teach until 1961. But this proved to be only the first stage in a restless odyssey which filled the next fifteen years, the odyssey which he has tried to trace in his novel *The Wanderers*, and which was to land him later as a professor in that citadel of Westernism, the United States.

It is a measure of how far the situation in South Africa had worsened during these same years that all the steps by which Mphahlele fought his way upwards from the slums have been struck away one by one, leaving no comparable ladder for his successors. St Peter's School and Adams College have both ceased to exist, destroyed by the Bantu Education Act which swept away all liberal and unsegregated education for Africans. The same fate has overtaken Kilnerton Institution, where he received his M A degree. Marabastad has also gone down before the bulldozers of the Group Areas Act – unlamented for its filth and sickness, but still a place where urban Africans could own and improve their own houses, instead of occupying the featureless identical barracks of the new townships. Many of his friends of those days are either dead, in prison or in exile. In an elegiac passage towards the end of his book, Mphahlele looks back and reflects how, even as a comparatively young man, he can see the landscape of his own past destroyed behind him:

Marabastad is gone but there will always be Marabastads that will be going until the screw of the vice breaks. Too late maybe, but never too soon. And the Black Man keeps moving on, as he has always done the last three centuries, moving with baggage and all, forever tramping with bent backs to give way for the one who says he is the stronger. The Black dances and sings less and less, turning his back on the past and facing the misty horizons, moving in a stream that is dammed in shifting catchments. They yell into his ears all the time: move, nigger or be fenced in but move anyhow. They call it slum clearance instead of conscience clearance – to fulfil a pact with conscience which says: never be at rest as long as the Black Man's giant shadow continues to fall on your house. . . . Rebone left us too, after mother. A mysterious disease swept her off in a whirlwind. I know now that she loved me and wanted me more than I imagined and that her married life was – what does it matter now? Like her father she had lived lustily. . . . More mothers will come and pass on but the African sage will tell you pain defies comparison. There are many more second avenues with dirty water and flies and children with traces of urine running down their legs and chickens picking at children's stools. I have been moving up and down Second Avenue since I was born and never dreamt I should step out of the nightmare. Often I wonder if I'm still alive or whether this is not really another way of 'crossing the bar'.[8]

In another, later passage Mphahlele comments on the strange feeling of release, accompanied by a lack of firm bearings, which he experienced in Nigeria. The habitual stabbing movements of his own prose are partly a constant and exasperated exploration of limits known to be narrow, restrictive and *there*. The higher the barriers piled between the races by the Nationalist authorities, the more starkly and acutely conscious they become of one another. The very absence of such known limits can create, for the South African exile, a sensation of floating which is not entirely comfortable:

I'm breathing the new air of freedom, and now the barrel of gall has no bottom any more. I shall soon know what to do with this freedom. For the moment, I'm still baffled, and my canoe still feels the momentum that launched it in Second Avenue. But what a glorious sense of release![9]

It was during those four years in Nigeria that Mphahlele achieved his greatest period of fertility as a writer. *Down Second Avenue*, presumably completed by 1958, was published in the following year. In 1961 the newly established Mbari Publishing House in Nigeria brought out a volume of his short stories entitled *The Living and Dead*. All of these stories, except the rather weakly melodramatic 'We'll Have Dinner at Eight', had already appeared in such South African magazines as *Drum*, *Student*, *Standpunte*, *Purple Renoster* and *Africa South*. But, although they are thus the harvest of his last four years in the Republic, the opportunity to publish them in book form was peculiarly the kind of opportunity brought to Mphahlele by his departure. The following year, 1962, brought the appearance of his book of critical essays, *The African Image*. The years since 1962 have seen no comparable burst of creativity, surely the fruit of that 'sense of release' of which Mphahlele wrote. His second collection of stories, *In Corner B*, published in East Africa in 1967, also contained hitherto uncollected stories from his South African days, as well as reprinting three of the stories already used in *The Living and Dead*. Mphahlele's main production since 1962, apart from various critical introductions, has been his largely autobiographical novel *The Wanderers* in 1971, a revision of *The African Image* and one further volume of essays, *Voices in the Whirlwind*, in 1972.

The earliest of Mphahlele's writing to appear had been a small collection of stories called *Man Must Live*, which appeared in South Africa in 1947. Writing of that book in *Down Second Avenue*, he appeared to have buried it in oblivion as 'escapist'. He also lumps together all the critical notices of this book, and he appears to have been rather fortunate in the number of these, as 'most patronizing in parts, woolly in others'. This comment may well be true of some of the opinions quoted, but by no means so of all. What of *The Johannesburg Star*, which wrote:

These stories owe little to the western European tradition . . . Mr Mphahlele writes like a Russian. . . . These stories are very coolly written. . . . The author stands a little away from this astonishing world he has set out to describe. . . . Yet his stories are full of feeling.[10]

These comments seem neither patronizing nor woolly, and are perhaps rather high praise for the stories themselves, if we are to judge by the one which Mphahlele finally decided to rescue from oblivion and include in *In Corner B*. This is the title story 'Man Must Live', which does rather stick out from its neighbours in that later collection, both by virtue of its improbable plot and some fairly dreadful overwriting. The author never really makes us believe that Sophia Masite, the rich and educated Mosotho widow, would wish to marry the simple-minded Zungu. If his attractions for her were merely physical, this seems an unnecessarily elaborate way of securing them. Yet it is hard to believe they are anything else as, once married, she seems to go out of her way to insult and humiliate him. As for the style of this early story, it is a mark of how far Mphahlele travelled in the next ten years that he could here commit himself to phrases full of confused idiom like: 'They soon found themselves sailing on the glassy sea of easy conversation', or ' . . . not without a pang of the sense of Time's ironic twists, this experience was not accounting for itself at the right moment'.[11]

I have discussed this particular story first because it is much the earliest of Mphahlele's writing to have appeared in this more permanent form, but I now propose to turn to a discussion of some of the stories in *The Living and Dead*, which contains the majority of his best work in fiction. When I first wrote of these seven stories, in the first edition of the present work, I formed a strong impression that the title story and 'He and the Cat' must be considerably later in composition than the others, and must represent a movement towards that 'reconciliation of protest and acceptance' for which he was striving. However, the researches of Professor Bernth Lindfors[12] have made it clear that 'He and the Cat' was published as early as 1953. It nevertheless stands out from the stories which surround it by reason of its economy of means and its introspective quality, as the narrator, obsessed with his own problems, focuses slowly and with difficulty on what is around him.

It is a deceptively simple story. The narrator goes to a lawyer's office to seek help with a problem that is consuming him. He takes his place in the waiting-room with about twenty others. The clients gossip in snatches, the clerk comes to summon them one by one. At a table a little apart sits a man sealing envelopes, with the picture of a black cat on the wall behind him. Gradually this withdrawn figure becomes more and more important, until he dominates the whole room, the whole mood of the scene:

An envelope fell to the floor. He bent down to take it up. I watched his large hands feel about for it, fumbling. Then the hand came upon the object, with much more weight than a piece of paper warranted. Even before he came up straight on his chair I saw it clearly. The man at the table was blind, stone blind. As my eyes were getting used to the details, after my mind had thus been jolted into confused activity, I understood. Here was a man sealing envelopes, looking like a drawing on a flat surface. Perhaps he was flat and without depth, like a gramophone disc; too flat even to be hindered by the heat, the boredom of sitting for hours doing the same work, by too many or too few people coming. An invincible pair, he and the cat glowering at him, scorning our shames and hurts and the heat. . . .

I went in to see Mr B. A small man (as I had imagined), with tired eyes but an undaunted face. I told him everything, from beginning to end.[13]

Whatever the chronology of its composition, this story shows a technical assurance not always evident in the rest of the collection. Here Mphahlele is content to write directly out of experience, without looking for the conventional type of 'plot'. The narrator's egocentric obsession with his legal anxieties is gently displaced by his slow awareness of the quiet presence of another man, more completely locked within the dark walls of his own experience than the narrator can ever be.

Several other stories in the collection show characters who, whether black or white, are borne helplessly along in a stream of events which they cannot master or understand. They seldom act, and when they do, like Mzondi in 'We'll Have Dinner at Eight' or Timi in 'The Suitcase', they act disastrously. In the first-mentioned story there is a somewhat inadequately prepared murder: Mzondi kills the sentimental white employer who has invited him to dinner, because he mistakenly believes that she is pumping him on behalf of the police. In the second, a desperate man steals a suitcase which a girl has left beside him in a bus. He is taken to a police station on suspicion of theft and is there found to be carrying a dead baby around with him. Although the story of 'The Suitcase' is apparently based on an actual event, these plots are rather too obtrusive in the neat way events are unfolded, and the stories suffer from a thinness of fictional texture.

'The Master of Doornvlei', first published in 1957 and reprinted in the same collection, is a more substantial story. The incident with the bull and the stallion which finally brings about the confrontation between Mfukeri and his master is convincing and appropriate, for this kind of projected conflict is precisely what we expect to find between two men who have no love for each other but have been held together by a certain mutuality of interest. The story is made all the stronger by the fact that the old, black foreman is not in himself at all a sympathetic character, though he comes to stand in sympathetic opposition to the Boer farmer.

But the other outstanding story in this collection is 'The Living and Dead'. Unlike most of Mphahlele's stories, this one is not unidirectional, and its greater length gives it that degree of amplitude which is almost essential to real achievement in this form. The structure is daringly unorthodox for a story of only a few thousand words. Mphahlele begins with the thoughts and experiences of two apparently unconnected people on a day in urban South Africa. Lebona, a railway sweeper, has just seen a man pushed backwards down the train steps and trampled to death by the rush-hour crowd. He has also picked up a letter which he found lying on the track. Thoughts of the letter and the casually abrupt death of the unknown man obsess him. Meanwhile Stoffel Visser, a middle-class white resident, has just completed a report to the Government urging that 'kaffir' servants should all be moved out of the white areas into their own locations. His obsession, very different from Lebona's, is the fear that white civilization will be swamped in a rising sea of black labour. But because his own servant, Jackson, has not returned in time from leave, Stoffel has overslept and has failed to send the report in time to the responsible Minister. A man comes to the door with a letter addressed to Jackson, saying that he found it on the railway line. He spills out a confused story of seeing a poor man killed at the station. Stoffel lends him half an ear, while impatiently longing for his departure. A moment later, Jackson's wife Virginia appears on the doorstep which Lebona has just vacated. She knows nothing of Jackson's whereabouts and is highly agitated by his disappearance. Stoffel fails to hand her the letter. Instead, he dismisses her and reports matters to the police, after which he guiltily opens the letter himself. By this time the reader has concluded that the dead man at the station is probably Jackson, and this suspicion is reinforced when the letter proves to be a desperate summons to Jackson from his dying father in Vendaland. He sends his son some photographs of his family for safe keeping and begs him to come and look after the farm. But the strength of the story is that the dead man turns out not to be Jackson and remains as unknown at the end of the story as at its beginning.

All these events are drawing Stoffel against his will into taking a personal interest in people, even people he does not know, like Jackson's father, like Virginia, like the railway sweeper:

So he couldn't at the moment answer the questions that kept bobbing up from somewhere in his soul; sharp little questions without ceremony; sharp little questions shooting up, sometimes like meteors, sometimes like darts, sometimes climbing up like a slow winter's sun. He was determined to resist them. He found it so much easier to think out categories and to place people.[14]

The similes here are ill-chosen and don't contribute to the effect. But the story is creating that effect of itself. At last Stoffel walks home and finds Jackson lying in bed, badly injured. He has been insulted and severely beaten up by the police whilst peacefully returning from an outing to the zoo with his children. This is the last straw for Stoffel's narrow, inflexible mind:

For four years he had lived with a servant and had never known more about him than that he had two children living with his mother-in-law and a wife. Even then, they were such distant abstractions – just names representing some persons, not human flesh and blood and heart and mind.

And anger came up in him to muffle the cry of shame, to shut out the memory of recent events that was battering on the iron bars he had built up in himself as a means of protection. There were things he would rather not think about. And the heat of his anger crowded them out. What next? He didn't know. Time, time, time, that's what he needed to clear the whole muddle beneath the fog that rose thicker and thicker with the clash of currents from the past and the present. Time, time. . . . And then Stoffel Visser realized that he did not want to think, to feel. He wanted to do something. Sack Jackson? No. Better to continue treating him as a name, not as another human being. Let him continue to be a machine to work for him. Meanwhile he must do his duty – despatch the commission's report.

That was definite, if nothing else! He was a white man and he must be responsible. To be white and to be responsible were one and the same thing.[15]

It would have been easy to make this story the preparation for a reforming of Stoffel Visser, the breaking of a new light into his bleak corridor of bigotry. Mphahlele's ending is truer and, as we come to see it, inevitable. This is how things happen in a society dominated by racial mythologies. And the way in which Mphahlele draws his apparently random, anonymous threads together into a significant pattern of unacknowledged human relationship, unaccepted human responsibility, shows an altogether new power in his imaginative resources.

Of the twelve stories issued in *In Corner B*, three of the best ('He and the Cat', 'The Living and Dead' and 'The Master of Doornvlei') are reprinted from the earlier volume. Two relatively slight stories date from Mphahlele's experiences in Nigeria, the more interesting being 'The Barber of Bariga', which does capture a kind of brash, ebullient depravity that has a distinctly Nigerian accent. The immature 'Man Must Live' has already been discussed, but the other new South African stories include two of considerable length and vitality, both apparently published here for the first time. 'Grieg on a Stolen Piano' contains a memorable portrait of the author's irrepressible paternal uncle, who had trekked in terror from the north, having fled from the brutal oppression of a white farm and been hunted by a posse of Boer horsemen. Starting from the kitchens of Pretoria, this uncle has made his way through teacher-training at Kilnerton and several years of teaching to a valuable opening as 'junior inspector of African schools'. Valuable, because he immediately attached to the post a profitable line in diamond smuggling. Combining cultural ambitions with a remarkable eye for the main chance, this man's character reaches its most intense expression in his touching performances of Grieg on a stolen piano. Having precipitately made an unlucky second marriage to a sulky woman, he abides that with the same even mind as the rest of his misfortunes:

So he was going to keep his wife, rain or shine. When her behaviour or her sullenness oppressed him, he went back to his whisky. Then he played excerpts from Grieg's piano concerto or a Chopin nocturne. . . .
   'If she knew this piano was lifted from a shop,' he thought often, 'this dumpling would just let off steam about the fact, simply to annoy me, to make me feel I'm a failure because she knows I'm not a failure and she

wants to eat me up and swallow me up raw the way she did her first husband. . . .'

The keyboard felt the impact of these passionate moments, and resounded plaintively and savagely. . . .[16]

Mphahlele also offers an interesting account of his uncle's efforts to conciliate an apparently malignant fate. These are uncompromisingly traditional, and owe nothing to the modern quackery of city diviners and astrology columnists. Instead he summons his relatives to partake of the meat of a slaughtered goat, whose bones he then buries in the yard:

At such times his mind searched the mystery of fate, groping in some imagined world where the spirits of his ancestors and that of his dead wife must be living, for a point of contact, for a line of communion.[17]

'Mrs Plum' is Mphahlele's most ambitious story to date, told entirely in the voice and within the imagined comprehension of Karabo, an uneducated girl from Phokeng who comes to Johannesburg and works in the household of a rich, white liberal. The girl wearies alike of Mrs Plum's enforced friendship (for a while she is even expected to sit at table and eat with the other guests) and the more unforced friendship which develops between her and the rebellious daughter of the household, Kate. The first is undermined when the girl realizes Mrs Plum's selfish dependence on her, a dependence which would be better expressed in a more generous monthly wage than in amiable chats. The second is exploded when the daughter falls in love with, and for a while threatens to marry, a black doctor for whom the girl Karabo has also, though distantly, fallen. Realized as a privileged rival, Kate suddenly becomes both hateful and unnatural to Karabo:

These white women, I say to myself I say these white women, why do not they love their own men and leave us to love ours.

From that minute I knew that I would never want to speak to Kate. She appeared to me as a thief, as a fox that falls upon a flock of sheep at night. I hated her. To make it worse, he would never be allowed to come to the house again.[18]

As for Mrs Plum, Karabo spoke truer than she knew in the few words with which she first introduced her:

She loved dogs and Africans and said that everyone must follow the law even if it hurt. These were three big things in Madam's life.[19]

The love of dogs (a somewhat perverted one, as it turns out) comes into collision with the love of Africans when a rumour sweeps the white suburbs that the black servants are going to poison their employers' dogs as an act of vengeance. Black Sash and liberal activism notwithstanding, Mrs Plum is really set back by this, because she had never realized that activities like hers can do no more than try to give a humane face to an inhuman social order. The coddled dogs, with their big diet and special status in the household, are a constant remainder of her real scale of values.

In Mrs Plum, Mphahlele anticipates the attempt he makes in the early chapters of *The Wanderers* to render the quality of Southern Bantu speech directly into English. This is particularly evident when Karabo is gossiping over the fence with her 'home-girl' Chimane, in some of the liveliest scenes of the story:

'I tell her I say, Oh daughter-of-the-people, more and more deaths. Something is finishing the people at home. My mother has written. She says they are all right, my father too and my sisters, except for the people who have died. . . . Mother says also there is a woman she does not think I remember because I last saw her when I was a small girl she passed away in Zeerust she was my mother's greatest friend when they were girls. She would have gone to her burial if it was not because she has swollen feet.'[20]

Critics and scholars have theorized for some years about the dearth of full-length fiction from black South Africans; on the face of it, this dearth is the more surprising in that South Africa made an early start with the novels of Mofolo, Platje, Dhlomo and others, in the first thirty years of the century. Since then the considerable achievements in poetry, short fiction and autobiography have not been matched by any novel of major scale. To insist that writers like Peter Abrahams and Alex La Guma are 'coloured' rather than black may seem like participating in the racial obsessions of the authorities, but it remains true that the world of experience tapped in a work like La Guma's *A Walk in the Night* (which is in any case a short novel rather than a novel) is not the same as that revealed in the journalism and short stories of the black writers. To the voluntary segregation practised by most coloureds has been added the enforced segregation which puts them in different townships, different schools, different universities and a different range of jobs. Hence La Guma's work is centred upon the world he knows intimately, that of coloured slum-life in and around Cape Town. Although we may discern at a deep, unrealized level a phenomenon we can call 'South African literature', the absence of common experience, common education and common communication in a country so deeply and bitterly divided does force us to admit that a novel by a white, or Indian or coloured writer, however sensitive and perceptive, cannot be regarded as cancelling the expectations which attend upon a new black South African fiction.

It was into this atmosphere of expectancy that Mphahlele, certainly the best established black South African writer today, launched his novel *The Wanderers* in 1971. The first thing that must be said about this book is that it is simply not a novel. Rather, it is a thinly disguised autobiography, which extends the story of *Down Second Avenue* to cover the author's last couple of years in South Africa (the years of *Drum*) and his subsequent wanderings in Africa and Europe. Comparison with the earlier book, however, can only damage *The Wanderers* as much as any insistence that it is a novel. As a novel it totally lacks shape and relevance; for the form of the novel demands rather more than an arbitrarily sawn-off section of the author's own experience. Incidents should be included only because they are important to the action, and not simply because they happened; events should be presented with some sense of their moral complexity, rather than in self-justification. The motive of self-justification is dangerously prominent in much of *The Wanderers*.

The range of experience presented in this book has faced Mphahlele with real problems of style. The prose of *Down Second Avenue* was angry and often abrupt, but, unlike the writing of many of *Drum*'s contributors, it never struck a note of wishful Americanism or a breathless striving for toughness of effect. Such a note does occasionally obtrude in *The Wanderers*, as in the paragraph which recounts the author's own move to *Drum* (here called *Bongo*):

I joined *Bongo* magazine as political reporter and sub-editor when I had gotten sick with teaching high school. The white government of South Africa had laid down the Negroes shall be taught only those things that would make them a willing follower of the white man's instructions. So I quit.[21]

The rhythm here, and the somewhat gratuitous 'gotten' and 'quit', don't really suit Mphahlele's rather weighty personality. The same uncertainty of tone weakens much of the dialogue. Here is an episode where the easily identifiable Emil (Professor Ulli Beier) is telling the author why he is leaving Africa. Neither of the speakers sounds remotely like his actual self, forced as they are to talk with a kind of frenzied jocularity:

'We've two offers,' Emil says. 'Malta and the Fiji Islands. We'll decide when we're in Singapore. By the way you owe us a word of congratulation – we've just got married.'

'Hey, why didn't you say so you son of a——? Of course hearty congrats! Are you just wanting a change?'

'Yes. But also Iboyoru's in turmoil right now and my position has become vulnerable because I've lived and identified mostly with the ethnic group that's teetering between two rival groups of the east and north. Also the people there – at any rate two writers – don't want a white promoter of African arts any more – not even when I offered to work under them.'

'Is it a bloody affair?'

'And how!'[22]

It is as hard to imagine Professor Beier using expressions like 'And how' and 'ethnic group' as it is to imagine Mphahlele offering 'hearty congrats'. The author has simply paraphrased this scene into the prevailing dialogue style of the book, rather than attended with a novelist's ear to the qualities of individual speech in English. Also, it is hard to see what purpose is served by giving Nigeria the transparent and comical name of Iboyoru throughout the book. Of course, if Emil were a genuine fictional character, it would be another matter; he might speak with whatever tongue the author chose to give him. But the disadvantage of all *romans à clef* is that the reader is bound to test the verisimilitude of the author's characters against their originals, and in the relatively small world of African literature he is likely to know who these are.

The Wanderers comes nearest to having a life of its own in the earlier chapters, and particularly in the section dealing with the author's visit to a Boer potato farm in the effort to trace a girl's missing husband, who has been sent there for forced labour by the police. This lacks the immediacy of the late Harry Nxumalo's celebrated *Drum* articles on the potato farms of Bethel, but Mphahlele's dialogue is at its most successful when he is rendering Bantu speech:

'You men, let us not speak as if we are the first people in this world to have children. Our fathers had us and they had their fathers. The trees that you see in this land, the corn, and everything that grows has been watered with the blood of people. . . .'

'You know, so many people here talk as if we were being asked to do anything, to fight the white man tonight or tomorrow, but we are just talking because to be alive is to talk. . . .'

'That is the man with a tongue as broad as the road. . . .'[23]

The effect of such reporting is to give a certain human weight to even the most simple speech. Mphahlele, however, appears to have no ear for the mannerisms or accentuation of educated black South African talk. Everyone in this reach of society 'talks like a book', and there is an unintended effect of condescension when such characters are confronted by Indian or coloured speakers, whose mannerisms Mphahlele seems much more anxious to observe. Here a coloured speaker confronts the author (who, incidentally, confirms my point that the generality of coloured and black writing cannot, unfortunately, be equated in present-day South Africa):

'Why don't yous peepel write more about us brown peepel in *Bongo*?' Domingo asked.

'When we get news, we do,' I replied.

'Most of what we reads is this brown pin-up girls, histories of dead brown politics leaders. You know, see what I mean?'

'We do our best. Remember we don't have so many coloured people – I mean brown people – reading *Bongo*.'

'Say more about them and then you see they reads more. You know, see what I mean?'

'Economics, my friend!'[24]

The dismissive last line only confirms the generally lofty, 'educated' tone of the writer here. The same patronizing effect creeps into the scene with Chandra, the Indian store-keeper, though Mphahlele is actually building up a point about up-country Indian store-keepers which recognizes their courage and endurance, and which is not entirely negative:

'. . . Vee Indians also take. Some peepel vill tell you all Indians don't take but t'ink of me, vat vill happen to me in dis part of de kuntry if I don't take little bit?'

'In actual fact, you take alcohol because you are Chandra,' Shuping said, as we were sipping our drinks. 'Don't conceal your real thoughts now!'

'Vat you mean?' He seemed to have been taken off guard.

'I mean, now look at it this way. In so many isolated parts of this country you'll find an Indian shopkeeper or a Jewish one. You may be the one solitary Indian for miles around and yet you survive with your spouse and children, giving nothing, taking nothing outside your shop life.'

Chandra nodded, looking impressed.

'There is something in you people deep inside there, something that never dries up, something that just keeps on and on which you can top up endlessly.'

'You mean like a car battry,' Chandra chipped in, laughing chubbily. 'It juss go on until it goes kaput.'[25]

I am not suggesting that there is anything wrong in this reporting of Indian or coloured people's English – it is the novelist's job to listen and record. But has Mphahlele listened equally hard to his African speakers? Do they never drop an article, mix up genders (which don't exist in Bantu verbal structures) or display idiosyncrasies which can be rendered phonetically? And do they really come out with words like 'spouse' in the middle of a *duka* drinking session?

The weaknesses of *The Wanderers* show as much in these kinds of detail as in its overall lack of fictional organization and authorial 'distance'. The disappointment is the greater in that this is the mature work of a good writer, the writer who above all might be expected to produce a black South African novel of real substance and achievement. Stories like 'Mrs Plum' and 'The Living and Dead' give us room to hope that Mphahlele will one day write a full-length work of fiction that displays a comparable power to organize and to project and develops more fully the style manifest in some of the short stories, now that the story of his wanderings has been told.

Mphahlele's importance in modern African literature has been as much in his roles as editor, critic and cultural *entrepreneur* as in his own fiction. He was one of the founders and moving spirits of the Mbari Writers' and Artists' Club in Ibadan in 1961 and was for some time co-editor of *Black Orpheus* with Ulli Beier. Was he perhaps instrumental in getting La Guma's early work published by the magazine at this time? Whilst based in Paris with the Congress for Cultural Freedom, he organized the first African Literature Conference held on the continent itself, which took place in June 1962 at Makerere College in Uganda. Soon afterwards, he moved to Nairobi to set up the Chemchemi Centre, which was roughly based on the ideas already worked out at Mbari. *African Literature and the Universities* (1965), edited by the present writer, was the product of two important conferences on this subject which he sponsored at Dakar University and Fourah Bay College in 1963.

In the midst of all this public activity came *The African Image* (1962, revised and expanded 1974), which was the first extensive work of criticism published by any Anglophone African writer. The liberalism which Mphahlele castigates in his political writings has left its mark on his own early criticism, and much of *The African Image* is a recasting of his South African M A thesis of the 1950s. Much more valuable as criticism are two long essays of the 1970s, in which he makes extended comparisons of black American, West Indian and African poetry, particularly in their bearing upon themes of conflict and revolution.[26] What survives of the liberalism in this much more committed criticism is a certain scrupulousness, a degree of awareness of the richness and contradiction to be found in the Western tradition itself, which make it impossible for him to indulge in the sort of heady gestures of dismissal so popular in radical circles. After examining the concrete evidence for the emergence of a black aesthetic truly distinct from the wide range of Western poetics, Mphahlele concludes:

Clearly, what is referred to as a black aesthetic has emerged as a *black point of view* so far.[27]

But of that point of view, the expression of that distinctive experience, he quotes and analyses many fine examples from both America and Africa.

The same essay contains a much more measured and telling attack on 'the African theatre of *négritude*' than some of Mphahlele's intemperate utterances of the 1960s. In its Caribbean antecedents, negritude had shown a genuine concern with assailing the citadels of white power. Too often in Africa, he concludes:

it is a dialogue between two selves in the African and only indirectly addressed to Western civilization. It moves on both a personal level and that of a small public – the elite; often so much on that level that there is a 'dissociation' of sensibility between what the poet really feels and thinks and does and what he is urging the public to do. . . . It speaks a language that does not touch, because it does not concern, the common man. . . . The Senegalese school of *négritude* seldom runs full tilt against white authority as white power. It is concerned with talking to an elite so as to instil in them a sense of self-pride as black people.[28]

What makes these strictures telling is the comparison with the new, populist language which is emerging in Black American poetry and theatre; where the language itself, and not merely what is said, is an act of revolt. But this is perhaps to ignore the differences of time as well as space separating the Paris–Dakar axis of the 1930s from the Harlem of the 1960s. Rather similar observations on negritude were, however, made by Sembène Ousmane at the 1963 conference in Dakar.

The contrast in tone between the two halves of *The African Image* has been, if anything, increased in the later revision. Whereas the second part, 'Literary Images', is a smoothly written, cool-tempered, rather polite account of how African characters are presented by white and black novelists respectively, the first half shows a much more unbuttoned Mphahlele who writes in the angry, staccato tone made familiar by *Down Second Avenue*. It is correspondingly more valuable as an insight to the mind and personality of the writer. In particular, the following passage may help us to understand why an intellectual who stormed definitively out of South Africa in 1957 should voluntarily return there some twenty years later:

Go back and teach where you know you'll be contributing something real, something relevant for your people. Teach the youth what the government syllabus says and use it to sow the seeds of rebellion, and set on fire the passions that are already raging, waiting for articulation. Charge them up till they explode under the asses of white folks, subvert their crooked, miserable lives. Thought of it because of the schooling the state-screened tribal colleges are giving the Africans. . . . What are the monsters doing to the minds of my people! I always cry out. And so the dream. The anguish. Who will atone?[29]

Perhaps Mphahlele has persuaded himself to believe that, operating in the Bantustan of the northern Transvaal (roughly where he spent those unhappy years of childhood), he will be able to achieve that integration of culture and education he has long dreamed of, without the handicap of being an exile and a foreigner which has dogged him from Ibadan onwards to Philadelphia. But will that 'state-screened' system really consent to be blown up as he envisages? Is there any classroom without its spies, any Bantustan without its quislings? No doubt Mphahlele himself will tell us the answer to these things, in his next book.

Mphahlele earns his place in this book because he is the most important black South African writer of the present age, by virtue of his all-round achievement and his lifelong commitment to literature. Others may have equalled or excelled him in autobiography, or in criticism, or in the short story. But Mphahlele's contributions in all three of these fields add up to a career of major distinction. If he cannot give us the great black South African novel which has been so long awaited, it seems probable that no one at present can. The fragmentation of creative achievement into the poems and short stories in which black South Africa has been so prolific must be seen as the obverse of those conditions which make major fiction so difficult of achievement there. The corpus of Mphalele's work remains rich enough, however, in qualities of insight, compassion and intelligence.

Sembène Ousmane

Born 1923 at Ziguinchor in Southern Senegal, son of a fisherman. After early schooling, he worked at many jobs and had a turbulent spell in the French colonial army. After 1945 Sembène worked for some years as a docker in Marseilles, until forced to give up by a back injury. His first novel, *Le Docker Noir*, appeared in 1957 and his best known, *Les Bouts de Bois de Dieu*, in 1960. Since then, he has been prolific both as a writer and film-maker. His films, all based on his own scripts and using many amateur actors, have been dogged by censorship in Senegal itself, but have won many international prizes. He now lives in Yoff, near Dakar.

3 The Primacy of Change

It is impossible to imagine a greater contrast between writers of the
same nation, with only seventeen years dividing their dates of birth,
than that between Léopold Sédar Senghor and Sembène Ousmane.
But the grounds of this contrast lie well beyond any abstract consideration of 'personality'; given the difference in the writers' class
background, upbringing and education, we could not reasonably
expect anything but a totally diverse attitude towards literature and
society. Senghor was marked out to be exceptional even before he
became a writer. He was exceptional in his Christian-bourgeois
upbringing, in his early schooling, in his move to France for higher
studies and in the level he reached in those studies, all before he had
published a single poem. There is a sense in which his creative work
is an expression of his sense of elitism, and of the need which this
imposes for self-justification and reconnection with the parent
society. Sembène's work seeks, rather, to be an expression of common
experience, common struggle and common exclusion from privilege.

Sembène Ousmane was born in 1923 at Ziguinchor in the
Casamance Region of Senegal. This region is cut off from the rest
of the country by the long finger of Gambia, and is further distinguished from it by its general character as tropical forest, rather
than open savannah. But Sembène's rather detached parents gave him
an insight into the whole sweep of Senegalese experience; learning
Wolof and the life of the city from his fisherman-father, while his
mother was rooted in the rural life on the Casamance and its Diola
language. As he grew up, Sembène's own experience took on the
representative character which makes him much better able to speak
of common life than any elitist writer of the region. After a minimal
education and some years as a wandering fisherman and trader, he
served as an ordinary soldier in the French colonial army, was
discharged in France (apparently for striking an officer) and then
worked for a long while as a docker in Marseilles. It was at this

period that he threw himself into union activities on behalf of his fellow black dockers and began to attend lectures on Marxism. His ambition to use the novel as a means of analysing and teaching from his own experience bore fruit during these years.

Sembène's work in both fiction and film, starting with the publication of his first novel, *Le Docker Noir*, in 1956, charts a steady progression away from a type of romantic individualism towards the communal struggle and communal consciousness celebrated in his later work. It is not that his work ever lacked an ideological content, of a generally radical tendency, but that the artistic means of expressing this content demanded many years and many experiments for their discovery.

The immaturity of *Le Docker Noir* as a novel may also be attributed to what finally proved one of Sembène's strengths – his very lack of that sophistication in education and experience which severed many of his contemporary writers from the lot of their fellows. As it happens, there is an earlier novel about black dockworkers in Marseilles, *Banjo*, written by the Jamaican Claude MacKay in 1928. But whereas MacKay gives his readers very much the black man they expect – shiftless, footloose and cheerful; ready to break into a song-and-dance routine at any moment – Sembène's book is more like a cry of pain for the poverty, wretchedness and discrimination they suffer. One of the chief concerns of Diaw Falla, the novel's hero, is to help them break out of this isolation, which is not only that of their blackness but that of the poverty they share with their white fellow-workers. Instead of holding aloof from unionism and political action as 'white men's business', they must throw themselves into both if they are to change their lot.

Here already is that insistence on the primacy of change which runs all through Sembène's work. But to some extent it runs counter to another tendency in *Le Docker Noir*. Diaw's concern to change his own condition by the use of the pen. This brings him up against the perpetual dilemma of the artist; the need for isolation and withdrawal in order to create seems at times a betrayal of that very comradeship in suffering which he seeks to celebrate. The generality of dockers do not read novels and cannot hence feel liberated by them.

Alone among Sembène's novels, *Le Docker Noir* begins with a flashback, so that we are aware before Diaw's story begins that he has come to grief in France and is awaiting sentence on a charge of homicide. In Senegal, the news precipitates the following exchange in a bus carrying Diaw's anguished mother; for it coincides with reports of a colonial massacre at Dimbroko on the Ivory Coast:

'You see Yaye Salimata? Her son is in France, it seems he's killed a woman, perhaps they'll kill him too or send him to prison. He has only one murder on his conscience, the whites have just massacred dozens of men, but they are not even judged . . . no-one asks them to justify themselves.'

'You're a fool, my friend,' cried the man in khaki. 'Everyone looked at him and he changed to French: 'You don't know how to tell politics from sadism. That man you're speaking of, we all know him, why did he go over there? To live by pimping. You see his poor mother? She scarcely looks like a living woman now. For fellows like him, the laws should hit hard.'

With a screech of the brakes, the bus stopped and hurled together the three rows of benches acting as seats.

'Get out!' yelled the driver brutally. 'Sterility is a blessing when one remembers that it's possible to give birth to creatures like you!'[1]

This lively opening is part of a whole series of scenes, showing us how Diaw's crime seems to himself, to his fiancée Catherine, to his friends and relatives, and to his judges. The trial scene that follows, and which is handled with passion and skill, reveals to us what is alleged against Diaw and what he refutes, but it is not until much later in the novel that we get a straightforward narrative account of what really happened on that fateful night in Paris.

This technique of delayed exposure is in general effective. The reader's interest in Diaw's fate is engaged right away and he longs to fill in the details. But the trouble with the way that fate is presented is the somewhat melodramatic, individualist turn that it takes as Diaw develops his ambitions as a writer. What does he really long for? Fame, certainly, for he resents far more Ginette's theft of his fame than of his money; but also enough money to enable him to marry his mulatto fiancée, herself a stranger to Africa. The winning of the major literary prize of which he has been cheated by Ginette would undoubtedly have altered his life profoundly, pushing him towards Paris and a literary career, rather than towards either his suffering mother in Senegal or his suffering comrades in Marseilles. Sembène's novel is hot with the flavour of insult. Diaw's bitterest reproach to Ginette is: 'Tu m'as pris pour un "noir"' (you have treated me as a 'coon'). But that flavour is so sharp upon his tongue that he fails to view his hero with the objectivity of art; his motives are not analysed through the eyes of those who share his poverty but lack his talent.

The same fault persists strongly in his second novel, *O Pays, Mon Beau Peuple!* (1957), which concerns itself with the movement of return to Africa – almost as if Diaw had in fact escaped imprisonment and had returned with his 'toubabesse'* to the Casamance. The ambitions of his new hero, however, are not literary but political and economic. Oumar is determined to liberate his people, even despite themselves. And this crusading zeal gradually isolates him, first from his family, then from his French wife Isabelle, then from all but a few like-minded friends. Oumar, in other words, is the first of those harsh iconoclasts who henceforth continue to occupy his work (one thinks of Bakayoko in *Les Bouts de Bois de Dieu* (1960); of Ngone War Thiandum in *Vehi-Ciosane* (1966); of Tioumbé in *L'Harmattan* (1964) and the beggar in *Xala* (1973). That Oumar already exhibits the traits of this world-changing character we may see in the painful exchange with his mother, whom he quits almost at the moment of his long-awaited return to Africa, refusing to spend more than a single night under her roof:

'. . .I will even wear shoes, as I hear one always does in the land of the toubabs. I will bring you food. I'll be your servant. . . . But don't leave me.'
She was now gripping him by the shoulders.
'Oh', groaned Oumar, in the depths of embarrassment and of a grief he also felt cruelly, 'mother, it is not that at all. If I stay in town, I stay with all of you.'
'. . . . I don't want you to belong to everyone. . . . I carried you, I sacrificed everything for you. . . . If I felt you moving within me when I was walking, I would stop. . . . I gave more than a thousand women give to have a child. I longed and still long for you to have things none of your comrades have. I will give them to you . . . But, oh my son, stay with me. . . .'
She was tired of standing. She let herself fall on a root, crossed her legs, refilled her pipe and lighted it, with her gaze still fixed on Oumar. Her eyelids were swollen. She let out a long puff of smoke.
'Mother, it's getting late, I must go now,' said Oumar.
The old woman had shut her eyes. Brutally, she got up. 'I hate your wife! I hate all her people! I'll have no peace as long as they live here!' she cried. 'As long as I look towards the East and the sun rises there, I shall have no rest. They have stolen you from me. . . .'
She went right up to Isabelle and tapped her, then, turning towards her son, she spoke again:
'She has made you eat her menstrual blood!'[2]

*White woman, a reference to Diaw's mulatto fiancée.

The real irony of this exchange emerges as the novel develops, for it is not the harmless Isabelle who alienates Oumar from his family, but his own proud and unaccommodating nature. Having immolated his mother to the demands of that nature, he follows up first with the sacrifice of his uncle Amadou, who has befriended him and re-introduced him to fishing, and then of Isabelle herself, whom he neglects outrageously, both for his work and, it is implied, for the mulatto girl Désirée. Far from having bewitched him, Isabelle strives in vain to keep him in some sort of touch with reality. To effect the kind of changes he dreams of in the Casamance demands tact, sympathy and patience; it demands the support of family, friends and all those who are not actively hostile to his ideals. But the real weakness of the book is that Sembène does not perceive his hero even slightly ironically. If we suspect this as we read, we become certain of it after Oumar's death, when the author goes into a rhapsody over the meaning of that event:

Oumar Faye was certainly dead and lying in the earth. But the criminal hands that struck him down were deceived. It was not the tomb which held him, it was the hearts of all the men and all the women. . . . He ran before the seedtime, he was present in the rains and kept company with the young in the harvest season.[3]

What are we to make of this romantic extravagance? The fact is that Sembène has already defined the force of character of this would-be world-changer, but has not yet discovered how to integrate that force with its social context. To do this, he has to show us both the need for radical change and a consciousness of that need within the bosom of the society, so that the burden is shifted from indi-vidual heroics to collective action; to the sense of a whole society in motion. It is this structural change which he attains in *Les Bouts de Bois de Dieu* and which makes that novel such a giant step forward in his development. Bakayoko, in that novel, is perceptibly the reincarnation of Oumar Faye, but the author does not place on his shoulders the whole burden of the strike, and he is not even instru-mental in its decisive climax – the march of the women on Dakar. In fact, there seems to be a correlation between Sembène's dis-covery of how to use his iconoclastic, aloof protagonists, and his discovery of African woman as the neglected force which can shift the whole society into the future. There is a kind of dialectic between Bakayoko, whose lack of warm human contacts is made to seem like a condition of his success as a union organizer, and a character like the prostitute Penda, all warmth and human frailty, who enjoys a freedom comparable to Bakayoko's because she does not share the domestic lot of ordinary women. We see this freedom come particularly into play during the women's march on Dakar, where Penda's generalship depends partly on sarcasm, irreverence and scepticism. One of the marchers, la Séni, has fallen into convulsions whilst another, Yaciné, has cut her toe on a sharp stone and is bleeding. The more hysterical of the women immediately insist that la Séni has been possessed by a devil and that it is already sucking Yaciné's blood. Both women are in danger from the hordes of marchers who descend on them with sticks and branches in their murderous panic. The immemorial superstitions of the village threaten to destroy the new political consciousness that has just emerged. Only Penda keeps her head and the very shock to their modesty she administers shakes them out of their panic:

'. . . It is you who are the devils! Leave that girl alone or I'll eat you all raw! Mariam! Go and get Boubacar and his men. Fetch Maïmouna too!'

She managed to free Yaciné, half-dead with fear and with all her clothes in rags. On the road, la Séni now lay on her back surrounded by women; her legs were completely stiff and straight. One could hear her teeth grinding. . . .

Maïmouna stooped over the prostrate woman. 'It's not serious,' she said, 'she must have a sniff of urine.'

'Go on, you sluts, go and piss!' yelled Penda. The women looked at her, stunned and motionless.

'What, there are hundreds of you here, and not one of you can raise a bit of piss?'[4]

By characterizations like this, Sembène breaks free from the trap of offering us only 'heroic' workers and cigar-smoking, moustache-twirling bosses. It is the social forces to which they are respectively exposed which make the workers, or many of them, capable of heroism, and the bosses capable of cruel stupidity.

Thus Bakayoko, though he is the nearest thing to an authorized *persona* in the book, is also viewed critically in the end. Sembéne builds him up skilfully by delaying his actual appearance in the action until the second part of the novel. Hitherto, we have merely heard of him in mysterious and slightly contradictory terms, and have perhaps built up a picture of some kind of aloof superman. But Bakayoko turns out to be all too human. He is, indeed, an exploiter of loyalties which he doesn't, on the personal level, return. He has no common touch, and is in this respect vitally dependent on people like Lahbib. His devotion to the cause is no greater than that of Doudou, who refuses a huge bribe in its service. The various types of devotion offered to him by Assitan as the traditional Moslem wife, and by the enamoured N'Deye Touti, mean very little to him. He falls short of expectations both as a husband and a lover. His warmest feelings are for his daughter Ad'jibid'ji, who is presented as a prototype of the new woman, articulate and aware, who will offer him the kind of relationship he dreams of. It is the authorial voice which tells us:

Truly if Bakayoko, with that manner he had of despising or forcing destiny, was the soul of the strike, then Lahbib, the serious, reflective, calm, modest Lahbib, was its mind. Lahbib counted God's bits of wood, weighed them, judged them and arranged them. But the sap which was in them came from Bakayoko.[5]

Although the texture of the novel is generally naturalistic, it has elements both of the epic and of the symbolic. The modern prose epic must generally avoid the supernatural and the marvellous which predominated at the birth of the form, but it must retain the heroic dimension and offer us the spectacle of a people transcending themselves before the challenge of extraordinary events. In this sense, as well as in the sheer scale of the action, *Les Bouts de Bois de Dieu* can be considered as the first epic novel to emerge in Africa, pointing the way towards the later examples of Mongo Beti's *Remember Ruben* (1974) and Ngugi's *Petals of Blood* (1977).

Symbolism is present in Sembène's description of the great glistening locomotives which stand in their sheds like sleeping monsters; in the way that the marching women form a kind of train which snakes its way from Thiès to Dakar when the railway itself is silent; or in the way in which the silence is evoked:

Thus the strike settled down over Thiès. An endless strike which, for many along the line was an occasion for suffering, but for many also one for reflection. When the smoke ceased drifting across the savanna, they realized that an age had returned, an age of which the ancients had told them, when Africa was a vast garden. It was the machine which now ruled over the land. By blocking its movement over more than fifteen hundred kilometres, they became aware of their force, but also of their dependence. The truth was that the machine was turning them into new men. It did not belong to them; it was they who belonged to it. By its present inaction, it taught them that lesson.[6]

The peasants who stand silently gazing at the empty rails at the times when the train was wont to pass are indeed the new men here described; the machine is no superficial excrescence on their lives and they feel its absence like a blow. But Sembène does not lament the coming of the machine age to Africa or hunger for the days when it was a vast garden. As a Marxist, he cannot lament the changes which colonialism has brought in its wake. Even the rise of the new bourgeoisie can be welcomed as a temporary stage leading to further, more drastic changes. The coming of the machine announced the inevitable end of the old feudalistic, caste-bound Western Sudan. In that sense, the impression that the strike has brought back a vanished age is an illusion; rather, it is the announcement of a new age, when industrial man begins to act as such, rather than in the old narrow categories. It is noteworthy that the train assumes something of the same importance in Ngugi's *A Grain of Wheat*, where the arrival of the Sunday Special at Limura Station is described as the social event of the week. In Kenya, too, the train was the first long finger of the industrial order, pushing across forest, plain and mountain.

In comparing Sembène's novel with Ngugi's later experiments in epic fiction, however, we do well to remember that *Les Bouts de Bois de Dieu* was very much a pioneer work in African literature as the state of the art stood in 1960. It seems probable that Sembène's model, insofar as he had one, was Zola's *Germinal*, which likewise offers us a big cast of characters divided between workers and bosses; a prolonged strike affecting the livelihood of a whole region and gradually embittering relations between the two sides as it continues; together with politicization of the conflict as its wider implications begin to be grasped. Sembène's work is, however, free from Zola's often intrusive theories about the nature of fiction and about heredity which plunge the later pages of *Germinal* into melodrama. He has been criticized for the sheer size of his cast, evidently designed to reflect every aspect of the strike and its participants. But he does generally manage to keep the lines of the main action clear and in motion, even if we do sometimes have to glance back to remind ourselves who so-and-so is within the general scheme. Apart from its intrinsic importance, then, Sembène's book now looks like the announcement of a trend which has become marked in both Anglophone and Francophone fiction. His shorter novels, such as *Le Mandat, Vehi-Ciosane* and *Xala,* may well be more successful as complete works of art, but they lack this kind of seminal function within African fiction as a whole.

Without *Les Bouts de Bois de Dieu,* Sembène himself would

scarcely have begun his next major novel, *L'Harmattan* (Part I: Referendum) with the powerfully described tracking-down and killing of a meddlesome government official. The reader is left to make the jump from this to the main action, concerned with the Referendum campaign of 1958, and to establish the connections between the overall strategy of neo-colonialism and its random manifestations in the bush.

In Sembène's next major novel, *L'Harmattan,* the role of iconoclast is filled by a woman, and the same sort of dialectic as we saw in Bakayoko's roles as organizer and lover is played out internally between Tioumbé's needs as a woman and her duties as a revolutionary. These needs and duties are briefly reconciled in her affair with Sori, but his imminent departure for Guinea at the end of the book forces her to choose between them, for Sori is about to return to Guinea because there alone the Independence campaign has triumphed:

'Why don't you come along, Tioumbé? You'll find work. They need teachers there.'

He fell silent and stretched his legs, Tioumbé saw his muscled back and the deep hollow of his neck.

'*Yo*, Sori, you understand nothing! Nothing. . . . Do you imagine I'm happy about your departure? No. . . . But I'm content that you are going back. I've often, so often, wanted you to tell me: "Tioumbé, I'm not going after all". But now, it's better that you go. That corner of the world is yours. It's natural that you want to go back there. As for me, I'm a teacher. I know quite well that I'd find work there – and I know there'd be work for everyone. But we fight in order to live; not just to rejoice in our victory. To build! There'll be plenty of work here, and to spare. You forgot that this country is still not independent, and that I'm a member of the first Marxist party to write the word Independence, and the first to utter it in this part of Africa. . . . The imperialists, in a way, ask nothing better than that we leave the field to them. But that, never!'

'I know. . . .'

'Let me finish, because you don't seem to understand. Don't stiffen up! Don't ask me to give up the very thing that makes you leave. I am African. The existing frontiers are the work of colonialism. Get that into your head. Turn over, we're going now.'

'But the others said, this evening. . . .', cried Sori, disarmed by the severity of her words.

'You are with me, but your spirit is already elsewhere. . . .'

She had drawn brusquely away from him. At a stroke, the room lost its intimacy. A malicious light glimmered in her eyes. She got dressed. Sori, muffled in his lappa, observed her haggardly.

'You understand, it's only. . . .'

'It's because of the independence of Guinea,' she said, cutting him short. 'What are you waiting for? You're going to be late. I'm going behind the house.'[7]

This, from an African girl in bed and in love, is a new tone in the literature of the continent. She is telling *him* that there are sometimes more important things than romance. Sembène writes here without a trace of the male chauvinism which lingers in so many African novelists, and which can be glimpsed even in his own early work.

At first sight, nothing might seem further from the educated, liberated girl Tioumbé than a poor, illiterate village woman like Ngone War Thiandum, but her role in *Vehi-Ciosane* (White Genesis) is even more of a break with tradition than Tioumbé's defiance of her parents, her political and sexual rebellion, and her final assertion of independence from her lover also. For Ngone has been reared in a society where women play no part in the discussion of public affairs, and has known no other. The most they might aspire to is to influence what their menfolk will say at the mosque or the weekly council. But the incest in Ngone's family festers not only because the deed is heinous in itself, but because the degenerate society lacks the will to acknowledge and purge it. Ngone's suicide does just that, and lends to the child of this unnatural union of father and daughter the character of a new and hopeful beginning. In a situation where men are no longer themselves, Ngone resolves that women must force the pace. As the new mother takes the road with her baby, the whole conversation with the lorrydriver points towards that future which Ngone's sacrifice has made possible:

In the cabin, the driver asked her:

'A girl, or a boy?'

'A girl.'

'Pity! Her name?'

'Vehi-Ciosane Ngone Thiandum.'

'I've never heard a name like that: *Vehi-Ciosane*. Of which Thiandum is the father?'

Khar Madiagua Diob gently squeezed the baby, drew her bundle under her feet and gazed forward. The man beside her looked at her; then, getting no response, started off.

The immensity of the *niaye* on one side, the immensity of the sea on the other, the truck advancing down the middle, leaving the wheel-tracks which the sea lapped up quickly.

This story has no other ending; it is a page in their lives. A new one begins which depends on them.[8]

That phrase, 'depends on them', might be taken as an epigraph to the whole output of Sembène Ousmane. His insistence on man's ability to change his fate is at the opposite extreme both from the fatalism of Islamic tradition and from the idea of inevitable destiny which runs through the singing of the *griots* of the Western Sudan. Perhaps an echo of that fatalism persists in the lot which befalls Diaw Falla, and the weary stoicism with which he confronts perpetual imprisonment in the long letter which closes *Le Docker Noir*. Thereafter, it is wholly absent from his work.

One factor in its disappearance is Sembène's discovery that woman has the greatest revolutionary potential in Africa, simply because she has the most to gain from a wholly new order. The blend of theoretical radicalism with social conservatism, so common in men, is seldom found in women. Once they are committed to change, they are wholly committed. Sembène had already explored this idea in some of the short stories of *Voltaïque* (1962) before he developed it in *Vehi-Ciosane*. Those stories show him to be as much at home as a *raconteur,* in tales like 'Un Amour de la Rue Sablonneuse' or 'Le Voltaïque', as he is on the larger canvas of the novel. In many of these stories, a wry humour finds more expression than in any of the novels, a humour which was later developed in the visual wit which marks many of Sembène's films.

Since the early 1960s, Sembène has been increasingly absorbed by his work as a film-maker, and the fiction he has written since then (notably *Le Mandat* and *Xala*) has shown the signs of this absorption. Unlike many film-makers of literary leanings, he has always recognized that the short novel provides the ideal basis for a film-script, because the film can then develop and elaborate visually what is offered by the text, instead of having to cut and brutally condense a full-length novel. Hence he has not attempted to film any of his major novels, His major films to date, *Emitai, The Money Order* and *Xala*, all show this strong sense of visual and dramatic situation and all produce a result which is probably in many ways richer than the literary text (in the case of *Emitai* this is a speculation, as the original text has never been published).

One of Sembène's earliest films, the delightful *Borom Sarratt*, tells its story almost entirely in visual terms. The shabby driver and his little horse-drawn cart (*borom sarratt*) are seen first in the popular quarters of the city, moving through a warm and human social environment, giving free rides to the very poor, helping to transport people and goods from place to place. Finally, he is approached by a besuited bourgeois with shiny suitcases, who is presumably too mean to hire a taxi. Against his better judgement, he is persuaded to penetrate the 'Plateau', the posh and white part of the city. We see them inching past skyscrapers and the guarded gates of great villas; until suddenly the police arrive, the bourgeois takes to his heels and the driver is left, fareless, to face a certain beating and a probable imprisonment.

More ambitious films, like *The Money Order* and *Xala*, also exhibit a single and simple story-line, concentrating upon one incident and pursuing it until it is in some way resolved. In the former film, we concentrate entirely upon the money order and its disastrous effect upon the poor but contented household of Ibrahima Dieng. The humanity with which Sembène presents the domestic scenes and the covert collaboration of Dieng's two wives is matched by the visual satire of other scenes, such as that in which the cousin's young wife paints her toenails under the nose of the dignified old man, while he humbly counts his chaplets. Scenes like these cannot easily be matched by a text on the page, because they make their effect without words. There is, in fact, no precise equivalent of this scene in the published story.

Xala (1973) is the closest of Sembène's novels to film form, and was clearly written with one eye already on the script. There is an abundance of dialogue and a relative absence of the sort of commentary or reflection which cannot be rendered visually. The plot concentrates solely upon the brief career of Abdou Kader Beye's third marriage, his immediate relapse into *xala* (impotence) and his eventual or supposed cure at the hands of the beggars.

Abdou is representative of the 'compradore capitalists' of Dakar, who have gleefully taken over the Chamber of Commerce but whose power is still limited to control over relatively petty retail trading. Senegal's major commerce, along with its banks, shipping insurance and industry, are still largely controlled by the big French companies; whilst the middle level of commercial activity, including even shops, bars, cinemas and restaurants, are largely owned by local whites, Lebanese or Mauritanians. Hence the pomposity of the novel's opening scene in the Chamber of Commerce is matched by the pointless ostentation of Abdou's third marriage and by the spitefulness of his expulsion from the chamber when his creeping *xala* leads to his business failure also. Only in that moment does Abdou suddenly see, or suddenly declare, the truth about himself and the others:

'What are we? Just shabby little agents, worse than sub-contractors. We handle nothing but distribution – distribution of the crumbs willingly left to us by the big fellows. Are we really businessmen? For my part, I say No. Dirty-arsed peasants. . . .'[9]

Abdou's impotence, then, is that of his class, and it has been fastened upon him by a man he sees every day, a beggar whose existence he ignores and whom he once ruined in his rise to wealth and petty power. But Abdou's suspicions dart everywhere else: to his senior wives, his enemies, his new in-laws; and his superstitions, genuinely those of a peasant, drive him to financially ruin himself with *marabouts* in search of a cure which in reality he can minister only himself.

His search for relief seems finally successful when, through the agency of his driver Modu, he visits the famous *marabout* Sereen Mada. His *xala* is indeed cured but on condition that the cheque he pays to the diviner will prove sound. Abdou's cheque is, however, as hollow as his status and the third marriage which was intended as the culmination of his career. His new bride has already been made inaccessible by her indignant family, so Abdou vents his rediscovered potency on his favourite second wife, only to find it dry up as rapidly as the money in his bank account. It is now that the despised beggar reveals himself as the master of the situation.

The climax of the novel is more effective on screen than on the page. The reader has somehow acquired a kind of sympathy for the harassed man, who is certainly no worse than his fellow-traders and who maintains a certain humanity in his dealings with his laconic driver Modu. We have also developed a certain fondness for his first wife Adja Awa Astou and her 'liberated' daughter Rama. All three are involved in the culminating scene, one of baroque cruelty, where Abdou's house is invaded by a host of beggars and cripples who induce him to strip and endure the torrent of their spittle. Only thus can he be cured, ordains the ringleader who has fastened his *xala* upon him. Meanwhile armed police surround the villa and await their opportunity to strike. But prison holds no terrors for the outcasts who swarm the streets of Dakar, except when a state visit requires them to be put out of sight.

This scene irresistibly recalls a similar one in Buñuel's film *Viridiana*, and the comparison makes us realize that its ferocious symbolism is visual and cinematic rather than literary, since the film can more easily persuade us to glide from realism to surrealism and back again. In the case of *Xala* the film has been allowed, just slightly, to wag the novel.

The effect of film upon Sembène's literary style, however, is more speculative than its effect upon the form and length of his fiction. This is all the more so because the film has provided a way for him to move away from French altogether. All his recent films have been scripted either in Wolof or Diola, with sub-titles in the appropriate foreign languages. He has also given direct encouragement to literature in Wolof through his sponsorship of the revue *Kaddu*, written entirely in that language. Rama, the eldest daughter of Abdou in *Xala*, is presented as a young adherent of the Wolof movement. Although in many ways the twin-sister of Tioumbé in *L'Harmattan*, Rama is presented as rather ridiculous and ineffective in the final confrontation with the beggars. It seems that the author has come to see that particular type of 'liberated' woman as very much a bourgeois phenomenon. He is now more concerned with the kind of liberation offered by Penda or Ngone Thiandum, which promises that of a whole people.

According to private information, Sembène originally conceived *Vehi-Ciosane* as a film and scripted it in French. The effect, using the kind of talented amateur black actors he always employs, was halting and stilted. The story as we have it was therefore rewritten in Wolof and then translated back into a French that 'works'. Sembène's work has always been notable for his ability to represent the different levels of French speech in Africa (see, for example, the French of Rokhaya in *O Pays, Mon Beau Peuple!*). The effect which can probably be attributed to his film-work is a greater use of dialogue, an elimination of authorial comment (such as that which mars the end of the same novel) and a sparing use of description, which offers enough to the reader's imagination but leaves free scope for the film-maker, who is invariably the author himself. This makes his work of the greatest interest to the comparatist of film and fiction.

For a writer of strong political and social commitment the film has obvious advantages over all other artistic media, as revolutionary Russia was the first to recognize in its sponsorship of Eisenstein, Pudhovkin and others. Films are popular in Africa, especially in the rural areas, where a mobile film unit can be sure of attracting most of the populace as soon as it appears in the village. By writing novels in French, Sembène was automatically excluding all those who cannot read French with fluency, and all those do not read novels anyway. Part of this problem of audience would remain even if he were to write in Wolof. By contrast, the status of Wolof as the real *lingua franca* of Senegal – understood by some 75 per cent of the population – makes it an ideal language for film, supplementing what can in any case be presented visually and dramatically, even without the aid of dialogue.

The weakness of film as a revolutionary weapon in a non-revolutionary society is that of being even more vulnerable to censorship than the printed book. The banning of a book does not prevent its circulation in even the most draconian system, and often assists its popularity. The banning or mutilation of a film prevents it from reaching the very audience for which it was most intended. The prestige of showings and prizes in the film festivals of Paris, London or Cannes will scarcely compensate for this. Sembène is now, however, a film-maker whose reputation is world-wide and whose chosen audience is at least as wide as Africa. He is to some extent, therefore, protected against these dangers. This did not prevent the authorities from trying to ban *Xala*, however, until a boycott of the cinemas forced them to permit its showing in Senegal. The French ambassador also made vigorous (in the end, too vigorous) attempts to have *Emitai* banned. The banning of his film *Ceddu* in Senegal in 1978 was ostensibly caused by a quarrel with the President about the Wolof orthography of the title, rather than about content. Sembène's refusal to submit was perhaps motivated by his belief that heads of state, however literate, should not meddle in matters like this, where they can use their authority to crush all disagreement.

Although he has published no major novel since *L Harmattan*, Sembène is now reputed to be hard at work on a new one. Those who relish the complexity and toughness of the novel's texture must applaud this, but there can be little doubt that, for the revolutionary artist in contemporary Africa, Sembène's choice of the film medium as a major vehicle of expression is important and probably correct. His cardinal importance as an artist is that his work was the first in Africa to move beyond 'protest' (whether satirical or indignant), to show people in the process of changing themselves, under the stress of oppression, into a force which can overthrow it.

Camara Laye

Born 1924 at Kouroussa in Upper Guinea, the son of a goldsmith. French schooling early drew him away from his traditional background, a process immortalized in his first book *L'Enfant Noir*, published in 1954 when he was working at the Simca car factory in Paris. Returned to Guinea as a qualified engineer, but later joined the growing band of Guinean exiles in Dakar. His most admired novel, *Le Regard du Roi*, was published in 1955 and has been one of the most frequently discussed works in African fiction. In recent years, has done much work on the Samory epics sung by Malinke *griots* throughout West Africa. His third novel, *Dramouss*, was published soon after his move to Senegal. Camara Laye died in 1980.

4　The Aesthetic Vision

There is sometimes a danger in thinking of writers too rigidly in terms of their generation, and the work of Camara Laye should remind us of it. Born only a few years before fiercely anti-colonial writers like Mongo Beti or David Diop, and a year later than Sembène Ousmane, his early writing seems to inhabit an entirely different world. In Diop's poetry, for instance, the menace and cruelty of Europe are never absent, oppression seems to enclose his writing on every side, making his talent spring like a tiger. Both Mongo Beti and Sembène Ousmane, even in their treatment of rural themes, write of an Africa profoundly degenerated by the experience of colonialism, and by the years of encroaching slavery and conquest which preceded it. That 'Africa of proud warrior on ancestral savannahs'[1] of which Diop sings is certainly not something recollected from personal experience, but an idealized vision of what once existed. Likewise, from their earliest writing, Beti and Sembène see Africa as having lost, irretrievably lost, its traditional values and historical innocence. It is not mere decolonization which can reverse the processes of degeneration begun over a century ago; African societies, in their view, cry out for revolutionary change; a change which will sweep away the vestiges of feudalism and traditional inequality as completely as those of colonialism and dependence.

In Laye's work, the colonial theme hardly obtrudes at all. The Africa he recollects and recreates had still its own authentic vision of the world, its integrity, its total system of values. These things vanished, not a century, but a mere generation ago. Many of them died, it seems, with the author's own father and his contemporaries. Can all these writers be speaking of the same Africa, the same historical experience? The answer is: not quite. Although it is legitimate to generalize to some extent about African indigenous cultures, or about the nature and impact of colonial rule, it remains true that Africa is the world's second largest continent, and that the same influences, even if everywhere felt, are not felt with the same intensity. Above all, what Wole Soyinka has recently called the African's 'self-awareness', the ability to experience and interpret the world for himself, did not suffer the same blows in, say, Yorubaland, Upper Guinea, the Dogon country of Mali or the Lo-Dagaa country of Northern Ghana, as they suffered in the mines and slums of Johannesburg, the rubber plantations of King Leopold's Congo, or the 'White Highlands' of Kenya. These differences in the quality and intensity of deprivation persisted, not only a generation ago, but into our own day. They help as much to explain certain aspects of Soyinka's own writing as they help to explain Camara Laye or *The Myth of the Bagre* or *The Mwindo Epic*. And they make the charge so often levelled against Laye, that he ignores the colonial impact, appear in some degree irrelevant. For to insist, as Laye does, that a certain kind of African authenticity has survived the colonial whirlwind, and will perhaps survive the whirlwinds that follow in its wake, is to make a much stronger apprehension of self than to be wholly absorbed in castigations of 'the Other'. Such castigations allow the Other to appear as the most important factor in one's experience.

Camara Laye was born in the ancient city of Kouroussa, which stands on the head waters of the Niger in the great plain of Upper Guinea. This part of the Western Sudan has known historical civilizations for a thousand years. Though conquered and administered by France, a city like Kouroussa was complex and self-sufficient enough to go very much on its own immemorial way. Its people, if we are to judge by Laye's writing, were not constantly obsessed with the alien presence of Europe in their midst, but were far more occupied with their own concerns of hunting, trade and craft. Above all, the city itself was not, like so many cities of Africa, the product of colonial settlement.

To make the contrast yet stronger, Laye's father was the town's leading goldsmith and blacksmith, a figure universally respected both for his skill and for his magical powers, as smiths so often were throughout West Africa. Growing up in such an environment, Laye was able to know intimately a life which was still intact, though beginning to disappear; a life which was not essentially changed from that of the empires of the Mansa Musa or Sundiata which had ruled these riverine cities six or seven hundred years earlier. Yet Camara Laye was born in 1924.

This vanishing world, so rich in dignity and human values, has been recorded by Camara Laye in an autobiography which will live as long as men are interested in Africa. *L'Enfant Noir* was published in Paris in 1953 and James Kirkup's fine translation, *The Dark Child*, in London the following year. It is a unique book in many ways, written with a singular and gentle sincerity, yet with very conscious artistic skill. Laye does not proclaim his negritude or announce the coming dawn; he records what his childhood was, what was the quality and the depth of the life from which he sprang.

I was a little boy playing round my father's hut. How old would I have been at that time? I cannot remember exactly. I still must have been very young: five, maybe six years old. My mother was in the workshop with my father, and I could just hear their familiar voices above the noise of the anvil and the conversation of the customers.

Suddenly I stopped playing, my whole attention fixed on a snake that was creeping round the hut. He really seemed to be 'taking a turn' round the hut. After a moment I went over to him. I had taken in my hand a reed that was lying in the yard and I thrust this reed into the reptile's mouth. The snake did not try to get away: he was beginning to enjoy our little game; he was slowly swallowing the reed; he was devouring it, I thought, as if it were some delicious prey, his eyes glittering with voluptuous bliss; and inch by inch his head was drawing nearer to my hand. At last the reed was almost entirely swallowed up, and the snake's jaws were terribly close to my fingers.

I was laughing, I had not the slightest fear, and now I know the snake would not have hesitated much longer before burying his fangs in my finger if, at that moment, Damany, one of our apprentices, had not come out of the workshop. The apprentice shouted to my father, and almost at once I felt myself lifted to my feet: I was safe in the arms of one of my father's friends![2]

This scene, so brilliantly alive in itself, prepares us perfectly for much that follows; the crowded intimate life of the forge where the apprentices lived like sons of the family; his father's magic protective presence; and the happy unconcerned child playing in the midst of this sufficient life from which he will be progressively estranged and which he must at last leave for ever. For Camara Laye was clever, and once he set foot in the local primary school he was embarked on a course which led him inexorably to Conakry and Paris. What matter that he was the eldest and favourite son, and as such the natural inheritor of all his father's skill and knowledge? The world was changing, even Kouroussa knew it, and nothing could prevent it from sweeping him away.

The same immediacy marks every scene in the book: the excited woman breathing in the firelight while his father bends over an intricate gold ornament and the praise-singer plucks at his kôra, urging his imagination from hyperbole to hyperbole: or the great ceremony of circumcision, with all its pain and significance never better explained. Writing in exile and loneliness. Camara Laye creates out of his deep need to remember and handle all these things again. Here he describes the rice harvest on his grandmother's farm. To this farm he went every year at harvest time and here, among his lusty uncles and cousins, he began even as a schoolboy to feel the first motions of his estrangement:

When the great day arrived, the head of each family would rise at dawn to go and cut the first swathe in his field. As soon as this first sheaf had been cut, the tom-tom would sound, signalling the beginning of the harvest . . . the reapers used to set out, and I would fall into step with them, marching to the rhythm of the tom-tom. The young men used to toss their glittering sickles high in the air and catch them as they fell, shouting aloud for the simple pleasure of hearing their own strong young voices, and sketching a dance step or two on the heels of the tom-tom players. . . . In our December, the whole world is in flower and the air is sweet . . . the countryside that for so long has been drenched in rain and shrouded in baleful mists now lies radiant; the sky has never seemed so blue, so brilliant; the birds are ecstatically singing; there is joy all round us – its gentle explosions are echoed in every heart. . . .

When they arrived at the first harvest-field, the men would line up at the edge, naked to the loins, their sickles at the ready. . . . At once the black torsos would bend over the great golden field, and the sickles would begin the reaping. Now it was not only the breeze of morning that was making the whole field sway and shiver, but the men also, with their sickles. . . .[3]

The day's work passes quickly, with young Camara Laye following eagerly on the heels of his Uncle Lansana's younger brother, who is the champion reaper of the village. A break for the midday meal of *couscous* and then back to the field:

The afternoon's work was much shorter and time used to fly. It would be five o'clock before we knew it. The great field would now be shorn of its precious yield, and we would walk in procession back to the village – the tall silk-cotton trees and the wavering smoke from the huts seemed to welcome us from far off – preceded by the indefatigable tom-tom player, and singing at the top of our voices the Song of the Rice. . . .[4]

Does Laye idealize the old life in passages like this? Perhaps, for his mood is frankly nostalgic and will naturally select the high spots of the past. Yet there is great authenticity about this description. The warmth of comradeship and shared labour, the simple joy of harvest, the sparkling blue weather of the dry season, these were real enough. No doubt some of the reapers got drunk and beat their wives, some of the children died, victims of superstition and dirt. But there is a curious inconsistency about the sort of chauvinistic criticism which, whilst asserting in the abstract the virtues of African civilization, can read a passage like this and ask indignantly: 'where are the horrors of colonialism?' The genuine writer is not a marionette; he dances to a music of his own, and not to one dictated by others. The vision of *L'Enfant Noir* is integral and only the crassest imagination can fail to register that integrity. As a concrete manifestation of an African civilization operating on every level of consciousness it can be compared only with that fine novel *Les Soleils des Indépendances* (1968),[5] by his fellow Malinke, Ahmadou Kourouma. Kourouma equally refuses to be pushed into orthodox postures of protest which would be inappropriate to his fictional aim. His hero's view of Malinke civilization may not be ours, but it is indisputably authentic and entire.

A distinguishing feature of all Laye's writing is his respect for people. It is this respect which underlies the tenderness and sympathy with which he recreates the past. He realizes, for instance, the depth of suffering caused to his parents by his long absences from home. After finishing primary school he goes to a technical college in Conakry, four hundred miles from Kouroussa, on the Atlantic coast of Guinea. Here he has the support of his father's brother, an educated business man, and the love of his beautiful friend Marie, with whom he enjoys a strangely calm and innocent affair. But for four years he is at Kouroussa only for his annual holidays, and at the end of that time, having passed out top of his year, he is offered the chance to study engineering in Paris. He breaks the news first to his father. That wise and good man has long understood the logical consequences of sending a clever child to school, and has long abandoned all hope of seeing his son follow in his own footsteps. Together they go in some trepidation to face his mother with the news that a definite offer has come:

We found her crushing millet for the evening meal. My father stood a long while watching the pestle rising and falling in the mortar. He hardly knew where to begin.

'What do you want?' she said. 'Can't you see I'm busy?' And she began pounding faster and faster. 'Don't go so fast,' father said. 'You'll wear yourself out.'

'Are you trying to teach me how to pound millet?' she said. And then all of a sudden she went on angrily: 'If you want to discuss our son's departure for France you can save your breath. He's not going.'

'That's just it,' said my father. 'You don't know what you're talking about. You do not realize what such an opportunity means to him.'

'I don't want to know,' she said.

Suddenly she dropped the pestle and took a few steps towards us.

'Shall I never have peace of mind?' she cried.

'Yesterday it was the school at Conakry; today it's a school in France; tomorrow . . . what will it be next? Every day there's some mad scheme to take my son away from me! . . . Have you forgotten already how sick he was at Conakry? But that's not enough for you: now you want to send him to France! Are you crazy? . . . And as for you,' she cried, turning towards me, 'you are nothing but an ungrateful son. Any excuse is good enough for you to run away from your mother – But this time it won't be as you want: you'll stop right here. Your place is here. What *are* they thinking about at the school? Do they imagine I'm going to live my whole life apart from my son? Die with him far away? Have they no mothers, those people? But they can't have mothers, of course. They would not have gone so far away from home if they'd had mothers.'

And she lifted up her eyes to the sky and addressed the heavens: 'He's been away from me so many years already,' she said. 'And now they want to take him away to their own land! . . .'[6]

Laye's conscious artistry is very evident in this scene. The descriptive detail, such as the sudden speeding up of the pounding pestle, is perfectly selected, and the timing of the mother's hopeless outburst matches perfectly the human rhythm of the encounter. But all this artistry is placed at the disposal of an exceptional sincerity and a compelling purpose. Laye, writing out of his loneliness as a worker in a Paris car factory (for such he became), is recapturing and weighing everything that he has lost, the deep natural heritage which has been taken from him, and which is the real price of his modern education.

Laye's second book, the symbolical novel *Le Regard du Roi* (The Radiance of the King), appeared only a year after his autobiography and was translated by James Kirkup with the same sympathy and skill. It has many of the qualities we should expect from the author of *L'Enfant Noir*; the same simple but beauitfully modulated prose. the same compassion, the same sense of mystery investing ordinary things. But it displays also some entirely new aspects of his art. Nothing in his first book has prepared us for this gift of sustained unportentous symbolism, this daring alternation of narrative speed and exploratory slowness, or the racy, cryptic humour of much of the dialogue.

The hero of this fascinating book is Clarence, a white man. We know nothing about him beyond that simple fact, except that he has arrived in Africa, after a long struggle to cross the reef which surrounds it, has lost all his money at cards and has consequently been flung out of the white hotel. Now at the mercy of his black inn-keeper, who covets the very clothes he stands up in, he goes desperately to seek the African king of the place and throw himself on his mercy. The king seldom appears in public, but today is one of those blessed occasions and Clarence pushes his way to the front rank of the great crowd which is waiting on the esplanade. They are watching the dancing:

Clarence watched the dancers for a long while. . . .
'They are dancing well,' he said at last. One of the black giants at his side looked him up and down in an unfriendly manner.
'You call that "dancing"?' he said bitterly. 'I call it "hopping", nothing more.'
'Well yes, they *are* hopping,' thought Clarence. 'They *are* hopping, but they're dancing too; that must be their way of dancing.'
'They don't know the first thing about dancing,' the black man went on. 'They. . . .' But he did not finish his sentence. He spat contemptuously on the red earth. 'You wait for a while, yes, you wait and you'll see some real dancing when the king. . . .'
'Will the king be here soon?' asked Clarence.
'He will be here at the appointed time,' answered the black man.
'What time will that be?' asked Clarence.
'I've just told you; at the appointed time.'
'Yes I know. But exactly what time will that be?'
'The king knows!' replied the black man. He spoke the words abruptly, cutting short the interrogation. . . .
'So you want to speak to the king?' said the black man, looking Clarence up and down a second time.
'That's what I came for.'
'But it's unheard of. Young man, do you think the king receives just anybody?'
'I am not just anybody,' replied Clarence, 'I am a white man.'
'A white man?' said the black man. He made as if to spit, but stopped himself just in time.
'Am I not a white man?' cried Clarence.
'The white men do not come here on the esplanade!' retorted the black man, using the same abrupt tone of voice as he had used before.[7]

This exchange is almost a miniature of the action of the whole book. The arrogance and imperception of Clarence are shown in his questions ('exactly what time will that be?'), but his goodwill shows his desire to remark on the dancing to his strange neighbour, and it is this same goodwill which finally proves to be his redemption. At the same time, the replies of the beggar (for it is he) show that confidence in another ordering of time and space ('the appointed time') which is later displayed by all Clarence's instructors. And the rising dust in the arena lends to the scene that quality of hallucination or vision which invests nearly every scene leading to Clarence's final acceptance by the king. Finally, the beggar's replies and the unfamiliarity of the scene begin that long process of breaking down Clarence's expatriate confidence and certitude, which stand between him and acceptance by the land to which he is now consigned. This process begins immediately, for Clarence, after being silenced for a moment by the beggar's last retort, soon perks up again:

'I shall present myself to the king as soon as he arrives,' he said. The black man beside him sniggered. . . .
'The guards won't even let you go near him!' he declared.
'Then what shall I do?' said Clarence. He suddenly felt overwhelmed with weariness.
'Perhaps I shall put in a word for you,' said the black man.
'What – you!' cried Clarence.
He looked at his neighbour in amazement: he was an old man, poorly clothed; a tall man, no doubt, like all those in the front rank, but dressed in rags – a sort of beggar.
'But you are a beggar!' he said.
'That is true: begging and soliciting, that's my trade,' said the black man. 'It's not an easy life; I began to learn the trade when I was very young.'[8]

This beggar, with his strange manner compounded of impatient arrogance and humility, is to be Clarence's companion on the greater part of his pilgrimage. Soon they are joined by his other future companions, the irrepressible boys Nagoa and Noaga, who stop dancing and take up their stations just in front of them. The turmoil and excitement increase every moment, but Clarence is half-asleep with the smell of sweat from the dancers:

'Come on!' the beggar was shouting, 'wake up!'
'Is it time?' asked Clarence.
'It's the appointed time,' said the beggar.
But the esplanade was still empty. . . . Then it was suddenly alive with galloping horses. . . .
'Don't get excited,' said the beggar. 'All these are nothing but petty

rulers who have come to do homage to the king. . . . The king. . . . How could anyone fail to recognize the king? . . . He is. . . .'

He was at a loss for words. Perhaps he realized that there are no words to express what the king is.

'He is. . . .' the beggar began again.

But a sound of drums and trumpets drowned his voice. . . . And suddenly the whole crowd – and it was immense, stretching all along the edge of the esplanade and leading almost certainly right down to the centre of the city; perhaps it had even, like the great red cloud, overwhelmed the city itself – the whole crowd began to shout and jump up and down. . . .

It was then that Clarence saw an adolescent boy dressed in white and gold, mounted on a horse whose caparisonings trailed on the ground – a caparison of green velvet, embroidered with white flowers. An attendant, with a drawn sword in his hand, was leading the horse by a bridle. . . .'[9]

After this brief glimpse of the king, who is so bowed down with gold that his arms have to be supported by attendants, Clarence is flung on his face by the sudden prostration of the crowd and becomes far separated from the bobbing parasol which marks the king's passage back to his palace.

The beggar, true to his word, disappears into the palace for a while, but returns to say that the king has no place available for him. He suggests that Clarence set off for the south, whither he and the two boys are also going. The king is sure to make a visit to his southern subjects before very long and Clarence may await him there. Meanwhile the great red wall of the palace shimmers and fades in the evening light, the crowd vanishes and everything is still. This transformation, something between a naturalistic and a dream effect, is brilliantly achieved by Laye. The excitement and swirling animation of the preceding scene, the knockabout humour of the insolent beggar and the cheerful impudence of the two boys are suddenly followed by a hushed and mysterious expectancy as the four companions re-enter the dark and silent streets of the city of Adramé.

There follows a rapid series of bizarre encounters. The sinister clown of an innkeeper insists on having Clarence's coat in settlement of his debt, but splits the seam in pulling it over his big back and so makes it easy for the two boys to creep back and whip the two halves off his shoulders. Clarence and the beggar, knowing nothing of this escapade, are arrested by the palace guard for stealing back the coat and brought before a judge who is counting his beads in a vast empty room of the palace of justice. The judge is just about to

sentence Clarence – though the coat has not been produced – when
the beggar advises him to run for it.

This Adramé sequence has pace and humour, but is perhaps
rather too close to similar sequences in Kafka's *The Castle*. It doesn't
directly contribute to the book's main action, which flows straight
from the opening scene on the esplanade into Clarence's long journey
to the south. This now begins, and again Laye manages one of those
perfect shifts of tone from the lunatic atmosphere of the City to one
of pricking mystery:

The dancer's father led them along a tortuous corridor to a door that was
much smaller than the others and had no inscription on it. He opened it.
Clarence saw that it gave onto the fields. The full moon was gently shining
on the ploughed acres and on the patches of fenced ground that looked like
market gardens. In the distance there was a long dark line; the forest,
perhaps, or mountains.

'If you go this way you won't have any unpleasant encounters,' said the
dancer's father. And he gave Clarence a very obsequious bow.[10]

As the four travellers now leave Adramé far behind and embark on
apparently endless wanderings in the tropical forest, they are over-
come by the odour of the south, 'a subtle combination of flower-
perfumes and the exhalation of vegetable moulds'. Clarence stumbles
half-asleep through all these days. He becomes so disorientated that
he loses all sense of time and direction. These pages mark the total
severance of Clarence from his past self. For the first time, be begins
to confront the fact of the sensual nature which he shares with all
men. He begins to deteriorate, eating and drinking a great deal and
growing self-indulgent and lascivious. At last they reach the little
town of Aziana, the home of Noaga and Nagoa. Here the old beggar
tricks Clarence by selling him to the naba, the chief of the place, in
exchange for a donkey and a woman. Clarence's duties are to
consist of sleeping with each of the naba's wives in turn, for the man
is now old and beyond such matters. Clarence knows nothing of all
this and supposes that he is simply waiting in Aziana for the king's
arrival. He is given a hut in the palace courtyard and a luxuriant
mistress called Akissi. He spends his nights in violent sexual play and
his days in drinking palm-wine with his fat friend Baloum, the palace
eunuch, or in escapades with the two boys.

A long time passes. Clarence is half aware that Akissi leaves his
hut every night and that another woman takes her place, but he
refuses to admit this knowledge to himself until his enemy, the

Master of Ceremonies, rubs his face in it. By this time, almost every woman in the harem has shared his embraces and borne a little coffee-coloured brat. Feeling utterly self-disgusted and weary, Clarence leaves the town and goes to see his friend Diallo the blacksmith. Diallo is making an axe: '. . . It has to be a very fine axe, the finest ever made, in fact; the strongest and sharpest I shall ever fashion, for the naba intends to present it to the king.'[11]

Clarence, under all his degradation, and humiliation, is also learning. Like the axe, he also is taking shape. Laye's writing is full of small touches which escape us at first reading. For instance, a short while before this scene the naba has presented Clarence with a new *boubou*. Clarence has chosen one made of green cloth patterned with white flowers, much to the disgust of his friends. But this is precisely the colour of the caparisons of the king's horse in the first scene. Unknown even to himself, he is preparing for the climax of his quest.

The encounter with Diallo yields its meaning quite easily and directly, since it is Diallo himself who tells us the meaning of what he is doing. This is not so in the ensuing encounter with the prophetess Dioki and with the Fish-Women. The interpretation of these episodes benefits from some understanding of the Malinke civilization to which Laye belongs, and of the place of dream and prophecy within it; for the Malinke believe that truth speaks to man in dreams, and that those who have the talent to summon dreams or visions at will (the prophets) can teach him both the meaning and the nature of events. An ignorance of Malinke culture, and of the curious interplay of Islamic and totemic belief within it, has hampered much criticism of Laye's work. Some critics, in discussing the meaning of the king, even assume that Laye is speaking of the Christian God, despite the evidence in his first book about the nature of the beliefs in which he grew up. *The Radiance of the King* is in fact a work highly characteristic of Malinke literature, as we can see by consulting the importance of prophecy in *The Epic of Sundiata*[12] and of dream in Ahmadou Kourouma's *Les Soleils des Indépendances*.

The Fish-Women are, of course, manatees, whose apparently dual nature of beast and woman reminds Clarence that he cannot renounce his physicality; he can only learn to control it by acknowledging, for the first time, its reality. In his exaggerated self-disgust at being told (in a dream) the truth about his nightly exploits, he has tried to renounce not only Akissi, but his true friends Samba Baloum and the twins, and has sought refuge in a 'desert without men'. Significantly, it is they who rescue him from his swoon.

His visit to Dioki in the following chapter reinforces the point, for it is in a semblance of sexual ecstasy that Dioki shows him the vision of the king's departure for the South. Indeed, to the watching boys it seems that Clarence is himself involved in that sexual embrace. Laye would applaud, perhaps, the words of William Blake: 'The Path of Excess Leads to the Palace of Wisdom.' At least, such excess is a necessary path for those who, like Clarence, lack humility and a proper recognition of their own humanity.

Despite all these preparatory signs, the moment of Clarence's redemption finds him prostrate in his hut. Naked but far from unashamed, he is unable to face the king. For the Master of Ceremonies had just called him 'a great cock' and he cannot wipe away the slur. Baloum, Diallo, Akissi and the two boys all plead with him to put on his *boubou* and come out into the square where the king is holding audience. In vain. Only when they have all left him does he suddenly take courage, walking naked through the wall of the hut, across the square, into the arms and breast of the king who is awaiting him.

The publisher's blurb announces confidently that this book is an allegory of 'man's search for God'. It is a tempting ascription, but it may be we shall do better to remember Laye's own words in covering the inarticulateness of the beggar, 'Perhaps he realized that there are no words to express what the king is.' Quite as much as a search for God, Clarence's pilgrimage seems to be a search for *identification*. He becomes more and more like his human companions, plunging far deeper into sensuality than they only in order to purge away his separation and superiority. The beggar not only bosses and tricks him, but teaches him a lesson in humility. For, as he says, begging is not an easy life. The two cheeky boys are faithful in their fashion and indestructibly gay. The fat mincing eunuch Baloum is the best friend he has. Only when he feels himself to be below even the least of these is Clarence ready to enter the service of the king.

Some interpreters have suggested that Clarence is not so much a white man as a 'been-to', an African whose soul has been whitened by over-exposure to European influence and values. Such a person is, in fact, often referred to as a 'white man' among his own people, whether ironically or in admiration. This interpretation cannot be dismissed; it should rather be considered as evidence of the multivalence of a work of art; but it certainly is not necessary to regard Clarence as anything but what he is described as – a white man entirely strange and new to Africa.

It is as well to say something also about the vexed question of Kafka and *The Castle*. The strongest charge of plagiarism has been levelled by Wole Soyinka, who enumerates various similarities of character and incident. He fails in that essay, however, to take stock of the far more significant differences of structure, tendency and meaning in the two works. In *The Castle*, K never gets anywhere, never comes near to understanding the meaning of any incident, never succeeds in stabilizing his relationship with anyone. Not only does he never reach the castle, but the reader realizes long before K himself that he cannot reach it; perhaps it is not even there to be reached. By contrast, every episode in Laye's novel, however mysterious it may seem to Clarence at the time, has a meaning and contributes to the total meaning of the work. Clarence succeeds in his quest, along with all those who similarly strive with good will. And the result is a work rich in humane insight and significance. Soyinka has not recanted his charge in a recent essay, but the pages he there devotes to *The Radiance of the King* show an understanding of its real importance and distinction. He summarizes:

The Radiance of the King remains our earliest imaginative effort towards a modern literary aesthetic that is unquestionably African, and secular.[13]

The art of symbolical fiction depends upon the interest and variety maintained on the immediate level of perception. The mind should not be continually aware of 'pregnant significances' as it reads, but should be fully entertained and absorbed by the story itself. The search for parallel or inner meanings should come later. This means that the surface narrative and dialogue may be largely naturalistic and even sprightly in tone, though the events and conversations described may be bizarre enough. A heavy, portentous style, drugged with its own significance and continually drawing attention to its own profundity must be abjured above all. In *The Radiance of the King*, Laye has avoided these dangers. He has written a book which we can read with enjoyment, amusement and keen absorption, but which occupies the mind in such a way that new perceptions keep rising to its surface when the reading is over.

After a silence of eleven years, Laye published his third book, *Dramouss*, in 1966. This novel is undoubtedly a disappointment after the level of achievement in his first two works, but although uneven and marred by too much authorial intrusion, it also contains some of the most intense and searching pages to be found in recent African writing. The weakness of the book stems mainly from Laye's failure to make up his mind whether to write a memoir or a novel; the early pages read like the former and the final pages, like the latter. The use of an authorial *persona* called Fatoman arouses expectations of a work of fiction, but the account of Laye's first return to Guinea in the late 1950s is not sufficiently distanced or transmuted to achieve the status of fiction. At the same time, Professor Blair's dismissal of the book as a 'political tract' is certainly wide of the mark and her account of it is inaccurate in several respects.[14]

Having expressed in his first two books a lyrical faith in the continued vitality of African humanism, Laye/Fatoman returns to a Guinea where it seems to be utterly denied; where arrest, detention and execution have become daily events; where arson and terror are actively promoted by political leaders as methods of strengthening their grip on the country. Lest Laye's account be thought biased, it can be checked against that given by Alioum Fantouré in *Le Cercle des Tropiques* (1972).[15] It is also validated by the number of distinguished Guineans who have been driven into exile, the number of political prisoners, and the known number of those who have died before the firing-squad. The last group includes Keita Fodeba, whose work as poet, musician and director of the Ballet Africaine had been a distinguished contribution to Guinean culture. After Laye himself had gone into exile in Senegal, both his wife and his father-in-law were seized by the regime. Only the most misguided progressive will feel compelled to defend all these actions on the grounds that they are socialistic. As the hero of *Dramouss* remarks:

I must say that a regime which founds itself in blood and the burning of others' houses is nothing but a regime of anarchy and dictatorship, a regime rooted in violence and which violence will destroy. It's all very well to cry 'Long Live Freedom', but we must recall that the Deputy of this country, [Sekou Touré] who has just voted in Paris for the crushing of fighting Algeria, has behaved like a colonialist. . . . I must say that the violence which you are implanting in this country will be paid for by each one of you, and most of all by the innocent. To build a viable society, we need more concrete and honest measures, fewer speeches, more respect for the views of others and more brotherly love.[16]

The high hopes aroused by Guinea's espousal of independence in 1958, and her laudable desire to avoid the client status which befell the rest of Francophone Africa, have bred a reluctance on the part of her defenders to admit that she averted one fate only to fall into another. The paranoia of an apparently independent leader can be no less intense than that of a 'stooge' president, though he will depend on home-grown 'Tontons Macoutes' to express it, rather than on French mercenaries and paratroopers. Laye writes as one who shared those high hopes and who returned to Guinea with every intention of remaining there. He depicts many of the friends and companions of his youth as still drugged with party enthusiasm, though others have already perished in the political terror of the times. Forced to choose between patriotism and fidelity to what he most deeply values, he resolves finally to depart. Up to this point, the tone of the book has been one of naturalistic dialogue and reporting but when Fatoman is about to leave Guinea again for France, his father gives him a little white ball covered with cowries to set under his pillow, so that he may dream the future of his suffering country. Symbolic dream or vision has always played a crucial role in Laye's work (one thinks of Clarence's successive dreams and stupors or of that remarkable story 'The Eyes of the Statue').[17] Dream also figures prominently in Kourouma's *Les Soleils des Indépendances*, where the hero Fama, is visited by a white-clad woman resembling the Dramouss of this book, who warns him of the terror and repression to come.

The resemblances between these two visions of wrath will speak for themselves. Here is the opening of Fama's dream:

First, an atmosphere, like a bush-fire in a harmattan afternoon. Reptiles. Snakes or crocodiles? Fama couldn't be sure, but all had scales, all slithered over the surface of a huge anthill covered with greenish moss. This anthill held the capital of the Ebony Coast. From its crater, from the edge of a gulf which resembled a tomb ravaged by hyenas, one could see the whole city lying in the bottom, lashed with flames. . . . Far away, two houses kept on smoking, like two pots of amber at the feet of the dead. But where were the dead? As if in answer to this question, a baboon leapt out of the smoke onto the ground; he had claws of flame, of darting flame, he chased a crowd of naked, muscled men who fled wildly in fear. The baboon caught one of them and mounted him as a dog does a bitch, came into him, then fell satisfied to the earth, bounced up, chased (his trail still lined with flame) and seized another man and mounted him likewise. Allah be praised! The repulsive ape spared Fama, but from the distant smoke where he vanished came a woman entirely veiled in white, save for her feet and her black hands, black as the plumage of a crow. Fama turned in terror, but he was quickly reached by the woman. 'Come', she cried to him, 'let's get away from here. Could I wish you any harm! Don't associate me with that creature', she continued, speaking hatefully of the ape and pointing to the place where he vanished. . . . 'To pass one door, a second door, a third door, and then stop before the fourth, is not to look for a house, but to seek a certain quality in man. . . .'[18]

Fatoman's dream is far more extended and we shall have to examine the sequence of events within it if we are to guess at its meaning. It begins with a vision of Guinea as a vast circular prison with immensely high walls, into which the dreamer is helplessly thrust. Starved, bullied, flogged and even eviscerated by their gigantic guard, the prisoners seem completely inured to their fate, but the dreamer insists on conducting a series of conversations with this sardonic, argumentative and bloodthirsty lout:

'You are nothing but a *linke*,' he yelled. 'Exactly like that huge tree which, instead of casting its shadow at its feet, throws it bizarrely round about, leaving its roots exposed to the sun, even though they have need of humidity to keep the tree alive.'

'But. . . .' I blurted.

'No,' he said, 'let me finish. I know that when you see the least of men, you attach yourself to him. And you even give him money and pledge your charitable feelings towards him. Even more, you think of him as a brother. . . . And you are so naive that you expect something of man. You await some recognition on his part. Only, in casting your shadow elsewhere, in depriving yourself for others, you condemn yourself. . . .'

'What I do for my brother, I do for myself and for God,' I replied.

'Nonsense!' he yelled. 'You're just a simpleton, you hear? A credulous ass!'

'It's my credulity and simplicity which earn me peace of mind.'

'It's that which condemns you!' he roared.

'Do what you like. Your prison can't change the basis of my ideas. I shall keep my convictions.'

'Does good-will ever pay? . . . Now you, you have a heart of such sensibility and sensitivity that it's incredible. . . . The heart of a mother for her children! . . . It's shameful to have such a good heart. Magnanimity ruins man.'[19]

Persisting in his questions and in his attempts to soften the guard's ferocity, the dreamer is condemned to death by public burning. Marched out before the assembled prisoners and fastened to the pyre, he finds himself ascending, like the smoke of a burnt-offering, high above the scene of his 'death'. In a series of rapid transformations, the dreamer now becomes a sparrow-hawk, but, his flight weakening, is in danger of falling back into the prison when he is rescued by a black serpent which shoots 'like a rocket' into the sky. This serpent, who appears in the earliest pages of Laye's *L'Enfant Noir* in Dioki's cavern and in an earlier scene of *Dramouss*, symbolizes the prophetic and protective wisdom of the ancestors. The dreamer is rescued because of his faith in man, the faith of the traditional African civilization in which he was reared.

There follows a scene in which the snake, descending safely to earth in a neighbouring land, assumes the features of the tall, commanding woman Dramouss. After wandering through the familiar but sadly changed streets of Samakoro, a village in Upper Guinea, the dreamer finds himself standing beneath a huge *kailcedrat* tree, at the foot of which hundreds of corpses lie ranged. Dramouss orders him to bring one more body to complete the rows, but he at first refuses, believing the man she indicates to be merely sleeping. Returning to gather up the body he finds it stiff and heavy with death, but, while he is setting it on his shoulder, the corpse awakens and vanishes like a lightning flash. Is this body his own, and its miraculous resurrection his own also? 'Everything passed as if I had myself been the awakened and reanimated corpse.'[20]

Finally, the vision closes with yet another movement of ascent. A flood of icy water gradually swallows the earth and drives the dreamer into the topmost branches of the tree.* There Dramouss reappears and lights for him a vision of judgement in the skies. Between the files of the damned and blessed appears a huge black tablet on which is inscribed:

ON EARTH MAN DOES NOTHING FOR ANYONE, AND NOTHING AGAINST ANYONE. HE DOES EVERYTHING FOR HIMSELF AND AGAINST HIMSELF.[21]

Dramouss tells him that the revolution has swallowed everything: she has been able to rescue only the gun, the hoe and the assegai, which she has entrusted to the Black Lion (another totemic figure, which may be compared with the panther totem in *Les Soleils des Indépendances*). For the dreamer she has nothing but a golden staff, which proves to be a propelling pencil, the tool of the artist. The moon now descends upon the surface of the great flood, and, balloon-like, opens its door to offer him rescue. Within sits the Black Lion, presiding over the moon's safe ascent towards the sun, to which it proves to be tied by a great cord. Ever more rapidly, lion and dreamer hurtle towards the great source of light. Gradually the moon

*c.f. a similar episode in 'The Eyes of the Statue'.

itself becomes conterminous with the whole redeemed, resurgent, illuminated world of Africa:

> Yes, I recognised these girls dressed in *temourés* and flowing cloths, these boys and old men, these girls and old women. I was looking at my Guinea, guided with wisdom by the Black Lion, the heroic and sage Black Lion.[22]

This complex and extraordinary vision (scornfully dismissed by Blair as a 'political tract'), with its constant transformations and repeated movements of ascent and descent, may be interpreted on many levels. At the most banal of these, the 'source of light' is merely the burning thatch of Fatoman's hut, which he awakes to find in flames (his father says it was burnt down by Dramouss in a jealous fit, because he forgot to warn his son to sleep without his wife that night). It also contains imagery of Laye's own escape from Guinea and his decision to live in adjacent Senegal. But would not anyone familiar with the symbolism of Manding and Malinke culture recognize its rearrangement here in a way that speaks of Laye's undimmed hope in the resurgence of a humane civilization, founded upon what seem to him, through every vicissitude, the most enduring things in the life of Africa? If the prison represents the Guinea of the 1960s then its final ascent under the guidance of the Black Lion speaks of Laye's confidence in its future and the resilience of its traditional humanism. Particularly striking is the concept of the moon as a kind of vehicle or intermediary between man and the sun. Is not the moon often regarded in the Western Sudan as a repository of the souls of the dead? Does not the sun speak, not merely of light but of the rekindling of life? And what of the juxtaposition of the tree, the serpent–woman and the seeker after knowledge? The antiquity and ubiquity of the imagery which Christians associate with *Genesis* are as evident here as in the *Myth of the Bagre*,[23] recorded hundreds of miles southwards, where the first woman learns the art of sexual intercourse with a serpent encountered under a tree, and subsequently teaches it to her husband. For these pages alone, *Dramouss* rewards attention. The broken structure of the book is the expression of a personality which Laye himself describes as divided:

> My being . . . was the sum of two intimate selves: the first, closer to my sense of life, fashioned by my traditional existence of animism slightly tinted with Islam, enriched by French culture, was in conflict with the second, who, for love of his native soil, would betray his own thinking by coming to live in the heart of this regime.[24]

In *Dramouss*, Laye has not found the overall structure which can contain and transcend this conflict. But his use of vision to express it is no sudden aberration; it is deeply consistent both with the whole tradition of the Malinke and of his own writing.

In the years of his exile, Laye has concentrated on compiling an ambitious *variorum* of Manding and Malinke accounts of the exploits of Samory, the great warrior of Western Sudanese resistance to French conquest in the nineteenth century. For this purpose he recorded and compared oral epics of many different *griots* in various parts of Mali, Senegal and Ivory Coast, preparing a text both in the original languages and in French translation. Laye's sensitivity to language and his closeness to the *griot* tradition made him peculiarly suited to carry out this task. But the ill-health and loneliness of these years of exile from his beloved Guinea have hampered the completion of his work on this great project. It can only be hoped that I F A N, the African Research Institute for which he has worked all this time, will carry this great project to its conclusion. But there are ominous signs that Laye, the artist and exile, has fallen among linguists. One can only pray that they, finding his work insufficiently 'rigorous', will not bury it in a pyramind of amendments.

Alex La Guma

Born 1925 in Cape Town, where his family was already active in politics. La Guma early threw himself into activity with the Communist Party and the Coloured People's Congress, which led to his involvement in the Treason Trial of 1956–61 and to several spells of imprisonment and house arrest. Began writing in prison and smuggled his stories out for publication in Nigeria and elsewhere. *A Walk in the Night*, published in 1962, established his reputation as a powerful, original writer, a reputation further advanced by the novels he had published since leaving South Africa for London in 1966.

5 Through Suffering to Resistance

The movement of the La Guma family through two generations might stand as representative of the evolution of the Cape coloured community over the same years. Jimmy La Guma, the father, though a life-long militant, enjoyed the sort of marginal privileges which the regime then allowed to that community. These were a relic of Cecil Rhodes's liberal imperialism, as practised in the Cape during the 1890s. Rhodes, with a political cunning lacking in his successors, had recognized that the long-term safety of the white regime must depend on collaboration with all the groups which might stand between it and the black masses. These groups included, in his view, the large coloured community, the Indians and the small educated black elite, many of whom were in those days notably anxious to co-operate.

These attitudes and ideals did not die with Rhodes but lingered on in a sickly fashion until extinguished by Smuts's deal with the Nationalists in 1924, which began the process of extinguishing group rights one by one. Thus Jimmy La Guma, though as a communist he was opposed to ethnic politics, still followed the tendency for each group to fight its own corner, and still served as President of the South African Coloured People's Congress. Politics in South Africa operated on apartheid lines, long before apartheid itself was enshrined as the official creed of the state. The long-standing notion that each ethnic group must develop its own institutions and work out its own political destiny is now enforced by segregation in housing, education and at work, but the rigour with which it is imposed has begun to produce a rejection of it amongst the young. In 1960, the blacks of Sharpeville died alone. In 1976, many young 'coloureds' were shot down in the streets along with their black comrades. Each death of this kind must bring nearer the emergence of a united resistance to apartheid and the abandonment of sectional politics.

When the Nationalists came to power in 1948, Alex La Guma was already 23. Ignoring the inner logic of that event, many black leaders continued to use the methods of the open society (meetings, petitions, demonstrations, etc.) to fight for their rights. This was still the age of Alan Paton and the rise of the Liberal Party which, although entirely white in leadership, managed to attract some black members. La Guma's own career began apparently within the orbit of his father's, with his election to the executive of the Coloured People's Congress and to the district committee of the Communist Party.

In 1955 came the first significant move towards the forming of a united political opposition to apartheid. This was the formation of the Congress Alliance, consisting of the African National Congress, the Indian Congress, the Coloured People's Congress and the white Congress of Democrats, which included many members of the now banned Communist Party.

The Congress Alliance proceeded to draw up a Freedom Charter, demanding equality of rights in a non-racial South Africa. This in turn led to the notorious treason trial of 1956–61, in which 156 leaders, including La Guma, were charged by the state and took five years of legal battle to free themselves. Although it ended with the acquittal of all the accused, the trial had the desired effect of ruining many of the accused both financially and professionally. In La Guma's case, this legal battle was immediately followed by a series of imprisonments, bannings and house arrests which lasted right up to his final departure from South Africa in 1966.

Whilst undergoing these long periods of enforced idleness, La Guma read widely and began to write short stories. During the intervals between imprisonment, he wrote for the radical journal *New Age*. Both his early short novels, *A Walk in the Night* and *And a Threefold Cord*, were also written whilst he was in prison or under house arrest. But La Guma's writing did not directly reflect his own involvement in active political struggle at this time, even though most of it was smuggled out of the country and published overseas. Not until the appearance of *In the Fog of the Season's End* in 1972 did La Guma produce a full-length portrait of a dedicated political activist in Beukes, the grass-roots revolutionary whose obscure course knits together all the lines of resistance which tyranny is still unable to snap. In his earlier fiction, his *personae* had registered suffering and endurance – the conscience of witness – rather than a quiet determination to go on burrowing at the foundations of white power, despite the death or disappearance of comrades, the dogging vigilance of BOSS and the nightmare terrors of the torture cell. The publication of *In the Fog of the Season's End* marked the convergence of his fiction with his own long-held position as an uncompromising revolutionary.

The reasons for that slowness of convergence may be sought in his choice of form. For La Guma's first published work consisted of the shortest of short stories, and this is not a form which can carry any strong ideological charge. The statements it makes are vivid and brief; they must be left to produce their own effect in the reader's imagination. At their best La Guma's stories do precisely that, drawing no attention to their art or to the artist's opinions, but leaving us with the raw, sharp flavour of experience in a society where racism is the very air we breathe. Such a story is 'Slipper Satin', first published in December 1960. In a few pages, this shows us the return of a young brown girl to her home after a prison sentence served under the Immorality Act. The girl is completely isolated in her belief that what she has done is no crime, and would not be considered as such in any decent society. Not only does her ignorant, unhappy mother load her with reproaches for disgracing them all, but her white lover Tommy, who also clearly regards their relationship as a disgrace, has shot himself at the moment of their discovery by the police, rather than face up to it. Only her heedless affectionate young sister Ada, intent on her own impending marriage to what their mother calls 'a nice coloured boy, one of our own kind of people', greets her with any sympathy or love. But Myra, the heroine, has come to the end of weeping, even to the end of bitterness. She lies on her bed thinking how she will buy Ada an evening dress of slipper satin. She feels almost apologetic for the suffering which her decent, simple morality has caused in a society where it is not only the law which deems her behaviour immoral:

Dear old Ada, with a whore for a sister. . . . She felt sorry for her mother, for Ada, for all those women up the street, for Tommy. Poor old Tommy. Tommy couldn't stand up to it. Him and his love. Him and his I love you. She had died, too, she thought, the instant Tommy pulled the trigger.[1]

'Slipper Satin' and a rather similar story called 'A Glass of Wine', which also looks ironically at the inhumanity of South Africa's race laws, were the first of La Guma's published work to appear outside the Republic. They appeared in 1960 in *Black Orpheus* (nos. 7 and 8) whose editor, Ulli Beier, brought out La Guma's short novel *A Walk in the Night* for Mbari Publications in 1962. This work, written when its author was under house arrest, and was shortly to be placed once more in solitary confinement, made a powerful and immediate impression. It established La Guma as a major figure in African fiction, whose work was quite unlike that of any other novelist then writing. His world was that of the sleazy clubs, bars, whorehouses and tenements of District Six, a coloured slum in Cape Town which was soon afterwards bulldozed by the Government and the site designated for white occupation. La Guma's prose lifts the glossy surface off Cape Town's tourist brochures like a scalpel, and shows us the swarming misery of existence for the majority of its citizens:

In the dark a scrap of cloud struggled along the edge of Table Mountain, clawed at the rocks for a foothold, was torn away by the breeze that came in from the south east, and disappeared. In the hot tenements the people felt the breeze through the chinks and cracks of loose boarding and broken windows and stirred in their sweaty sleep. Those who could not sleep sat by the windows or in doorways and looked out towards the mountain beyond the roof tops and searched for the sign of wind. The breeze carried the stale smells from passageway to passageway, from room to room, along lanes and back alleys, through the realms of the poor, until the massed smells of stagnant water cooking, rotting vegetables, oil, fish, damp plaster and timber, unwashed curtains, bodies and stairways, cheap perfume and incense, spices and half-washed kitchenware, urine, animals and dusty corners became one vast, anonymous odour. . . .[2]

The landscape of early La Guma is invariably urban and un-relentingly sordid. Not for him is there any escape to the white suburbs or to the noble landscapes where one can momentarily forget the South African tragedy. And for his characters too, there is often only the escape of death. Their poverty and abandonment have no other end. *A Walk in the Night* begins as the story of Michael Adonis's aimless journey through District Six, but in the course of the narrative we have a sense of all its characters locked in similarly random and wasting motion. Willieboy's own journey ends in the back of a police-truck and Doughty's at the end of a bottle. Adonis is clearly destined to drift into violent crime and towards a violent end. Foxy and his depraved gang move through the plot like a sinister chorus, looking vainly for Sockies. Only the orphaned Joe, the most destitute of all, has any sense of dimension extending beyond Hanover Street, with its filthy alleys and the illusory promise of its neon signs. But he is unable to convey his sense of this to the damned spirits who walk the dark labyrinth of these streets. His sense of wonder is as lost upon them as his sense of nature:

'I got a big starfish on the beach yesterday. One big, big one. It was dead and stank.'

'Well, it's a good job you didn't bring it into town. City Council would be on your neck.'

'I hear they're going to make the beaches so only white people can go there,' Joe said.[3]

Joe crosses Michael Adonis's path several times during the night, drawing from him his single act of charity and warning him against the brutality of Foxy's gang. But there seems to be something fateful about the young man's drift to disaster. At the very threshold of his crime, he fails to respond to the broad hints of the girl who is setting off alone to see a film called *Love Me Tonight*. Ten minutes later, with a murder on his hands, he is beyond any such innocent diversions. He is ripe for Foxy, the long prison sentence or the police bullet. But what really drives him onward is not abstract fate; it is his rage at a wrongful dismissal for answering back to the white foreman. There is thus nothing mystical about Adonis's doom. On the contrary we perceive a direct causal connection with the racist character of the society, which provides so many of the book's characters with this impulse towards self-destruction.

Whereas many of the short stories exhibit an ironic humour, *A Walk in the Night* is a sombre work, as dark as the streets through which its action is threaded. Those exhibiting random acts of charity, like Adonis, are also capable of random acts of violence. Constable Raalt is capable of little else but brutality, through which he channels all his rage at his inadequacies as a husband. The young police driver will, we are sure, soon pick up the brutal attitudes and corrupt practices of his senior. The only glimpses of a fuller humanity are in the marginal characters of Frankie Lorenzo and his wife (who play no part in the action) and Joe. And, significantly, it is they to whom La Guma gives the closing lines of the book:

Somewhere the young man, Joe, made his way towards the sea, walking alone through the starlit darkness. . . . And in the rock pools he would examine the mysterious life of the sea things, the transparent beauty of starfish and anemone, and hear the relentless, consistent pounding of the creaming waves against the granite citadels of rock.

Frankie Lorenzo slept on his back and snored peacefully. Beside him the woman, Grace, lay awake in the dark, restlessly waiting for the dawn and feeling the knot of life within her.[4]

This short novel, and the three full-length novels which followed, have allowed scope to La Guma's exceptional gifts for description and evocation, gifts which were scarcely displayed in his short stories. In a few pages, these usually take a single scene or incident (the shy white boy of 'A Glass of Wine' coming to see his girl in a black shebeen; the two men in 'At the Portagees' picking up a couple of young, giggling girls) and handle it largely through dialogue. This technique keeps the writer more firmly in the background than in the novels, where his extended descriptions are themselves a kind of commentary. But La Guma's distinctive dialogue, with its scattering of Afrikaans words and its peculiarities of style, is already fully displayed in the early stories:

'You can have the green,' Banjo said.
'She's got pimples.'
'But she got *mos* knobs, too. Don't I say?[5]

La Guma's use of the short story, however, was very much as an apprenticeship to the novel. His interest in the form is limited and he has never attempted to give it the sort of elaboration we find in even early Mphahlele pieces, like 'Grieg on a Stolen Piano' and 'The Living and Dead'. Mphahlele's success here, which makes him one of Africa's best short story writers, matched with the failure of his one attempt at the novel, prompt us to see him as a writer for whom the short story is the perfect medium. The same could not be said of La Guma, who both attempts and achieves all his best effects in the more extended form. It is probable that he has put the short story behind him since *A Walk in the Night* and turned his attention entirely towards the novel.

Unlike the ironic commentary which characterizes the early stories the increased scope of the novel brings from the author a greater degree of commitment. If *A Walk in the Night* shows us characters caught up in an inexorable fate, *And a Threefold Cord* (1964) indicates more possibilities of choice and development, even though its actors are sunk lower still in poverty and abandonment than those of the earlier book.

Structurally, the new novel also differs considerably from its predecessor. *A Walk in the Night*, as befits its title, is confined to the events of a single night as well as those of a single district. But, although it starts by following the footsteps of Michael Adonis, it soon broadens out to show us other actors who are likewise 'doomed to fast in fires', so that the centre of the narrative's attention is continually shifting. *And a Threefold Cord* offers the same concentration of venue and concerns the events of a few days only, but it is more exclusively centred upon the consciousness of Charlie Pauls. In this sense, it may be said to have a 'hero'. All the other figures who appear in the book, from the Pauls family through their African and coloured neighbours to Susie Meyer, the poor-white wreck George Mostert and the white policeman felled by Charlie's heavy fist, are connected with his movements around the shanty-town in the brief time-span of the plot.

Charlie Pauls wakes to the sound of rain, and rain is the *leit-motif* which runs through the whole book. If the sticky watchers of District Six were waiting for the South-easter to blow, here they are waiting vainly for the rains to stop. And these shanty-dwellers are considerably more at the mercy of the elements than the lodging-house denizens of *A Walk in the Night*. Rain flows as constantly through the dialogue as through the many descriptive passages of the novel:

'Still raining?' he asked, putting the brush away on a shelf made of a tomato-box nailed to an upright of the wall. There was a small, dusty jar of thick, green pomade on the shelf, beside the brush, and the skeleton of a plastic comb, dry entrails of hair clinging stubbornly to its broken ribs.

'*Ja*,' Charlie said, and sat down on his bed. . . . 'But not so much. Just a little. It will hold up later I think.'

'How you know it's going to hold up?' Ronald asked, with a little scorn in his voice. 'How you know such a lot about when the rain will stop and how long it will go up? You's *mos* clever, man. Don't I say?'[6]

Rain impels Charlie to make his visit to Mostert, calling *en route* upon his neglected mistress Freda, and fighting on behalf of his sullen brother Ronald. Rain contributes to his father's death and to the enforced idleness of his drunken Uncle Ben. Rain falls into his father's grave and over the torn features of Susie Meyer, dying under Ronald's knife. Even the raiding policemen have the effrontery to complain about the weather, as they kick down doors and break open lives.

Charlie Pauls's simple humanity is the main antidote to events which, on the naturalistic level, are as depressing as those of the earlier novel. He does not give up, and as long as he doesn't, the current of life, even the current of hope, seems to flow through these wretched streets. We are soon made very much aware of his presence and of a kind of personal force within him:

Charlie's face, brown-skinned, glowed in the light which picked up the wide curves of his high cheekbones and the thick, solid jaw running into a chin as curved and hard as the toe of an army boot. There was a dark stubble in the hollows of his cheeks, and deep grooves bracketed the wide, heavy, humorous and sensual mouth. He had a wide forehead, and low, with the dark, thick, kinky hair growing far forward. There was a mole on his right cheekbone. His eyes were dark-brown, the colour of chestnuts, gleaming in the lamp-light, the eyeballs yellowish.[7]

This is the figure who will have to deal with the aftermath of his father's death, with Ronald's probable execution, with the burning of Freda's children, with his own prolonged unemployment. It is a measure of the book's success that we feel confident he will indeed deal with it all. But we feel this because of what he is, rather than what he says. La Guma has sought to show in Charlie the dawnings of an ideological consciousness, but he has weakened this by making it only a recollection of some half-understood words spoken by a 'slim rooker' with whom he once worked. The introduction of these recollections is forced and self-conscious. La Guma could equally well have shown Charlie as coming to certain decisions by himself (as in his striking of the policeman and his taking in of Freda), without the aid of these rather adventitious appeals to the rooker and his opinions. Such an effect of direct experience and reflection is shown in this speech:

'Listen, Uncle Ben, one time I went up to see Freda up by that people she work for, cleaning and washing. Hell, that people got a house, *mos*, big as the effing city hall, almost, and there's an old bitch with purple hair and fat backsides and her husband eating off a table a mile long, with fancy candles and *dingus* on it. And a *juba* like me can't even touch the handle of the front door. . . .'[8]

Charlie does represent, however, the first emergence in La Guma's work of someone who is fumbling his way towards a philosophy of resistance rather than one of endurance.

If La Guma's first novel is cast in a darkness as profound as the first scene of *Hamlet* or the lowest circle of Dante's Hell, the world of *And a Threefold Cord* is one of daylight, however rain-sodden. Its range of mood is also far wider, embracing tenderness and love, responsibility and concern, as well as tragedy and violence. Above all, the book is shot through with humour, both in the dialogue and in a description like this concerning the funeral procession of Daddy Pauls:

Up ahead, in front of the hearse, walked Mister Sampie, the undertaker's agent. He was a small, brown, knobbly man, like a peanut. Off duty he was chirpy, but now he had assumed the guise of an attendant upon death, and he plodded along at the correct pace, with an air of sadness, hands clasped professionally behind his back. . . .

And beside him walked Brother Bombata. Woolly-haired, and black as a beetle, he trudged ahead with his own professional air, clutching a dog-eared Bible against his side; and with his flaring nostrils and long, gloomy face, looking for all the world like an ageing horse in a white celluloid collar.[9]

As already suggested, each of La Guma's novels establishes a distinctive, closed world and confines its action entirely within it. This confinement reaches its logical extreme in his third novel, *The Stone Country* (1967). The panorama of fiction can be internal as well as external, and we need not traverse the steppes of Russia or the battlefields of Napoleonic Europe in order to encounter examples of every sort of human personality in action. It is a true if sad comment on twentieth-century literature, that many of its finest novels have accepted the walls of a prison, a labour camp or a hospital as the limits of a sufficient world; for the prisoner or patient at least knows precisely what he longs for, which is often more than the free man can boast of.

With the exception of one short flashback showing how George Adams and Jefferson were arrested, *The Stone Country* exhibits this kind of austerity. The prisoners do not even spend much time in dream or reminiscence; the novel's dramas are not internal, but are played out in the grim yards and cells of the gaol itself. This after all, as the epigraph reminds us, is the world inhabited by a daily average of 70,351 South Africans. An even more interesting statistic would be that showing how few South African blacks have never seen the inside of a police or prison cell. The logic of the whole Pass System seems to be to ensure that they do.

La Guma's short stories had already introduced less developed versions of some of the characters in *The Stone Country*. 'Tattoo-Marks and Nails' had shown us the prototypes of Butcherboy (the prison bully) and Yusef the Turk; in 'The Creature' and 'Ahmed the Turk'. There is too the relentless emphasis on heat, for prisoners can be more or less indifferent to the alternations of day and night, and even to rain (which had provided the elemental dominance of the first two books), but summer still touches them with its sweaty finger:

The heat was solid. As Ahmed the Turk remarked, you could reach out before your face, grab a handful of heat, fling it at the wall, and it would stick. . . .

'I know only one place hotter than this,' said Ahmed, alleged house-breaker, assaulter and stabber. He smiled, flashing his teeth the colour of ripe corn in his dark handsome face. 'And I don't mean Hell,' he added.[10]

Here are the lineaments of that friendship which develops in the novel between the educated, relatively innocent 'political', George Adams and the lean, wiry Turk, veteran of a hundred street-fights. Without perhaps comprehending exactly what moves George Adams, the Turk senses in him a kind of superiority which he is determined to protect against the uncouth lunges of Butcherboy:

Yusef the Turk laughed. 'This is *good* people, man. Not your kind, not my kind, even. You know this John? No.' The easy voice changed suddenly, and the Turk said dangerously, 'Leave him.'[11]

Well though the Turk is characterized and vital though he is to the balance of life in the cells, the triumph of the novel is in the depiction of the Casbah Kid, the nineteen-year-old boy with ancient eyes and sealed lips who is awaiting sentence for murder. The Kid provides a measure for the fates of the other inmates, who are at least not destined to hang; who may hope for a term they can see the end of; who do not have as their earliest memory the horror and complicity this boy has never been able to bury. For the Kid has not only been the terrified, helpless witness of his mother's suicide, but has said nothing to prevent his father hanging for the crime. In one of his rare bursts of confidence to George, there is a sense that he has probably deserved this turn of events, from the fatalism he expresses.

George Adams looked across at the boy and shook his head sadly. He said, 'Maybe it is too late, but don't you feel sorry about that one you stabbed?'

The boy looked at him. 'What one? Oh, him, Sorry? What is sorry? I tell you, mister, his death was put out for him . . . he don't give up straight. He want to struggle, *mos*. So the next thing the knife is in him. Okay, mister, I'm not squealing. It was put out don't I say?'

'But, listen – '

The Casbah Kid broke in surlily: 'Forget it, mister. You's clever. You got things to talk about and brains. Okay. But leave it, hey. Me, I'm going to swing. Who cares? My old man was hanged, so what about it?'

George Adams said: 'Your father? Your Pa?'

But the Casbah Kid had turned away onto his side, facing the wall, withdrawing into stubborn silence.[12]

Poignant exchanges like this, and the final parting between George and the Kid at the book's end, are the most effective things in the novel. The many descriptive passages, though usually vivid and exact, are occasionally overdone. Butcherboy, whose death at the hands of the Kid ends Part 1, attracts too many epithets. He is variously described as 'anthropoid', 'ape-like', 'neolithic' and 'ugly and brutal as a Neanderthal'; which is a popular but inaccurate use of language, since anthropoid means man-like and hence conflicts with ape-like, whilst Neolithic man was no different physically or mentally from ourselves. As for the Neanderthal, I suppose it is a matter of taste, as William Golding found them so endearing in *The Inheritors*.

The same weakness of overemphasis can be found in the following paragraph which contains no fewer than one metaphor and three diverse similes (and when did the stars ever look like cheap jewellery, anyway?):

Above him, the darkness writhed and undulated with the wild, vast caresses of the South-east wind, and the starlit sky, dark purple, glimmered like a blanket strewn with cheap jewellery. Away, beyond the outer walls of the prison, the city glowed like a dying bonfire in the night haze, and along the harbour front the silhouettes of cranes rose like the dark, un-covered forms of petrified monsters.[13]

The great set-pieces of the book are, however, free from this sort of strained effect. The defeat of Butcherboy by the Turk has the quality of fresh, direct observation, whilst the conflict of cat and mouse which punctuates Gus's efforts to get hold of the hack-saw blades that promise his own liberty is full of tension, humour and irony. The final escape of the battered, terrified mouse anticipates that of the unwilling Koppe, who is the only man to get away in the ensuing gaol-break.

The segregation which moulds public life in South Africa is perfectly mirrored in the stone country of the prison, so that George and his black comrade Jefferson, who were arrested together for the same crime, never see each other once inside its walls. The counterpoint of their separate suffering is the theme taken up in La Guma's fourth book, *In the Fog of the Season's End*, and becomes the chief element in its structure. Here again we have two main protagonists, the African Elias and the coloured Beukes, who are activists and organizers in the freedom struggle. In the age of B O S S, the repressive statutes of the 1960s and the rise of guerilla warfare in Southern Africa, this struggle has become far grimmer and more demanding than in the far-off days of meetings and petitions. The whole book is framed by the agony of Elias, who is arrested on its opening page and mercifully dies, after prolonged torture, towards its end. His more extreme suffering thus runs through the whole novel as one element of its theme, to which the controlled but nagging fear of Beukes provides a counter-element. The two are tied more tightly together because Elias's silence is designed to protect Beukes, one of the few organizers still at large, whose identity is still unknown to the police. His fidelity is the more admirable because he doesn't know for certain whether Beukes has got away. In this book La Guma is able to depict for the first time a solidarity which goes beyond black and brown attending one another in moments of need and crisis (as we saw in the shanty-town of *And a Threefold Cord*), to one which is as strong as death itself. If Elias dies to protect Beukes, then Beukes at the end of the book chooses to remain in South Africa, organizing the escape of others who will become freedom-fighters, at the cost of sharing, almost certainly, the fate of Elias before long.

La Guma's way of building this story of resistance and dire suffering is altogether bolder than any he has used earlier. We begin with the arrest and initial interrogation of Elias without learning his name or his connection with the main action which follows. Then we jump directly to a nursemaid called Beatie Adams, sitting in the municipal park where she is spoken to by a tired-looking brown man who is sharing the same bench. She goes off at the end of the chapter and we see her no more, but the tired man turns out to be Beukes, and for the main body of the action his movements are the thread that we follow around the city, as he moves from contact to contact, sleeping little and never in the same place. Beukes has already been obliged to leave the young wife he loves, in order to avoid easy arrest, and is living a kind of half-life of ceaseless movement, secrecy and infinite precaution which is the only way to keep a step ahead of the security police. Later we learn that he was actually with Elias at the moment of the latter's arrest, but managed to escape with a wounded arm and get treatment for the gunshot wound from a discreet doctor:

'Well, it's like this . . .' Beukes started to say.

But the doctor broke up the smoke with a small, plump hand and said through the gap: 'Mister Beukes, I can tell a gunshot wound, even a flesh wound, when I see one, although I do not have the opportunity of treating many . . . The police?'

Beukes nodded. The doctor said, 'Yes, one could guess so. . . . Well, the law says I should report suspicious wounds and so on.'

'Will you obey the law?'

The doctor looked at his cigarette and then back at Beukes. 'If the community is given the opportunity of participating in making the law, then they have a moral obligation to obey it,' he said.

'But if the law is made for them, without their consent or participation, then it's a different matter . . . Injustice prevails, and there are people who have the nerve enough to defy it. Perhaps I have been waiting for the opportunity to put my penny in the hat as well.'[14]

Beukes's contacts range from sophisticated sympathizers like this to obscure activists like the messenger Isaac and naive acquaintances like Tommy, the ballroom-dancing fanatic, who offers him a bed occasionally out of sheer uncomprehending good-will. All are necessary to the design of resistance and secrecy. The last piece in this design that we encounter is the least idealistically motivated of all. He is the mechanic Henny April, who makes money on the side by transporting stolen or smuggled goods, illegal immigrants, and all who might have reasons for crossing the frontier discreetly. The tableau with which the novel closes ranges from the venal but co-operative April to the committed young Africans who are escaping in order to join the guerrilla armies on the border. In the midst, as usual, stands Beukes, the most unheroic and persevering of heroes, more exposed than ever after the disappearance of Elias, but going quietly back to the city to resume the round of his loveless exhausting existence.

In this mature novel La Guma has restrained the exuberance of his descriptions and has developed the ironic juxtapositions which we encountered in *The Stone Country*. One of the best of these is the scene where the wounded Beukes slumps against the garden wall of a posh white house, desperately easing his arm out of the jacket-sleeve so as to conceal the blood, whilst the frivolous, drunken conversation of a suburban party floats over his head. This is a far more telling way of depicting the infinite separation of South Africa's social worlds than any amount of polemics. Experience, depicted at this level of authenticity, is the most eloquent denunciation:

Using his good hand and his teeth, Beukes knotted the handkerchief around the bloody shirtsleeve. Somebody was laughing and saying, . . . 'champagne' . . . and he thought, I could do with some of that right now, or a stiff brandy. Can't remember when I last tasted brandy. He could not

see where the wound was and was afraid of making any sort of examination. Behind him the voices still argued. 'I'd like to be left alone, thank you. Why don't you go and find that Helen Stuttaford?'
   Somebody said, 'She's pissed and passed out in the joint.'[15]

The confinement of this novel is that forced upon Beukes's life-style by his dedication to resistance. We move around the city and the suburbs with apparent freedom, by day or night, encountering a variety of characters, settings and métiers. But every so often our footsteps cross with those of the two white detectives who have already caught and destroyed Elias, who have missed Isaac by a hair's-breadth, and are circling ever nearer to Beukes himself. The confinement, then, is not physical but psychological; it is the confinement of well-founded fear, which makes a man study his every move, his every word, his every gesture. La Guma here attempts a range of characterization, including the African Elias and the white doctor, for beyond anything in his other work. By showing us, without fuss, just what resistance now means and costs, he has written his finest and most moving work.
   In 1979, after a silence of seven years, La Guma published a short novel which marks, in some respects, a return to the manner of his short stories and of *A Walk in the Night*. Whereas *In the Fog of the Season's End* traces a developing situation which begins with the arrest of Elias and ends with his death and the safe departure of the young guerillas, *Time of the Butcherbird* centres upon a single episode. That episode is the murder – or perhaps the execution – of the Nationalist politician Hannes Meulen. We sense its approach from almost the first page; thereafter we merely follow the gradually converging movements of Meulen and his assassin until their explosive encounter. The interim has shown us why Murile cannot rest until his brother's murder has been avenged upon the one surviving culprit, and why Meulen does not really deserve any alleviation of his fate. Direct responsibility for the death of a fellow human being has taught him nothing; he is in fact about to share responsibility for the probable death of others, displaced from their meagre acres in the midst of a season of drought by their 'God fearing' white neighbours:

'As soon as the kaffirs are moved – '
'We call them Bantu now, boy,' Steen said and smiled again. 'Things have changed.'
Meulen smiled, 'As soon as the Bantu have been moved, the develop-

ment of the area will commence. As you know, by the request of the people here I myself went to the magistrate to ask that they be moved . . .'

'Those black things will move, of course,' Steen remarked.

'Naturally. . . .'[16]

La Guma's dialogue in this story is peppered with the kind of irony we find here. Not only does Steen's remark that 'things have changed' run counter to the way the two men casually discuss the destruction of a human community, but he himself quickly slips from the official word 'Bantu' to 'those black things'. The removal of the black community from the neighbourhood is another episode, far more typical than the murder of Meulen with which it coincides, around which the story unfolds. And here La Guma offers us a structural irony corresponding with the more detailed ones in his dialogue and descriptions. The story ends with a heroic gesture of resistance to removal by the handful of aged black inhabitants and their women folk. If the ending should leave us in any doubt of the immediate outcome, this has been resolved already by the story's opening paragraph, where the arrival of the deportees in their wretched new desert is described. But the resistance is important as a symptom rather than a material blow to white authority. On a local level, both the resistance and Meulen's murder underline for the little *dorp* in the Karroo the same lesson that the mass demonstrations are giving to the cities: that, if times have not yet changed, they certainly are a-changing.

A more extensive structural irony is offered by the sub-plot of Edgar Stopes and his wife Maisie. Stopes's presence in the town is as random as his frequent encounters with Meulen in the squalid little hotel and his presence at the very moment when Meulen is killed, which earns him the other barrel of the shotgun. But his death coincides with the very moment when his wife is considering, and perhaps renouncing, the idea of getting rid of him by violent means. The tawdriness of this whole sub-plot is perhaps La Guma's way of situating the English-speaking petty bourgeoisie, also the target of Athol Fugard's satire in a play like *People are Living There*. It is because the grip of Hannes Meulen and his like upon South Africa is so strong that it has to be loosened; they have no other reality and must learn to modify the only one they know. Stopes and his Maisie are Identikit characters who could be reconstructed in Pittsburgh or Peterborough without any change being necessary in their horizons or their vocabulary. La Guma may be implying that their involvement in the South African tragedy, which is in essence the struggle between

Boer and Bantu for mastery of the land, is as random as Stopes's involvement in the death of Meulen.

Time of the Butcherbird is remarkable not only for the density with which it recalls rural South Africa after thirteen years of exile and for the sureness of its touch with all the inhabitants of the wretched little *dorp*, but for the poetic interpretation of landscape and action. This is particularly evident on the first page and the last, and in all those intervening sequences which involve Murile with the old shepherd Madolena. The story ends with these two setting out across the scorched *veld*:

The sun, a smear of bronze, turns the light of the world a cruel metallic yellow in the furnace–hot time of the day. Now there is a harshness and a hardness in the land that foretells little sympathy for the weak.... It seems that the air, heavy with heat, begins to move. It has weight, it moves soundlessly and heavily, gathering momentum.... The movement of the wind builds up and carries the stinging dust; the veils of dust cross the land like the smoke from lines of artillery and the moaning of the wind rises to a roar.... Then the thrust of the wind lessens and the difference in the air makes life possible again. The roaring dies away.

The yellowing afternoon light puts a golden colour on the land. A flight of birds swoop overhead towards a water-hole.[17]

These are the concluding words of the novel. It is to achieve that 'difference in the air' that men and women endure torture, imprisonment, death and exile. In that afternoon light a water-hole becomes a symbol of refreshment and renewal for a land which has come near to death. But for the desolate deportees of the opening page the official watertank had resembled nothing but 'an empty glove clenched against the flat and empty sky'.[18]

Chinua Achebe

Born 1930 at Ogidi in Eastern Nigeria, son of a catechist and early Christian convert. After Umuahia Government College, Achebe went to the new University College at Ibadan as one of the first generation of undergraduates there. His first novel, *Things Fall Apart*, appeared in 1958 and made an instant impression throughout Africa. Until the outbreak of the Nigerian civil war, Achebe worked for the Nigerian Broadcasting Corporation, rising to the position of Director of the External Service. Since 1970 he has pursued an academic career in the United States and at Nsukka, where he edits the literary journal *Okike*. Achebe has published no major fiction since *A Man of the People* in 1966, but has continued to work as a poet and story-writer.

6   Unless Tomorrow

The appearance of *Things Fall Apart* in 1958 won for its author a position of eminence in African literature which for a long time led to his being elevated above his fellows, in his own and the succeeding generation. The book was quickly recognized as a classic and tended to be used as a yardstick with which to measure the many Anglophone novels, Nigerian and other, that followed it. It was, indeed, the first African novel of real weight and substance to appear in English. For reasons explained in *Seven African Writers*, I do not consider Amos Tutuola's major books to be novels in the proper sense; they are more comparable to the prose epics or romances of the late medieval or Renaissance periods in Europe which, like them, were largely composed of folk materials. The 'novel', as Ian Watt has argued, is so called precisely because it is something new; a substantial departure from the rehandling of already familiar oral narratives which preceded its emergence. Much more truly a novel is Cyprian Ekwensi's *People of the City* (1954), and Ekwensi can be profitably compared with an early journalist/novelist such as Daniel Defoe, just as the new petit-bourgeois reading public in the Nigeria of the 1950s can be compared with that of Augustan England.

But, although Ekwensi's example in creating a popular fiction for these new urban readers was important, his early novels do possess the flaws often associated with that genre: improbable plots with rather contrived happy endings; sentimentality combined with sexual titillation; and a somewhat spurious condemnation of the free-wheeling, amoral urban life which his readers crave to join. These same weaknesses can be found, of course, in Defoe's *Moll Flanders*, yet they do not prevent its being seen as a classic of early English fiction. Improbable plots and happy endings remained a feature of the English novel long after Defoe. Perhaps it is too soon to determine Ekwensi's final status as an African novelist, but a comparison with *Things Fall Apart* shows the latter to be a more sustained work.

Achebe's task was not merely to look back to the Africa of his childhood, but through that childhood into the Africa of some two generations earlier. At the beginning of *Things Fall Apart*, the white man has not even been heard of, let alone seen. By its end, he has already destroyed the delicate equilibrium of the traditional world. Camara Laye, from the work-bench of the Simca factory in Paris, could look back upon the vanishing life of his savannah childhood with a loving and somewhat idealizing eye. But Achebe had to strive for objectivity in evoking a life that he personally had never known. Furthermore, Achebe's childhood, as the son of a leading Christian convert, had been spent in considerable isolation from the vestiges of traditional culture still surviving around him. It was only as an adult that he gained the orientation which made him frequent the old, the shrines, the festivals, and all other available means towards the recreation of a credible, actual past.

Achebe's theme is suggested by his title, chosen from Yeats's celebrated poem 'The Second Coming':

Things fall apart; the centre cannot hold;
Mere anarchy is loosed upon the world,
The blood-dimmed tide is loosed, and everywhere
The ceremony of innocence is drowned;

But although he sees the disintegration of Igbo* society as a communal and personal tragedy for those who lived through it, he does not allow this theme to distort his account of that society as it was. We perceive its strengths as well as its weaknesses; and we perceive that these weaknesses contributed to its fairly rapid collapse, once the process of penetration was really in motion. In Achebe's own area, this first thrust was surprisingly long in coming. The Anglican missionaries were established at Onitsha, on the Niger, by 1857, but they made few converts during the next thirty years or more. It was only towards the end of the century that they, swiftly followed by the British Administration, began to make deep inroads into the Igbo heartland behind them. It was Achebe's own grandfather who welcomed the first missionaries to Ogidi, only six miles up the road from Onitsha.

Achebe's hero, Okonkwo, may be supposed to have lived roughly between 1850 and 1900, in an inland village rather further from the European presence than Ogidi. There are many such villages where

*I have followed Achebe's more recent practice in preferring this spelling to 'Ibo'.

even today one may meet old people who remember 'the coming of the white man' as an event of their childhood, but none today can recall the pre-colonial society as a living, daily reality; it is just too long ago. Hence the problem of recreating that society as experienced by someone like Okonkwo, who was already an elder when the first cracks appeared in its structure.

It is here that the novelist's manner is all important. Achebe's brief, almost laconic style, his refusal to justify, explain or condemn, are responsible for a good deal of the book's success. The novelist *presents* to us a picture of traditional Igbo life as just as he can make it. The final judgement of that life, as of the life that replaced it, is left to us. Only Achebe insists that we should see it as a life actually lived by plausible men and women before we dismiss it, with the usual shrug, as nothing but ignorance, darkness and death. His people win our full respect as individuals whose life has dignity, significance and positive values. Only they were as ruthless as the members of most societies in rejecting whatever seemed to threaten their security. Being a tense and somewhat pessimistic people, the area of light within which they could live in confidence was a rather narrow one. Everything which by its abnormality appeared to threaten that area was literally cast out to perish in 'the bad bush'. This went even for such a happy phenomenon as the birth of twins, welcome to many other African tribes. It was not quite common enough to rank as 'normal', and was consequently looked upon with special fear and abhorrence.

In order to highlight Okonkwo's fall from hard-won fame and eminence to exile and a death deemed abominable by the clan, Achebe first introduces him at the height of his prosperity. We learn retrospectively of his rise and we witness his downward career. But before concentrating upon narrative, the novelist must first set the scene, not only for the foreigner but the modern Nigerian reader. So each of the first ten chapters, though slightly advancing the plot, also introduces one of the events of the Igbo calendar: the rituals of welcome in chapter 1; the mode of settling a blood-feud in chapter 2; the Week of Peace which precedes the planting season in chapter 4; the New Yam Festival and its attendant wrestling bouts in chapters 5 and 6; a judgement by the masked spirits in chapter 10: these are some examples of how Achebe fills in the social context of his main action. For some curious reason, however skilfully this is done, the African novelist is always accused of 'putting in too much anthropology' if he attempts to show us the texture of daily living in traditional society. Of course, this type of exposition can be done clumsily and obtrusively, though Achebe generally avoids these dangers. But the Western reader in particular is likely to scent anthropology in the breaking of kola, but not in the rituals of tea-drinking in a Jane Austen parlour or a Russian country house.

In the meantime, we are beginning to build up our picture of the proud, fierce Okonkwo. We perceive that he is not quite as strong as he seems, since he is a man driven by a fear of failure, who feels the constant need to prove himself more manly than others. His beating of Ojiugo during the Week of Peace is just the first evidence of a vein of recklessness which can make him occasionally transgress the very traditions he is trying to embody. The comments of the Ezeani on that affair are ominous: 'The evil you have done can ruin the whole clan'.[1] The tone is echoed soon afterwards by his friend Obierika on the slaying of his adopted son Ikemefuna: 'It is the kind of action for which the goddess wipes out whole families.'[2] In retrospect, we shall come to see this beating of Ojiugo as the first in a chain of actions which makes Okonkwo's exile from Umuofia seem like divine justice rather than arbitrary misfortune. In any case, the society in which he lives does not recognize the possibility of a misfortune that is not rooted in one's actions or one's personal fate, one's *chi*.

Everything in Okonkwo's driven nature contributes to his striking down of his ward Ikemefuna, his heavy threats to the wretched Nwoye to hide his sense of guilt in this affair, or his shooting at another wife in blind anger. That time, he aimed and missed; next time, it is perhaps Ani the Earth Goddess herself who ensures he will unwittingly kill a clansman when firing his gun at a funeral. Despite their evident difference in character and reputation, there is a fateful similarity in the deaths of Okonkwo and his father Unoka, for suicide is if anything deemed even more abominable than the swelling sickness, and likewise forfeits the right of honourable burial. Thus Okonkwo's lifelong struggle to be as unlike his father as possible brings him full circle, to the 'evil grove'. There is more here than simple tragic irony; for it is Okonkwo's excessive harshness, his cult of virility at the expense of tenderness and understanding, which contributes to the string of offences that prepares his fate: the beating of a wife during the Week of Peace; the slaying of Ikemefuna; the shooting at Ekwefi and the destruction of Nwoye's natural love and respect for his father.

Okonkwo's exile marks the end of his good fortune. Although his sulky behaviour there is an insult to his mother's clan, whose 'son' he truly is, Okonkwo is right in feeling that he will never recover his former position in Umuofia. The seven years of his exile have, in any case, so changed and divided the old community that the former position of an eminence recognized by everybody no longer exists. Okonkwo's futile attempt to bring back the old heroic age with a single hatchet-blow may look noble in retrospect; at the time it only causes fear and embarrassment:

Okonkwo stood looking at the dead man. He knew that Umuofia would not go to war. He knew because they had let the other messengers escape. They had broken into tumult instead of action. He discerned fright in that tumult. . . .[3]

A point missed by many commentators is that Okonkwo is not 'a typical Igboman'. If he had been, his example would have been followed by others. It is Obierika who really represents the more typical role. Okonkwo is more like a sort of super-Igbo; an exaggeration of certain qualities admired by his people, but at the expense of others which the rounded man is expected to possess. The clue can be found in Okonkwo's attitude towards his father. He is unable to see any merit in a man who has at least the virtues of kindness, generosity (when he has something to be generous with), an artistic joy in the created word, and the courage to bear his lonely, agonizing death with an even mind. It is Unoka who speaks to his impatient son words which will prove prophetic for both of them:

'A proud heart can survive a general failure because such a failure does not prick its pride. It is more difficult and more bitter when a man fails alone.'[4]

Things Fall Apart was originally conceived by the author as part of a trilogy which would trace Igbo historical experience through the fate of one family, bridging some four generations and roughly one century. On the advice of his publishers, he decided to issue the first part of the trilogy as a single, self-sufficient novel. The second part was recast as *Arrow of God* (1964), which is set in a different village and concerns an entirely different set of characters, but does fill in the chronological gap between the pre-colonial Nigeria of the first novel and the quasi-independent nation of *No Longer at Ease*. This last title, published in 1960 and set in the years 1956–7, represents the third and contemporary part of the original trilogy. Set partly in Umuofia and partly in Lagos, it traces the fate of Okonkwo's grandson Obi, which is marked by a similar circularity. Like his grandfather before him, he is ultimately forced to embrace everything he has most dreaded and avoided. Okonkwo's seven-year exile lost him the coveted position of eminence he had won for himself in the clan. The manner of his death cost him even the honour of formal burial – the occasion above all others when a man's achievements are praised and celebrated. Obi returns from Britain to a Nigeria where new types of eminence are in vogue: the 'senior service' post; the car; the European-type house; all the allowances and privileges which had hitherto been reserved for the white man. Like Okonkwo, he achieves them only to lose them. But Achebe makes a structural innovation by introducing his new hero at the moment of his disgrace rather than of his triumph. The novel thus begins with a question, 'Why did he do it?', and then proceeds by recapitulation to tell us the answer.

Obi's career reminds us as strongly as his grandfather's of Novalis's dictum, 'character is fate'. The first novelist to quote it was Thomas Hardy, in relation to the equally circular destiny of Henchard in *The Mayor of Casterbridge*. We have seen how Okonkwo, by running away so hard from the image he has created of his father, brings himself both exile and abomination. Obi likewise runs away from a certain image of Nigerian reality which he has formed for himself. Not for him the use of 'influence', the convenient bribe, the easy, free-wheeling morality of Lagos, the arranged marriage which keeps the village people happy. But by striving to do better than his fellows, he does worse, His quick temper and resentment cause him to quarrel both with his true friend Joseph and with the tribal union which could have offered him real support and protection. Having sacrificed Clara to his mother, a sick and dying woman, he fails to attend the latter's funeral. Like his grandfather and great-grandfather, he is ultimately alone with his fate. It is the cyclical fate of the Okonkwos which makes one suspect that, although Conrad is often cited as one of Achebe's major influences, and is specifically referred to by him in *No Longer at Ease*, perhaps Hardy's masterpiece, which is particularly popular with African students, may have been a stronger one.

Both Achebe's early novels are full of clues which, though we may ignore them in passing, help finally to show up their tragic ironies. Unoka's words to Okonkwo were one example. The warnings of the Ezeani and Obierika seem to look forward in time to the total obliteration of Okonkwo's compound and name at the time of his exile. Similarly, Achebe seems to anticipate the reader who may find Obi Okonkwo's fate rather tepid after that of his grandfather, by making the young man give us his own view of the nature of tragedy, when he is interviewed for a job quite early in the novel;

'You think that suicide ruins a tragedy,' said the Chairman.

'Yes. Real tragedy is never resolved. It goes on hopelessly for ever. Conventional tragedy is too easy. The hero dies and we feel a purging of the emotions. A real tragedy takes place in a corner, in an untidy spot, to quote W. H. Auden. The rest of the world is unaware of it. . . . There is no purging of the emotions for us because we are not there.'[5]

At first reading we may think that Obi, with his display of cleverness and his literary allusions, is simply characterizing himself here. But the words are really designed to make us think about his own later decline, his slow death by the 'thousand cuts' of emotional, financial and professional failure, contrasted with the more conventional tragic end of Okonkwo. Even more ironic is the direct comparison made soon afterwards by the elder, Odugwu, when Obi first returns to his father Isaac's village:

'He is a son of Iguedo. . . . There are nine villages in Umuofia, but Iguedo is Iguedo. We have our faults, but we are not empty men who become white when they see white, and black when they see black.'

Obi's heart glowed within him.

'He is the grandson of Ogbuefi Okonkwo who faced the white man single-handed and died in the fight. Stand up!'

Obi stood up obediently.

'Remark him,' said Odugwu. 'He is Ogbuefi Okonkwo come back. He is Okonkwo *kpom-kwem*, exact, perfect.'

Obi's father cleared his throat in embarrassment. 'Dead men do not come back,' he said.[6]

By this point in the novel, we are already aware that Obi's rather shallow idealism and his blustering when confronted by the least hint of corruption are signs of weakness rather than moral strength. But the passage is doubly ironic, because we perceive how the shame of Okonkwo's suicide has been retrospectively transmogrified into a kind of single combat with the white man in which he heroically perished. As a matter of fact, the most truly strong of the four successive Okonkwos is Isaac (formerly Nwoye). He has made a painful and difficult choice early in life, has abided by that choice through thick and thin, and remains a man whose moral certitude is unwavering, even if we think it sometimes misguided. He alone of the Okonkwos seems to have escaped the bad *chi* that destroys

Unoka, Ogbuefi and Obi with what looks like a kind of savage glee. As he later tells Obi, whose flabbiness he seems to detect already:

'I left my father's house, and he placed a curse on me. I went through fire to become a Christian. Because I suffered I understand Christianity – more than you will ever do.'[7]

The difficulties which destroy Obi are largely common and inescapable ones. A young man sailing the seas cannot be expected to seek romantic involvement only with a girl acceptable to his family. Returning to Lagos, he cannot expect immunity from the financial claims of his relatives and his tribal union, nor can he expect these people to be indifferent to his choice of partner. Least of all can he expect to avoid altogether the claims of bribery and influence. Obi's outright rudeness towards those who wish him well, and his air of injured innocence towards Mr Mark and his daughter, are all signs of inner incertitude. When he meets implacable opposition, as from his dying mother, he just takes to his bed for the rest of the day. Achebe is not showing us a situation in which an idealistic young man is bound to fail, but a situation in which a weak and indecisive one will. Obi's moments of silence when first told by Clara that she is *osu* show us that he is really trying to prove to himself, rather than to his father and his friends, that such superstitions are outdated. From that moment onwards, their rupture is inevitable, as Clara herself realizes in her occasional flashes of realism. Achebe is, in any case, carefully ambiguous about Clara's real character, for we see her only as and when Obi sees her. Is her involvement with Sam Okoli a bit deeper than she pretends? Is it perhaps from him that she got the fifty pounds (a tidy sum for a young nurse) which she gives to Obi? The questions serve to remind us that Obi really seems to know very little about Clara or her motives, though the ambiguity allows us to think well of her if we wish. Her violent hostility towards Joseph, however, argues a certain false sophistication and inability to read character which do not promise well.

Much has been written about Achebe's mastery of language in *Things Fall Apart*, where he is on the whole felicitous in his introduction of Igbo words and proverbs into the flow of the text. An early example can be taken from page 7 of that novel:

Okonkwo had just blown out the palm-oil lamp and stretched himself on his bamboo bed when he heard the *ogene* of the town-crier piercing the still night air. *Gome, gome, gome, gome*, boomed the hollow metal. Then the crier gave his message, and at the end of it beat his instrument again.[8]

At the end of the first sentence the non-Igbo reader has very little idea what an *ogene* is, except that it is some sort of sound. It could even be the distinctive cry or song of the messenger. But the second sentence tells us that it is made of hollow metal and the third that it is beaten to announce a message. The chapter opening is simple and dramatic, yet it conveys a body of information without apparent effort. A few pages later, we find another example:

. . . he still remembered how he had suffered when a playmate told him that his father was *agbala*. That was how Okonkwo first came to know that *agbala* was not only another name for a woman, it could also mean a man who had taken no title.[9]

Again, the explanation is delayed until the second sentence; and when it comes, it follows the shape of own thought, as he first hears the word and then ponders its application in a strange context. Thus the reader is not over-conscious of being instructed by the novelist.

Although *No Longer at Ease* naturally contains fewer Igbo words and phrases, it is no less a linguistic *tour de force*. In this short novel, Achebe not only conveys the abiding strength of village conversation, but the inflated rhetoric of the President of the Umuofia Progressive Union, Mr Green's irritable pomposity and the light-hearted banter of Obi, Clara and Christopher as they slide from 'pidgin' into colloquial modern English. The following passage from Odugwu's praise of Iguedo village is a good example of the first:

'Who ever planted an iroko tree – the greatest of the forest? You may collect all the iroko seeds in the world, open the soil and put them there. It will be in vain. The great tree chooses where to grow and we find it there, so it is with greatness in men.'[10]

A few pages earlier, we have heard the President greeting Obi Okonkwo with phrases like these:

'The importance of having one of our sons in the vanguard of this march of progress is nothing short of axiomatic.'[11]

The love of rhetoric is still there, but the borrowed phrases boom with incertitude and hollowness. In modern Nigeria such a speech is more likely to be peppered with English proverbs and biblical phrases than with illustrations drawn straight from the storehouse of Igbo speech, like those of Odugwu. The points of reference have changed.

The same dexterity in the handling of speech is found in Achebe's third novel, *Arrow of God*, and in some ways it reaches its apotheosis there. The action of this relatively long book takes place entirely in two adjacent village clusters of Igboland in 1921. The contrasts between these groups of villages resemble, in some ways, those developed by Ngugi wa Thiong'o for his two adjoining ridges in *The River Between*; for Okperi is already a government station complete with resident white administrators, trading store, mission and school; whereas Umuaro is only just beginning to feel the disintegrating effects of the new political authority and the new religion. The colonial authorities, in fact, have only recently abandoned military 'pacification' of the interior in favour of civil administration. Okperi, then, has already fallen under the authority of a mission-educated Warrant-Chief, who styles himself 'His Highness Obi Ikedi the First', a spurious title imposed upon his fellows only with the aid of colonial police and tax collectors. In the bungalows of Okperi, the pidgin English of the servants can be heard interspersed with the clipped, semi-military jargon of the white officials and the mangled speech of their interpreters. Umuaro, on the other hand, still conducts its affairs in an Igbo fashion as yet untouched by these influences. Only occasionally, and reluctantly, does it converse through inter- mediaries with the new sources of power. Its political authority resides with the Ezeulu, the Chief Priest of its federal deity Ulu, but it is expressed through religious ritual rather than administrative fiat. Power of the latter kind has never been acknowledged there.

Arrow of God is a more ambitious novel than *Things Fall Apart* and gives both a deeper and a fuller account of traditional Igbo civiliza- tion in decline. As befits these intentions, its hero Ezeulu is also a more complex and enigmatic character than the tempestuous Okonkwo. He is also less often in the centre of the stage, though when he is there his presence is unforgettable. His eminence is not based on physique or wealth, however, like that of Okonkwo, but on his awesome status as a priest, 'half-man, half-spirit', who has in his care the political unity and health of the six villages which compose Umuaro. Ezeulu is well aware of the limitations of his power and somewhat resentful of them; the early pages of the novel find him brooding upon that very point:

Whenever Ezeulu considered the immensity of his power over the year and the crops and, therefore, over the people he wondered if it was real. It was true he named the day for the feast of the Pumpkin Leaves and for the New Yam feast; but he did not choose the day. He was merely a watch- man. His power was no more than the power of a child over a goat that was said to be his. As long as the goat was alive it was his; he would find it food and take care of it. But the day it was slaughtered he would know who the real owner was. No! the Chief Priest of Ulu was more than that, must be more than that. If he should refuse to name the day there would be no festival – no planting and no reaping. But could he refuse? No Chief Priest had ever refused. So it could not be done. He would not dare.[12]

As it turns out, the transitional days in which Ezeulu lives actually bring him the opportunity for such a refusal. He does dare; but the attempt costs him much of his authority, and finally his sanity. For the ruminations in this extract indicate that he understands the nature of his authority but does not sufficiently remember its origin. If the six villages created their collective deity Ulu to serve their well-being, his priest can hardly be expected to do less than serve that same interest.

As in *Things Fall Apart*, the novel offers an early warning to Ezeulu of the dangers inherent in forgetting the social origins of his role. Akuebue warns his friend, just before the arrival of Winterbottom's messenger and the central crisis of the novel:

'. . . you forget one thing: that no man however great can win judgement against a clan. You may think you did in that land dispute but you are wrong. Umuaro will always say that you betrayed them before the white man. And they will say that you are betraying them again today by sending your son to join in desecrating the land.'[13]

Akuebue's traditional wisdom and instinct are here shown to be far sounder than Ezeulu's lonely, innovative intellect. There is in fact no way in which Ezeulu's inherited power can be preserved, now that new power-centres of church and state have established themselves a few miles away. The most he can do is to go down fighting, and the only way to achieve that is to present himself as a clear, uncompromised alternative to those authorities. In the eyes of his people, however, Ezeulu's position has been fatally compromised by his claim to be the friend of 'Wintabota' and by sending one of his sons to the Christian mission. To ask Oduche to be his 'eyes and ears' at the mission is to give the boy as impossible an assignment as Waiyaki's father was giving him at about the same time, in Ngugi's *The River Between*. It is not possible for the young, in search of a passionate allegiance, to maintain two antagonistic ones at the same time. The one shared by their teachers and their schoolmates will surely prevail. Thus Ezeulu can be seen as a man who has long been preparing the fate which finally overtakes him, when his rejection by the clan ends in the total solitude of madness.

The fact that Ezeulu inherits his status from his father and his madness from his mother adds to the richness of the action depicted in the novel. We have here a number of intersecting dialectics, in all of which Ezeulu is involved as one of the poles: there is the dialectic between his individual character and his inherited office; the political dialectic for the control of Umuaro between himself and Ukpaka; the dialectic between traditional quasi-religious authority and the new separated authorities of District Officer and Christian priest; even the dialectic between Ulu and his priest. Ezeulu's madness ends all these dialectics in favour of the new dispensation and of Ukpaka, who will surely be far more willing than the Chief Priest to have his authority bolstered by a warrant from the white man. *Arrow of God* is, among so much else, a study of the process by which colonialism and Christian proselytism triumphed. Ironically enough, it is Ezeulu himself who analyses this process, during his dispute with Akuebue:

'How many white men went in the party that destroyed Abame? Do you know? Five. . . . Now have you ever heard that five people – even if their heads reach the sky – could overrun the whole clan? . . . Who showed them the way to Abame? They were not born there; how then did they find the way? We showed them and are still showing them.'[14]

All Ezeulu's actions are, however, wrapped in ambiguity. His eldest son Edogo suspects that the sending of Oduche to the mission was designed to disqualify him from inheriting the office of Chief Priest, which must then pass to his favourite son Nwafo. Likewise, Ezeulu's revenge against the clan is first conceived in Umuaro and then refined while he is imprisoned in Okperi, far away from the altar of Ulu:

his greatest pleasure came from the thought of his revenge which had suddenly formed in his mind as he sat listening to Nwaka in the market place.[15]

The same pleasure is evident when he rebuffs his assistants in Umuaro, who come to propose the announcement of the New Yam Festival:

If anyone had come into Ezeulu's hut after the men had left he would have been surprised. The old priest's face glowed with happiness and some of his youth and handsomeness returned temporarily from across the years.[16]

Even more decisive appears to be the passage where Ezeulu decides that the longer he stays in Okperi, 'the greater will be his grievance and his resources for the fight'.[17] The reader's attention has not yet been focused on the surplus yams, but there can be no doubt that Ezeulu's mind has already fastened on them as his most devastating weapon for revenging himself on his people.

Yet we are told, once we are acquainted with the surplus, that Ezeulu is anguished by the sufferings of Umuaro and by his own growing isolation. Ulu tells him, or so he believes, that it is the god's quarrel, not just that of his priest, and that he cannot dispose of it by any convenient accommodation like eating the extra yams. And what, anyway, is Ezeulu's mind if it is not the mind of Ulu? These reflections, however, prompt us to wonder what happened in the past when the Chief Priest fell ill at the appropriate lunar cycle and was unable to eat the sacred yam on the appointed day, an event which must surely have occurred during the generations of the priesthood?

All these questions remain in the mind after the novel is finished and contribute much to its fascination. Ezeulu's actions are probably not susceptible to a simple either–or explanation. All that seems certain is that Ulu cannot be turned into the scourge rather than the saviour of his people without some perversion of his role. If Ezeulu believes that his own will cannot be separated from his god's, that belief is clearly not shared by the people of Umuaro.

The social fabric of *Arrow of God* is also denser than that of any other Achebe novel. The novelist concentrates less exclusively upon his hero's development, though that is always a theme within the narrative, and gives us many scenes which enrich our perception of Igbo village life at a time when its rituals and belief-system are still largely intact. The Festival of the Pumpkin Leaves in chapter 7 is a high point in this social realization, as well as in Ezeulu's proper fulfilment of his role as the protector of the six villages. If Achebe here exceeds his earlier achievements in the evocation of Igbo life, he also attains a new level in his rendering of its speech. This exchange between Akuebe and Ezeulu may stand as an example of nimble repartee which is nevertheless careful to situate itself in terms of what is done or not done in the matter of breaking kola. Akuebue is sorting seed-yams when Ezeulu comes to visit him and is offered kola by the host's son:

'Thank you,' said Ezeulu. 'Take it to your father to break.'
'No,' said Akuebue. 'I ask you to break it.'
'That cannot be. We do not by-pass a man and enter his compound.'

'I know that,' said Akuebue, 'but you see that my hands are full and I am asking you to perform the office for me.'

'A man cannot be too busy to break the first kolanut of the day in his own house. So put the yam down; it will not run away.'

'But this is not the first kolanut of the day. I have broken several already.'

'That may be so, but you did not break them in my presence. The time a man wakes up is his morning.'

'All right,' said Akuebue. 'I shall break it if you say so.'

'Indeed, I say so. We do not apply an ear-pick to the eye.'

Akuebue took the kolanut in his hand and said: 'We shall both live,' and broke it.[18]

Achebe's ear is equally sharp when it comes to recording the clipped, world-weary English of Captain Winterbottom, or the more tentative remarks of his young assistant, Clarke. The immense gap in understanding which separates these men from Ezeulu is one of the central ironies of the novel. Yet Achebe, like Ngugi, accepts that such limited men can idealize their role in a way which actually hampers understanding, because that very idealism precludes the possibility of Africa's having anything to teach them. They are there, not to listen, but to perform a certain imperial duty. If things go wrong, it is because of some interfering 'desk wallah' in Lagos; not because that duty is itself misconceived.

Arrow of God, then stands pre-eminent among Achebe's novels by virtue of its complexity, richness of texture and moral depth. As things fell out, its reputation was temporarily eclipsed by the slighter *A Man of the People*, which appeared a few days after the January 1966 military coup in Nigeria and was hailed as a remarkable prophecy of that event. Africa had, however, seen several civilian regimes overthrown by the military before the Nigerian coup, and Nigeria itself had been thick with rumours of a take-over for a good twelve months. Poems like Christopher Okigbo's 'Path of Thunder' sequence are, in fact, more fully accurately predictive of the wrath to come than Achebe's novel, whose closing pages make the army sound like high-minded saviours of an indifferent, cynical populace. The mood of the people was neither indifferent nor cynical in January 1966, when civil order in the Western Region had virtually collapsed and the Balew government was on the brink of imposing martial law. And, as events were to show, the army was neither uniquely high-minded nor ideologically united in its desire for change. A certain military impatience with 'politicians' should not be mistaken for altruism. As Okigo's warning goes:

POLITICIANS are here in this iron dance of mortars, of generators –
The eagles are suddenly there,
New stars of iron dawn;[19]

But to be fair, Achebe is perhaps suspending judgement by staging
his coup at the very end of the novel, so that it remains an untried
reality. And he certainly avoids the common trap of dismissing the
politicians as a peculiarly corrupt and self-seeking group who
battened themselves upon an innocent society. Were they not, rather,
a mirror image of that society and its aspirations? That is the
question posed throughout the novel:

Some political commentators have said that it was the supreme cynicism
of these transactions which inflamed the people and brought down the
government. That is sheer poppycock. The people themselves, as we have
seen, had become even more cynical than their leaders, and were apathetic
into the bargain. 'Let them eat', was the people's opinion, 'after all when
white men used to do all the eating did we commit suicide? Of course not.
And where is the all-powerful white man today? He came, he ate and he
went. But we are still around. . . .'[20]

This passage is characteristic of the rather knockabout, high-
spirited satire of the book; a startling change after the gravity of
Arrow of God. The word 'poppycock' dismisses the genuine capacity
for critical appraisal which was shown by sections of the Nigerian
press and public in the pre-coup period; correspondingly, it ignores
the increasing degree of censorship and repression practised by the
Balewa government and some of the regional governments, particularly from 1964 onwards. These realities are far more apparent in
Wole Soyinka's novel *The Interpreters*, published a few months
earlier. Achebe might argue that he was not specifically writing about
Nigeria, but the argument will not carry conviction. There are, in
fact, structural reasons for Achebe's insistence on public apathy and
cynicism, to which we shall now return.

The moral ambiguity of *A Man of the People* is, of course, deliberate. Achebe's hero Odili Samalu is, if not 'a typical Nigerian', at
least a typical member of the young elite. At first, he seems to despise
and envy Chief Nanga in about equal measure, and is perfectly
happy to accept his friendship and sponsorship until the Elsie
episode inflames his *amour propre*. That episode, however, far from
exposing some new depth of moral frightfulness in Nanga, merely
shows him to be a mature man confronted by the childish petulance
and rudeness of Odili. Achebe's strategy is to show us a young man

who is potentially another Chief Nanga himself (though of a more recent model), but who grows morally as he learns more about himself and the society he lives in, until the book's end shows him at a new level of awareness. The strategy is to avoid adopting a tone of lofty moral superiority in the narrative; a tone which would ignore the symbiotic relationship between Chief Nanga and the society that sustains him. It is a bold strategy, but one not without its penalties, for it prevents Achebe from having a voice of his own in the book (as he does through the third-person narrative of all the other novels). He is obliged to speak always through Odili, yet the last pages of the novel leave us with some doubt as to whether it is Odili or Achebe who is addressing us, and whose authority is behind the word 'poppycock'.

The Elsie episode by which Odili sets so much store and which changes the direction of his career, is one from which he does not emerge with much credit, though he clearly expects the reader to share his sense of outrage. We have already seen that both Odili and Elsie are entranced by the aura of wealth and luxury around Nanga in about equal measure. Take, for example, the scene where Odili proudly drives to her hospital in the chief's car:

'Wetin be the name of your friend's car?'
'Cadillac'.
'Ah! This na the famous Cadillac? I no think say I done see am before.' She was full of girlish excitement. 'Na tough car! Eje-je-je! You think say these people go another heaven after this?'
'My sister I no know-o. Anyway make me follow them chop small for dis world. . . .'[21]

Furthermore, Odili has gone out of his way to assure Chief Nanga that Elsie is a good-time girl who means nothing serious to him. Given the ridiculous scruples which prevent the young man from simply taking Elsie to himself, we can only be amazed that Chief Nanga waits a whole hour before acting on his behalf.

It must be admitted that Odili shows many signs of wry self-questioning: he rightly criticizes Max for accepting Chief Koko's money under false pretences; he develops a real affection for Edna, though he started off by treating her as a mere pawn in his game of revenge, and he learns to make a more just assessment of his father's character. On the other hand, his rudeness to Chief Nanga when leaving Bori is merely weak and childish; he worms his way into the confidence of both Mrs Nanga and Edna's family by posing as the

Chief's friend, when he is in fact his deadly enemy; he never seriously questions either the ideology or the financial basis of the CPC; he dismisses his former teacher Nanga as a 'bushman' and an 'illiterate', which is clearly untrue and smacks of the most unpleasant kind of educational snobbery. We have to remember that Nanga instantly remembered his former pupil and invited him to Bori. Would Odili do as much for his pupils in a few years' time?

Much of this is intentional on Achebe's part, and perhaps those critics who find Odili an 'attractive, unidealized hero' have completely accepted his fictional schema. But there can be no doubt that Odili does idealize himself, even when his creator does not. The reader, at any rate, is left with a real doubt as to whether Odili in power would be any less corruptible than Nanga, and whether he would even succeed in developing the same common touch, which stems from the fact that Nanga really *was* one of the people until yesterday. Odili strikes us as having prided himself from the first on not being one of them. Witness his description of his father's *obi* as an 'outhouse', and his general lack of interest in anything but his own fulfilment or advancement, both before and after his entry into politics.

Has Achebe, then, gone a bit too far in his efforts to avoid a super-hero or a superior moral tone? There can be no doubt that *A Man of the People* is a sour book. A people who are as apathetic and cynical as Odili/Achebe insists they are, cannot hope to be redeemed either by themselves or by the military. Can they then be redeemed by the likes of Odili? Perhaps one fault with the book is that it introduces no one who could be described as formidable, unless it be Eunice, and her we scarcely know. The attempt to explore this central theme of recent African fiction entirely through a hero as slight as Odili was interesting and original, but must finally be judged as inadequate. Take Odili's attempt to examine his political ideas:

A thought sneaked into my mind and told me it was futile now to try and go through with my political plans which in all honesty I should admit had always been a little nebulous – until Edna came along. She had been like a dust particle in the high atmosphere around which the water vapour of my thinking formed its globule of rain.[22]

Now what, 'in all honesty', has Edna to do with anything that could coherently be called a political plan? And, in any case, she did not 'come along'. Odili's political plan, if it can be graced with the name, was never anything but a scheme of revenge centred on Edna and Anata, in which she was as much a cipher as the village itself.

These are the reasons why *A Man of the People*, despite its topical success in 1966 and its easy, colloquial style and masterly use of pidgin, is something of a disappointment after the tragic grandeur of *Arrow of God*. Like all topical novels, it suffers the penalty of being rapidly outmoded, and therefore is not a book to which the reader is likely to return for nourishment or enlightenment.

In the years since 1966, Achebe's output has consisted of a slim volume of short stories, a collection of critical essays and a book of poems. For a writer who produced four novels between 1958 and 1966, this relative silence is striking, and it suggests that he has not really found a way of situating himself as a novelist in the Nigeria of today. One possible reason for this is Achebe's whole-hearted support of Biafran secession in 1967–70. Like many at that time, he seems to have pinned his hopes on a collapse of the whole Nigerian experiment, in which Biafra's example would be followed by West and North. The defeat of Biafra and the survival of the Nigerian Federation has thus presented him with something of a dilemma as a national spokesman. It may be significant that all Achebe's fiction, whether rural or urban in setting, has concentrated upon Igbo characters and their interaction with other Igbos. It would be possible, for instance, to read both *No Longer at Ease* and *A Man of the People* without realizing that Lagos is, at the popular level, a Yoruba city. The elite class there spans the breadth of Nigeria in its origin, but the social context it inhabits does not. We could learn this from Ekwensi or from Soyinka, who are both more interested in Lagos as a phenomenon and who make it a presence in their work.

Girls at War, first published in 1972, contained stories spanning some twenty years. Although some of these, notably the title story, 'Vengeful Creditor' and 'Civil Peace', are of high interest, it remains a thin harvest for two decades and indicates clearly enough that the short story has never been Achebe's favourite medium. Four of the stories in the 1972 edition were in fact products of his undergraduate days, before he became a novelist. They are slight affairs and give little hint of the talent which was later to flower in the novels. 'Marriage is a Private Affair' and the slightly later 'Chike's School-days' do, however, read like early sketches for the marriage theme in *No Longer at Ease*. In the latter story, though, it is the fanatical Christian father, Amos (as it could be, Isaac Okonkwo), who has insisted on marrying an *osu* and has thus himself become a slave in the eyes of the village. This idea is a germ well capable of sustaining a whole novel, since it would have enabled Achebe to explore consequences and ramifications which are only hinted in *No Longer at Ease*, with its Lagos setting and Western-educated hero. Elechi Amadi has since developed a comparable idea in his village novel *The Slave* (1978), where the *osu* theme broods over the whole plot and finally destroys the hero's dream of escape from his destiny.

With 'Girls at War', Achebe turns to the civil war itself and traces the collapse of the early idealism and self-sacrifice that character-ized the Biafran cause into widespread disillusion and self-seeking. He does this through the complex interaction of two characters: Reginald Nwankwo, an official in the Ministry of Justice, and the girl Gladys who is scarcely out of school. In their first encounters, early in the war, it is she who challenges his complacency with her obvious seriousness and dedication. Nwankwo is one of those high-ups who intends to have a good war, even though he avoids the worst examples of profiteering and privilege. He reckons to have a car and a driver, a good supply of relief foods for his family and a general aura of respect for his position. Furthermore, he expects these things to be retained, no matter how badly the war may go or how extreme the sacrifices demanded of others. He tells us that the encounter with Gladys at the check-point shook him out of his flippant attitude towards girl volunteers. But on his next meeting with her, towards the end of the war, he manifests exactly the same flippancy:

'. . . You don't recognize me?'
'Oh yes, of course. What a fool I am. . . . You are. . . .'
'Gladys'.
'That's right, the militia girl. You've changed, Gladys. You were always beautiful of course, but now you are a beauty queen. What do you do these days?'
'I am in the Fuel Directorate.'
'That's wonderful'.
It was wonderful, he thought, but even more it was tragic. She wore a high-tinted wig and a very expensive skirt and low-cut blouse. Her shoes, obviously from Gabon, must have cost a fortune. In short, thought Nwankwo, she had to be in the keep of some well-placed gentleman, one of those piling up money out of the war.[23]

It soon turns out that Gladys has indeed abandoned her early idealism in the quest for good things (popularly known as 'survival') and has adopted the sexual laxity common, and often so convenient, in some girls at war. But Nwankwo's immediate reaction is to boast about the gay bachelor existence he leads in Owerri, safe from his evacuated family, and to promise her 'a real swinging party' that night. He then concentrates on getting her into bed. Yet, when they reach the party later, he begins to adopt a high moral tone, refusing to dance 'until this war is over', and constantly taunting her with remarks about her frivolity in contrast with the sufferings of others. This attitudinizing even makes him stop the car next day to pick up a crippled soldier, something he would evidently never do normally. Yet, when the car is bombed, it is Gladys who tries to rescue the soldier and dies in the attempt. Beneath the wig and new-found sophistication she has in fact retained decent instincts which never seem to have found much play in the career of Reginald Nwankwo.

This is a painful and subtle story, the more so as it is told from the point of view of Nwankwo in a condescending manner as though he is confident of retaining the reader's support and moral approval. Achebe manages to tell the truth about the debilitating effects of war and shortage without lapsing into a bitterness that denies the survival of human qualities too. 'Vengeful Creditor' is another substantial story, told with a more objective irony that leaves the new bourgeoisie squirming at the tip of the writer's pen and forces us to sympathize with a young girl who has done an apparently awful thing. Achebe shows us how completely some of the old colonial vocabulary about 'those people' has been taken over by women like Mrs Emenike:

From that day Mrs Emenike hated the words 'free primary' which had suddenly become part of everyday language, especially in the villages where they called it 'free primadu'. She was particularly angry when people made jokes about it and had a strong urge to hit them on the head for a lack of feeling and good taste.[24]

Another deeply moving story, 'Civil Peace', shows us the typical struggle of a family that has emerged from the war with nothing, but is grateful enough just to be alive. The little the family members have accumulated by ingenuity and hard work is then put at risk by a party of armed robbers, to whom they are obliged to hand over their *ex gratia* payment (known as 'egg rasher'). It is the sardonic leader of the gang who gives the story its title:

'. . . Trouble done finish. War done finish and all the *katakata* wey de for inside. No Civil War again. This na Civil Peace. No be so?'[25]

In these stories of the immediate post-war era, the latest of which was published in 1971 in Achebe's literary journal *Okike*, he brings to short fiction all the art he has learned as a novelist. They hit hard but they are still vignettes, and we still await the kind of major statement which the novel offers.

Just before *Girls at War*, Achebe had published locally a volume of poems, *Beware, Soul Brother* (1971), which are mainly the product of the war years and their immediate aftermath. The stress and hurry of those times evidently pushed Achebe into a form of expression new to him. The poems disclose no great lyrical gift, no capacity for sustained song, but they do occasionally make their effect by virtue of a certain clipped restraint. Pain, expressed with this raw sincerity, can find its own route into poetry, as in 'First Shot':

That lone rifle-shot anonymous
in the dark striding chest-high
through a nervous suburb at the break
of our season of thunders will yet
steep its flight and lodge
more firmly than the greater noises
ahead in the forehead of memory.[26]

The last line is marred by the surely unintentional clumsiness of 'ahead' and 'forehead', but this is not fatal to the poem. We hear the shot, in the ringing night, and we tremble for what is to come. It is, on the whole, the very short poems that work best; those which exceed twenty lines or so tend to lose impetus and draw too much attention to their prosaic diction. 'Mother and Child' and the closing lines of 'Love Song' have the same kind of felicity as 'First Shot':

I will sing only in waiting
silence your power to bear
dreams for me in your quiet
eyes and wrap the dust of our blistered
feet in golden anklets ready
for the return someday of our
banished dance.[27]

Taken as a whole, however, *Beware, Soul Brother* does not seem to mark the sudden emergence of a poet. It is in prose fiction that Achebe has won his distinction and it is probably there he must look to further it. A little later than these collections of stories and poems came his volume of essays, *Morning Yet on Creation Day* (1975). This too assembles the work of over a decade, and hence lacks the energy and unity of concern which mark Soyinka's *Myth, Literature and the African World*, for instance. Each of Achebe's essays stands alone and nearly all of the fifteen pieces had already been published in periodicals. 'The Novelist as Teacher', for example, had been available for some ten years and had already been much featured in criticisms of his work. *A Man of the People* may be seen as marking, to some extent, the practice of Achebe's new dedication to a more didactic type of fiction, which would avoid the metaphysical subtleties of *Arrow of God*. More rewarding to those who had followed Achebe's work and thought over the years were essays like 'Colonialist Criticism', 'Language and the Destiny of Man' and '*Chi* in Igbo Cosmology', all of which were here made available for the first time. 'Colonialist Criticism' is a spirited and well-aimed attack on some of the more fatuous attitudes which still sometimes obtrude in foreign criticism of African literature, and even influence African critics themselves. Achebe is particularly incensed by the cult of 'universalism' as an objective towards which African writers must strive if they are ever to come of age:

I should like to see the word *universal* banned altogether from discussions of African literature until such a time as people cease to use it as a synonym for the narrow, self-serving parochialism of Europe, until their horizon extends to include the whole world.[28]

The point is well taken, and it is worth mentioning that these pedlars of the universal are only a thinly updated version of the evolutionists of old. One wonders what is universal, in the sense they use the word, about Count Vronsky or Huckleberry Finn. Achebe is equally good on the somewhat nasty chorus of praise and the shower of prizes which greet books like Yambo's *Le Devoir de Violence* or the novels of V. S. Naipaul, where self-contempt can be identified by a foreign taste eager to have its prejudice confirmed rather than challenged.

The other two essays referred to are more exploratory and less polemical, that on the Igbo concept of *chi* being of exceptional interest and value. In an area more filled with darkness than illumination, Achebe manages to link, at least tentatively, the two meanings of the word: sunlight, and spiritual double or personal destiny. Achebe has that virtue, rare among writers, of being able to enter controversy without bitchiness and to demolish stupidity with good humour. But his essays never leave us in any doubt as to what he means or the force with which he means it. This absence of dogmatism is, however, the positive aspect of a certain ideological deficiency in these essays. They do not, like Ngugi's *Homecoming*, for example, indicate the direction in which Achebe would like to see his country move. We are not quite sure what he wants to put in the place of the past he has exposed, or the bourgeois nationalism of the First Republic which he dissects in *A Man of the People*. The novelist who aspires to be a teacher must visibly participate in the choices which face his people. The dominant debates in African countries today are between the authoritarian, one-party state and the relatively open, multi-party system to which Nigeria is returning; also, between the capitalist system implanted and sustained by the West, and the socialist alternative. There stands also the question of how, without authoritarianism and a strong, united political movement, Nigeria can solve the problems of indiscipline and squalor in its sprawling cities. Achebe's earlier writings have encouraged his readers to look towards him for at least some tentative answers for tomorrow. Since he is committed to a certain degree of didacticism in fiction, his next novel, when it comes, may be expected to embody a vision which opens towards the future.

Tchicaya U Tam'si

Born 1931 at Mpili in the then French Congo, Tchicaya was taken to Paris at the age of 15 by his father, one of the first black Députés from that territory. He took the *baccalauréat* in France and began his poetic career with *Le Mauvais Sang*, published in 1955. Since then he has published a further six volumes of poetry and several plays. Apart from a short spell in Leopoldville in 1960 as Editor of the Lumumbist paper *Le Congo*, Tchicaya has lived most of his adult life in Paris, where he is a permanent official of UNESCO, but the Congolese imagery and imaginative world of his poetry remain unmistakable. His work is not easy at first to encounter, but his reputation is steadily growing and he is highly esteemed by other poets. His plays have been staged at the Avignon Festival, in Paris, in Martinique and elsewhere.

7 The Uprooted Tree

Tchicaya U Tam'si is not only the most prolific of Africa's modern poets, but the one whose work displays the most sustained energy and intensity. He has been steadily engaged with the development of his art for a period of nearly thirty years, during which he has published seven major collections of poetry.

A rather crude division of African poets working in the former colonial languages might place them in two categories according to the way they interpret their relationship to the language used. In the first category would be placed all those who bring to their work an intense involvement with their indigenous poetic traditions and forms, so that many of the refrains, image-clusters and formal structures used in their own poetry are derived from those traditions. in such cases it is reasonable to assume that these poets' first intense, emotional involvement with words came through their participation in African verbal-musical events, rather than through the early study of a European literature. Thus they bring their minds to the reading of, say, Baudelaire or Yeats, with an already clearly formed idea of what poetry is in their own cultures.

Notable in this first category are certain important poets of Anglophone Africa, such as Kofi Awoonor of Ghana (the Ewe People), Mazisi Kunene of South Africa (the Zulu), Okot p'Bitek and Okello Oculi of Uganda (the Acoli), or the Nigerian poets Romanus Egudu and Okogbule Wonodi (the Igbo/Ikwerre). Examples of this kind are rather harder to find among Francophone poets, perhaps because the educational policies still followed by most of the former French colonies many years after independence militate against the serious study of indigenous language and poetry. The intellectual climate produced by these policies also obstructs the sort of sustained involvement with this poetry by which young educated poets can produce work which extends their own poetic traditions into another language. Something of this kind does appear to have been achieved by the Cameroonian poet E. Epanya Yondo in his *Kamerun! Kamerun!* and the young poets collaborating with Sembène Ousmane on the Wolof revue *Kaddu* may be able to produce a genuine neo-Wolof poetry even in much-assimilated Senegal.

Our second category, much the larger of the two, would group together all those poets who appear to have come first to poetry through an excitement with the works of French or English literature studied at school or university. Their early work is marked by imitation of certain chosen masters and only later do they seem to reorientate their writing towards a native poetic tradition which has existed all the while outside the walls of their elitist institutions. Among leading Anglophone poets, one might hazard here the names of Lenrie Peters, John Pepper Clark, Christopher Okigbo, Gabriel Okara and Mbella Sonne Dipoko; among Francophone writers, those of L. S. Senghor, Diop Birago, David Diop, Joseph Bognini, Jean-Baptiste Tati-Loutard and Paulin Joachim.

It must be no surprise that this second passage seems to have been the way through which Tchicaya U Tam'si passed to find, incredibly quickly, a voice and a tone entirely his own.

Brought to Paris in 1946 at the age of 15, he was exposed at an even earlier age than Senghor to exclusively French surroundings and educational processes. What probably saved him as a poet was that from the Lycée Janson-de-Sailly he proceeded, not to the narrow elitism of the '*grandes écoles*', but to several years of odd-jobbing as a warehouseman, farm hand, and restaurant porter. Only after the publication of his second book in 1957 did he move to one of those occupations usually associated with French-educated African poets, a writing and producing post in radio.

But the initial move to France, no doubt well-intended on his father's part, left the deepest possible mark on his early poetry, which is charged with an overwhelming sense of loss. Whether literally or metaphorically, he feels deprived of his country, a mother and even of a genealogical identity. These are some of the recurrent themes throughout the first collection, *Le Mauvais Sang* (*Bad Blood*), published in 1955 at the age of 24. All his poetry, however, is haunted by the figure of this 'mère inconnue', and he reverts continually to the idea of something strange and alienated in his parentage:

Né de mère inconnue, vénale
Ma faute grandira l'oubli
Je fus troqué contre le mal.[1]

[Born of an unknown mother, venally
My fault swelled the oblivion
I was swopped for the wrong]

Is this the venal fault of the child whose birth coincides with his mother's disappearance, or is it some deeper and more mysterious sorrow? Tchicaya had in fact been brought up in ignorance of his mother's identity, and even of her continued existence.* The figure of the father in his poetry is also enigmatical, charged with tension and with perhaps a sense of opposition. This is the father who brought the poet to Paris at the age of 15 and who thus both connects him with Africa (by his existence) and separates him from it (by his action). Tchicaya's father was the first elected, black deputy for Moyen Congo to take his seat in the French National Assembly under the new constitution of 1946. It was for this reason that he came to Paris and brought the young Tchicaya with him. In the ironical poem 'Entendu dans le Vent', which describes a visit to a fortune-teller and ends with the words 'Monsieur, I want to take a look at your entrails', we find these lines, again weighed down with deprivation:

Open your mouth and your hands: nothing but cockroaches!
I see neither father nor mother nor brother. . . .[2]

Tchicaya's second and third collections, *Feu de Brousse* (Brush Fire) (1957), and *A Triche-Coeur* (A Game of Cheat Heart) (1960), are haunted by the figure of 'the child' or 'the 'orphan', who wanders everywhere seeking the tree or root of his origin, the source of his very being. The same orphan figure meets us already in the concluding title-poem of *Le Mauvais Sang* written, like Rimbaud's poem of the same title in *Une Saison en Enfer*, in prose:

Fleuve non mer non lac non, arbre oui arbre mauve à
l'endroit du soleil rond, arbre la nuit mille et mille
lucioles en font un diamant brut comme la naissance et
j'ouvre mes bras pour me chercher une mère-Misère! Pitié!
Splendeur! Clopin-clopant infernale cadence! Fleuve mer
lac non viendra l'orfèvre je fermerai mes bras pour
retrouver un coeur de pierre. Crève donc! . . .

Ils marchent à pas lents des orphelins nus de honte comme
si avec le sens que nous avons du monde il est permis à
des orphelins privilégiés d'être sans père. Quelle comédie! . . .[3]

*Personal communication.

[River no sea no lake no, tree yes tree mauve in the place
of the round sun, tree the night a thousand thousand fire-
flies deep down a diamond crude as a birth and I open my arms
seeking a mother-Misery! Pity! Splendour! Clip-clop infernal
cadence! river sea lake no no the goldsmith comes I will
close my arms to find a heart of stone. Die then! . . .

They move with the slow steps of orphans naked with shame as
if with the sense we have of the world this was permitted to
orphans privileged to be fatherless. What a comedy!]

In this passage we note the bitter word-play not only on *mer/mère/
misère* (sea/mother/misery), but also on *père/pierre* (father/stone).
The theme of an infant cursed with ill even in his very birth is present
here, not only in the words 'clip-clop' (Tchicaya has a club-foot)
but in the opening arms of the newborn child, which close upon a
stone.

   This particular theme is taken up in another poem of this first
collection, 'Le Mal' (The Wrong), which must also be quoted in
French in order to bring out the richness of its rhyme and word-play:

Ils ont craché sur moi, j'étais encore enfant
Bras croisés, tête douce, inclinée, bonne, atone.
Pour mon ventre charnu, mon oeil criait: aumône!
J'étais enfant dans mon coeur il y avait du sang.[4]

[They spat on me when I was still a babe,
Arms bent, soft head inclined, dull and good.
For my plump belly, my eye begged: alms!
I was a child with my heart full of blood.]

Tchicaya's blood, it seems, is 'mauvais' in a double sense. The
orphan's blood carries the heritage of a bitter destiny founded in
ill, but it is also the 'gros sang' (strong blood), of a new race, full of a
rebellious urgency which breaks and remakes the physical world.
Perhaps it is this 'gros sang' in both senses which makes Tchicaya
recognize a companionship in ill and in world-shaping creativity
with Arthur Rimbaud. The prodigious French poet Rimbaud
(1854–91), though born in and of Europe, felt himself always displaced there because of his 'mauvais sang'. Rimbaud's too was an
orphaned adolescence of revolt and restless departures. He yearned
for a pagan identity which would renew his existence under tropical
suns, far from the sick war-torn Europe of 1870–71. Fate had cast
him to play a part in that Europe and he spent his brief life in

endeavouring to change that role, at whatever cost in terms of isolation and pain.

One of the final poems in *Le Mauvais Sang*, entitled 'Le Gros Sang', also elaborates upon the idea of a blood whose 'badness' is now only an ironic way of referring to its strength and rebellious urgency. Here the associations with some profound guilt, opprobrium of scandal are shed, and the poet is ready to burst his bonds:

I have disrupted the winds to make myself heard
To rediscover all bloody the desires they sell me
I am the tempered blade, the fire of new races
In my coarse red blood troubled rivers lie foaming.[5]

Does the connection with Rimbaud, born exactly 100 years before the book appeared, extend beyond a biographical identification? A more precise formal influence might be seen at work in this first volume. Here, in a way uncharacteristic of his later work, Tchicaya writes predominantly in regular stanzaic form (generally in sonnets or in quatrains with a predominance of twelve-syllable lines), and in rhyme. He also makes much greater use of punctuation and of clear sentence-structure than in his later poetry. The last poem of the volume, 'Le Signe du Mauvais Sang', whilst perhaps acknowledging Rimbaud's *Une Saison en Enfer* in its prose form, marks a departure from the rest of the book in its unbroken flow, its freer association of sounds and images, as may be seen in the passage quoted above.

By the time Tchicaya published his second collection, *Feu de Brousse*, he had moved decisively away from this relative conservatism of prosody and form. If we wish to chase influences, we might adduce a direct one from the French Surréalistes, or an indirect one through the work of Aimé Césaire. However that might be, Tchicaya swings into his new volume with an amazing, sustained *élan*, a torrent of freely associating images which flow backwards and forwards within the poems, without the barriers of punctuation or capitals to separate them or demarcate their areas of reference. The occasional mannered weaknesses of the earlier poetry are avoided by the absence of any regular demand for a formal gesture of conclusion. In *Feu de Brousse* the individual poems are much longer than before and each is shaped as it emerges, upon the page, rather than being submitted to the demands of any previously selected model. The poems are also more unified within the whole volume, making it in effect one sustained poem. Indeed, the poet has indicated as much by sub-titling it a 'Poem spoken in seventeen visions'. Here, to give an idea of these new qualities in Tchicaya's work of the later fifties, are the opening lines of the first poem, 'A Travers Temps et Fleuve' (Across Time and River):

One day I must be caught
whirling above the winds
like leaves from trees
across dungheap and fire
no matter
if future times shall turn our souls
to flints
threatening naked feet
we shall lie on all roads
threatening thirst
threatening love
threatening time[6]

It will be noted that the poet here fulfils a vision only glimpsed in his earlier work, the vision of a manifold physical existence which corresponds to, intermingles with and transforms all the elements of the world around him. Even more striking examples of this identification with the physical world will be quoted from his later poetry, but the process is certainly at work throughout *Feu de Brousse*.

Given the unity of the collection, it may be more rewarding to quote extensively from one of the 'visions' which exemplifies the special qualities of this new style, arrived at without any apparent transition, than to attempt any comprehensive account of a volume running to some eighty pages. In the poem 'Présence', which forms the seventh vision of the book, Tchicaya unfolds a number of themes which are to dominate his next two collections also. In the opening lines we find one of the most striking of all his expressions of physical identification with the river, forest and ocean of his native Congo. The very strength of this impulse towards physical unity may be seen as a product of his exiled situation. Then follows one of the many ambivalent references to Christ, a figure with whom the poet feels indissolubly linked and even implicated. Christ was betrayed by his own companions, but also by his followers, who systematically destroyed the Congo kingdom and enslaved, brutalized or exploited its inhabitants in his name. The stench of this historical betrayal clings inescapably to Christ himself. But the figure of the sacrificed god retains nevertheless an extraordinary fascination for the exiled poet who has also both betrayed and been betrayed by his country; 'betrayed' because he does not fully share its experience, and 'been betrayed' because robbed by destiny of this fuller Congolese experience. Thus Christ appears in his poetry as a 'nailed fetish'; a description which is not a mere insult but an acknowledgement of his profound, intimate relevance. The image stuck all over with nails is also a common feature of the sculpture of the Bakongo, Tchicaya's people. The nails in Christ's flesh are, Tchicaya tells us, 'my vices'. The gentle, forgiving Christ is mocked as a 'fakir', the prophet of an 'invertebrate religion', but it is to music of Christ's 'slow sadness' that the poet chooses to waltz his poem.

These references, gathered together from various parts of *Feu de Brousse, A Triche-Coeur* and *Epitomé*, are necessary to build up a picture of the complex, ambivalent and even contradictory image of Christ and Christianity as it emerges in the whole corpus of Tchicaya's work. And each specific reference, as in stanza 3 of 'Présence', is best seen as a facet of that image. Indeed, the same is true of any of the master-images of this poet, which gradually deepen, enrich and complicate their total meaning as they recur in new situations, moods or applications. Thus, one could not say definitively what Tchicaya means by 'following my river', because here the river is eternalized, thereby stressing its analogous relationship to the bloodstream, whose salt content matches that of the rejuvenating ocean when its waters thrust into and mingle in those of the Congo. The river is here the companions of the poet in his wanderings and in his search for rebirth. But in a poem such as the great threnody 'They are dead' from *Epitomé*, the river is more externalized as the tragic process of Congolese history itself. It is the war dead of 1960–1 who are mingled with its transforming waters, rather than the poet who stands upon its shores to give them a memorial.

So much by the way of preparation, for some of the recurrent *leit motifs* which make their appearance in 'Présence', some of them for the first time:

Having found no men
on my horizon
I played with my body
the ardent poems of death
I followed my river
to the cold and surging billows
I opened myself to the world
of sea-weeds
Where solitudes crawl
open the thickets to solitudes

to the sun
open my flesh
to the ripe blood of riots
the breath of sperm mingles me
with the yeast of leaves and storms

and my hair roughened by all the winds
stands on edge
my hands moist to all seeds
carry my feet deep into space
and I resemble slow death with its rich suns

faked presence I shall be unfaithful
for christ the god of armies
has betrayed me
when he allowed his skin to be pierced
offering us the mere proof of his death

treacherous christ
here is my flesh of bronze
and my blood closed
by the numberless – I copper and zinc
by the two stones of my brain
eternal by my slow death
coelocanth of the deep. . . .[7]

The imagined process of death in the magnificent opening lines is
one forced upon the poet by his isolation in a white world which
cannot share his concerns or comprehend his anguish. The sense of
isolation grows still deeper in *Epitomé* (1962), when feelings in the
West began to run high over the Congo tragedy, but in a direction
absolutely contrary to those of any radical, informed African; more
especially, any Congolese African. But these earlier lines give us
already a powerful impression of the poet's inner exploration of a
body, a physical 'presence', which is his only link with the landscape
and people of his own country. And since death is above all the
process by which we mingle our elements with those from which we
came, it is this process which dominates the opening stanza of the
poem. But the impression is far from deathly, for the imagery of
'breath of sperm', of 'yeast' and of 'rich suns' stresses that the path
is more one of renewal than of disappearance.

Connected with this belief in the total, suggestive power of the
human body is the common practice of multiple metre in African
dance. Robert Farris Thompson has shown in *African Arts in
Motion*,[8] how multi-metric dancing, where different parts of the body

are moved to different rhythmic strands in the music of the orchestra, is matched by similar chracteristics in African sculpture and in the complex sounds of many African instruments (for example, bells or vibrating wires attached to stringed lyres and bows). He goes on: 'Ideally speaking, multiple metre in the dance is a means of articulating the human body more fully than is possible in ordinary discourse; it makes a person blaze as a living entity at the centre of understanding.' In fact, Tchicaya often moves from imagery of physical auto-exploration to imagery of dancing; moving the whole body in sadness, exultation or praise:

Christ
I will waltz to the tune of your slow sadness.[9]

It is this pagan, organic conception of death and rebirth that is contrasted in the third stanza with the dualism of Christianity, which can conceive of a death of the body, and an immortality for the soul alone. The frail body of Christ may be pierced, but the poet's body is cast in bronze, as though the mortal clay were only a mould into which the hot alloy of the blood is poured. Thus the poet is rendered eternal, not by separation of the soul, but by 'my slow death'. Like the coelacanth* he will lurk unguessed at in the deepest oceans of Africa, stirred by the currents of rebirth.

The transition from the concerns of *Feu de Brousse* to those of *A Triche-Coeur* (A Game of Cheat Heart) is marked by a sharper concentration upon the quest for origin. The new collection, published in 1960, is dominated by the poet's search for the 'key to dreams', introduced in the very first line. The search is conducted exclusively beside the waters of the Congo, but the passionate restlessness of the seeker is gradually transformed into the positive discovery of resurrection. The familiar images of the orphan's bereavement occur again and again early in the sequence. In the second poem, 'Étiage' (Low Watermark) we find:

My own head is a ploughshare
but upon my earth
not a groove not a furrow
Where is the breast of my mother
that I may throw my head high there
before the new moon
and the high tide. . . .[10]

*A prehistoric fish, thought to be long extinct until discovered to be still living in the deep ocean trenches around Africa.

and again a few lines later:

> open the breast of my mother
> that I may throw my head high there
> and blessed be the bread that is taken from me
> blessed be the thirst that is taken from me. . . .[11]

In a later poem, 'Equinoxiale', the same pattern of imagery (head as ploughshare, breast as earth, moon as sexual symbol associated with intercourse, menstruation and childbirth) is taken up and re-worked as a kind of spiritual biography of the mother in death. Here it is the moon which seizes the newborn child and the woman who wages war upon it. The opening lines are full of a moon-bathed stillness which grips the tableau of death:

> The moon spread out
> all the blood of a woman
> in guise of a holocaust
> to the stars of the sea
>
> The moon took the child
> of a woman
> curling with its blue
> light of death
> that mother's hair
>
> The same woman. . . .
> held out against a moon
> murderous and accursed
> she fought victoriously
> dragging at her heels
> a moon in tribute. . . .[12]

Fighting against the moon's innate influence towards death and negation, the woman opens her 'musician-sex' to the ardent blackening of the sun's rays. Intent upon a new fructification of 'the sadness of her opened flesh', she wrestles the crescent moon into the shape of a ploughshare; and the furrow thus opened within her becomes a shining river of rebirth.

The transformation of the images of death, stillness and negation which dominate the opening lines of the poem into the great hymn for 'a furrow to write eternity' which closes it makes this one of Tchicaya's strongest and most complete visions of wholeness and continuity. And the resurrection here achieved by the dead mother becomes a means of enabling the poet to separate himself from the 'orphan my accomplice'. The orphan becomes now, not his current, but his dead self, from which the poet bursts free and rises in a triumphant assertion of immortality. Thus in the next poem, 'Le Corbillard' (The Hearse), we find:

the orphan is dead in the storm. . . .
A flash of lightning showed me joy
I saw nothing of the living but that orphan resurrected. . . .[13]

Another feature of *A Triche-Coeur* is a greater element of child-hood recollection and autobiography, often using imagery of a highly sexual character – a kind of purging-through-release of his obsession with something scandalous or obscure in his begetting:

then
an idiot virgin opened her sex for me
to piss upon my already putrid sorrow
god alone knows how sweetly I came then
and returning more bravely in my tracks
I met nothing but trees
which carried one another's fruit
trees none the less
but no-one of my family
in their branches. . . .[14]

It seems almost fortuitous that Tchicaya thus resolves a part of his personal dilemma before embarking on his more active involve-ment with that of his people. It is already suggested in 'Equinoxiale' that the mother's vindication of her flesh will be that of the suffering Congo also, for the poem speaks of 'discovering in sorrow/three centuries of her life'. The poems in the main sequence of *Epitomé* (published in 1962, but evidently written mainly in 1960) each carry a superscription identifying them with particular phases or events of the struggle which raged on the banks of the Congo in 1959–61. In the midst of this period, Tchicaya was for three months Chief Editor of the Zaire daily *Le Congo*, published in Kinshasa. He was thus an anguished and immediate witness of Patrice Lumumba's virtual imprisonment in his own capital; of the ambiguous role of Dag Hammarskjöld and the United Nations in that affair; and of its culmination in the attempted escape, capture, torture and martyrdom of the Prime Minister, who seemed to carry to the grave with him all hopes of a genuinely united and independent Congo. The first part of *Epitomé* reads like a poetic diary of these events, in which their initial impact is recreated, their meaning sought in the deeper perspective of all other events suffered by the same or other colonized peoples. The vision nurtured during those perilous but heady days in Kinshasa was something very different from the American-dominated dictatorship which later rose upon the wrack of Lumumbist hopes. It could even be dreamed, as Tchicaya dreamed in some of those poems, that the Congo's five centuries of anguish since the Portuguese arrival might be resolved at last into freedom and unity for its peoples. The poet taunts Christ to share to the full the specific agony and division of his people, wrought by such 'Christian' enslavers, colonizers and intriguers:

Walk on this road of my people where I limp
You will tell me in what Egypt my people groan
My heart is no desert speak oh Christ speak
Was it you who put living gold in my wine of joy
Do I owe to you my twin sources
And my soul and my heart
Was it you who set at my heart two ventricles
such tiny ones
Tell me why I should suffer this love in my heart. . . .[15]

Contemplating the dead of the Congo and viewing their deaths in the perspective of a colonial history peculiarly disastrous even by African standards, Tchicaya is able to see his personal situation as something transcended by the fate of others apparently more 'typically' Congolese. So, the superscription to the poem 'they are dead', already referred to, invites the poet to wash off his deep sense of personal guilt in the waters which carry the Congolese dead to the sea:

Live; wash off your guilt
They are dead. . . .[16]

But at other times, where the poem is imaginatively situated in Paris rather than Kinshasa, Tchicaya looks ironically at his own predicament and contrasts it with the other forms of 'betrayal' offered by his Congolese brothers, whose caution and bourgeois commitment leave the nation to the care of foreign powers even more rapacious than the classic colonists of Belgium:

The disasters unfold in silence . . .
and a grey rain serves all our dreams
forcing me to become a forger
and holy assassin

despite the equinox
despite myself
despite the sorcery of the smiles
of my obedient black brothers

And then
What would you say of this silence
squatting beside my own conscience?[17]

and in the very next poem:

I am elastic like all honest hearts. . . .[18]

It is this ironic note, this ability to focus on the complex of African attitudes towards the Congo crisis, which prevents any sense of messianism from overwhelming Tchicaya's poetry even at its most passionately involved. If he sees himself here as the poet of his people, he is incapable of castigating them without seeing the ambiguities of his own situation. The perception of these ambiguities is far more honest in his work than we shall find it in other exile patriots like Birago Diop and Léopold Senghor. When the Parisian situation of writing is evoked in their work, it is invariably lamented as something inescapably imposed on the poet, who yearns helplessly for the village hearths. Tchicaya's irony accepts that there is an element of choice in his exile, which answers the choice of those 'at home' who fail to match all the challenges of the hour with adequate courage or commitment. The poet can even mock himself as being: 'more French than Joan of Arc', and therefore, perhaps, all the better equipped to recognize the compromises and betrayals of others.

This quality of self-irony grows even stronger in his next two collections, *Le Ventre* (1964) and *L'Arc Musical* (1970). The first is a volume still dominated by the Congo experience. The belly, turned uppermost in both acts of love and birth and also in a watery death, becomes here the crucial image, whose meaning must be allowed to express its full horror before being made to yield also its potentialities for renewal. Even more than *Epitomé*, these poems are driven by an impulse to understand imaginatively the experience of those terrible months in the Congo. In this respect they might be compared with the 'Massacre' sequence in Wole Soyinka's *Idanre* (1967), which is similarly engaged with the mind-beggaring facts of massacre and civil war in Nigeria. Soyinka uses an imagery of harvest to deepen our sense of everything that is abortive and dismaying in the spectacle of a new nation tearing itself apart. This is a seed-time which sows only violence and reaps only the victims heaped by tractors into putrid lakes or common graves:

There has been such a crop in time of growing
Such tuneless noises when we longed for sighs
Alone of petals, for muted swell of wine-buds
In August rains, and singing in green spaces.[19]

Instead of contrasting the Congo's harvest of death with the vital harvests that independence might have brought to fruition, Tchicaya muses intensely over the distended bodies of the slain, striving to see within them the lineaments of rebirth as well as of denial and decay. And once again, it is often his own body that he uses as an interpreter and mediator for this experience of death:

Nothing is lonelier than the belly
and the heart!
Alone in that solitude
Whose edges burn our living sores;
tearing out our milk teeth
with the first disillusion of the heart!
We must keep beside us this music
Which trickles with blood
So that we may never see
the soul spill over with all the blood
at Kin!

Now that the sky is darkened with these flakes
only the hot skeletons
are safe from response to the call
Now as for me I am armoured white
to lose myself in the first assault
of laughter
or in this music
Which trickles with all the blood
at Kin![20]

Here even the very warmth of the living belly links it with the hot stench of putrefaction. In the last lines of the same poem, the 'music' of the spilling blood at Kin(shasa) is compared with that in which the poet tries to find refuge. The flakes which darken the sky above the city are the parachutes of the returning Belgians which snowed upon the city only a few weeks after independence. In these terrible days, there is even a certain safety in death; ironically it is the 'hot skeletons' which display the quality of warmth in the midst of this white blizzard of destruction. Is it the poet's sense of complicity – as an *assimilé* normally resident in Paris – which makes him 'armoured white' to withstand this new assault from the skies?

Alongside this ironical portrayal of the poet as someone who, despite himself, has inescapable elements of complicity and 'black obedience' within him, there develops another comparison. Far more than *Epitomé*, these poems are haunted by the martyred figure of Patrice Lumumba. No Congolese leader since his murder has gathered into himself so many aspects of the struggle for a meaningful Congolese and African unity; for the use of the Congo's wealth to free rather than to subdue its people; for a real departure from the five-century history of foreign manipulation and exploitation, which is practically the only relation the Congo has ever known with the West.

In these poems, then, the physical exploration of experience is conducted through the broken body of Lumumba as much as through Tchicaya's own physical witness. It is what *dies with* Lumumba that remains uncertain at the time of writing these poems; hence, perhaps, the offer of a 'Funeral Flamenco' for the burial of the fallen leader, whose death may mark only a phase of a developing struggle. It is notable, too, how the themes of betrayal, flogging and martyrdom link Lumumba here with the images already developed of Christ and of the betrayed–betraying poet himself:

He falls beneath the flails
Then four or five planks
his companions are outside
or else a common grave
under a light covering of earth. . . .
While my belly is warmed
only with wine!
He falls beneath the flails!

Yes! (A strident yes
for this rattling
of souls, axles and waves!)
A funeral flamenco for him![21]

After all, the poet is able to force out a painful cry of assent, even 'If the yes tears the throat of the dove!' A myth can sometimes wield more positive force than its own progenitor, and one has only to recall how the dead Lumumba instantly became the hero of a thousand anonymous ballads, funeral dirges, broadsheets and passionate recitations up and down the length of Africa to perceive the meaning of this '*Oui!*' across the years which already separate us from it.

It will be seen that the poetry of *Epitomé* and *Le Ventre* is on the whole more public in its concerns than the intensely self-communing volumes that preceded it. And this more public orientation is matched, particularly in *Le Ventre*, by a slight simplification of style. A more stanzaic form reappears on the page, after the boiling cascades of images which pour through *Feu de Brousse* or *A Triche-Coeur*, and there is a return to a limited use of punctuation, capitalization and closed sentences within each poem.

Tchicaya continues to search for the tree of his origins, he pummels and dissects his own belly to find the meaning of rebirth within the giant fact of death in the Congo of those years; the great river flows as ever through his pages, carrying, changing and delivering up the burden of a tragic historic experience. Thus all the elements of continuity are present; only the poet's preoccupations begin to take on a more representative character; he is both literally and imaginatively closer to the experience of his people than the brilliant young Parisian poet of the 1950s.

This quality of passionate involvement makes possible the assertion which ends the long dialogue poem 'The Bodies and the Benefits':

Whoever survives
Will see the Congo
Riding astride the Congo
Or floating amid the water-hyacinths. . . .[22]

It also informs the sombre magnificence of the final poem 'Le Ventre Reste' (The Belly Remains), into which Tchicaya gathers many of the themes of the whole volume, with a focus of extraordinary intensity and power. Here the dead of the Congo become 'the seers', every one of them prophesying the Congo that shall be, after the anguish and loss of our day. Their posture is that of love and birth as well as death, and there will be 'benefits' from these countless corpses which scatter and disfigure the land. Just as Soyinka's imagery of harvest, even of the aborted harvest, nevertheless reminds us of the green harvest that can and should and ultimately must be; so Tchicaya's long physical exploration of death and martyrdom leads him at least away from despair:

Certainly the belly remains chaste
beneath a treasury of white bones
then open to a soldier's song
losing body and joys
in the flames of his passion. . . .

Certainly the belly remains,
Is it more soiled than chaste?
Because of its heartbreaks?
But love for love
is surely more desolating than the rest.
But love for life
he who was dropped from the belly
is taken by the earth
God be praised the prophets fall
most often on their backs
most often with arms opened wide
most often
their bellies to the sky![23]

Tchicaya's next collection marks another change of direction or emphasis within the stream of his development. This is *L'Arc Musical*, published as part of the two-volume *Collected Works* issued by Pierre-Jean Oswald in 1970. In some ways this volume marks a move towards African poetic tradition, since the poet here conceives of himself more as a *griot*, a poet-musician who sings as much through his instrument (the bow harp) as through his voice, but one who is compelled to practise his craft in an alien city and for an alien audience. The imaginative centre of his work now seems to have shifted once again to Paris and the situation of the exile is made ironic in a way reminiscent of his earlier work, where 'my city' referred usually to Paris rather than to Kinshasa or Brazzaville. Although the regime in the author's native République du Congo is a leftist one and represents something closer to the ideals of 1960 than what has emerged across the river in Zaire, it seems that he nevertheless prefers at present to experience it as an annual visitor rather than as a citizen. The intense excitement and immediacy of his work of 1960–4 gives way, therefore, to a more lyrical vein and at time to a more definite ironic poise, a kind of protective detachment. Characteristic of the first might be these lines, which still carry the conviction that everything must be experienced through the channels and structures of the body. The poet has already carried his death:

tie a stone to my death
which hangs heavy upon me[24]

His 'improbable genealogy'; his tyrannous mistress with her grinning fakir of a Christ. Let fraternity be built also into the walking skeleton which informs his poems:

La fraternité fut un mot
j'en fais un os de plus
à joindre à mon squelette. . . .[25]

[Fraternity was just a word
I make of it another bone
to fasten to my skeleton. . . .]

This detachment, which is only another aspect of the saving laughter which pours through *Epitomé*, here takes the form of a professional skill. If the poet cannot warn or terrify, he can at least entertain:

A curse on the typsy bird!
What use is yapping?
It is the bow harp
that we must play in this country.[26]

The use of the bow harp here as something which stands between the poet and the listener, the art to some extent detachable from the artist, has also been prepared for in the figure of 'the passer-by' who moves mysteriously and enigmatically through the pages of *Epitomé*. 'The passer-by' is a foil to the poet's own desperate involvement, just as the harp is his poetic skill rather than his mortal life.

Allied perhaps to this withdrawal into a recognizable traditional role as the professional poet singer, is an even greater economy and precision of form than Tchicaya had already achieved. The poetry is at times almost tersely controlled; there are fewer of the great 'cries of passion' earlier saluted by L. S. Senghor.[27] The poet is less totally self-exposed, but for that very reason his sarcasm can be even more deadly. Tchicaya had already written in *Epitomé*:

my assassin's laughter
aping the savage king's
made the butcher also laugh. . . .[28]

Here that laughter often pierces more than it burns. Tchicaya now once again inhabits a society where his passionate concern for the victims of racism and imperial ambition, whether in Louisiana, Algeria, Vietnam or the Congo itself, can appear eccentric to those who still clutch an illusory white security and complacency. The shape of the world is simply very different when viewed from the Quai d'Orsay than from the shores of the River Congo. This is something that even the most sympathetic and informed white too often fails to realize. And it creates an acute problem for the exiled poet, even when he knows that many of his eventual readers will be in the black world. It is the immediacy of human response, and equally shared response, that he must lack. There are glimpses too of a more intimate pressure upon the poet to surrender the Promethean fire of his art; to accept Christ's suffering in place of his own:

One flesh made my flesh sad
One fire made my soul liquid
One wind wanted my hands porous

A love scarcely more sweet
than the jew's death I demand
promises me peace of heart
if I restore the stolen fire
and recover my blood from the night.[29]

Many of the poems in *L'Arc Musical* also seem to offer more insight into what the poet seeks immediately in his life; the search is less cosmic, less all-embracing than the whirlwind which drives through *Feu de Brousse*, for example. Instead of tree, river, blood or sun, we have attempts to define the sort of faith which might be acceptable to the poet, the sort of house he wishes built for him by faith. The very titles of the poems – 'Collectes du Sang', 'Communion', 'Funèbre', 'Noces' – reveal this incessant use of religious imagery (particularly that drawn from the Eucharist) and this urge to move beyond mockery of the bourgeois, compromised church and Christ of *Epitomé* towards a definition of his own creed. In 'Pourquoi donc dieu est-il mort?' (Why then is God dead?) he sings:

I want his two hands forming
a watertight thatch for my head;
his kiss a second sun
his mouth a second door. . . .[30]

In both *L'Arc Musical* and the following collection *La Veste d'Intérieur* (1967) there is a relative absence of direct reference to public events, which formed the 'trip' or starting point for many poems in *Epitomé* and *Le Ventre*. The events are there all right; they form part of the complex of experience which presses in upon the poet from every side, and they demand his witness. But the search continues for a way of structuring his life that will take account both of the isolation of the artist and that of the exile living among alien peoples. Contrary to one of the clichés of African literary criticism, it is not true that traditional African poetry never registers this kind of isolation. The songs of Adokto recorded by Okot p'Bitek in *The Horn of my Love*,[31] and those of Akpalu recorded by Kofi Awoonor can be cited as evidence that the traditional poet often registers his sense of isolation and neglect in a heedless, uncaring world. Often he longs for death, and turns the funeral ceremonies of others into occasions for contemplating his own. Thus the fine poet Akpalu sings:

I shall sing you a song of sorrow,
When my turn comes, who will sing for me?
There is silence, deathly silence.
This way they said is how the poet dies.
Alas for someone who will bear him over the gulf
And he will come bearing along his voice. . . .[32]

We might compare this with Tchicaya's valedictory poem 'Legs' (Legacy), in *L'Arc Musical*, which closes with the lines:

the earth more ardently
wishing us at rest
within her milkless sides
will lap us with humus.

And if this harp cannot follow me
there where the spirits wait
this is my testament:
I leave you the fire and the song.[33]

This mood, then, is one which often besets any poet, whether singing in the midst of his indigenous folk or issuing his poems through the silent medium of the printed word. In a poem from *La Veste d'Intérieur* the poet's feeling of claustrophobia, of being shut in with his song, becomes stifling:

The song I pour out of the window is sticky
The sunlight clings
Sex and blood sacrifice themselves
There is a great plain on the road

The rain too tense with blackness shelters
The dead resume their absence

This morning the wind will not yield
Ashes and hemp
The window is walled up
The sunlight clings

The death has a foul odour
Which expatiates thus in the song

The window forbids itself promise.[34]

Tchicaya's humour and irony, however, prevent him from ever lapsing into self-pity. They are strongly evident in the reflections, entitled 'Notes de Veille' (Waking Thoughts), which close this volume. Tchicaya has always mingled the lyrical with the dramatic, and has always made use of an aphoristic, reflective, more prosaic style from time to time. He does so in the closing sections of *Le Mauvais Sang* and of *Epitomé*. 'Notes de Veille' carries us back to those volumes, and it is impossible to read the following cryptic dialogue between God the Father and Christ without being reminded of the theme of deprivation which runs through them:

CHRIST: Father, Father, why hast thou forsaken me?
THE FATHER: Son, Son, what sin of pride is this?
Fraternity, for an only son, is the worst.[35]

The dramatic elements just referred to as a constant strand in Tchicaya's work reached their fulfilment in the plays which he began to write from 1976 onwards. His debut as a dramatist took place at the Avignon Festival in the summer of 1976, with the première of *Le Zulu*, an intense re-examination of Chaka's character and the meaning of his life. The play, which was repeated in Martinique and at the Théâtre Oblique in Paris the same year, was published in 1977 with the addition of the short dramatic monologue *Vwène le Fondateur*.

Le Zulu invites comparison with the earlier dramatic poem 'Chaka' of L. S. Senghor, to whom it is dedicated. Whereas Senghor's poem is a kind of post-mortem trial of Chaka, prosecuted by a white voice, defended by himself and triumphantly vindicated by the choir, Tchicaya internalizes the whole debate about Chaka's motives and achievements within a taut, fast-moving drama of three acts. Instead of debate we have action. The only disembodied voice is that which is addressed by his genuises Ndlebé and Malounga as 'the Master' in the opening scene, and which appears to Chaka in the form of a hero's staff, prophesying his glory but warning him of the perils which attend that destiny:

VOICE Behold, I am your servant!

CHAKA What will your salary be?

VOICE It is written on this shield, with the point of the assegai.

CHAKA This blood, is it mine?

VOICE That of your ambition. That of your design. Unity of the sky like that of the earth. . . . The threshold of Nobamba is open. But. . . .

CHAKA But what?

VOICE Let nothing white appear to the southward. . . . Beware the foam of the sea.

CHAKA The foam of the sea. What is that? What is the sea? What is the foam? (*looking at the shield with terror*) This blood, is it also mine?

VOICE Yes, if it is ever spilt upon you.[36]

All the main lines of the ensuing action are indicated in this short exchange. The first blood upon the shield is that of Chaka's ambition (the betrayal of his patron Ding'iswayo and of his ally Zwidé). But Zwidé's dying curse, that Chaka's own blood will choke him, not only preys upon the all-powerful conqueror but fulfils itself with inexorable force. Both his mother Nnandi and his wife Noliwé are kinswomen of Ding'iswayo and brood upon his unrevenged death. Chaka first kills Noliwé, with his own unborn child in her womb, and then the conspiring Nnandi. But, in the manner of classical tragedy, his doom is approaching him from another direction, that of his brother Ndingana. When even his familiars, Ndlebé and Malounga, desert him, his destiny deserts him also. But he dies at the hands of black stooges in white men's uniforms, and can say in dying:

A dawn is always heavy with something which fatally escapes man. . . . Man. . . . What kind of man have I been? . . . Poor country! It's not even a consolation to know that I'm dying. . . . To die! That's the inevitable stop, but before the horror that is coming, what can I do? And after all it was freedom. . . . This legacy of slavery is not from me. No.[37]

Tchicaya has deepened Chaka's crimes, whilst also explaining their motivation. The chronicles do not attribute to him the deaths of either Zwidé or Nnandi.

Chaka's most debatable acts are here the logical consequence of his urge to unify the Zulu nation. But his motives are not understood by others, and his actions bring nemesis upon him in the form of clan vengeance. His enemies collaborate with the very forces which will soon destroy or enslave them all. Thus Chaka stands as the last and supreme embodiment of an enlightened black resistance, carefully building a power which can match the swelling menace from the south.

No more than Senghor is Tchicaya writing a historical play. For, in the historical record, Ndingana did not collaborate with the Boer invaders (in fact, he massacred Piet Retief and his party), and Chaka did receive white visitors favourably at his court. But his imaginative recasting of these events has its own kind of coherence, its own teaching virtue, in an age when the struggle in Southern Africa is again between black collaboration and black resistance.

There is a crispness and thrust about Tchicaya's dialogue which distinguish his sense of language for the stage. Consider this exchange between three of the conspirators:

NNANDI You are with us and you are with him to betray us.

NDLEBÉ The mother who dreams of her own son's death prepares her grave. . . . Let her beware then of suspecting others.

EPERVIER Stop this quarrelling. . . . How is he now?

NDLEBÉ Stupid as all those who seek repose in sleep. . . . and not in death.[38]

It seems likely that, having established himself so swiftly as a dramatist, he will turn increasingly towards writing for the theatre. His *Le Zulu* must soon be translated into English and must find its way on to the stages of Africa, for which it was surely designed. This is not to suggest that Tchicaya will cease activity as a lyric poet. The discovery of his gifts for the stage is merely an additional channel of expression for an imagination which remains innately poetic in its concentration and daring.

Okot p'Bitek

Born 1931 at Gulu in Northern Uganda, son of a schoolmaster. Okot was educated at Gulu High School, King's College in Budo and later at the universities of Wales and Oxford. After early years as a schoolmaster and athlete, he studied law and anthropology in Britain and soon distinguished himself as an authority on African oral literatures and indigenous religions. After some years as an extramural tutor in Uganda and Kenya, where he founded the Gulu and Kisumu festivals, Okot moved to the Literature Department of Nairobi University. His earliest published work was a Lwo novel written in his early twenties, but his literary reputation was established with *Song of Lawino*, published in English in 1966 and in the Lwo original in 1969. Okot p'Bitek died in 1982.

8   The Horn of the Grasslands

Few events in the development of modern African literature have been as dramatic as the appearance of *Song of Lawino*, late in 1966. From the very first line the poem established a distinctive tone which appeared to owe nothing, and in fact did owe nothing, to any earlier African poetry in English, whether in East Africa or elsewhere:

First take a deep look, brother,
You are now a man
You are not a dead fruit!
To behave like a child does not befit you!

Listen Ocol, you are the son of a Chief,
Leave foolish behaviour to little children,
It is not right that you should be laughed at in a song!
Songs about you should be songs of praise![1]

These lines alone, from the first movement of the poem, are enough to establish how wrong the publisher was to add the subtitle, 'A Lament by Okot p'Bitek', for the poem cannot be classed as a lament; still less is it a lament in the authorial voice. The first point to grasp about this work (and some reviewers found this remarkably difficult to do) is that Okot has created a dramatic *persona* who is not himself, whose life experience and horizons are not his own, and whose song is just as full of anger, scorn and triumph as it is of lamentation. Lawino runs the gamut of the emotions suggested by her position as the rejected first wife of the aspiring bourgeois, Ocol. From complaints about her lot she soon moves to biting sarcasm about her rival:

Her lips are red-hot
Like glowing charcoal,
She resembles the wild cat
That has dipped its mouth in blood,
Her mouth is like raw yaws

It looks like an open ulcer,
Like the mouth of a fiend!
Tina dusts powder on her face
And it looks so pale;
She resembles the wizard
Getting ready for the midnight dance.[2]

The power of the insults here does not spring from any sense of
inferiority or inadequacy. When she is in her normal vein, Lawino
makes no apologies for being what she is – a typical Acoli woman,
brought up in the values and rich culture of her people. After con-
demning the promiscuous intimacy of night-club dancing, where the
couples cover their bodies, cling together and 'dance silently like
wizards', she springs into the great paean of praise for her own youth
and beauty of yore, for the decorum of Acoli dancing, which is at
the same time an exposure of one's physical presence and a demonstration of control. This movement, 'My Name Blew Like a Horn
Among the Payira', is one of the most sustained and passionate of
the whole poem:

When Ocol was wooing me
My breasts were erect,
And they shook
As I walked briskly,
And as I walked
I threw my long neck
This way and that way
Like the flower of the *lyonno* lily
Waving in a gentle breeze.

And my brothers called me *Nya-Dyang*
For my breasts shook
And beckoned the cattle
And they sang silently:

> *Father prepare the Kraal,*
> *Father prepare the Kraal,*
> The cattle are coming.[3]

What are the sources of this extraordinary style, with the unfailing
freshness and sharpness of its images, its range of mood, its ability to
gather up and convey to us a whole distinctive way of life in work and
play, in sorrow and in joy? Nothing remotely comparable had yet
appeared in East Africa; but for the scale of its organization, *Song
of Lawino* was also something new in Anglophone Africa as a whole.

The answer lies partly in the special nature of Okot's preparation as a poet. Born in 1931 at Gulu in the north-west of Uganda, he was in his youth an outstanding singer, dancer and athlete. Whilst still a schoolboy at King's College, Budo, he had composed and directed a full-length opera. At the age of 22 he published a novel in the Lwo language of Acoli,* *Lak Tar Kinyero Wi Lobo* (Are your Teeth White? Then Laugh).[4] In 1956 he wrote the first draft of the Lwo original, *Wer pa Lawino* (Song of Lawino), though he was then unable to find a publisher for anything so outspoken and uncompromising. Soon afterwards, he was playing football in England for Uganda's national team. This in turn led to his studies in education, law and social anthropology, which culminated in his Oxford B Litt. thesis, devoted to the oral literature of the Acoli and Lango. Thus Okot was occupied in both the study and practice of Lwo poetry for many years before he attempted to write in English. More important still, perhaps, he did not study English literature at the post-secondary level, which can be a distracting experience for a poet seeking to master his own tradition. His literary studies between leaving Budo and finishing the final version of *Wer pa Lawino* in 1966 were devoted entirely to the poetry of the Acoli and Lango. These studies and experiments reinforced the early influence of the poet's mother, Lacwaa Cerina, herself an accomplished singer who probably played a part in the formation of Lawino's character. The Acoli are exceptional among Ugandan people in the extent to which they have maintained the artistic side of their culture, despite the inroads of missionary activity and many changes in the material base of that culture. A number of teachers, as far back as the 1940s, were themselves singers and players of the 'nana', the seven-stringed boat-zither which is the favourite instrument of the Acoli poet. These teachers were just in time to collect songs from some of the great pre-colonial singers, as well as composing many new ones of their own. Hence, schooling in Gulu was not the invitation to turn one's back on traditional culture which it often became elsewhere. The schools even acted, to some extent, as a theatre for the transmission of this culture. Equally remarkable is the fact that one of the sons of a chief, notorious for his collaboration with the British and whose family thus became a sort of early local elite, not only taught himself to play the nana but developed a new poetic style in Lwo, using rhyme and

---

*The 'c' of the Lwo language always has the value of a hard 'ch'. The Lwo language spoken in Northern Uganda should not be confused with the separate but related Luo language of Kenya and Tanzania.

regular metre. Thus, the new educated class in Acoliland contained many who refused to let their English education turn them aside from the language and literature of their own people.

Another reason why *Song of Lawino* is not a lament is that Okot's language and imagery are drawn from the whole range of Acoli song, including the satirical songs of the beer-party (especially when Lawino is attacking Ocol, Clementina or the Christians); the victory songs of the *bwola* dance; the war songs and the praise songs. Even her self-praise is deeply consonant with the whole Acoli tradition, where praising oneself is not merely permitted but required. In the villages, every male Acoli carries an animal horn around his neck, on which he is expected to blow his own praise-name as he approaches any inhabited compound, as a way of announcing himself. Girls, too, when they mount the anthills on a moonlit night, are expected to praise not only their lovers but their own charms:

I was the Leader of the girls
And my name blew
Like a horn
Among the Payira.
And I played on my bow harp
And praised my love.[5]

Towards the end of her song, Lawino even turns to the funeral dirges for inspiration and, as a supreme insult to the culturally dead Ocol, summons her kinsmen to sing a dirge for him:

O, my clansmen
Let us all cry together!
Come,
Let us mourn the death of my husband,
The death of a Prince
The Ash that was produced
By a great Fire!
O, this homestead is utterly dead.
Close the gates with *lacari* thorns,
For the Prince
The heir to the Stool is lost![6]

Every phrase here might be found in many of the splendid funeral dirges which are sung and danced at the second burial ceremonies of the Acoli, known as *Guru Lyel*. But what lends them especial poignancy and force here is that they are being sung for a still living man. Lawino's own rejection of her rejecting husband could not go further.

To appreciate the extent of Okot's involvement in the stream of Acoli song, it is necessary only to look at his collection, *The Horn of my Love*, published in 1974. Equally revealing of the living context in which his song has grown is his more recent collection of Acoli folk-tales, *Hare and Hornbill* (1978). Both collections will reveal the extraordinary strength and vigour of indigenous Acoli tradition, compared with the hesitations, apologies or exaggerated justifications which often afflict those writing exclusively in English, or exclusively from an English literary stimulus. In the pages of *Song of Lawino* we are never in any doubt that an African sensibility is in charge, a sensibility which will judge everything according to its own priorities and its own involvement with the struggle for articulation. This is as little in doubt in Okot's poetry as in the following lines from an Acoli love-song:

Woman of my bosom,
If anybody touches my beloved,
He will be struck by lightning,
Oh, oh, my heart is on fire for her,
Oil of my youth. . . .
[She] keeps my eyes from sleep.[7]

Part of the background to *Song of Lawino*, then, is total participation by the poet in the still flourishing culture of his people; but more important still has been the mode of its composition. G. A. Heron has demonstrated in his study of Okot's poetry[8] how the writer first developed a new prosody for Lwo, using an a–b–a–b rhyme scheme and a more or less regular metrical beat of some eight to ten syllables per line. This style was already present in the unpublished 1956 version of *Wer pa Lawino*, which ran to only thirty-one pages, but was much further developed in the full-length version which the poet finished in 1966 (not published until 1969).[9] At the same time as he finished work on the final Lwo original, Okot began the task of rendering it into English. He was under no illusion about the losses involved, deciding that he must inevitably 'clip a bit of the eagle's wings' in the process. In the English version, he wisely resolved to abandon both rhyme and metrical regularity, since to have stuck to them would have forced him to move far away from the mainly literal translation which enabled him to preserve the force and character of the original imagery. English is also more lengthy and wordy than Lwo, which makes abundant use of prefixes and suffixes to modify root words. Okot therefore decided to adopt a short, fast-moving line in English, since a line-by-line translation would have become clumsy and long-winded. A comparison of the opening passages in the 1969 Lwo original and the English version will illustrate these changes:

Ilanya, ipako ya bong'imita	Husband, now you despise me. . . .
Ya arom ki gigu ma wi obur	You say you no longer want me
Iyeta, ibuku dogi ki buru	Because I am like the things left behind
Ya bong'angeyo wa ki 'a'	In the deserted homestead.
Ya bong'akwano i cukuru	You insult me
Ni an pe amako nying'a	You laugh at me
Ipora ki la-gwok kurukuru	You say I do not know the letter A
Gwokke larema, la-lwak omera,	Because I have not been to school
Gwok lebi jal, gwok dogi. . . .	And I have not been baptized
Wer pa Lawino, pp. 11–12	You compare me with a little dog
	A puppy.
	My friend, age-mate of my brother,
	Take care,
	Take care of your tongue,
	Be careful what your lips say.
	Song of Lawino, pp. 13–14

What survives in the translation here is the urgency of Lawino's rhetorical style. As the poem advances, she keeps changing the target of her apostrophes, exactly like an angry woman in the village. Sometimes she addresses her husband directly, sometimes she describes him mockingly in the third person, sometimes she turns to appeal to her clansmen, or reminds him of his complex relationship with her and her family (for example, 'age-mate of my brother'). Hence, the poem is not so much a soliloquy as a dramatic monologue.

Now let us consider what is lost. The reader will immediately notice that Lwo abounds in strong consonants and open vowels, which assist the process of rhyming. It also displays many duplicated sounds ('kurukuru') and is particularly rich in possibilities of assonance and alliteration. Consider for example the rich effects in the line 'Gwokke larema, la-lwak omera', and see what is lost in 'My friend, age-mate of my brother'. Finally, the natural economy of the Lwo language imparts a certain conciseness to its poetry.

Comparing the English version, however, with many African poems composed in English, we become conscious of the gains in Okot's method of composition. The Lwo original, though then unpublished, had already been performed by the poet up and down

Acoliland; it was already a well-known poem which had elicited much response and had modified Acoli poetic tradition in a certain direction. Whereas the African poet composing directly in English has often to rack his brains for the sort of appropriate imagery which comes so spontaneously in traditional poetry, Okot's poem is still linked organically with that tradition, and draws much of its imagery from a common source, since behind every phrase there lies an established way of expressing this particular emotion in the poetry of the Acoli people. The result is a kind of economy of expression, a refusal to elaborate or explain, which very properly leaves something to the imagination of the reader. When Okot writes:

I threw my long neck
This way and that way
Like the flower of the *lyonno* lily
Waving in a gentle breeze[10]

do we really suffer from not knowing the shape, or even the colour, of the *lyonno*? When Lawino calls on her kinsmen to close the gates with *lacari* thorns, do we need any sharper or more precise expression of mourning? Indeed, how can we, since the whole context gives meaning to these words?

But having established this kind of confidence between himself and his language, Okot is able to extend it to cover situations which were certainly not encountered in the poetry of the ancients. Thus Lawino's comments on the style of independence politics have the same pungency as when she ranges over the familiar life of the village. It is because we know so clearly where she is standing, from what angle she is viewing events which bear heavily on the lives of the people, that her remarks have a peculiar force:

And while the pythons of sickness
Swallow the children
And the buffaloes of poverty
Knock the people down
And ignorance stands there
Like an elephant,

The war leaders
Are locked in bloody feuds
Eating each other's liver. . . .[11]

The rough strength of these images is typical of Lawino's language. As in the poetry of her people, there is no squeamishness here;

whatever is seen and known in the community is a fit subject for song. Lawino's description of a night club lavatory spares nothing of its squalor, whilst her catalogue of the various type of human dung has a certain earthy humour (pages 39–40). The advantage of a poet who works quite consciously within the confines of a rich and ancient poetic tradition (instead of at the outer limits of an alien one), is that he can raid at will the body of imagery and allusion which that tradition has slowly generated. There is no question of 'plagiarism' here, for within such a tradition the artist is judged by his knowledge of it and his ability to manipulate it. The Western concept of originality is essentially post-classical and has no relevance here. Thus, not only does Okot embody several songs from the Acoli repertoire in his text but much of his imagery elsewhere is, as it were, sanctioned by usage. The familarity of some of it (though in other contexts) can only assist the reception of Okot's poem in its original language and among its original audience. The same might be said of certain other poets, who have a comparable relationship to an African traditional poetry; notably Kofi Awoonor within the Ewe poetry of Ghana and Mazisi Kunene within the Zulu poetry of Natal. But Okot's example appears wider than theirs, in that he derives his references and images from the whole range of Acoli poetic expression, whereas Awoonor depends heavily upon the funeral dirges of a few famous singers. Kunene, too, appears to draw mostly upon the dirge and the praise song for his resources. Take, for example, these lines from a well-known Acoli song, as they occur in *Song of Lawino*:

When a woman has brought
death in a bundle. . . .
And Death has felt the inside of the victims
And found them clean,
It bounces back
And destroys the bringer![12]

The lines sting sharply enough of themselves, but the application they are given here is to Lawino's search for the root of the misfortune which has stricken her homestead. The theme of witchcraft still links the two applications, for Ocol has been in some way bewitched.

It is shortly after this that Lawino swings into the funeral dirge which forms the twelfth movement of the poem. But she is mourning more than a husband here; she mourns for a whole age-set which was:

. . . . finished
In the class-rooms,
Their testicles were smashed
With large books![13]

It is probably pure accident that Okot's English poem is written in thirteen movements, the number of months in the lunar year. But, if the poem reaches its lowest point in the mock-death of Ocol in movement 12, then, as befits the auguries of the New Year, movement 13 is full of the sense of resurgence. Ocol can yet be cured of the foreign madness which has eaten up his head. Imagery of convalescence and of gradually returning strength culminates in the last lines of the poem, where Lawino once again appeals to her husband in the rich language of the Acoli love-song. All her anger and bitterness are swallowed back in this last surge of tenderness and reconciliation (I must disagree with Heron in finding her words here humble; Lawino is celebrating her husband's imagined recovery from cultural death):

Let me dance before you,
My love,
Let me show you
The wealth in your house,
Ocol my husband,
Son of the Bull
Let no-one uproot the Pumpkin.[14]

By ending the poem in this way, Okot left the reader with a faint hope that Ocol might yet really recover his senses, and with them his love and respect for his first wife. For when Lawino first 'mourns' her husband and then seems to celebrate his returning strength, she has left behind all sense of humiliation. It is not she who is rejected, but Ocol who no longer properly belongs to his people. But four years later Okot came out with the *Song of Ocol*, and here we see a completely unrepentant husband, whose own words justify everything that Lawino has said of him. As she has already told us, Ocol is not merely asking his wife to pack her things and go; he is sending the whole of his traditional culture along with her. But here we come across a difficulty and it is one which is almost fatal to Okot's second poem. For whereas Lawino sings always in the words which she might actually utter (since so much of her song is drawn from the poetic *corpus* of the Acoli), Ocol often seems to tell us what he really thinks, rather than what he would dare to say. By 1970, when this poem was published, it had become almost impossible for any educated 'been-to' to publicly dismiss his race and his culture in this open way:

Timid,
Unadventurous,
Scared of the unbeaten track,
Unweaned,
Clinging to mother's milkless breasts
Clinging to brother,
To uncle, to clan,
To tribe

To blackness

To Africa

Africa
This rich granary
Of taboos, customs,
Traditions. . . .

Mother, mother,
Why,
Why was I born
Black?[15]

Other writers, most notably Ayi Kwei Armah in *The Beautyful Ones are not yet Born*, have attributed this sort of psychosis to the modern African; accusing him of being in love with whiteness and the gleam of all things white. But in Armah's novel, it is not an articulated desire. It is one which he reads beneath all the rhetoric of nationalism and racial pride. A song, however, is nothing if it is not a passionate and public articulation of our feelings and desires. And because the feelings expressed by Ocol here are not such as would ever be uttered in traditional Acoli song, Okot's language here does not have that rich and durable plane of reference lying always behind it. The song stands alone (and we do not feel anyway that Ocol is a man who would ever sing). And yet there are many places where Ocol's words do come alive; most notably in his mockery of African woman for allowing a few sweet words by a poet to blind her to her real position in society:

Woman of Africa
Sweeper
Smearing floors and walls

With cow dung and black soil.
Cook, *ayah*, the baby tied on your back,
Vomiting,
Washer of dishes,
Planting, weeding, harvesting. . . .
Cart, lorry,
Donkey. . . .

Woman of Africa
What are you not?[16]

Is Ocol here (the whole of the third movement) only feeling sorry for himself for having been born black; or is there a genuine compassion moving in these pages for the lot of African woman? Who has not occasionally felt the same, seeing a woman bent double beneath a heavy load walking the pathways in rain and sun, old before her time, carrying the burdens, it sometimes seems, not only of herself but of her man as well? Once he walked behind with a spear to protect her. Nowadays, he just walks behind.

If Ocol's song stands alone as a public utterance, whereas Lawino's is only the visible part of a huge poetic iceberg extending into the life of her people, we can also say that Ocol's voice is very much his own. Okot is now so much at ease within his discovered style that he no longer needs to appeal to traditional utterance as a kind of authority. But this ease does not find an adequate theme in most of Ocol's denunciations of the life around him. His fierce denunciation of East Africa's pastoral nomads, however, is scarcely an exaggeration of what public officials have often said. Patience with the remaining nomads must soon run out, especially as former nomadic peoples like the Nandi and Kipsigi have adapted so successfully to settled life:

We will not simply
Put the Maasai in trousers
To end twenty-five thousand years
Of human nakedness. . . .

We will arrest
All the elders
The tutors of the young
During circumcisions,
The gathering of youths
In the wilderness for initiations
Will be banned,

The Council of Elders
Will be abolished;
The war dance. . . .
The blowing of war horns
Will be punished
With twelve strokes
Of the cane
For each blast;[17]

Such sentiments have been found perfectly consistent with nationalism, for the unrepentantly traditional nomad has been found an embarrassment to governments anxious to present a modern image. The Maasai's way of doing so is to simply hang a transistor radio on the end of his spear, rather than to throw away his weapon and his way of life. But as long as he wanders, it is impossible to provide him or his family with the facilities which otHer citizens enjoy:

Believing you were
The richest of the earth. . . .
You continued to jump
Up and down
Up and down
As you dance,
Firmly holding to the spear,
The symbol of your backwardness.[18]

The Song of Ocol, then, is not simply the articulation of an inner psychosis; parts of it are a satirical treatment of those who praise African culture only in the most generalized terms, but denounce many concrete manifestations of it as backward. At the end of the fifth movement of the poem, the young warrior and his girl are invited to walk proudly into the city with Ocol; there is clearly no place left for them in the countryside. The physique which they owe to their traditional diet and athletic way of life can be turned to good account in city courtships:

Do you see
The eyes of the girls
Glued on you?
Here you do not have
To kill a man or a lion first.[19]

Ocol finds in the entire African past no theme of praise. The great heroes of the past, he says, have left nothing to their successors except a legacy of defeat. His hurry to catch up with the rest of the world leaves no time for idle indulgence and he ends his 'song' with a dismissal of every singer and poet in the business of celebration:

What proud poem
Can we write
For the vanquished?[20]

Okot could have perhaps written a more interesting and complex poem by presenting Ocol as someone whom Lawino does not understand and, to some extent, misrepresents. If Lawino expresses one side of a dialectic which rages within the breast of the poet himself (who may love, but cannot truly live the traditional Acoli way of life), then Ocol is too bigoted and blind to express the other side of it. Far from leaving us with any feeling that Lawino has misrepresented him, we end his poem with a conviction that he is even more foolish and second-rate than we had suspected. This may well have been Okot's intention, but it is an intention that produces a poem notably poorer and slighter than his earlier masterpiece.

One reason for this is that Ocol's targets are generalized (he addresses 'Africa', 'African Woman', or the whole Nilo-Hamitic group of nomads), except for those few passages where he addresses Lawino herself. By contrast, Lawino's song is always personal and passionate, whether addressed to her husband or to her clansmen. In this connection, Heron has rightly remarked:

Lawino's use of oblique respectful titles reflects the fact that she is . . . living within a peasant community in which the titles and praise-names are still meaningful. . . . At the beginning and end of the poem particularly, Lawino stresses everything that binds her to Ocol and leads her to expect from him a certain kind of behaviour.[21]

It was with the publication of *Two Songs* in 1971 that Okot found themes of a passionate concentration to match his perfected style. The hypocritical persecution of the prostitute and of the assassin, both of whom are secretly used by those in power and then publicly spat upon and condemned, provides all the fuel necessary for Okot's scorn, anger and compassion.

The initial impetus for the writing of 'Song of Prisoner' may have been an apparently minor episode when Okot was arrested for a single night on his way home from Nairobi to Kisumu, where he was then living. If this is so, then it contributes to the principle on which the whole poem is written, which is one of steady escalation and expansion, through which the lot of one prisoner becomes that of every prisoner of conscience in the world. His anger becomes theirs, he shares the injustice which condemns them, and the narrow limits of his cell seem to swell to embrace them and their multifarious causes.

In the opening lines of the poem, the prisoner is prostrate, still overwhelmed by the suddenness of the fate which keeps him from his wife and children, from the cool breezes of the lake and the music of its night-sounds. The mother-image which infuses the cold, damp materials of his cell only renders their embrace more bitter:

The stone floor
Lifts her powerful arms
In cold embrace
To welcome me
As I sit on her navel.

My head rests
On her flat
Whitewashed breasts.[22]

From this supine mood the poet moves swiftly to one of blazing anger. The uniformed oafs who beat and kick him, the magistrate in his brain who keeps shouting, 'Guilty or Not Guilty?', all contribute to his sense of raging helplessness. He is:

A young tree
Burnt out
By the fierce wild fire
Of Uhuru.[23]

His whole family shares the dishonour which has fallen upon him. He imagines his young wife in the arms of a chief, his children howling like mad dogs, and a wizard dancing silently on his father's grave. He curses his parents severally for each failing to choose a better partner. But suddenly he changes his plea from 'intoxication' and 'hunger', to 'hatred'. We seem to see him rising slowly upright, shaking the doors and even the walls of his prison to announce his cause to an unlistening world. He complains no longer of the cold embrace of the stone floor. He complains of those who, now that he has served their purposes, find it convenient to forget him. Is Okot here glancing at the obscure political assassins who kill famous men, certainly not upon their own initiative, but whose sponsors are never identified? The hypocrisy of the great is even harder to bear than the brutality of their stupid instruments. The prisoner's belief that those who hired him will secure his release, that he will soon be hailed as a national hero who has rid the land of a tyrant, quickly gives way to a sense of betrayal and abandonment.

His anger, however, continues to expand the scope of the poem. Soon it is not this prisoner alone we are considering, but every victim of power-sadism everywhere. This expansion is aided by the extent of the prisoner's imagination and the range of his desires. Soon the direction of his energies shifts from anger and reproach against his masters to the untrammelled expression of these desires:

I want to drink
With the peasants
In the fields,
And with the old women
In my constituency,
I want to suck *lacoi* beer
And share the sucking tube
With the old men
Around the fire.

Let the French girl
Bring her sexy cognac
And I will drink it
I will cover her
With my broken kisses.

Let the Munyoro girl
Bring her sickly *amarwa*
And I will share it with her,
I will touch her unbroken breasts.[24]

From these drunken embraces, the prisoner soon turns once again to remember his family. Even the cattle egret can flourish his long tail and dance between his wives and chicks. But the prisoner's fatherless children will never go to school; the teacher's cane will never touch their buttocks. The prisoner pleads guilty to pride and remembers his prowess as a singer, drummer and dancer. He longs to join the village girls in the love-dance and to stamp the dusty earth at his father's *Guru Lyel*:

Let me beat the rhythm
Of the *orak* dance. . . .
I want to join the youths
At the 'get-stuck dance'
I want to suck the stiff breasts

Of my wife's younger sister,
I want to wrestle
With my wife-in-law
And crush the young grass
Beyond the arena. . . .

Is today not my father's
Funeral anniversary? . . .
Men drink *Kweke* beer
Women cook goat meat

And make millet bread,
But I am not there
To distribute the dishes
Among the elders. . . .

I want to join
The funeral dancers,
I want to tread the earth
With a vengeance
And shake the bones
Of my father in his grave![25]

Although so much more eclectic than *Song of Lawino*, since the prisoner's desires range from the garlanded Vietnamese girl to the Eskimo's 'snowy song', this whole sequence, from movements 12 to 14, is remarkable for its evocation of a culture based on dance, where every rite of passage from the cradle to the grave has its appropriate music. Whereas Lawino reproaches Ocol for what he cannot do, the prisoner yearns for all that participation which he is denied, and in the final movement, in a last thrust of frustration, he seems to burst out of his prison and leap into the arena with his fellows:

Open the door,
Man,
I want to dance
All the dances of the world
I want to sleep with
All the young dancers.
I want to dance
And forget my smallness,
Let me dance and forget
For a small while

That I am a wretch
The reject of my country

A broken branch of a Tree
Torn down by the whirlwind
Of Uhuru.[26]

Thus the poem closes with the whirlwind image which also occurred in the last movement of *Song of Lawino*, where Lawino warned Ocol that by trying to cut down the *Okwango* in the sacred family shrine he was threatening to cut himself loose, to be blown here and there about the world. But the most extraordinary feature of this last, fifteenth movement of 'Song of Prisoner' is the evocation of black suffering in the tragic decade of the sixties. It is through the various types of music in the night-club where he imagines himself to be dancing that the prisoner hears 'the cutting throbs/in your wounded song' of the American blacks; the Nigerian high life wails to him like 'Bombs/bursting in the market place'; the Congolese cha-cha-cha suggests images of rape and death in obscure corners of the forest. And his identification with all that suffering becomes total in the lines:

Sing Brother
Sing,
Cover me with the bile
From your heart. . . .[27]

The prisoner whom we first discovered prostrate on the cold floor of the cell, full of self-pity and humiliation, has become a representative figure whose emotional energy reaches out to touch the anguish of all those likewise overthrown by the whirlwind of Uhuru.

Apart from this steady expansion of its concerns, Okot's poem is held together by several thematic elements. The chief one is the reiteration of the magistrate's stern demand, 'Do you plead Guilty or Not Guilty?', and the prisoner's imagined replies, in which he pleads guilty to everything from intoxication to pride, thus setting the emotional tone of successive movements of the poem. There are also more localized refrains, such as that which punctuates the last movement of the poem: 'Who are playing in the night club/Tonight?' Having lived outside Uganda since 1967, Okot now writes without the daily contact of Acoli life and language which accompanied the composition of *Lawino*. By the same token, he no longer composes his poem first in Lwo, because the poetic style discovered in the 'Englishing' of that poem now sits naturally upon him. Already, in producing the English version of Lawino's song, Okot had displayed a freedom denied to the mere translator; adding certain passages and omitting others (such as the original fourteenth movement) entirely. In 'Song of Prisoner' the short, unrhymed line first adopted to avoid the relative long-windedness of English and to maintain a fast tempo is still further developed. In the use made of this short line for the composition of long poems, Okot can be compared with the West Indian poet Edward Kamau Brathwaite, but he does not make use of the split words, internal rhymes or staccato effects employed by the latter. The nearest he comes to it is in this early passage of the poem, where we are forced to weigh the sound and meaning of individual words:

And I
Trembling,
Hungry,
Mad,
Sit,
Spit,
Shit,
Hate,
Wait. . . .[28]

Another innovation in 'Song of Prisoner' is the use of extended metaphors which are not specifically linked to the main argument, but which stretch it into other theatres of experience. In the midst of an argument with himself about the inevitability of his own acquittal and vindication, the prisoner suddenly produces these rather sinister images:

A python enters
Into a dead termite mound
And swallows the edible rat
And all its young.
An ostrich races
Across the dry plain
To cover her eggs
As the storm threatens. . . .[29]

The effect is to modify our own reception of the prisoner's optimism. At these points, the poem steps slightly aside from personal rhetoric.

The second of the *Two Songs*, 'Song of Malaya' (Prostitute), also makes use of a thematic structure, with each movement introduced by the girl's address to a different type of customer ('You vigorous young sailor', 'You sweating engineer', 'But you/Big Chief') or to their wives, who are foolish enough to be jealous, instead of grateful, towards those who help to keep their husbands happy:

And you
My married Sister
You whose husband
I also love dearly. . . .[30]

Most of the seven movements also end with a variation upon the refrain:

Sister Prostitutes
Wherever you are,
Wealth and Health
To us all. . . .[31]

It is this general address to her profession, and the sheer range of the singer's own clientele, embracing every race and class in Kenya, which give her song a comprehensiveness comparable to that of 'Song of Prisoner'. Her mood, however, is less often angry than exultant, mocking all those who affect to despise her and clamour for legislation against her, whilst secretly pestering her with their flabby instruments and embraces. It is the honest-to-goodness customer who is spared the lash of her tongue, for he matches his avowed needs to her avowed requirements. In her unsophisticated way, the *malaya* is telling us that we cannot have the other symbols of progress (skyscraper hotels, night clubs, vast new cities) without her ostensibly unwelcome presence as well. After seventy years of deliberate urbanization, it's a bit late to start lamenting the lost virtues of the village. The harlot is scarcely a new phenomenon, after all:

We'll drink to the
Daughters of Sodom
And to the daughters of Gomorrah
Who set the towns ablaze
With their flaming kisses. . . .
Let's drink to Rahab
With her two spy boy friends,
To Esther the daughter of Abigail,
To Delilah and her bushy-headed
Jaw-bone gangster.[32]

The *malaya*'s target (and Okot's) is the hypocrisy and brutality which cheers when the girl you were with last night is stripped and beaten in the street or fined (and with whose coin does she pay the fine?), or locked up in the police cell (and with whose coin does she secure her release?). After recounting all the sickening devices by which society projects and then punishes its own guilt, she asks, with the prophets of old:

But
Who can command
The Sun
Not to rise in the morning?[33]

In his anxiety to castigate these follies, Okot is perhaps tempted to dwell overmuch upon the supposed pleasure of the prostitute in her own skill and her own body. The profession is, after all, not without its own horrors, quite apart from those inflicted by a prudish society. Except for the choosey, high-priced call-girl, there can be scarcely a night without fear of the kinky, violent or thievish customer; scarcely a day without its anxieties about disease, old age, or social rejection in the village which still represents the only real security for those who have drifted to the cities. Taken alone, 'Song of Malaya' is perhaps too much on one note, but as a complement to the harsher and more wide-ranging 'Song of Prisoner' it helps to make up a volume as striking as *Song of Lawino*. It establishes that the initial impact made throughout Africa by Okot's first poem was no heady and precipitate enthusiasm, but the recognition of a formidable poetic talent which has changed the face of African poetry in English, giving it a range, energy and authority which it had seldom attained before.

Mongo Beti

Born Alexandre Biyidi in 1932 at Mbalmayo, in what was then the French Trust Territory of Cameroun. After early years in a seminary, he took his *baccalauréat* in Yaoundé before moving to the University of Aix-en-Provence. His first story, 'Sans Haine et Sans Amour' was published by *Présence Africaine* in 1953 and his first novel, *Ville Cruelle*, was issued by the same publishers in 1954, when he was 22 years old. He gained both fame and notoriety with his first major novel, *Le Pauvre Christ de Bomba*, published in 1956, where the pseudonym Mongo Beti was used for the first time. Between 1954 and 1958, Beti published four novels. A silence of sixteen years was broken in 1974 with the publication of two major new works, followed by another novel in 1979. Since the late 1950s Beti has made his career in France as a teacher in various *lycées*, but has recently assumed a new role as director of the journal *Peuples Noirs, Peuples Africains,* founded in 1978.

9 From Satire to Epic

Nowhere on the continent of Africa was there a more sudden explosion of literary activity than in the former French Cameroons, now the Cameroun Republic. This area had a relatively early exposure to Western education, owing to the activities of German missionaries in the period 1884–1914, but no secondary schools were established during the first thirty years of French rule which followed. By 1954, despite the rapid growth of a fairly large educated group, there was nothing to show for it in the field of modern literature. By the end of that decade, Cameroun had established itself as one of Africa's most artistically prolific countries, as well as one of the most politically active and aware. Those years saw the publication of four novels by Mongo Beti, three by Ferdinand Oyono and one by Benjamin Matip. They also saw the rise and fall of Ruben um Nyobé, the dynamic leader of the Union des Peuples Camerounaises, who led his movement into a direct challenge of French neo-colonialism and the emerging client-state of Cameroun. That challenge did not end with his death by firing squad in 1958, but raged on as a full-scale guerilla war until the mid 1960s.

Interestingly, the novels published during the fifties do not bear the direct marks of that struggle, being more concerned with a satirical treatment of the classic colonialism which Cameroun had experienced in the past. Only in his work of the 1970s did Mongo Beti, the youngest and most formidably talented of these novelists, turn his attention to the meaning of the dire contest which was in full swing while his earlier novels were being published. The same comment might be extended to Algerian literature in French, which also began to blossom during the 1950s, but for some time bore no marks of the war of liberation launched in November 1954. The comparison seems to tell us something about the nature of the emergent fiction of the late colonial period, which takes some time to turn its attention directly to contemporary events, focusing first upon a re-interpretation of the past and a vindication of its people in the eyes of a foreign readership. It is no accident that all these early Camerounian novels were published and for the most part written in Paris.

Beti's real name, used in signing most of his political writings, is Alexandre Biyidi-Awala. He was born in the small town of Mbalmayo, some thirty miles south of Yaoundé, in 1932. After a brief tussle with a Catholic upbringing aimed at the priesthood, he left the mission and entered the newly founded lycée, where he took his *baccalauréat* at the age of 19. In 1951 he went to France to continue his studies, first at Aix-en-Provence and then at the Sorbonne. Later he took his doctorate and became a teacher in various French lycées. He has never returned to the Cameroun, except for one brief visit, which led to his imprisonment and interrogation by the white security police of the 'independent' republic. Gradually, Beti has emerged as the intellectual leader of the growing group of Camerounians living in exile in France. This position was signified by the founding of his radical revue *Peuples Noirs, Peuples Africains* in Paris at the beginning of 1978, following the publication of three important books in the preceding four years.

In conversation, he mingles courtesy, vigorous humour and the fiercest radicalism in a flow of rapid idiomatic French. In life, as in his writing, he expresses uncompromising opinions with great sincerity and force, so that his personality makes a deep impression.

At the age of 22, while still a student at Aix, Mongo Beti offered his first novel to Présence Africaine. After publishing a key chapter in the review, they decided to issue the whole book, though Beti himself already had doubts about it. *Ville Cruelle* (Cruel Town) was duly published by Éditions Africaines in 1954, under the pen-name of Eza Boto. The author has since indicated his opinion of the novel by jettisoning this *nom de plume* and taking that of Mongo Beti for all his subsequent books, though it is for the first time listed among his publications in *Main Basse sur le Cameroun* (1977).

Ville Cruelle is a rather bad novel, but it is manifestly not the work of a bad writer. It appears to be the trying out of a young talent, as yet loose and uncontrolled, but open and rich. If the book is sentimental, its very naïvety is often disarming; if its action is melodramatic, it bears everywhere the marks of feeling and experience. As it is out of print and unlikely ever to be reissued, I will offer the reader a brief synopsis.

The book begins well. The first chapter, in which the young hero Banda casually throws off his mistress and declares his intention of marrying a girl more acceptable to his dying mother, does not fully prepare us for the orgies of filial sentiment which are to follow. The next chapter, devoted to the cruel town itself, is certainly the best thing in the book. This, one of the few pieces of extended impersonal description in the novel, is beautifully built up and displays a gift for compassionate irony which is seldom apparent in the later pages. Tanga is the familiar double-town of colonial Africa. Along the dark fast-flowing river lies the commercial town, greedily devouring raft after raft of timber. This is Tanga South, 'the kingdom of logs'. Up the hill, beyond the street of Greek 'factories', lies the government station, aloof and inviolate. But on the northern slopes of the hill is the real town, if such it can be called; a huddle of crowded wards, each with its own life, though peopled entirely by unfledged townsmen whose hearts and thoughts lie still half-rooted in the surrounding forest, and whose urban existence is a matter of a few years or even few months: 'Two Tangas . . . two worlds . . . two destinies!'

Between these two poles flows the black life of Tanga, draining by day into the shops, factories and offices of the southern town, returning by night in a river of cyclists and pedestrians to the crowded alleys and yards; the bars, brothels and hovels of the northern quarter.

They came from every corner of the country. But they tended more and more to think of themselves as inhabitants of Tanga, rather than as children of the south and east, the north or west. One saw them about the streets, laughing and arguing with gestures that would bury the whole world. They ran and walked, jostled and fell from their bicycles, all with a certain spontaneity, the sole relic of their lost purity. They bustled in the sunshine, danced and sang under the anguished eyes of the police, who walked always in groups, as if the town were in a state of emergency.

At night, life flowed back into the popular quarter. Tanga North reclaimed its own and exploded with unbelievable effervescence. It was fiesta every night for these prodigal children. One would have thought that they were trying to glut themselves with something that they would perhaps soon lose for ever: joy, real joy, joy undisguised, naked and original. But they themselves would scarcely understand that. Already they could only tell whence they came by naming their tribe and village. They no longer knew where they were going, or why they were going at all. Astonished to find themselves so many they were not less astonished at this strange isolation from their native forest, in which each felt himself to be alone.[1]

If this brilliance of observation were maintained, *Ville Cruelle* would be a novel indeed. It is a foretaste of what has always remained an outstanding quality of Beti's writing, that intensity of evocation which often distinguishes the exile. However, we are soon plunged into the raw and often tiresome emotions of young Banda, who now arrives in the town to sell his seasonal crop of cocoa. Before doing so he must have it approved by the Control, but for some reason, perhaps because he is not sufficiently obsequious, the Controller orders the whole of Banda's crop to be thrown on the fire as rejected. When Banda protests violently he is arrested, beaten and led off to the police station. To his great surprise, the white superior indignantly orders his release, but a new skein of bitterness has been added to the confused web of his emotions. He wanders through the town, visiting his old uncle the tailor, witnessing an accident in which the lorry driver is threatened with a beating by the mob, seeing a white man carried by an angry group of Africans and thrown into the gutter when the police van arrives. Finally he takes shelter from the rain in a bar, where he drinks a great deal of maize beer and muses upon his misfortunes. He has no money and cannot after all marry. He contemplates stealing 10,000 francs from a Greek trader, but does not know how to set about it. His musings are interrupted by the entry of the young girl Odilia, who instantly appeals to him and enlists his help. Her brother Koumé has been the ringleader in the attack on the European. The man had persistently refused to pay his employees and was being bodily carried to the Commissioner of Police when the police squad intervened. In his sudden fall he has been badly injured and is dying. All the police in the district are now looking for Koumé and all the roads from the town are blocked. Odilia takes Banda to where Koumé is hiding, and he offers to lead them both through the forest to a safe obscurity in his own village. While crossing a slippery log in the darkness Koumé falls into the river and is drowned. Banda takes Odilia to his mother's house and leaves her there while he paddles Koumé's body downstream and leaves it under the town bridge, but not before feeling in the pockets and finding exactly 10,000 francs in notes. It is the money taken from the dead European.

On the way home with the loot, Banda stumbles upon a suitcase which a Greek has lost from his car and for which he is offering a reward of – 10,000 francs! So Banda is able to hand over all Koumé's money to Odilia – no mention is made of a share-out to the other employees – and virtuously claim his reward. Meanwhile Odilia and his mother have got together and fixed up for him to marry Odilia; this is all the more convenient because there is no bride-price in her area, so he can get her free. So Banda's mother dies happy and the fortunate couple prepare to set off for Fort Nègre, the great city of the coast. The original virtue of the bush is not for them, and they are pushed inexorably into the cruel maw of the new urban Africa.

All through this string of improbabilities runs the interior monologue of Banda. Often the naïve exclamations, repetitions and self-questionings of the hero are happily natural and unforced, but gradually they become tedious and, finally, infuriating. We have had enough of Banda. This is a fair specimen of his ruminations as he moves through his adventurous day.

Banda, aren't you ashamed of yourself? Do you have to rob a corpse in order to get married? That lad there, he was a tough one, a man; and never while he lived could you have rifled his pockets like this. He was a real tough, while you – you're just a corpse-robber! Pouah! . . . aren't you really ashamed of yourself? Think of Koumé, he wasn't afraid of Madame's bullets while he was robbing the till, though he'd fought and suffered enough already. He wasn't afraid of Madame's bullets. Ah! he was a tough! And instead of doing as he did, you just plunder his body![2]

Ville Cruelle, then, combines a novelettish plot with a brilliance of observation and a quality of pain which we associate with a major novel. Strangely enough, it was precisely by the more controlled and skilful use of exclamatory, naïve monologue that Mongo Beti developed some of the most effective passages in his second novel, *Le Pauvre Christ de Bomba* (The Poor Christ of Bomba). With this book, published only two years after *Ville Cruelle*, the writer emerged as a formidable satirist and one of the most percipient critics of European colonialism. For now the naïvety of his hero, instead of being presented subjectively, becomes the pure mirror through which we see the greed, the folly and the tragic misunderstandings of a whole epoch in Africa's history. Used in this more distanced way, the monologue becomes a weapon of devastating satiric force.

Le Pauvre Christ de Bomba is written entirely in the form of a diary, the diary of an acolyte who accompanies his master, the Reverend Father Superior Drumont, on a missionary circuit through the land of Tala. Tala is a remote district of Cameroun which has been deliberately abandoned by Drumont for three whole years because of its 'backsliding'. He is now revisiting all the stations in the hope of finding the thirsty souls crying out for solace. In fact, of course, he finds nothing of the kind. The men of Tala have forgotten

God and turned to bicycles. Even the women have fallen short on their cult payments. The churches are broken and empty, but the bars are full and the new money from cocoa is beginning to flow through the land, for we are now in the late 1930s. Drumont is an austere man of obstinate courage, choleric and impatient, moving with all the authority and confidence of twenty years' missionary work in Africa. But even his faith wavers before the spectacle of Tala. As the circuit progresses he questions himself and his purposes more and more deeply. For the first time he enters into dispute with his parishioners and listens to their arguments, instead of quelling them with his own energy and authority. Meanwhile the young administrator Vidal, who is also touring Tala, continually appeals to him as an ally. Is he not a fellow white and a Frenchman? Vidal assures him that all will soon be well, for a road is to be built through Tala by forced labour: the sufferings of the road gangs will soon fill the churches to bursting, as they have already done in those areas which lie along the main routes, under the heavy hand of the administration. The whole system of forced labour is a true friend of the Catholic Church, for is not contentment the great enemy of religion?

Chafing against this hateful doctrine and already deeply shaken by his weeks of disappointment in Tala, Drumont returns to his home mission at Bomba, only to face a dreadful scandal there. Raphael, the catechist–director of the 'sixa', (an institution supposed to prepare fiancées for Christian marriage), has been systematically debauching the girls in his charge and infecting them with syphilis. A full medical inquiry reveals that the dormitories are dirty and airless, the food is poor, the girls are cruelly overworked and constantly intimidated by the catechists. Broken finally by these discoveries, Drumont abandons his mission and sails for France, never to return.

This disastrous course and revolutionary conclusion are shown to us entirely through the faithful, unquestioning eyes of Drumont's acolyte 'boy', Denis. Not for him the doubts that assail his beloved master. He is utterly confounded by the wickedness of man, but still more so by this unsuspected 'weakness' in his living God, who finally leaves him to wander alone through the grass-grown compound of the silent mission. Every action and word of the father is meticulously recorded, so that we have eventually a far better understanding of the man than his uncritical disciple has, much augmented by the speeches of his enemies; for these are likewise set down, albeit indignantly, by the faithful scribe. Here he is reporting, poker-faced as usual, on Drumont's attitude towards unmarried mothers:

This business will certainly drive him mad one day. Poor Father Drumont! Sometimes I feel so sorry for him! He has spoken so often to our stupid villagers about the awful situation of the unmarried mother. Personally, I don't see why he thinks it matters so much. Anyway, at least the Christian girl-mothers come to baptize their babies at Bomba, and pay a special fee fixed by the father himself. After all, isn't that a source of revenue for the mission coffers? And we need so many things. . . . But the father will certainly kill himself over these girls. To think that we, the blacks, will all be damned for loving babies so much! . . .[3]

Denis and Drumont are accompanied through Tala by the father's cook Zacharie and (unknown to Drumont) by a plump young beauty from the sixa called Catherine, who is Zacharie's mistress and who secretly joins him every night for the most vigorous amours, conducted within a few yards of Drumont's bed. Denis at first mistakes the nightly racket from Zacharie's room for the throes of dysentery, but his virgin innocence is shattered one night when, Zacharie being absent, the indefatigable Catherine joins him instead. There follows a seduction scene of splendid bawdy, culminating in an orgasm which leaves Denis absolutely dumbfounded. With agonized conscience and excited senses he confides it all to his diary, unable to face Drumont with a confession.

Zacharie acts in the diary as a kind of devil's chorus, and his mordant comments on Drumont's spiritual fantasies and exertions run through its pages in a sour trickle of denigration. When Denis runs to him with complaints about the abominable wickedness of Tala, he cries out in exasperation:

What does it matter to them, your confession, your communion, your – God knows what? I ask you, what is it to them? They are busy with something else, my little father. Money, money . . . that's the great business of life, you little clot! Open your eyes and look about you. You're pretty green, aren't you! But, since you're so keen on religion, perhaps you'll be a father yourself one day. Then you'll know what money is. Then you'll see why we all run after it, the priest just as fast as anyone else, perhaps faster. Do you think that everyone here is as dumb as the people along the main roads? No, no, my lad! They're smart enough around here. Count yourself lucky that they've dashed us six chickens![4]

It is the discovery of Catherine's nightly antics that finally leads Drumont, on his return, to look thoroughly into the real state of affairs at Bomba. Catherine is soundly thrashed by a catechist and Zacharie prudently runs off for a few days until things have cooled down. Drumont and his young vicar Le Guen now begin a systematic interrogation of the nubile girls of the sixa. Each one is solemnly brought in, bent over, and beaten by the under-cook Anatole, whose sexual inversion gives him a particular pleasure in the task. After a good beating, each girl is subjected to a close inquiry into her sex life while at the mission. Le Guen soon sickens of this business, but Drumont is driven on by his usual intemperate obstinacy until every single girl has been thrashed and grilled.

The unsavoury violence of this scene, which matches that of many scenes in the novels of both Mongo Beti and Ferdinand Oyono, is a commentary on the savagery which has distinguished the colonial regimes in Cameroun, both French and German, and which has not yet spent itself. But more tragic than the violence is the incomprehension of Drumont. Throughout these disgusting interviews he keeps exclaiming to Le Guen, 'What a race! They are riddled with the worm of lust. You see for yourself what they are like!' Although he abandons his mission in despair, it is largely a despair at the innate wickedness of the 'native'. Never once does he consider how the very institution of the sixa places these girls under a system of unpaid labour and at the complete mercy of their instructors; while, had they remained under the pagan dispensation, they might perhaps have slept with their future husbands but would at least have been safe from being debauched against their will. Never does he blame his past unwillingness to listen to complaints or argument; his own ignorance of human (not African) nature under temptation; or his gross negligence in supervising effectively the life of the sixa. The tragedy of misunderstanding is as deep at the end of the book as at the beginning, and Drumont has only left to make way for a lesser man to continue his work.

Le Pauvre Christ de Bomba adds up to a radical and final rejection of white missionary activity in Africa, at least as practised within a white colonial order. As Drumont observes to Vidal towards the end of the book – for on this matter at least he grows enlightened:

I should prefer not to defend colonization before God. I shouldn't like to be in your shoes. You tell me that I'm an exception amongst missionaries? Alas, it's true, and you see what it has cost me! Look, there are only two courses open for me now. Either I stay here in Africa with you, close to you, and help you to colonize it – 'soften up' the country ahead of you, keep it docile behind you – and that's how you conceive our role, isn't it? Or else I truly Christianize it. In that case, the best thing for me would be to get out of it, at least as long as you're still here.[5]

This point of view, unpalatable as it must be to many people, is driven home with great force, ironic skill and insight. The book is too long and is often repetitious (Drumont and Denis undergo essentially the same shock at station after station in Tala), but it marks a tremendous advance in the author's confidence and it remains a formidable challenge. Perhaps it is not surprising that its publication provoked a storm in Paris. Supposedly literary critics rushed into print to defend the French record in Africa and to attack this miserable reviler of those who had only gone there 'to do good to the natives'! None could grasp the simple fact that these things look different through African eyes, and that at last Europe was beginning to hear authentic voices from a continent long stunned and muted by the shock of conquest.

By one of those exquisite ironies born of the Cold War, Russia expressed a keen interest in translating the book, but wanted to leave out the more 'naturalistic' passages. This referred, of course, to the seduction of young Denis by the enterprising Catherine, probably the only scene in the book of which its French readers wholeheartedly approved.

If *Le Pauvre Christ de Bomba* astonishes us by its increase of power, Mongo Beti's next book achieves an equal surprise by an entire change of tone. The earnest sentimentality of *Ville Cruelle*, the ironic simplicity of *Le Pauvre Christ*, now give way to a note of rumbustious comedy. It is true that, on reflection, we find a foretaste of this in such scenes as the seduction of Denis, but we are scarcely prepared for so morally committed a writer to laugh from the bottom of his lungs through two hundred pages.

Some critics have suggested that this change of tone was forced upon Beti by the hostile reception of *Le Pauvre Christ de Bomba*. This seems most improbable. The greatest compliment one can pay to a controversial writer is a scream of rage, and Beti would have undoubtedly been disappointed to hear anything else. Even the immediate banning of his book throughout French Africa cannot have done him much harm. Banned books, like drugs, have a way of circulating just the same. And many of Beti's black readers in 1956 would have been in France anyway. Paris was to remain the centre of African intellectual, political and literary life for many years to come. Furthermore, Beti published a true sequel to *Le Pauvre Christ* only two years later, in *Le Roi Miraculé* (1958), where we see Father Le Guen's missionary career also come to grief. The most likely explanation for the uninhibited rustic comedy of *Mission Terminée* is that Beti was simply developing his talents. It was his third novel published in the space of just four years, and the novelist was barely 27. At this rate of development, it seems probable that *Mission Terminée* was already in draft by the time its predecessor was published.

Mission Terminée was published in Paris in 1957. It was the first of Mongo Beti's novels to be translated into English, appearing in London a year later as *Mission to Kala*. Peter Green had translated with evident enjoyment and had perfectly preserved the speed and gusto of the original. In his new hero, Jean-Marie Medza, Beti gives us a more autobiographical figure than any in his earlier novels. Medza is a young Lycée student who returns to his native village on holiday, after failing his *baccalauréat* examination. Instead of enjoying a rest which he, at least, considered well-earned, he finds himself despatched on a difficult errand. The wife of his feckless cousin Niam has run away to her home village of Kala and, since Niam is quite helpless without her, Medza is sent off by the local elders to retrieve the truant. It is felt that a 'scholar' is more likely to succeed in this delicate task than an ordinary villager. Medza is given a bicycle (since Kala is not on any motor road) and told to entrust himself on arrival to his uncle Mama and his cousin Zambo. He sets off in some trepidation, for Kala is a notoriously 'bush' village. As he cycles into the outskirts of the place his worst fears are confirmed.

Just outside the village a remarkable spectacle presented itself to my astonished gaze. It was not the setting which struck me, so much as the primitive savagery which animated every participant in the business. . . . On the sports-ground were about twenty big toughs, bare-legged and bare-chested, engaged in a game whose war-like nature even the Spartans would have recognized. Each team consisted of ten or twelve young men lined up in single file, Indian fashion. Thus only the leaders of the two sides were actually facing each other, at two or three yards distance; their supporters backed them up from behind. Each man carried a long, whippy, heavy assegai, its point carefully sharpened. They brandished these weapons in a most dangerous fashion. Right at the end of each file, as far as possible from the captain that is, stood the strongest man in the team. This man would pick up a ball about the size of a football, made of some hard, heavy, yet porous wood, spin round two or three times like a weight-putter and throw the ball as hard as he could along the ground. It sped away at tremendous speed, bumping and bouncing over the rough ground; and as it went the long pointed assegais whizzed out at it so hard and quick that it was a miracle no one was hit each time. Often the ball was stopped in mid-flight, pierced clean through by a particularly accurate shot. Then the team's supporters would cheer like mad, and all the lucky marksman's companions smother him with kisses. . . .

Having taken a bird's-eye, panoramic view of the scene, I now began to examine it in detail. The first thing that caught my eye was a great hulking devil in the Kala team who had such enormous muscles I concluded he must have bought them on the instalment system. . . . He was tall and flat-footed, with a disproportionately lengthy torso which he carried very badly. His buttocks were incredibly slender, yet he retained the country native's slight pot-belly, due to a habitually rough and meagre diet. He was like a kind of human baobab tree. Naturally, he was the one who threw the ball for his team. Every time he threw the ball, the spectators shouted his name in chorus, as though he had been a friendly God to be supplicated at the siege of Troy.

'Zambo son of Mama!' they yelled, 'Zambo son of Mama! Zambo! Zambo!'[6]

Medza is soon overwhelmed, however, by the warmth and friend-liness of Zambo's greeting. The huge youth is like a child with a fine toy as he shows off his scholar-cousin to the 'simple' villagers. The names of Zambo's friends are rendered by the translators as Duck-foot-Johnny, Petrus Son-of-God and Abraham the Boneless Wonder. They spend most of their time in wenching and deep drinking of palm-wine, pursuits in which the unfledged Medza finds himself at a great disadvantage, though he is anxious enough to catch up. Fortun-ately for him, his new friends are unshakably convinced that he is not only a scholar but a city slicker, to whom the fleshpots of Kala must seem very tame stuff indeed. When the most desirable and stand-offish girl in the place comes to his room at dawn and offers herself openly, embarrassment and inexperience render him quite impotent. He then has to convince the astonished Zambo that he finds the fast type unattractive nowadays and would prefer someone younger and more virginal.

Meanwhile his uncle Mama is dragging him round on visits night after night. Each visit is followed by a flood of presents from the host, and Mama's compound is soon overflowing with livestock, of which he fully intends to keep half as a reasonable return for his enterprise. Since Niam's wife has gone off again and cannot be found, Medza is obliged to stay on and yield to Mama's plans for yet another round of lucrative visits.

The obliging Zambo has now found a girl young and virginal enough to suit Medza's specifications. She is Edima, a daughter of the Chief of Kala, and she allows Medza to make the running from the first. When she finally visits his room one night during a wedding party at the palace, he has no difficulty in achieving a triumphant seduction. But Medza's bliss is short-lived, for very soon the naked couple are the victims of a staged discovery by the girl's mother, who goes through all the motions of heartbreak, outrage and even corporal punishment as she drags the wretched Edima out of bed.

By this time Niam's loose wife has turned up with her lover. A meeting is held at the chief's palace to consider the case, as a result of which the oafish lover is fined two thousand francs and the woman agrees to return to her husband. All is now apparently set for Medza's departure, but the chief persuades him to stay for a final meal. The trap closes on him with a satisfied click:

First of all the Chief ordered the young girls to begin dancing. . . . Then a motley collection of people swarmed in, some carrying musical instruments, others staggering under demi-johns of palm-wine or claret. . . . The Chief was in a jovial, almost hilarious mood, which I put down without a second's thought to the presence of his new wife. . . . Anyway, there was the same stupefying din going on outside as there had been during the bridal delegation's visit. . . . The usual procession of women was coming slowly up the steps: by now I was positively panting with curiosity. They advanced in leisurely fashion as far as the doorway, then defiled into the room itself. In the middle of the procession walked a bewildered, frightened, shame-faced girl, a girl about the same age as Edima – My God, it *was* Edima. When I regained my senses, I saw the Chief had taken Edima by the hand and was coming over in my direction. . . .[7]

So after all Medza returns to his home a married man. But he has just two weeks before the arrival of Edima's bridal procession in which to think things out. In these two weeks he discovers himself. He ignores the displeasure of his mean, tyrannical father and makes it clear that he will not tolerate reprimands on the subject of the *baccalauréat*; he also resolves that he is too young and unproved to saddle himself with a bride, even one so sweet as Edima. So when the Kala procession arrives, bringing Niam's shop-soiled wife, Medza's fresh young bride and a great quantity of bleating livestock, Medza is out of town. He shows up two days later, very drunk, and creates a scene of wild comedy in which he kisses Edima, defies his father, dodges a beating (much assisted by Mama and his Kala friends) and finally sets off with the faithful Zambo towards a life whose promise he has just begun to guess.

Only in the last few pages of his narrative does Mongo Beti deepen his tone, showing us that this is not just a ribald reminiscence, but is a moment of youth which he is still exploring, to which must he return again and again:

The more I think about it the more certain I am that it is I who owe him [Niam] a debt of gratitude for sending me on a journey which enabled me to discover many truths. Not least among them was the discovery – made by contact with the country folk of Kala, those quintessential caricatures of the 'colonized' African – that the tragedy which our nation is suffering today is that of a man left to his own devices in a world which does not belong to him, which he has not made and does not understand. . . . That is the end of my story. I have no notion what you will make of it, but I have reached a point at which I have no alternative but to write it down. It obsesses me so completely that at times I fear I may never find any other theme as long as I live. I am haunted by the story of my love for Edima, which is also the story of my first, perhaps my only love: the absurdity of life.[8]

In the whole pattern of Beti's career, however, it is important to note another aspect of *Mission Terminée*. The comradely relationship of opposites which develops between Medza and Zambo in the village is, by authorial comment, extended over the many unwritten years which separate the Kala adventure from the moment of writing:

What did we do together? We shared the same food and drink, made love to the same women, were imprisoned and tortured together, experienced the same miseries and disillusionments, shared the same joys. He is always there at my side; but he says little and I never entirely understand him. Above all, I have no idea what he really wants, his illusive goal.[9]

This marginal comment seems to promise an epic novel, as yet unwritten, about the adventures here referred to so cryptically. That novel was to appear seventeen years later in *Remember Ruben* (1974), and Zambo can be recognized as in many ways the prototype of the more fully developed Mor-Zamba of that novel. All Beti's early books are brief in temporal span and relatively narrow in spatial compass: *Ville Cruelle* is occupied essentially with events of a single day; *Le Pauvre Christ* with those of a single tour; *Mission Terminée* with one short excursion to Kala; *Le Roi Miraculé* with the events immediately following from a chief's deathbed conversion. Beti's talents for handling the epic sweep of events covering many locales and many years lay dormant until the publication of his two major novels of the mid 1970s.

Before turning to those books, however, it will be well to turn to *Le Roi Miraculé*, published only a year after *Mission Terminée* and completing the tableau of his astonishingly varied early work. *Le Roi*

Miraculé (King Lazarus) is set in a remote district very like the Tala country of *Le Pauvre Christ*. But the centre of our attention is no longer the Catholic mission; it is the court of a powerful pagan king. True, the mission impinges upon this life, with results which form the story of the novel itself, but we see them from the viewpoint of a narrator who stands, as it were, outside the conflict altogether.

The priest in charge of the mission is our old friend Le Guen, who as Drumont's vicar had ten years before witnessed the final collapse of his work at Bomba. Le Guen has no intention of being defeated like Drumont.

Between the great Chief of Essazam and Le Guen there subsists an uneasy truce, seasoned with a good deal of banter on both sides. But Le Guen is only awaiting his moment. Soon the splendid old pagan, who has never had a day's sickness before, falls into a desperate fever and lingers for days on the threshold of death. The conservative people of Essazam, men, women and children, flock to the palace from all parts of the land. They sit on the narrow benches of the audience chamber or squat in the shadow of the palace walls, silent and helpless before the impending calamity. The king falls into what seems the final coma and since Le Guen is away on a visit to his Bishop, he is about to die unbaptized and unrepentant. In this extremity his old aunt Yosifa, who is a fervent convert, rushes into the death chamber and pours jug after jug of water over the head of the helpless invalid. He is saved! And from that moment he steadily recovers.

Le Guen is not slow to put about a whisper that the king's recovery is miraculous, and by no means unconnected with his baptism, whose authenticity the Father is far too shrewd to question now. To clinch the matter, he gives the king a new Christian name, Lazarus. And during the king's convalescence Le Guen is an assiduous visitor at the palace, spending long hours closeted alone with him. Before long he is able to announce the king's full conversion and this news is hotly followed by orders from the king himself that all his wives, whom he now regards as no better than concubines, must quit his palace immediately. One only is to remain and join him in Christian marriage. He adds cryptically that 'she herself' will know who is the chosen one.

There are two notable contenders: the formidable old Makrita, the king's first wife, and the delectable Anaba, his latest. Scrawny and threatening, Makrita first tries to intimidate the king's brother and confidant, Mekanda, who is set upon and brutalized by her disappointed children. She then tries matters with Le Guen himself, again without success. Le Guen considers himself to be made of sterner stuff than Drumont; he has already written to his mother of his hopes in this royal conversion:

Think of our Bantu king accepting baptism! Oh, mother! This is Christ the King entering in great pomp and by the biggest gate into his new Jerusalem. It is Jesus, always triumphant, despite the millennia unrolled since his Ascension; Jesus triumphant despite nations, men, races, times. Ah! A triumphal procession, an exultant army of the devout drunk with faith, draped in white! The crystal voices of children celebrating the advent of the true God, chanting the death of deceitful superstition! . . . Mother, do you remember how Father Drumont wrongly exaggerated a personal check until it reached cosmic dimensions? . . . What I remember most bitterly about him is that he tried, unconsciously no doubt, but in any case wrongly, to make us young ones bear the responsibility for the failures of a generation which acted on a false and unchristian view of the world. I owe nothing to that generation – nor do any of the young priests now more and more numerous in Africa, with whom a sincere love of the black precedes any desire to baptize him![10]

Makrita soon sees that she is wasting her time in this quarter. But she is not alone in her resentment of the new order of things. Every clan which has a representative in the king's marriage-bed feels insulted now by her rejection. The king has shaken the whole basis of tribal life by taking up this monogamy nonsense, with twenty-three respectable married women already in his household. The angry clans gather and encamp themselves at the gates of the palace. And into this explosive mixture a spark is flung by Medzo, the luscious and provocative younger sister of Anaba, who flaunts herself in the midst of the clan dances and teases the rejected wives on their ugliness. A free fight breaks out and soon involves everyone in the town. Medzo makes her get-away, but Anaba, who is buried at the bottom of the central scrimmage, miscarries the king's child. Le Guen rushes into the mêlée and is soundly beaten by both sides for his meddlesomeness. He takes to his bed, groaning, 'Of course, they didn't recognize me!' while his fellow priest rushes off to call the forces of law and order. By the time these arrive, headed by the Chief Administrator of the region, M. Lequeux, the king himself has restored calm.

Lequeux orders a full inquiry into the causes of the trouble, but this turns out to be simply an oratorical display by the clan elders which leaves no one any wiser. However, Lequeux has already formed the view that Le Guen's excess of zeal is a threat to the peace of Essazam, and he suggests to the missionary that he relinquish his efforts to turn the king from the path of his ancestors. Le Guen flatly refuses and Lequeux departs in considerable dudgeon.

Soon nature reasserts itself in the breast of the monarch. One by one his wives are recalled to the palace and Essazam settles into the familiar tenor of its slow decline. Meanwhile an official letter has reached the hands of Le Guen. In the name of High Commissioner of the French Republic, he is reminded of: 'the fundamental unity of the mission with which we have been charged, both you and ourselves, by gentle France our incomparable mother, among this disinherited people'. Since Le Guen appears to have lost sight, temporarily no doubt of that unity, the government has suggested to the Catholic hierarchy that he be transferred to other duties. This suggestion will shortly be acted upon.

So once again the essential unity of France's 'civilizing mission' has revealed itself and Le Guen, ten years after his much-criticized elder Drumont, has learnt for himself the reality of his position as an agent of colonialism.

Into the tissue of these events, Beti weaves the adventures of two highly-contrasted young men: Kris, like several of Beti's early heroes, is an angry individualist, impatient with tradition and openly contemptuous of the elders. He has already been stripped of his bursary, on the eve of taking his *baccalauréat* for opposing a white instructor. Hence he has been forced to shift for himself, and this has only increased his individualist tendencies. He feels compassion for his aunt, one of the chief's rejected wives, whom he accompanies to Essazam, but seems equally impatient of his grandmother, his father and his half-brother Ntolo. At Essazam, he spends his time seducing Medzo and brewing illicit gin to raise money for his fees.

His friend Bitama is an idealist, both in politics and sex, who has acquired a wide knowledge of Cameroun by following his father in his civil service assignments. He is an enthusiastic supporter of the PPP (Beti's usual pseudonym for the UPC, the militant nationalistic party of the period). But Kris has no time for anything beyond his own affairs, as he makes clear in the following exchange with Bitama:

'How is it that the most intelligent of our young men, the best educated, in a word the elite, are so cold towards the PPP?... Look, here one is on this lousy planet; one is black, but looking all around one, reading the books, searching the faces of the famous, well, what's the use! There isn't a single one like oneself. Then you feel yourself incredibly alone; you'd like to invent men who are black like you, whom you could see all around you, men who really exist, not so? You would make yourself God, just for that. Haven't you ever felt the same way?

'The PPP offers us, for the first time in our history, the chance to develop great men of our own. I love the PPP. Isn't that natural, Kris? If you saw your brother among a dozen long-distance runners, wouldn't you suffer if you saw him come in last?'

'Me! Oh, certainly not! I'd more likely tell him "Poor old chap, you're nothing like a long-distancer. Run and see if mother has a nice piece of porcupine for you, and enjoy the spectacle of my health." That's what I'd tell him. There are non-viable races, just as there are non-viable individuals: we have to explain why in both cases. They are not like others, they lack vitality, to put it in a nutshell. . . .'[11]

Beti is content here to offer us two contrasted images of the young which we may set beside the dying society of Essazam. He leaves us with an uneasy suspicion that he identifies more with the cynical iconoclasm of Kris than with Bitama's bubbling enthusiasm. The irony is that his early novels appeared during the very years when the UPC, led by Ruben um Nyobé, was struggling bitterly against French plans to perpetuate the colonial presence and influence in the Cameroun. Yet the only echo this struggle finds in his work of the fifties is in this one exchange. Not until the appearance of his two major novels of 1974 did Beti's personal commitment to the UPC find reflection in his work.

The explanation might be sought in the fact that all his early novels are set in the past: *Le Pauvre Christ* in the 1930s; *Le Roi Miraculé* specifically in 1948; and the other two novels in a time of youth roughly corresponding with the 1940s. But such an explanation would be superficial, for it behoves us to ask *why* African novelists of the 1950s (one thinks also of Ferdinand Oyono and Chinua Achebe) were concerned with a redefinition of the past, almost to the exclusion of any direct statement about the present. The reason, in Beti's case, does not lie in any lack of political commitment, since he was writing militant articles for *La Revue Camerounaise* at the very period when his fourth novel appeared. The explanation must lie in the impulse behind so many early novels of the colonial period – the impulse to set the past to rights, which often smothered the more urgent task (one might think) of setting the present to rights.

The silence of sixteen years which followed *Le Roi Miraculé* was the very period in which Beti found the means to make his fiction a revolutionary instrument. It was broken by the simultaneous appearance of two novels drastically different, both from each other and from all his earlier work. But these changes of direction in his work should not blind us to the elements of continuity. The two heroes of *Remember Ruben* both bear some traces of earlier characters; Abena's ruthless impatience with an outworn rural world may remind us to some extent of Kris, despite the switch from cynicism to radical commitment; likewise, Mor-Zamba certainly has something in common with the Zambo of *Mission Terminée*, although he is so much more deeply and feelingly rendered.

But when all this has been noted, the originality of *Remember Ruben* is still astonishing. As already mentioned, all Beti's earlier novels were concerned with a single episode (the tour of Tala, the mission to Kala, etc.); they were limited spatially to events covering a few villages, and temporally to anything from one day to a few weeks. *Remember Ruben*, by contrast, is a novel of epic sweep, which gives us a representative account of Camerounian experience over some forty years, culminating in the civil war and the pseudo-independence of 1960. *Perpétue*, in its entirely different style, continues the story down to the 1970s. Beti's descriptive power, always one of his most outstanding talents, reaches new heights in *Remember Ruben*, both in the rustic scenes of the first part and in the evocation of urban life of the forties and fifties which follows. A powerful new element in the structure of this novel is its vision of destiny. The destiny which moulds the contrasting, diverging and finally converging careers of Mor-Zamba and Abena is the principal element in that structure – the backbone of the novel. Mor-Zamba ('Man of God', or 'Providential Man', in the Beti language of Cameroun) first appears to us as a figure of the wild; precocious, strong and apparently dumb. His sudden appearance in Ekoumdoum has all the air of the marvellous and his youthful career there, culminating in his triumphant wrestling against the Zolo, never loses that marvellous quality. As a stranger of unknown antecedents, however, he never succeeds in gaining real acceptance, despite the consistent patronage of the 'good old man' and of the fierce young Abena. After his enforced departure from Ekoumdoum, he exchanges this champion/pariah reputation for one of relative anonymity. In the cities his only marvellous feat is the rescue of Ruben um Nyobé from his executioners. His role now is not to astonish, but to bear witness; to be the typical new citizen, uprooted from the bush, uncertain of his bearings, suffering and striving to make a living, following Ruben's brilliant leadership with more faith than understanding. His companions observe his evident goodness, his fidelity and strength, but are inclined to dismiss him as a simpleton, a 'bushman'. Yet it is these very qualities which equip him, as Abena points out in the closing pages, to return to Ekoumdoum and begin the patient work of transformation which that decadent community cries out for. It is appropriate that his real identity (the son of a brutally deposed, long-lamented Chief of Ekoumdoum) emerges at the very moment when he is ready to assume his real task.

Abena's fate is in every respect contrasted with Mor-Zamba's. Starting in the village as the son of a respected family, he first distances himself from the community by his espousal of that unlucky prodigy's cause. To go in pursuit of Mor-Zamba, he ruthlessly breaks with his family and clan; and even his spell as the 'good boy' of Father Van den Rietter is really aimed at seizing the priest's gun. Failing to release his friend from forced labour, he embarks on a nineteen-year odyssey of colonial warfare, all aimed at preparing himself for the revolutionary struggle against the French in Cameroun. And to cap the contrast, when he finally returns to Cameroun, he does so with a new identity, that of the guerilla leader Hurricane-Viet, which has largely replaced the old Abena of Ekoumdoum.

Matching this structural innovation is Beti's new departure in narrative technique. He had previously tried the diary form (*Le Pauvre Christ*), the first person narrator (*Mission Terminée*) and the omniscient narrator who is outside the story altogether (*Le Roi Miraculé*). But *Remember Ruben* wishes to chronicle the impact of heroic conduct on ordinary sensibilities, and for this purpose Beti needs a narrator who is inside the story but somewhat peripheral to it. In Part I this narrator, who is an anonymous villager, gives us his own recollections of Mor-Zamba's mysterious appearance and all that locally followed from it. But for the rest of the tale he narrates at second-hand what he has since heard, from Abena and Mor-Zamba, about all that transpired during their long absence from Ekoumdoum. This technique has the advantage of constantly reminding us (like the narrator in classical epic) that the twin heroes are not as other men; that they have been marked out from the first for an exceptional destiny, and for each other.

Yet this deep comradeship is of a curious kind, for it is one of those complementarities whose members must remain almost always apart – *aware* of each other but not *with* each other. Only the weeks together in the forest preparing to build Mor-Zamba's house (their 'initiation') evoke the quality of immediate communion:

After each of their journeys, we witnessed the heaps of material swell, evidence of an effort which seemed beyond ordinary men, more like that of figures in a fable. And several times a day the inhabitants of Ekoumdoum would form a circle to admire without restraint, even with cries of passionate and voluble enthusiasm, the fruits of a truly gigantic labour. The two companions became the symbol at once of energy, brotherhood, and determination, so that the city* adopted this saying: 'Abena and Mor-Zamba are united; what mountain can they not lift from its base?'[12]

All this admiration, however, does not bring one finger of assistance to the pair. The community in need of redemption does not always welcome or even recognize its redeemers. We might compare with the primitive energy of this scene, that later one where, like a degenerate Virgil, Jean-Louis guides Mor-Zamba through the underworld of night-time Kola-Kola:

They soon arrived in front of a dance-hall whose entrance was blocked by a queue waiting for tickets. The two men benefited from some privilege whose nature Mor-Zamba couldn't guess, which saved them not only from queuing but even from buying tickets. Mor-Zamba was immediately abandoned by Jean-Louis, who seized one girl after another, alternately plastering them to his stomach and spinning them round, with his teeth fixed in a dazzling smile; or else went here and there to chat with his cronies. Meanwhile Mor-Zamba, dominating the crowd and recovered from the dazzling glare of the electric lights, gazed upon the scene so totally new to him. . . . Ecstatic girls surrounded the platform, on which the musicians toiled in their shirt-sleeves. A tall, thin mulatto, with pomaded hair, seemed to carve at his fiddle with the bow to produce the most ravishing melody whilst, at every pause, he stooped down and offered his face and neck to a fat girl, who mopped them with a wet towel.[13]

It will be seen at how little advantage Mor-Zamba appears in the second scene, compared with the heroic exploits of the forest. Yet it is in the obscure struggle for life and freedom in the cities that he finally proves his mettle and earns his status as a representative hero of modern Cameroun. It is as such that Hurricane-Viet despatches him on the return journey to Ekoumdoum as the agent of its renewal. This is the character whom Dorothy Blair describes as 'a shadow-hero, his misfortunes the pretext for a political tract'[14] (her fondness for this last phrase will be noted).

The end of *Remember Ruben,* as published in 1974, gave no indication that the novel was to be continued, and the appearance of Beti's sixth novel, *Perpétue,* a few weeks later, treating in an entirely

*The narrator always refers to Ekoumdoum in this flattering way.

different style the years since independence in 1960, seemed to indicate an abandonment of the quasi-naturalistic, quasi-mythical style of the earlier book. But the founding of his new journal *Peuples Noirs, Peuples Africains* in 1976 has given Beti a chance to begin serializing the sequel, *La Ruine Presque Cocasse d'un Polichinelle* (The Almost Farcical Ruin of a Clown).* The sequel begins exactly where the earlier novel left off, with Mor-Zamba's return journey through the forest to Ekoumdoum. He is accompanied on this journey by Joe the Juggler, the irrepressible buffoon of *Remember Ruben*, and an innocent young brother of Jean-Louis', called Evariste. The published episodes resume entirely the style, tempo and character of the earlier novel, except that the predominance of Joe the Juggler's role increases the element of ironic humour and diminishes that of the marvellous, for we are now in the Cameroun of 1960, no longer in the semi-legendary days of Mor-Zamba's forest childhood. As the giant Mor-Zamba retraces the steps of the journey which, twenty years before, brought him from Ekoumdoum to the city, we are able to measure the distance which the Cameroun itself has travelled. The countryside seems not so much in the grip of civil war as in that of petty uniformed tyrants, who make their exactions unchallenged by a peasantry still too inclined to deference and passivity. As the three travellers draw nearer to Ekoumdoum, so Joe the Juggler's exuberant cynicism and quick-wittedness are slowly eclipsed by Mor-Zamba's reappearance as the master of the forest and all its crafts. The disadvantage which always dogged him among the nimble spirits of the city now falls away and exposes his personality in all its monolithic grandeur.

The belated appearance of Beti's historical chronicle *Main Basse sur le Cameroun*[15] in 1977 (the edition 1972 having been seized by the French government, which also attempted to strip the author of his passport and nationality) enables us to juxtapose it with his fictional treatment of some of the same events. In *Remember Ruben* we see most of these events through the eyes of Mor-Zamba, who does not always fully comprehend them. But the difference is not merely one of viewpoint; Beti has also fictionalized some of the events themselves, so that they resemble, but do not correspond with, actuality. With the exception of Ruben um Nyobé and one or two lofty actors like Generals de Gaulle and Leclerc, Beti has also changed the names of the principal figures. Although his motives for this were probably

*The completed novel was published in 1979 by Éditions des Peuples Noirs, too late for detailed consideration here.

artistic, he nonetheless achieved a strategic effect, for *Remember Ruben* did not suffer the fate of his chronicle, suppressed two years earlier.

Within a few weeks of *Remember Ruben*, as already mentioned, Beti published his sixth novel, *Perpétue*. Here again is one of those startling innovations of style and technique which have marked his career as a novelist. Despite the air of the marvellous which clings around the early scenes, *Remember Ruben* is in general a highly naturalistic novel, characterized by brilliant detail and evocative power. *Perpétue*, by contrast, has the slightly dream-like atmosphere of the quest. Most of the characters are presented as a type rather than filled out in detail. The object of the novel, as of Essola's quest, is to discover what has poisoned the springs of independence at their source. Essola, a former PPP militant, returns from six years in a concentration camp to discover that his beloved sister Perpétue has been sold to an official by their mother and has died an obscure and early death. The venal mother seems to stand, as the novel progresses, for Beti's vision of the Cameroun of the sixties, alike in her gross favouritism of her drunken son and in her callous indifference to virtue and integrity where they exist. Perpétue's fate becomes more than a personal tragedy, more even than an indictment of the brutal materialism to which girls like her are often sacrificed. She comes to represent that quality in the life of a nation for which Essola has suffered six years of purgatory, and which he returns to find in eclipse.

The compassionate concern of the novel, so strong in the middle chapters, is marred by the sadism with which Essola disposes of his brother at the end, a sadism without parallel in any other work of Beti. This exultant cruelty, of which there is no trace in *Remember Ruben*, may be justified in terms of the novel's more allegorical and representational character, which deprives its actions of literal, naturalistic meaning. But, just as likely, it may stem from the frustration of watching two decades of political militancy, international agitation and devoted struggle come to nothing. One by one, the UPC leaders had been either murdered or executed (the latest being Ernest Ouandié in 1971), their followers horribly tortured or left to rot in one of the country's many concentration camps. As Essola himself ponders, towards the end of the novel:

If only we had won! . . . The only thing which might compensate a man for time lost and for his loved ones who disappear in the most absurd way, is success; that's to say, in politics, the absolute triumph of the party to which one is devoted, of the comrades at whose side one has fought.[16]

Essola's quest for the lost Perpétue becomes also an exploration of the petit-bourgeois society which has done well out of independence. Debauched by a police officer with the connivance of her ineffectual husband, Perpétue herself finally abandons the virtue which no one values, throws herself into a passionate affair with a young footballer and dies in pregnancy with her first love-child. There is pain and sweetness in the evocation of Perpétue's radiant character and unhappy fate, but the novel seems to me inferior in power and scope to *Remember Ruben*. Nevertheless, the publication of two novels of this calibre and contrasted quality in a single year finally confirms Beti as a master; one who, unlike many of his contemporaries, can make the transition from the relatively innocent 'protest' novel of the 1950s to the harsh realities of contemporary Africa.

Wole Soyinka

Born 1934 at Abeokuta in Western Nigeria, Soyinka was educated at Government College, Ibadan and at the new University College there, before moving to Leeds University in 1954. After graduating in English at Leeds, Soyinka worked for some time as a supply teacher and as a reader and scriptwriter at the Royal Court Theatre in London, where his first dramatic sketches, poems and songs were performed in the late 1950s.

In 1960 he returned to Nigeria as a research fellow in drama and quickly established himself at Ibadan as a dramatist, actor and director of exceptional talent. His *Three Plays* was published by Mbari in 1963. Since then Soyinka has been prolific as a writer of drama, poetry, fiction and criticism, though it is as a dramatist that his fame has spread most widely. Soon after his imprisonment during the Nigerian Civil War, Soyinka spent some five years living in Europe and in Ghana, where he became editor of *Transition*. In 1976 he returned to Nigeria and took up the Chair of Drama at Ife University.

10   Across the Primeval Gulf

Wole Soyinka is probably the most prolific of modern African writers and the most varied in his achievements. Though he will be most admired and most remembered as a dramatist, he has established an important place for himself in fiction, poetry and criticism. In just seven years following his release from detention in 1969 he published four plays, two volumes of poetry, a novel, a memoir and a collection of critical essays. To a degree unusual in a continent where famous men find it difficult to avoid stultifying public commitments, he has always managed to remain first and foremost a writer. This makes the task of saying something worthwhile about each of his works, and relating them all to one another, impossible within the space available here. It will be more profitable, I believe, to consider certain general and consistent qualities of his imagination. We shall then see how far those qualities persist from his earliest writing into his very latest. Soyinka has refined his art both as a dramatist and as a poet, but we shall not find in his work the sudden changes of orientation and method which we have noted in Mongo Beti, and shall later note in Ngugi wa Thiong'o.

The reason for this absence of a certain kind of development may be related to the absence of any direct imprint of history on his governing ideas. The cast of his mind is sythesizing and idealizing rather than analytical, as the Nigerian theatre critic Biodun Jeyifo recently pointed out in reviewing Soyinka's latest book, *Myth, Literature and the African World*. He comments on 'the entirely unrelieved idealist foundation and direction of his arguments' and goes on:

Notions, conceptions, symbolic actions and relations are all lifted clean from their material, historical contexts and fused into an ideal world-view whose coherence is purely conceptual. Thus for Soyinka, the labour of the gods in the cosmos, which the myths recount, and their ambiguous relationships with mortals, reveal ideal ethical and social paradigms for Africa, now and for all time.[1]

The same substitution of mythic for historical consciousness has been deplored by other Nigerian radical writers like Femi Osofisan and Kole Omotoso, though all acknowledge the scope of Soyinka's talent. There can be no doubt that his imagination has been fuelled from the first by this idealizing tendency, and it is impossible to believe that he can suddenly abandon it. Soyinka has, perhaps, always been more of a rebel than a revolutionary; a believer in the heroic individual act which can save a society, rather than in a society capable of saving itself by collective will. This belief seems no less prominent in a recent work like *Death and the King's Horseman* (1975) than in an early one like *A Dance of the Forests* (1960). In the earlier play the heroic act is that of Demoke the carver, who seizes the Half-Child and thereby seeks to bring into existence the frustrated potential of history, as well as the repeatedly still-born child himself. For Soyinka, therefore, history is not a process with an innate tendency towards change, but rather with a tendency towards cyclical repetition, which only a heroic individual act can deflect. Even Demoke's act is not assured of success. It is probably himself, rather than the Half-Child, whom he has redeemed by it. We see this in the exchange between Forest Head and his lieutenant Aroni:

FOREST HEAD   The fooleries of beings whom I have fashioned closer to me weary and distress me. Yet I must persist, knowing that nothing is ever altered . . . hoping that when I have tortured awareness from their souls, that perhaps, only perhaps, in new beginnings. . . . Aroni, does Demoke know the meaning of his act?

ARONI   Demoke, you hold a doomed thing in your hand. It is no light matter to reverse the deed that was begun many lives ago. The Forest will not let you pass.[2]

To Soyinka, it seems, the heroic gesture is an assertion of will which has value, whether it succeeds in its objective or not. For him, as for the German poet Goethe, it is ceaseless striving rather than actual achievement which marks the hero. His notion of history is too pessimistic to allow of any more rosy view of the heroic vocation. In a world where most of mankind is blindly intent upon repeating the follies and crimes of the past, it is the hero/artist alone who hazards his own existence in one desperate effort to disturb the cycle of fate, to alter in some way the repetitive pattern of events.

This peculiar view of the hero and his role in history may seem to European readers to smack of Nietzsche and his Superman, but it can in fact be traced to a traditional Yoruba view of the world and the task of the gods within it. As an artist, Soyinka made an early identification of himself with Ogun, god of iron and war, the chisel and the forge. Ogun played the Promethean role of bringing to man the knowledge and use of metals, with the ambivalent result that he was able to transform his technology and at the same time kill his fellows with greater efficiency. The same ambivalence can be traced in the duel character of Ogun himself, who is both inspiring and terrible, full of creative energy and destructive rage. Naturally, his adherents display the same duality, which Soyinka has depicted with particular clarity in the character of Egbo, in his novel *The Interpreters* (1965). Egbo has the temperament of an artist without his vocation; his creative energies are frustrated (like those of his fellow 'interpreters') by the corruption and sloth of modern Nigerian society, but his destructive potential is alert and dangerous, as his friend Kola recognizes by depicting him as Ogun the blood-crazed killer rather than as Ogun the artist.

The introduction of the character of Demoke in *A Dance of the Forests*, is in fact the only occasion in Soyinka's work when his Ogunian hero is distinctly portrayed as an artist. Eman in *The Strong Breed* (1961) is in flight from his hereditary role as a ritual 'carrier' for the sins of the people; Egbo is a civil servant, whilst the Ofeyi (Orpheus) of *Season of Anomy* (1973) is not a musician but 'a custodian of the grain', a figure associated with social renewal. As for those enigmatic heroes Professor and the Old Man, of *The Road* (1965) and *Madmen and Specialists* (1970), they seem to represent something different from the Ogunian principle. That principle might be defined as the effort, as it were, to earth divine energy and shape it for creative ends, recognizing that if not so earthed it may bring destruction rather than blessing. Professor and the Old Man seem more intent upon self-knowledge. They exploit their followers in order to feed this knowledge, though they both claim, with some justification, that these same followers will in the process acquire a little self-knowledge too. Professor taunts his drivers and their touts as men who trade in death (because of the accidents their driving provokes) without understanding or caring about its nature. Professor himself quite frankly trades in death with his accident store, his forged licences and uprooted road-signs. The method, as so often in Soyinka's drama, is one of parody: by the brutal spectacle of his own trading, Professor hopes to make his disciples recognize their participation in the business. Kotonu has in fact begun to make this realization, and has renounced driving for ever because of his recent brushes with death:

KOTONU   A man gets tired of feeling too much . . . Where is Zorro who never returned from the North without a basket of guinea-fowl eggs? Where is Akanni the Lizard? I have not seen any other tout who could stand on the lorry's roof and play the samba at sixty miles an hour . . . Where is Sergeant Burma who treated his tanker like a child's toy?

SAMSON   All the same. . . .

KOTONU   Sergeant Burma was never moved by these accidents. He told me himself how once he was stripping down a crash and found that the driver was an old comrade from the front. He took him to the mortuary but first he stopped to remove all the tyres.

SAMSON   He wasn't human.

KOTONU   But he was. A man must protect himself against the indifference of comrades who desert him. Not to mention the hundred travellers whom you never really see until their faces are wiped clean by silence. . . .
   You know, Professor is a bit like Sergeant Burma. He was moving round those corpses as if they didn't exist. All he cared about was replanting that signpost. To see him you would think he was Adam replanting the Tree of Life.[3]

In *Madmen and Specialists*, parody becomes a major vehicle of expression. The Old Man's method with his mendicants can be summed up in his phrase: 'Disgust is cheap. I asked for self-disgust'.[4] Under his influence, they parody everything, from Dr Bero's brutal methods of interrogation or the pantomime played out by visiting heads of state, to the Old Man himself. These parodies indicate a dawning critical awareness in the mendicants (who may be taken as representing typical members of an exploited and deceived society), and the awareness is a threat to all such as Dr Bero, who seek to control not only the actions but the consciousness of others. If the Professor and the Old Man can still be considered in any sense as artists, then their raw material is not wood or stone, but the common man.

This manipulative role, however, is one which properly belongs to the gods, and in this sense Soyinka's rather demonic old men are blasphemous. Professor parodies both the Christian Communion (with his evening palm-wine ceremony) and the Egungun masquerade, another bridge between god and man (by asking Murano to dance again in the mask in which he was knocked down). Both perish in the very moment when their manipulation of others reaches its highest pitch of intensity. Sharing the duality of Soyinka's earlier heroes, they present the same problem to the sort of playgoer or reader who is in search of clear-cut 'goodies' and 'baddies'. Although Soyinka was born into a Christian family in Abeokuta, seat of the first Christian mission in Nigeria (1843), his thought has been shaped far more by the traditional Yoruba world-view than by any alien influence. That view is one of a dynamic interaction between the gods and man, who complement each other. Man is the 'mask' through which the gods manifest themselves on earth. It is a view which is both profoundly religious, in the sense that everything is permeated with the divine essence, and profoundly humanistic, in the sense that man stands at the centre of its value-system. The continuity and vitality of the human community are what counts above all.

To this foundation Soyinka has added by his wide and various reading, his travels, his work in the theatre in many countries and with actors of many nationalities. The fact that he spent three years taking English Honours at Leeds University (1954–7) and another two years on the literary staff of the Royal Court Theatre in London also gave him an early and complete mastery of the language. Instead of swallowing him up in English mannerisms (though there are occasional Shakespearian echoes in his early plays), that mastery has enabled him to develop a greater variety of levels in the language than any other African writer. Both *The Road* and *Madmen and Specialists* offer innumerable examples of this ability to fit each character with an appropriate English speech, ranging from the creative exuberance of Professor or the Old Man to the broken vowels of, say, Tokyo Kid or the sinister ranting of Aafaa.

Like many major dramatists, Soyinka's range of formal expression is also very wide, stretching from a sombre tragedy like *Death and the King's Horseman* to the deft comedy, *The Lion and the Jewel* (1958) and the broad farce, *The Trials of Brother Jero* (1960). But Soyinka is too much of an entertainer to present these elements unmixed. Even the tragedy just mentioned contains a comic parody of colonial ritual (contrasted with the serious drama of ritual suicide), whilst the surprise ending of *The Lion and the Jewel* presents a substantial moral – 'Man, be thyself'! In his novels, too, the elements are mingled, though the humour in the early scenes of *Season of Anomy* (1973) is swept away by the torrent of catastrophe.

For reasons stated earlier; namely, the size of his output and the continuity of his ideas, I shall not attempt in this chapter to give an exhaustive account of Soyinka's work. By concentrating on some of the major works in drama, fiction and poetry which he has published since his release from prison in 1969, I believe we can trace both that continuity and a certain deepening of the strain of tragic pessimism which has always been present. Soyinka has always been a spokesman for political commitment, right from his involvement in the 1965 political crisis in Western Nigeria to his championship of Pan-Africanism, the Swahili language and intellectual freedom, as editor of *Transition* from 1973 onwards. But the peculiar cast of his ideas does not enable critics to categorize him as either 'progressive' or 'reactionary'. In the following pages I hope to show why.

In *Death and the King's Horseman*, Soyinka imposes upon his hero a crucial test. He must face personal extinction in order that the continuity of the community and its values may be assured. The choice is his own voluntary death or the death of all those traditional values which preserve it. The Elesin, (the King's Horseman), fails in that crucial test because the traditional world has begun to be corrupted and he has been touched by that corruption. Yet the society, and apparently Soyinka too, thinks it right that the Elesin should bear the whole weight of social expectation and the whole responsibility for failing that expectation. By neglecting to take his own life, he has taken life away from the civilization of his people. He feels it, his people feel it and, ignoring the objective changes which had taken place in Nigerian society by the 1940s, the audience is expected to feel it too.

ELESIN   My powers deserted me. My charms, my spells, even my voice lacked strength when I made to summon the powers that would lead me across the last measure of earth into the land of the fleshless. You saw it, Iyaloja. You saw me struggle to retrieve my will from the power of the stranger whose shadow fell across the doorway. . . .

IYALOJA   You have betrayed us. We fed you sweetmeats such as we hoped awaited you on the other side. But you said No, I must eat the world's leftovers. We said you were the hunter who brought the quarry down; to you belonged the vital portions of the game. No, you said, I am the hunter's dog and I shall eat the entrails of the game and the faeces of the hunter. . . .[5]

The Iyaloja (leader of the market women) taunts the Elesin because he insisted on tasting a young girl on the eve of his death and allowed the taste to weaken his resolve. That this insistence was in itself startling, even unprecedented, is indicated in the earlier scene where he hints at his desire for the girl, who is already promised to the

Iyaloja's son. The Iyaloja 'dare not understand' him, but he clarifies
his meaning beyond doubt:

> My wish
> Transcends the blotting out of thought
> In one mere moment's tremor of the senses.
> Do me credit. And do me honour.
> I am girded for the route beyond
> Burdens of waste and longing.
> Then let me travel light. Let
> seed that will not serve the stomach
> On the way remain behind. Let it take root
> In the earth of my choice, in this earth
> I leave behind.[6]

The Elesin's speech is sophistical, with its imagery of earth, seed
and plantain shoots, its scorn of mere desire, its insistence upon his
sanctity as a man already dedicated to death, and hence upon the
sanctity of his wishes. But his desire is nevertheless apparent, and it
is one which holds him to life instead of freeing him from it. It is
also, although Soyinka does not emphasize this, profoundly contrary
to the usual rituals of preparing oneself for a great spiritual task;
rituals which stress abstinence, whether from food, drink or sex,
rather than indulgence of senses which may cloud the will. Yet the
Iyaloja grants his wish without a struggle, because she appears to
accept his argument for its sanctity as coming from one 'already
touched by the waiting fingers of our departed'. Only when preparing
him for the marriage bed does she remind him that it must also be
the bed of death:

IYALOJA Now we must go prepare your bridal chamber. Then these same
hands will lay your shrouds.

ELESIN (exasperated) Must you be so blunt?[7]

The Elesin's outburst exposes all his sophistries for what they are.
Yet he is very ready, when the District Officer's prohibition of his
suicide provides an ostensible reason for his failure of resolve, to
transfer the whole guilt to 'the ghostly one' who burst in upon him
at the critical hour. The whole pattern of this last scene is created by
the torrent of reproaches which the Elesin directs upon Pilkings,
only to be overwhelmed himself by a greater torrent when the Iyaloja
enters with the body of his son, who has taken his own life to retrieve
the honour of his line. While the Elesin tells Pilkings:

The end of this night's work is not over. Neither this year nor the next will see it. If I wished you well, I would pray that you do not stay long enough in our land to see the disaster you have brought upon us.[8]

The Praise-singer directs all his blame for this cosmic disaster upon the King's Horseman:

Elesin, we placed the reins of the world in your hands yet you watched it plunge over the edge of the bitter precipice. You sat with folded arms while evil strangers tilted the world from its course and crashed it beyond the edge of emptiness. . . .[9]

Meanwhile, the Iyaloja is not slow to turn the Elesin's vegetable imagery against him:

. . . tell me, you know so well the cycle of the plantain: is it the parent shoot which withers to give sap to the younger or, does your wisdom see it running the other way?[10]

All are united at least in their insistence that we are not dealing with a single incident, however poignant, but with a climacteric in the failure of African civilization to maintain its integrity and hold its own course. Do not all of them exaggerate? In the language of myth, the Elesin's dishonour might spell all these things. In the language of history, it was the process of change, at every level and in every corner of Yoruba society, which made such an incident inevitable. Was not the Rev. Samuel Johnson, historian of the Yoruba, already installed as Pastor of Oyo when he finished his great book, *fifty years* before the affair of the King's Horseman? The historian in Johnson would have recorded such a ritual suicide as an interesting feature of his people's culture, but the Christian minister would have deplored it. The accusations levelled against the Elesin could with equal, perhaps greater justice, have been aimed at Afonja, the general whose ambition betrayed Yorubaland to its enemies and turned the northern provinces of the Oyo Empire into a desert, so that elephants now roam where Shango once held sway. But that was one hundred and thirty years before the Elesin's wedding night.

The historical imagination has to grapple with complexities like these; thus it cannot see human time as a series of unique world-shattering or world-generating events, as Yeats saw the birth of Helen of Troy and that of Christ. But the mythic imagination must simplify and dramatize, imposing its own meaning on events, even at the cost of some violence to the evidence, in order to make them teach a special meaning.

The mention of Yeats is important, because it was he who wrote that the modern poet must find or invent a mythology which will embrace all his work and impart meaning to everything within it. This is undoubtedly the role played by mythology in Soyinka's development. Like Yeats's own, where Irish gods rub shoulders with nationalist heroes, and Heraclitus with Plotinus, Soyinka's mythology is eclectic; partly founded in Yoruba tradition and partly invented too, out of other pretty miscellaneous materials.

But the analogies extend beyond Yeats, and remind us how many great dramatic poets, not only in our own century, have been mythologizers. They have preferred to hold a mirror up, not to contemporary reality (with its 'ugly face'), but to a heroic, ideal age which will give us the measure of our own depravity. Corneille and Racine cannot find any substitute for the models of classical antiquity, which had already fascinated the Renaissance. Ibsen infuses his doctors, bankers and builders with the spirit of old Norse heroes, whilst his heroines increasingly seem like destructive avatars straight from legend. Yeats's threnody, 'Romantic beauty's dead and gone', is matched by Eliot's cry, 'Where are the eagles and the trumpets?'

Because of its tendency to locate moral energy, romance or heroism uniquely in a world which is past and irrecoverable, the work of the mythologizing poet is often reactionary in its impact. It tells us to despise modern life rather than to transform it. By showing us how puny we are in comparison with its exaggerated heroes, it seems to tell us that the world today does not have the energy or the vision to change itself. We are nearing the end of a spent cycle, and so forth.

Death and the King's Horseman provides an ideal nexus for seeing the mythic imagination at work, because Soyinka's raw material here is a well-recorded historical incident which occurred in the town of Oyo in 1946. The event was resonant enough in itself, and an earlier Nigerian dramatization (*Oba Waja* by Duro Ladipo) had been content to re-create it very much as it was. Not so Soyinka. The whole business of the funeral wedding-night is a pure invention, whose function is perhaps to motivate the Elesin's failure of resolve in a more complex way than mere yielding to an official prohibition by the District Officer. Likewise, the son who died in his father's place in 1946 was a trader living in Ghana, still very much part of the traditional world and its values. Soyinka's Olunde is a highly articulate, Western-educated protégé of the District Officer; hence the last person one would expect, on a strictly naturalistic level, to take this kind of decision. The 'been-to' of 1946 would have been far more likely to join the District Officer in deploring such a custom as a relic of barbarism. Lastly, though this is far less significant, Soyinka has shifted the whole incident a few years earlier, to make it coincide both with the War of 1939–45 and with a royal visit by the Prince of Wales, who did in fact visit Nigeria in 1935. We must overlook the improbability of such a visit being arranged in the midst of a war and a submarine menace, to note only that it does enable the dramatist to have great fun with his macabre masquerade of colonial ritual in Act IV.

We see then that, like many a dramatic poet before him, not least Shakespeare, Soyinka feels quite free to rearrange the material of history to bring out the message he wants. He would have wished very much that someone of Olunde's background, freshly down from Oxford, should have made such a gesture or renunciation towards his whole education; such a total espousal of the ways of his fathers. History, therefore, becomes myth; and the Elesin is made to bear a greater burden of responsibility than, by naturalistic criteria, seems just. The Praise-singer charges him, 'You have left us floundering in a blind future'. We are asked by the play to believe, and under the spell of its poetry perhaps we do believe, that a world of pristine Yoruba values was shattered in mid-career by a single act of dereliction. We must suppress our knowledge that this world had been undergoing modification for a century and that such acts of dereliction were as old as the first Christian conversions in Abeokuta. It is no accident that the greatest traditional carvers in Ekiti and Igbomina finished their best work about the same time as the Oyo episode. The religious context was simply no longer there; the joint onslaughts of Islam and Christianity had reduced their real followers to a fragment of the population, instead of its very core. Authentic Yoruba sculpture had become as bizarre as ritual suicide.

And yet Soyinka does not reject modern life, in the manner of Yeats, Eliot or Pound. He believes that it can only recover its meaning and its soul by a full-hearted espousal of African values and civilization; an espousal of which Olunde's death is meant to serve as an image. The political, social, religious and even economic arrangements of Yorubaland offer a system which only needs re-interpretation to act as the blueprint for tomorrow. And it is precisely this belief that so many of his fellow countrymen reject. Whatever checks and balances it may have incorporated, that system was, for them, essentially feudal. A man or woman remained in the station in life to which their fate had called them. The blacksmith did not become an

Oba; nor did the action of a ruling house revert to being a mere peasant, even if the crown passed him by. The social and class mobility which urbanization and industrialism are imparting to Nigeria; the growth of huge multi-ethnic communities like Lagos, Kano or Benin; the emergence of serious class-conflict for control of the levers of state power; all these apparently irreversible developments seem to make Soyinka's vision more of a pipe-dream than a prophecy. It is no use castigating socialism as a 'foreign ideology' if one does not level the same charge at capitalism, which has already transformed the face of Yorubaland.

But the vision is not without its nobility, and the passionate eloquence of this play shows how deeply it is held. *Death and the King's Horseman* is a threnody (Soyinka, in a somewhat turgid phrase, speaks of its 'threnodic essence'); it shows us an ancient and comprehensive civilization faltering in its path. In the terms of the play, the future is not really separable from the past, and must suffer whatever contamination today's events may spill upon it. It is only in this restricted sense that the Iyaloja can tell us, in the play's closing words: 'Now forget the dead, forget even the living. Turn your mind only to the unborn'.[11]

For a model of what that future might be, we must turn to Soyinka's novel *Season of Anomy*, published two years earlier. The problem of scale is here evaded, because the only time we see the model actually working is in its original abode of Aiyéró, a village-state rather than a city-state, which is clearly based on an actual Christian community called Aiyetóró, in the creeks of coastal Yorubaland. Significantly, Soyinka makes his own community a neo-pagan breakaway from that parent, precisely on the issue that Christianity is an alien religion:

'We have observances,' Ahime conceded. 'We have our rituals. We are a farming and fishing community, so we acknowledge our debts to earth and to the sea. And when a great man dies, a founder, we pay him homage. If we wish to take one full year burying him it is still less than his dues. For a people who own everything in common what we spend merely returns to us.'[12]

In part, the novel is simply the story of Ofeyi's attempt to transform the larger society (Nigeria? Africa?) in the image of Aiyéró. In part, it is the story of Ofeyi's (Orpheus') quest to find and redeem Iriyise (Eurydice), who has been carried off to the underworld of military imperialist tyranny. There is no necessary dependence between these two motifs; but the Orpheus-Eurydice motif provides the mythic element which Soyinka's genius demands. With its cyclical and seasonal imagery (reflected in the chapter-headings: Seminal; Buds; Tentacles; Harvest; Spores), it transcends the inexorable machinery of history and enables the novelist to give an implication of hope – because the cycle must continue and fresh seeds be forever sown – to a situation which seems to deny it. As so often in Soyinka's work, his principal actors are artists, but ones who have not yet found their real function or métier. Whereas the 'Interpreters' (in the novel of that name) never really break free of the corrupt embrace of their society and never make the critical choices which will leave the old life behind them, Ofeyi the spoiled poet and Iriyise the dancer make this choice at the very beginning of the novel. The corrupted function of their art is shown in the early scene where they put it to the uses of the Cocoa Corporation. Iriyise's anguished struggle to burst out of the giant cocoa-pod, to serve the mere purposes of a publicity stunt, is prophetic of her final appearance in the novel as the sleeping seed of a new world within the pod of apparent death. But it is also, like the whole of that scene, a parody; Soyinka the ironist having his fling, with his merciless eye for the absurdities of contemporary life.

The transformation of Ofeyi and Iriyise to perform their new roles as heroic redeemers of their society is effected by means of ritual – the ritual of their initiation into the Aiyéró community – which shifts the burden of realizing the future onto the shoulders of Ofeyi and turns Iriyise into a figure symbolic of fructification and promise:

In wrapper and sash with the other women of Aiyéró, her bared limbs and shoulders among young shoots, Iriyise weaving fronds for the protection of the young nursery, bringing wine to sweating men in their struggle against the virgin forests. . . . Her fingers spliced wounded saplings with the ease of a natural healer. Her presence, the women boasted, inspired the rains.[13]

This is not bad for someone who was a 'bitchy', sophisticated, urban beauty a few days before. The strained language and effect here, as in many other passages of the novel, show the author's difficulty in placing it somewhere along the plane between naturalistic and mythic action. The trouble is probably that the mythic element in *Season of Anomy* is too insistent, whereas in a novel like Armah's *Fragments* it has to be teased out, after a first reading of what appears to be a naturalistic account of a young man's return and breakdown. Myth in fiction reposes more easily at the level of structure (the pattern of episodes and their development) than at the level of dialogue and narrative style.

The fabrication of the Aiyéró community also begs a number of questions. Soyinka manages to create the impression that there is something deeply and intrinsically Yoruba about the community's arrangements. But the fact is that the original vision of the Holy Apostles sect, which founded the historical Aiyétóro, has far more in common with other ideal Christian commonwealths, in Africa and elsewhere, than it has with a hierarchical and rather specialized society, like that of a traditional Yoruba city-state. This was communistic only in the sense that every freeborn son was entitled to the land he could farm – not necessarily the same amount as his neighbours – and that the wealth which accrued to the Oba and the chiefs was consumed within the community, much of it in the form of hospitality to the citizens. But enjoying an occasional calabash of palm-wine with the Oba does not make one in any sense his equal in the enjoyment of whatever wealth the region affords. The system was paternalistic rather than communistic. As Peter Morton-Williams remarks:

Ranking was characteristic of all levels and forms of Yoruba social organization.[14]

Soyinka's dream is presumably of a state made up of many small communal units, each resembling Aiyéró. In this respect, his thought resembles that of William Morris, and like Morris he leaves us to guess what sort of apparatus of coercion or control might exist at the centre. What we do witness within the scope of the novel is the cataclysmic failure of Ofeyi's attempt to peacefully export the ideas and methods of Aiyéró to the larger society. This failure seems to shift the burden of realizing the future on to the shoulder of his 'alter ego,' the Dentist, a professional assassin who believes in 'taking out' the enemy forces like so many bad teeth. If the Dentist is in some way Ofeyi's Bad Angel, then he has a Good Angel in the shape of the Indian girl Taiila (the author specifically refers to this Morality Play pattern). Soyinka apparently wants us to believe that both the element of loving-kindness and a saving violence are needed to make Ofeyi's humanistic enterprise succeed the next time round. But by externalizing and personalizing these elements, as Taiila and the Dentist, he has enabled Ofeyi to remain apparently separate from them. This leaves the reader uninstructed about the real modification of Ofeyi's character and motives which might be affected if the espousal of violence had been internalized instead, so that we saw Ofeyi's own nature change with the developing situation of the novel. It also has the disadvantage of creating cardboard characters who perform only one function and exploit only one line of thought. Once we know what they 'represent', they can no longer surprise or convince us as human beings. Consider, for example, this exchange between Taiila and Ofeyi:

She sighed. 'We pass and re-pass each other but you will not step off your circling path. You are trapped on your violent circumference. Ofeyi, why won't you rest?

'Mire and mud, for some these are the paths to beauty and peace. We may meet at several intersections, you and I, the mystery virgin of a transit lounge. . . .'

She came forward and took his hand.

'But you still don't believe it was fated. You think it was all an accident. Can't you see I am meant to save you?'

Ofeyi tried to infuse his voice with all the sincerity he felt. 'Believe me I envy you your glimpse of redemption. I really do. Only you must believe also in my own commitments. Leave me to track my own spoors on the laterals, Taiila. Moreover,' he added, 'if we were destined to meet so was my meeting with the Dentist. . . .'[15]

Charged, poetic dialogue like this is difficult to accommodate in the novel, especially one whose prevailing tone is still naturalistic. The passage makes it clear that both Taiila and the Dentist are functional characters, whose fated purpose is to subserve the destiny of Ofeyi. Correspondingly, and disappointingly from a dramatist, they tend to talk in an undifferentiated 'high' style, without the false starts, hesitations and perversities of ordinary conversation which we have come to expect of the novel. A sentence like, 'leave me to track my own spoors on the laterals', is quite a jaw-breaker too, and this results from the significant style in which Ofeyi's two mentors are made to speak – they have no existence independent of their relationship to him, and every word in their exchanges must be pointed in such a way as to underline this.

Soyinka, in fact, has not got away from his long-standing belief in the lone hero, the world-changer, deified in Ogun and personified in so many of his other works. Despite the Aiyéró model, which appears to hold forth a small-scale communal ideal, that model still needs the instrumentality of someone like Ofeyi (modified by Taiila and the Dentist) to rescue it from obscurity. We see this clearly enough in an early exchange between Ofeyi and the Custodian of the Grain, the reigning leader of the community:

'You have earned the right to your contentment,' Ofeyi said. 'But even the state of content can become malignant. Like indifference. Or complacency. Already you are near stagnant . . . please do not take offence. . . . It's admirable but . . . it encourages inbreeding. They [your sons] seem untouched by where they have been, by the plight of the rest of mankind, even of our own people.

'We find no virtue in aggression, son. Evangelism is a form of aggression.'[16]

The problem posed here is central to the novel. An ideal community is born out of withdrawal from and reaction against 'the plight of mankind'. Should it rely upon attracting adherents by simply existing as a visible, working alternative; or should it evangelize? The aggression implicit in evangelization is personified in the Dentist, but the apparent failure of the enterprise leaves this central question unresolved, though Soyinka tries to resolve it by later revealing that the Dentist himself is a son of Aiyéró, hence a product of its philosophy under stress. The idea of building up the nation from an agglomeration of small, semi-autonomous and democratically controlled units was originally common to both the Soviet Communist and Maoist ideologies. In both states, however, it seems to have foundered because it conflicts with the growth of an apparatus of interventionist state power (army, secret police, bureaucracy, central party committee, etc.), which comes to see that very autonomy as a threat to its rights of control. In *Season of Anomy*, Soyinka comes nearer than anywhere else in his writing to subscribing to a 'foreign ideology', in Ofeyi's commendation of Mao to Pa Ahime and latter's positive response:

'I like your Mao', he commented. . . . He is unique this Chinese isn't he? A man of simple truths and a large experimental farm. For the first time I feel like undertaking a journey to meet a man I have only encountered on the pages of a book. . . .[17]

But we are made to feel that this meeting, if it ever took place, would be a meeting of equals – the African way encountering the Chinese way – rather than a visit to the fountainhead of contemporary practice. The foundation of Mao's thought is scientific Marxism, reinterpreted in terms of Chinese historical conditions. The foundation of Soyinka's thought is his vision of Yoruba (African) humanism, reconstructed from the ruins of a colonized and exploited

society. Where, for instance, Mao saw traditional Chinese family
loyalty as a drag upon social cohesion, Soyinka would certainly not
see it that way, though he is well aware of the perils of clannishness
in public officers. Like many other Africans, Soyinka would like to
see probity in public life, whilst at the same time passionately
defending the extended family and its group loyalites. This is a
difficult, though probably not an impossible, combination to achieve.

In a tribute to Julius Nyerere, the poet reveals a social and political
vision which is close to that represented by the cult of the Grain in
Season of Anomy.

Sweat is leaven for the earth
Not tribute. Earth replete
Seeks no homage from the toil of earth.
Sweat is leaven for the earth
Not driven homage to a fortressed god.
Your black earth hands unchain
Hope from death messengers, from
In-bred dogmatoids that prove
Grimmer than the Grim Reaper, insatiate
Predators on humanity, their fodder.
Sweat is leaven, bread, Ujamaa
Bread of the earth, by the earth
For the earth. Earth is all people.[18]

Again, the labourer must see, enjoy and be surrounded by the products of his labour. That labour is not some homage which he owes
to an inexorable monster, called the state. The pun on 'Bread of the
earth' and the echo of Lincoln's Gettysburg Address extend the
meaning of the poem without weakening its insistence on organic
process, the cycle of restoration and replenishment. In this sense,
seasonal myth obtrudes as much in Soyinka's political thought as in
all his other work. It must make him resistant to any unilinear,
progressive version of history, whether Christian of Marxist. The
same note which is struck in 'Ujamaa' at the end of *A Shuttle in the
Crypt* is found at its very beginning in 'O Roots!', a poem written in
imprisonment, where Soyinka's favoured imagery of the Ogun
cycle is used to establish that connection with the elements which
seems to be denied him by the prison walls:

Receive the roots of lighting from the sky
Storing light of their departed eye
Draw to earth all lethal pulses, that my cup
Of hands may echo fiery harmonies, and sup

At wedding-feasts of sky and earth. Thread my
hands to spring-rites, to green hands of the dead.[19]

The same poem contains a reference to the Orphic quest, which is
equally concerned with resurrection and renewal:

Pathfinder to the underworld, lead
My feet to core, to kernel seed. . . .[20]

Soyinka's use of the Orphic myth in *Season of Anomy*, already
glanced at here in a poem written some years earlier, has been
described by some critics as an abandonment of Yoruba mythology
in favour of Western. But what is involved is not abandonment, it is
simply the establishment of analogous patterns. The Orphic myth
(which is anyway more Asiatic than Greek) is concerned with 'the
ordered movement of the Earth herself', to quote Jane Ellen Harrison.
Exactly the same may be said of the Ogun cycle, whose iron staffs
symbolize the harmless discharge of terrible divine energy through
lightning, which enters and symbolically fertilizes the earth for new
harvest.

A similar pattern of analogy is teased out by Soyinka in his
adaptation of *The Bacchae* of Eurypides, written for the National
Theatre of Great Britain in 1973. Dionysus is perhaps a more comprehensive figure than Ogun, in that he comes to represent the whole
affective, emotional side of man's nature; so terrible in his revenge
against those who deny him, so gentle in his possession of those who
accept. It would be an exaggeration of Ogun's role in the Yoruba
pantheon to make him represent all that. There is also the element of
the intrusive and exotic about the Dionysiac cult, an alien religion
introduced by Asiatic slaves which, like Christianity later, became a
threat to the established official cults. But enough of the analogy
stands to make Soyinka's *Bacchae* a work full of originality and
insight, containing some of his finest dramatic poetry:

I am the gentle comb of breezes on the slope of vines
The autumn flush on clustered joy of grapes
I am the autumn sacrament, the bond, word, pledge
The blood rejuvenated from a dying world
I am the life that's trodden by the dance of joy
My flesh, my death, my rebirth is the song
That rises from men's lips, they know not how.
But also,
The wild blood of the predator that's held in leash. . . .[21]

It is this duality in the divine nature of Dionysus, insisted on equally by Eurypides and Soyinka, which links him most specifically with Ogun, and with the whole system of Yoruba religious belief. This is a system which, like that of Ancient Greece, *contains* contradictions, rather than trying to polarize them into opposed systems of Good and Evil, or Progressive and Reactionary. The denial of contradictions is one of the most dangerous of human follies, punished as terribly by Ogun as by Dionysus. It is the same duality which renders the future 'ambiguous':

> OLD SLAVE   Dare we surrender to what comes after, embrace
> The ambiguous face of the future? It is enough
> To concede awareness of the inexplicable, to wait
> And watch the unfolding. . . .[22]

In confronting that ambiguous face, Soyinka has almost invariably had recourse to myth, and it is this which makes its consistent use in his work over some twenty years more crucial than its occasional appearance in the work of other African writers. History in itself does not yield any positive meaning to him; it offers back only 'a mocking grin'; and this is because he rejects any notion of history, such as the Marxist one, which sees it as having a certain inbuilt tendency, a pattern of development, even a destination. Only through the analogy of myth, which celebrates the resurrection of nature after the death of winter, or of the hero from the self-annihilation he suffers during his quest, can history be made to yield a positive meaning. This puts Soyinka at the opposite pole from a writer like Sembène Ousmane, who takes an actual historical event (the Dakar-Niger Railway strike of 1946; the referendum campaign of 1958; the bloody wartime episode recounted in his film *Emitai*) and makes that event itself show the direction and purpose of change. Equally strong is the contrast with a work like Beti's *Remember Ruben*, which uses the structure of heroic epic, but the fabric of naturalism and history. Both the latter writers believe that history, as shaped and pointed by the artist, can itself teach the people the way to their redemption. Soyinka seems to believe, as ever, in the heroic transcendence of history as the only way forward. Hence, even his poem *Ogun Abibiman*,[23] written in celebration of Mozambique's virtual declaration of war against the Smith regime in 1976, uses the same mythic-heroic apparatus. Zimbabwe will be freed, it seems, under the joint heroic leadership of Chaka and Ogun. Another writer might have been content to extol the actual, historic sacrifices and achievements of Machel's and Nugabe's guerillas, which provide a sufficient image of human heroism.

I have concentrated upon the dialectical struggle of history and myth as manifested in Soyinka's post-Civil War writings, because of their nearness in time to one another and their common body of imagery, much of which can be traced to his prison journal, *The Man Died*.[24] Also, because the increasing radicalism of his public utterances has led many young leftist critics, such as Biodun Jeyifo, Femi Osofisan, Kole Omotoso and Omolara Leslie, to draw attention to the apparent paradox between them and the tendency of his creative writings. It is tempting to conclude that Soyinka as an artist is a combination of tragic pessimist and exuberant satirist (the latter stream again coming to the fore in his Africanization of *The Beggars' Opera* as *Opera Wonyosi* in 1977). The experiences of 1966–70, both national and personal, have tended to stress the former attribute, without eclipsing the latter. But the full force of his genius is felt more in lines like these, from 'Flowers for my Land', than in even the most adroit of his satires:

Sun-beacons
On every darkened shore
Orphans of the world
Unite! Draw
Your fuel of pain from earth's sated core.[25]

Kofi Awoonor

Born 1935 at Wheta in the Volta Region of Ghana, son of a trader Awoonor studied at various mission schools in Eweland before moving to Achimota and then to the University of Ghana, where he graduated in English. His early poems appeared in the journal *Okyeame*, of which he was the first editor. He became successively a research fellow at the Institute of African Studies and Chairman of the Ghana Film Corporation, before going to London in 1967. There followed nine years of study and teaching, first at London University and later at the Stony Brook campus of New York State University, where he became Chairman of Comparative Literature. During these years Awoonor published his major collection of poems, *Night of my Blood* (1971), his first novel, his critical work *The Breast of the Earth* and his study of three leading Ewe poets. He returned to Ghana in 1975 to take up a post at Cape Coast University, but was soon imprisoned for a year in alleged connection with an attempted coup. Released in 1976, he became Professor of English at Cape Coast soon afterwards.

11 The Neglected Gods

Few African writers distil in all their work so intense a sense of place as the Ghanaian poet Kofi Awoonor. For him the traditional ritual of burying the child's birth-cord in the very place where it was born has taken on a symbolic importance which echoes through almost everything he has written. Rhetorically, the writer demands in an early poem: 'Cannot we find where they buried our birth-cord?'[1] bestowing on it the same kind of significance as Tchicaya U Tam'si gives to 'the tree of his origins'. But that very comparison indicates an important difference; for Awoonor does in fact know the exact spot, in the village of Wheta, in which his cord was buried. The search for it is a paradigm for the return to a lost self; the self which was torn away from home and childhood companions and carried off to the mission school. Tchicaya, on the other hand, was brought up in genuine ignorance of his origins and even of his mother's identity. To this ignorance was added the more drastic severance from the Congo and from Africa, when his father carried him off to Paris and a French education at the age of fifteen.

How do we then account for the intensity of Awoonor's feeling of deprivation? It is not that that feeling in itself is rare among African writers of his generation; rather, it is almost the rule. But as a theme it dominates in only a few of their works: an early novel celebrating the pastoral innocence of the village, such as Laye's *L'Enfant Noir*; or an early poetic sequence like Okigbo's *Heavensgate*. In these and other writers it is succeeded by other and apparently more urgent themes.

This is how Awoonor describes the consignment of his eight-year-old hero Amamu to school, in his novel *This Earth, my Brother*:

His father had decided he must go and live with some people from the interior now in a town on the coast. . . . His mother did not agree. Her husband's word was law. . . . Suddenly he began to cry. He was clutching a loaf of sixpenny sugar bread. The children of the household led him to the lorry which was to carry him away. His mother and everyone began to cry. She sobbed convulsively. His father became annoyed at waiting. He hoisted him into the lorry with a curse. The lorry sped away into the dust and the future.[2]

Both from that novel and Awoonor's work as a whole, we get the impression that the long adventure of missionary and colonial education was like a process which turned the poet's feet inexorably away from the soil of his origins, while his head remained obstinately turned upon it. What happens at the end of the novel is that Amamu's feet are finally able to follow the promptings of his head.

Although born in his mother's inland village of Wheta, Awoonor was in fact brought up mainly in Keta, on the coast of Ghana and within a few miles of its eastern border. Keta is a town of the Anlos, a coastal group of the Ewe people, the majority of whom are to be found in the adjoining Republic of Togo. The Anlos are predominantly fishermen, both in the turbulent Atlantic which fronts Keta and in the big lagoon which separates it from the mainland. Not only is the town perched on a narrow sandspit between these waters, but it is steadily encroached on by the sea. Parts of the town which were central during the German administration of 1884 to 1914 are now far out beneath the waves. In the streets, one is never out of earshot of the heavy thud and roaring withdrawal of the big Atlantic rollers, for these ocean beaches are never quiet. One of Awoonor's first published poems evokes the townsfolk's constant and losing battle with the waves:

At home the sea is in the town,
Running in and out of the cooking places,
Collecting the firewood from the hearths
And sending it back at night;
The sea eats the land at home.[3]

That image of the sea collecting the firewood and 'sending it back at night' could hardly evoke more powerfully the sense that this is a daily, not an occasional menace. The cry of the waves becomes like a mourning song for the land that has been lost and for all those whom the sea has taken. And indeed this note of mourning, which also predominates in the traditional dirges which form the richest part of Ewe poetry, is struck ever and again in Awoonor's work. The sudden, agonizing death of the childhood sweetheart Dede when she was twelve and the poet somewhat younger, is the cause of the trauma which dominates the circular career of his fictional hero Amamu and which is likewise ever-present in the early poetry collected in

Rediscovery (1964). That death prompts the questioning of the true African meaning of resurrection and salvation which we find in poems like 'Easter Dawn', 'Salvation' and 'The Nim Trees in the Cemetery', which ends with the following words:

Yet I know that I love the nim trees in the cemetery
And the gravestones with arms of angels outstretched to the winds
And in the pagan colony a yawning untenanted grave is open
The grave I've known since birth, beside where the forget-me-not is the
  only flower that blooms
And memory becomes a lie, a falsehood
Twisted and cracked in an unfulfilled repose.[4]

These lines puzzle with their concentration, even while they haunt us with the sombre beauty common in Awoonor's poetry. The Christian cemetery evoked here is the theatre for many discussions and ruminations on death, but the poet has no doubt that his true resting-place is in 'the pagan colony' where he was born, where death does not break the continuity and communion with the living and the unborn. Hence the decayed angels in the Christian cemetery become the images through which the memory of that burial which severed boy and girl is seen as 'twisted and cracked in an unfulfilled repose', like the angels themselves. Awoonor, one feels, would applaud Becket's terrible pronouncement: 'They gave birth astride a grave',[5] but that grave has to be the very one which contains the cord of our origins, the cord which links us to the earth and our ancestors.

In 'Salvation' there is a dialogue which begins by questioning the nature of human salvation and gradually extends the inquiry to include the whole people who have followed false paths and false doctrines, neglecting the resolution of all their questing which awaited them in their birthplace and their own culture:

The funeral drums beat from the Eastern houses.
Where lies our salvation? You asked.
We do not need any salvation.
Does our end lie on this beginning shore?
We cannot stop the search and join the mourners. . . .
The sea you said talked to us,
The moon flakes on storm's horns shiver
With the tenderness of birth cords.
And in the season of search
When discoverers land on far off shores
And the others who took the big boats return
We shall find our salvation here on the shore asleep.[6]

This quotation shows clearly enough the freedom with which Awoonor achieves what he wants in English, writing in a long-breathed line which eschews both rhyme and metrical regularity. According to my reading, the number of strong stresses per line in this passage runs: 5; 2; 2; 2; 4; 3; 5; 2; 2; 4; 5; 5. This is a more important clue to Awoonor's English style than the counting of syllables, which will show an equal variability, ranging from seven to thirteen. This boldness speaks of a confidence derived, not from the orthodox English Literature course which Awoonor pursued at the University of Ghana in the 1950s, but from elsewhere. We shall not understand the strength of his verse unless we see it, as he did, as an extension into English of a Ewe poetic tradition which is not a mere subject of study, but the pulse of his being and the source of his poetic vocation.

This tradition is centred upon the funeral dirge, composed by professional poets (*heno*) but often performed by women. Two poets are particularly important in the formation of Awoonor's work, Akpalu and Ekpe, both of whom flourished in the years when he was growing up and beginning to practise his craft. Akpalu is pre-eminently the dirge-singer who draws attention away from the corpse to the fact of death itself, and from thence to his own death, childless and poverty-stricken, which will be infinitely sadder than the one he has come to celebrate. It is Awoonor himself who has drawn our attention to what he owes these poets; who has recorded, translated and annotated their works. Hence we are able to set these lines of Akpalu's beside a comparable passage from Awoonor's early poetry:

They put an evil firewood in my hearth
So I am all alone
No child to carry my sleeping mat.
And yet they say I must be mute.
I must not say it, I must not proclaim it.
Vinoko [Akpalu] says he is lost in thought
So all his songs are lamentations.
It is my own mother's children
Who placed an evil wood in my fireplace.[7]

In this dirge, Akpalu does not even begin, as he often does, with some general reflections upon death. He plunges straight into lamentations of his own lot, which symbolize society's exploitation of the poet.

Writing for the page, Awoonor has to find means of compensating for the absence of the performance situation in which the original dirge would be sung. Hence the stresses within his lines may be taken to correspond with drum-beats and may even, if the poem is read aloud, be underlined by single drum-taps. This is what the poet himself recommended when he first published the short poem called 'A Dirge',[8] with a footnote speaking of taps at 'one-second intervals', although this note was omitted when the poem reappeared in *Night of my Blood* (1971), in favour of one identifying Ashiaghor's house as that of Awoonor's mother's clan:

Tell them, tell it to them
That we the children of Ashiaghor's house
Went to hunt; when we returned
Our guns were pointing to the earth,
We cannot say it; someone say it for us,
Our tears cannot fall.
We have no mouths to say it with.
We took the canoe, the canoe with the sand load
They say the hippo cannot overturn.
My fathers, the hippo has overturned our canoe.
We come home
Our guns pointing to the earth
Our mother, our dear mother,
Where are our tears, where are our tears?
Give us mouth to say it, our mother.
We are on our knees to you
We are still on our knees.[9]

Pain and solemnity here are enhanced by the heavy mid-line pauses, the repetitions and the refrain: 'Our guns pointing to the earth'. In a traditional dirge that refrain might be repeated many times in a performance lasting far longer than this short poem. Such a use of the refrain is achieved by Awoonor in his later, longer poems which form the second half of *Night of my Blood*. In particular, the periodic refrain: 'Hush! I heard a bird cry' in the poem of that name contributes greatly to its unity and poignancy. Although Awoonor here still utilizes the imagery characteristic of the Ewe tradition (canoes, guns, funeral drums, the splash and moan of the sea, the rituals of death and rebirth), the experiences which lie behind the poetry, those of a highly educated poet living in American exile, are diverse and strange, when compared with those normally expressed in that tradition:

Hush! I heard a bird cry!

Look for a canoe for me
That I go home in it,
Look for it.
The lagoon waters are in storm   5
And the hippos are roaming

But I shall cross the river
And go beyond.

Where are the canoes?
I broke my paddle in the marshes   10
Mad dogs chased me
I left my cloth on the dunghill,
The fetish drums are beating from Ghost's Head.

And the priests are in trance.
My people, listen;   15
Listen, and I will sing a song of sorrow

My people and I went fishing
And met the evil god on the water.[10]

Awoonor still makes much use here of direct quotations from Akpalu and other poets: lines 5 to 8 and 15 to 18 can be identified as such, but he has moved a long way from his earliest published poems, 'Songs of Sorrow' and 'Song of War',[11] which were often straight translations of traditional poetry. Awoonor's closeness to that tradition enabled him to realize that such a practice would never be labelled within it as plagiarism; rather, it is the approved technique by which the poet learns his craft. Every *heno* has at least one assistant or apprentice, and Awoonor was functioning as such an apprentice in the new situation created by Western education of the young.

By the time he wrote *Rediscovery*, Awoonor had developed many of his poems around themes and situations entirely of his own. The irony of 'The Weaver Bird' or 'We have Found a New Land'; the personal loss expressed in 'The Return' or 'The Longest Journey'; and the reproaches against his alienated generation in 'What Song Shall We Sing?' or 'Easter Dawn' may stand as examples. But he could still make telling use of quotation in a new context, as in the lines which end 'The Years Behind':

my life's song falls low among alien peoples
whose songs are mingled with mine
and the tuneful-reverberate is reborn

reborn on the tabernacle of my father's temple.
Sew the old days for me, my fathers
sew them that I may wear them
for the feast that is coming
the feast of the new season that is coming.[12]

The last four lines here are such a quotation, but they take on entirely new reverberations because they are set within the life-experience of a modern poet who has to fight to retain his sense of traditional identity.

The long poems in *Night of my Blood* mark to some extent a return to the communal tradition of Ewe poetry, after the more personal and often romantic lyrics of *Rediscovery*. Awoonor returns in these poems to the mode of address ('My people, listen,' etc.) which comes naturally from a tradition where the poet actually addresses the assembled people, and exists as a poet only then. Both Akpalu and Awoonor use the funeral dirge as an occasion to make general reflections upon life, fortune, fate and the poet's métier; these, rather than the body actually lying at the wake, are the true subject of the poetry. It will be noted that Awoonor's lines are now shorter than those generally employed in *Rediscovery* (for example, in 'The Nim Trees in the Cemetery' or 'Salvation'), but the tempo indicated is still solemn and slow, quite unlike the impetuous energy which drives the short lines of Okot p'Bitek, for example. And this difference is perfectly appropriate to that which separates the dirge from the sort of wide-ranging, general entertainment song which Okot is creating. The following lines from 'I Heard a Bird Cry', which are an example of general reflection within the dirge, will show what I mean:

If you turn your neck
Look at the whole world
The heat and the restlessness
How drunken dogs are
Tramping precious things underfoot
And stray hyenas carry their loot
To the cleared patch in the forest,
Tears will gather in your eyes.
What has not happened before?[13]

Many of the poems in both *Rediscovery* and *Night of my Blood* (which republishes twenty of the thirty poems of the former volume) are difficult of interpretation, because Awoonor shows us only parts of the memories and experiences which unify them. With the exception of a few poems celebrating, albeit with a touch of irony, the hopes of the Nkrumah era in Ghana, such as 'March, Kind Comrade, Abreast Him' and 'What Song shall we Sing?', those memories and experiences centre around the years of growing in Keta and Wheta. The sea-music of the former mingles with the funeral drums of the canoes bearing the dead across the lagoon to Anyako, or with memories of hunting and bird-catching in the woods around his mother's village. In that village both his maternal uncle and grandfather were important priests of the traditional Ewe religion, whilst his mother and aunts knew all the cult songs and the famous dirges. His first cousin, Vedo, is also a well-known *heno*. It was the poet's father, a trader and traveller with ambitions for the boy, who represented that innovating spirit which tore him from the shrines, the sandy paths and the companions of home to embark on an education of which he resented both the colonial bent and the inculcation of an alien religion.

To understand all this better and return to the poems with a richer sense of their meaning, it is important to read them side by side with *This Earth, my Brother*, which appeared in the same year as *Night of my Blood* (1971). It is to be hoped that the American publisher's blurb to the novel: '. . . Africa is, in effect, indicted and proven guilty with no extenuating circumstances', will be taken as lightly as it deserves, for *This Earth, my Brother* is not a work which sets out to prove anyone or anything guilty, least of all Africa. Awoonor's task is rather to show that temperament and historical destiny can combine to produce a life which must seek the cyclic nature of death and rebirth sooner rather than later. In the conventional sense, there is no way forward for Amamu at the book's end (which is also its beginning). But the belief in the traditional African concept of rebirth which sustains it, and the insistence that Amamu's fate embraces that of Ghana, can be seen as an insistence that Africa can and must be reborn. The book does not offer us blue-prints for revolutionary action, such as a realist writer might provide; it works entirely by allegory and metaphor, and is in fact as much a poem as a novel.

Central to its action and, as one comes to see, to much of the poetry, is that child's death already referred to, which forced its hero to confront at a tender age the fact of loss, the inadequacy of the Christian teachings about it, and the promise within his own tradition of a richer and more meaningful view of death as part of the process of continuity and renewal. The watermaid who rises from the sea at the beginning and end of the novel embodies that promise of rebirth which the hero yearns for. His relations with all other women are dominated by that experience and, in the 'present' of the novel, his mistress Adisa seems temporarily to offer a connection with his watermaid. But, in such moments, it is not really Adisa that he sees, but the meaninglessness of temporal connections and entanglements.

Just after the first vision of the watermaid's emergence, the boy Amamu also sees the ritual funeral of a whale, cast up on the shore. This ceremony, common all along the Ghanaian coast, is not just a gesture of respect to the greatest of all created beings. The whale, cast up by the sea to those upon the shore, seems to be a covenant of their interdependence – a gift of the elements which must be acknowledged. It is also a manifestation of Dalosu, the god of thunder. Finally it is the tomb and womb from which Jonah was reborn. Alongside this passage of the novel (pages 7–8) we may set these lines from an early poem, which are too enigmatic when read alone:

The hot breath of wearied love
Changes its beat for the renewal
The research and perhaps the rediscovery.
I must go and wash myself in the salt lagoon
And change the cloths on my father's gods.
Then I can come and call you . . .

Return, my heart did return
To see the prostrate figure on the shore
Sprawled in messy majesty
Covered with tears, little glistening tears:
Dear one, hold on, for I come.[14]

This poem is almost a paraphrase of the equivalent lines at the beginning of the novel; but not every reader will have recognized, on first encountering them, either the watermaid whom the poet is promising to call or the whale sprawled on the beach. It is not only his closeness to an allusive poetic tradition which makes early Awoonor sometimes difficult of penetration; it is also his use of certain highly personal moments of vision which are there presented to us only in fragments. The novel enables us to fit most of these fragments together, to see how 'the hot breath of wearied love' can suddenly give place to the re-emergence of the watermaid.

Whilst it is important to remember that Amamu is not Awoonor, it is perhaps true to say that he has Awoonor's temperament and formative experience, but a different destiny. He has no creative outlet for a temperament which constantly demands it. His work, his marriage, his social life, his status as a 'big lawyer' – none of these offers him any real meaning for existence. It is the shell of life, not life itself, which he walks out of at the book's end to fulfil that promise of return: 'Dear one, hold on, for I come.'

The relationship between Amamu and his creator Awoonor is reflected in the way the novel has been constructed. It begins with the unnumbered chapter first referred to, where we start with a visit to Adisa and are then simultaneously on the beach of boyhood vision and in the insane asylum of the book's end. Then follow twelve numbered chapters, each written in two parts: the first part being an 'external' narrative – roughly chronological – of Amamu's life, told in the third person and in a colloquial style which is often satirical and sometimes funny; the second being a poetic reverie inside Amamu's head, which associates images, tags from the Bible, the Mass, Ewe poetry and other sources, with complete freedom across space and time. As the crisis in Amamu's life deepens, after his visit to Nima, these two modes come together into a single narrative stream, which flows through the short Chapters 13 to 15 that end the novel. In these last chapters we no longer inhabit the mind of Amamu. The narrative is entirely in the third person, describing both Amamu's pilgrimage back to Keta and the search for him by his friends and relatives. This search, of course, echoes that at the beginning of the book, when his family sought him for three days while he was wandering with his watermaid. And that search again echoes the ritual search for the dead which formed part of the pagan funeral ceremonies for Dede. In the same way, Amamu's crossing of the Volta River with his last coin, to enter Eweland, echoes the crossing of the river of death which is so often evoked in the funeral dirges:

The men I met have turned salt drowned in the river
Not even one grain can I pick up.
My boat has arrived upon the shore.[15] (Akpalu)

Since the numbering described above can scarcely be random, it can be no accident that the unnumbered chapter, added to the fifteen that follow, completes the perfect number sixteen. This is the number on which the whole Afa system of divination is based, and is thus probably the most important number in Ewe cosmological belief. The sixteen chapters have taken us from Amamu's conception in the womb, through parturition to birth ('the darkness deepens into light'), on through boyhood and schooling to the empty prime of lawyer Amamu in Accra, and finally back again to the visionary moment which annihilates time and restores the promise of rebirth. Amamu has already prefigured that final renunciation in Chapter 2a, which begins by evoking the millenarian hopes aroused by Ghana's independence in 1957 and 'the ceremony of oneness' it seemed to offer:

Bricks cement mortars pounding. A nation is building. Fart-filled respectable people toiling in moth-eaten files to continue where the colonialists and imperialists left off.

The poor are sleeping the sleep of the hungry under the nims. Benevolent one, thou who hast begged us with tears in your eyes and soot on your face, Follow my laws my children, follow my laws, for I am the one who brought you from the dust of degradation.

And he cast us back into degradation. With the rage of the elements and the dissonant cry of mortars from saladins he cast us into degradation. With the cry of Long live the Party, the Party is supreme, he cast us into degradation.

Woman, behold thy son; son behold thy mother. This revolting malevolence is thy mother. She begat thee from her womb after a pregnancy of a hundred and thirteen years. She begat thee after a long parturition she begat thee into her dust and you woke on the eighth day screaming on a dunghill.[16]

This passage presents the new nation as blasted from infancy, since it was begotten by colonialism (that 113 year parturition stretching from 1844–1957) and was unable to renounce that parentage. The effect of the fourth paragraph is to qualify the condemnation of Kwame Nkrumah and the CPP in the second and third. What hope is there, then, for a rebirth of Ghana which can match the one promised to Amamu by the vision of whale and watermaid? Immediately after these bitter thoughts Amamu reflects:

I am able by my own strength to renounce everything and then to find peace and repose in pain.[17]

Is an equivalent renunciation possible for the misbegotten nation? The name Amamu means: 'The man has fallen, do not help him to rise; if he rises, he rises against you.' If Amamu's career is allegorical, how are we to interpret it in terms of what Awoonor wishes for his nation? Perhaps the book would have benefited from more discussions of this issue in its realistic passages, for the work as a whole is so intensely introspective that the allegory remains somewhat undeveloped. Crudely, we might say that it is an appeal to Ghana to renounce the neo-colonial trappings and structures which tie her to a corrupted inheritance, and return to her true self. But that might involve returning a lot further back than 1844, by which date the slave trade, with its accompanying social and political effects, had been in full swing for three hundred years. It is true that the subtitle 'An allegorical tale of Africa' may be the American publisher's own, since it does not reappear in the English edition published by Heinemann in 1972, but the passage quoted above does clearly establish an allegorical connection between Amamu's birth and divided growth, and that of Ghana as a nation.

An additional problem is that Amamu is not quite situated as a fictional hero. However wearisome it becomes to him, the life-style in which we find him, complete with formal suits, aimless club conversations, conventional marriage and obsequious policemen, is diametrically opposed to Awoonor's own. On the other hand, many of his memories and experiences, whether in Keta, Oxford or Moscow, are clearly the author's. The picture we begin to construct of Amamu 'the big lawyer' after reading Chapter 2, scarcely fits with this rather ribald conversation, which is very much one between writers and Bohemian intellectuals:

Here we are drinking March in a glass of Teachers while our totems fall. . . . In my room we talked about the changes that must come, that Africa needs spiritual, psychological, mental revolution. Look at African education. Look at the moral decay that has engulfed our beloved homeland. Yes, Africa needs a revolution. Long live Africa. . . . There can be only one revolution. The permanent revolution. So said the Gambian Trotskyite who fled from Moscow when the Soviets were beating Africans in Sochi and Tashkent. And they say they have no colour bar. Hypocrites. All Communists are hypocrites, just like the capitalist hyenas! Long live Africa.[18]

As a way forward, this is not much help. No recognition that material conditions must change before there can be this, among other things, spiritual revolution. No recognition that Russia has, for whatever motives, consistently supported revolutionary movements and regimes in Africa, just as the West has consistently opposed or undermined them. If there is no help in the conversations, then we can only turn to images of future perfection such as this, from one of Amamu's reveries:

Someday, by some rivers, the elephant grass shall spawn food, the sands of the shore shall grow grain for the granaries to grind into our small pots that will cook for a whole nation to eat.[19]

When finally confronted with the brutalization of the poor, however, Amamu's reaction is to renounce everything, including life itself. But the class which he represents is not about to renounce anything. If their grip on affairs is to be loosened, it must be by other means.

These judgements may sound diminishing, but *This Earth, my Brother* lives by the real pain and anguish it distils, and by its evocation of an alternative African view of existence, even if it is not able to show us how this can be recovered for the present age. It will be fairest to close my account of the book with a passage which displays these qualities – the emergence of the infant Amamu from the spirit world of his first seven days on earth into the world of those 'ghosts' who inhabit our darkling plain:

Dark, dark the grave's darkness as ghosts walk in purple velvet provoking laughter from me by poking their finger in my armpits and saying I believe he laughs he laughs when he laughs his penis gets up we are sure he wants a woman we are sure he does want a woman. Clutching at globular breasts firm spring fountain nipples of raining milk cooing little goat little little goat your mother is not at home your father is not at home for whom are you crying.[20]

As it happens, another Ghanaian novel published a year earlier, provides an interesting comparison with this one. Ayi Kwei Armah's *Fragments* (1970) presents a general surface of naturalistic, fairly colloquial narrative and dialogue, but in structure and characterization it is as symbolic as Awoonor's. The hero, Onipa Baako (Only Person), is likewise a disillusioned 'been-to', but he is one who makes no compromise with Ghana's elitist expectations from the first. His 'watermaid' is the Puerto Rican doctor Juana, who is presented both as a 'healer' and as a goddess linked with the sea and the phases of the moon. The thirteen chapters of the novel correspond with the months of the lunar year. Both the first and last are titled 'Naana', presented as the name of Baako's blind grandmother, but really indicating a link with the ancestors in general. These framing chapters are written in a monologue of poetic reverie resembling Awoonor's 'a' chapters. In Chapter 1 she is preparing herself for Baako's return from overseas, for 'each thing that goes away returns and nothing in the end is lost'.[21] The last chapter finds her ready to rejoin the ancestors in death, conceived as a rebirth into the spirit world. In between, Baako's adventure of return has waxed up to Chapter 6, subtitled 'Gyefo' (Full Moon), where he and Juana make love in the sea, her element. Then it wanes to Chapter 11, 'Iwu' (Death) which depicts both the death of his sister's child, wantonly sacrificed to the family's materialism, and Baako's own descent into despair and madness. It also corresponds with the absence or eclipse of Juana, who has returned to Puerto Rico on vacation. Chapter 12, 'Obra' (Life), finds Juana returning to Africa and Baako apparently on the way to recovery. Armah thus seems to have made the lunar *year* correspond with the *monthly* cycle of its waxing and waning, which presides over Baako's state of mind. The whole structure is pre-figured in Baako's folk-tale (told to Juana on the beach) of a musician who loves a sea goddess and meets her 'at long, fixed intervals only'. These periodic meetings resemble Amamu's fleeting rediscoveries of his emergent watermaid and, like those, are specifically linked to the full moon. Both Ghanaian novelists seem to embody in more or less the same imagery the promise of regeneration from madness or death.

Armah's novel, like Awoonor's, appears to urge a return to the true spiritual values of his people, without taking account of those values being rooted in a way of life which has itself vanished. It is no acci-dent that his hero is named Onipa Baako, since he is throughout the only person in step with these values. The others are either sunk in corruption or, like Ocran, tired of the struggle. It may be expedient that one man should die for the people, but can any real change be achieved where there are so few points of light; so few aware of their own damnation? Also Armah, like Awoonor, cannot resist satirical attacks on highly identifiable individuals which are not germane to his purpose and weaken its tragic urgency. But his pain is as real as Awoonor's; his book is another highly original attempt to infuse fiction with some of the qualities of poetry. There is, for example, a complex use of colour symbolism, in addition to the symbolic naming and structuring already referred to. Both writers see contemporary Ghana as a dungheap, variously decorated with Awoonor's butterfly or Armah's *chichidodo* bird (*The Beautyful Ones are not yet Born*). A dungheap, however, is also compost for a new growth.

With the publication of these novels in the space of a few years, Ghana strode suddenly into the forefront of African fiction. The heady years 1957–66 had produced in Ghana almost nothing worth-while in the genre. The hangover of the ensuing years, with their repetitive coups and ever-mounting economic difficulties, has induced all the introspection and truth-seeking which made these books possible. In 1975 Awoonor published in the Nigerian journal *Okike* a fragment of a new novel, *Comes the Voyager at Last*, running to some 25 pages. It is hazardous to form any judgement of this new work on the basis of a single extract. One is struck at first by the startling change of tone from Awoonor's earlier prose. The first person narrator, whose character and circumstances bear a deepening resemblance to the author's own, adopts a swashbuckling, cynical and often facetious style. Much of the extract is taken up with a fairly crude satirical attack upon Ayi Kwei Armah, presumably in revenge for Armah's portrait of 'Asante-Smith' in *Fragments*. That attack was unfair, but a good deal more dextrous, and even decorous than this:

he came home, and with the help of friends got a job on the National Newspaper as a feature writer. They couldn't use anything he wrote because no-one understood it. His supporters said it was because he was actually a genius. . . . Everybody and everything at his newspaper was wrong. The Editor was a clot, a sycophantic nincompoop who didn't understand him. Even the members of his family who by natural instincts expected support from this Jason were evil because they had hoped for monthly hand-outs. Above all, Kwame Nkrumah and everybody connected with the Government were corrupt, evil-minded, mindless morons. . . . To cut a long story short, our friend went back to America the beautiful, the only country which he knew and loved. . . . I already gave you the titles of his books, real tough books which set out not only his hatred for everybody and everything – his country, his mother, and even those who secretly admired him, but also for himself.[22]

This is sad stuff! That 'evil-minded, mindless' doesn't improve the passage, even though Awoonor is trying to give an impression of garrulity. Later, the night-club scene which occupies most of the extract hots up, and there is a somewhat gratuitous attack by a black American on a party of whites, in which one of their African companions is actually killed. The African girls who accompany the whites are described as 'nubile and innocent', though there is presumably more evidence for the former than the latter. The narrator's one concern, anyway, is to get the assailant safely out of Accra. He now becomes less garrulous and much more like Awoonor, shedding his flippancy as he runs. With what he himself calls a sort of 'inevitability' they head eastwards towards his native village in Eweland. Hereabouts the flippancy is replaced by something dangerously like sentimentality. Altogether, the extract doesn't whet one's appetite for the new book in the way it should. The lapse of time since 1975 even suggests that Awoonor may have set it aside in favour of other work. As a work written in exile (Awoonor spent the years 1967–76 in Britain and America) it is perhaps less aware of the contradictions which will beset the traveller on his return to Africa. We may expect these to be one of the themes of Awoonor's future writing.

Another work of the exile years is the short collection of poems *Ride me, Memory* (1973). It is here that we encounter the influence of the *halo* (satiric) poet Ekpe, rather than the tragic genius of Akpalu. The eye which Awoonor casts about him in America is often either satiric or baneful. Confronting the reality of American experience with the movie images formed of it in childhood, the poet asks:

Where did they bury Geronimo,
heroic chieftain, lonely horseman of this apocalypse
who led his horsemen across the deserts of cholla

and emerald hills
in pursuit of despoilers,
half-starved immigrants
from a despoiled Europe?[23]

The same ironic tone, presenting a mirror to the country's face which shows, not an ad-man's glossy confection, but the visage which greets the black visitor, prevails through the first section of the book, 'American Profiles'. Roaming Harlem in a winter's dusk, the poet hears:

. . . the dark dirge of America . . .

mean alleyways of poverty
dispossession, early death
in jammed doorways, creaking elevators,
glaring defeat in the morning
of this beautiful beautiful America.[24]

After the brooding melancholy of *Night of my Blood*, published only two years earlier, this change of tone and technique is quite startling. It confirms the belief that most of the long poems in that book, including the passionate and moving elegy for Christopher Okigbo, were written or drafted in Africa, or soon after Awoonor's departure in 1967. Their melancholy is indigenous, home-grown as it were, and expresses itself in the refrains, repeated segments and returning themes which he took from the Ewe tradition, as developed by Akpalu. The main link with that tradition in the new volume is evident in the direct and vitriolic insults which Awoonor pours upon his victims in his 'Songs of Abuse'. Here is a typical example of his opening salvoes to his 'Uncle Jonathan':

Sir, you stink.
Your nose is covered in fifty ugly warts.
You are a hairy bastard without a father.
My father sent to tell me how you are walking my beaches
In Bermuda shorts, and cursing my sacred name,
You fucker of sheep and goats,
a pederast in bloomers,
a whiskered fool with an obscene mouth.
What wrong did I do you and you curse my name?[25]

Here, as with much African abuse poetry, what matters is not the accuracy of the epithets, but that they should overwhelm the opponents with superior violence or more deadly venom. Pope would have appreciated the idea more easily than most modern poets. Here for comparison is the opening of a song of abuse by Ekpe, in Awoonor's own translation:

Hm hm hm. Beware,
I will place a load on Kodzo's head. . . .
Kodzo, winding in the air, his anus agape
his face long and curved
like the lagoon egret's beak. . . .
He is the man from whom the wind runs,
the man who eats off the farm he hasn't planted;
His face bent like the evil hoe
on its handle.[26]

Despite its retrospective title and this link with the *halo* tradition of the Ewe, however, the volume, taken as a whole, is sharply contemporary in flavour. Its racy colloquialism and freedom of style mark a completely new departure in Awoonor's poetry. Intense reverie over a personal past and landscape is replaced by an eye alert for everything around him in a strange land where he is, as he ironically remarks, 'the token African on Faculty'. His satiric portraiture is more economic and more telling here than in the fiction, often pinning his victim with a single line, like a moth in a display case: 'He was the boss, this short creature of our pity now'.[27]

The contemporary flavour is even more pronounced in Awoonor's second volume published with the Greenfield Review Press in America, *The House by the Sea* (1978). The experiences central to this volume are those immediately preceding the poet's return to Ghana in 1975, the political crisis which led to his imprisonment in December of that year, and his twelve months of solitary confinement in Ussher Fort Prison, 'the house by the sea' of the ironical title. It is thus a sequence which broods over the meaning of exile and return, of tyranny and the perpetual struggle for freedom. The obsession with a particular place, past and culture as the gauge of authenticity is far less evident than in the earlier poetry; the only eruption of Akpalu and his characteristic images of mourning is the memorial poem specially addressed to him in the year of his death:

The lagoon, the mat
the eyes upon the earth
despair that none shall come
over the void
to stretch even the short rope
for you on your journey.[28]

But this proves to be no more than a point of departure for expressing Awoonor's very different destiny. Whereas Akpalu found all the materials for his tragic vision of life within twenty miles of his native Anyako, Awoonor's has to embrace a mid century awareness of suffering elsewhere. The matter of his song has extended far beyond the lagoons and beaches of Eweland:

For a song please vomit Blood
in Capetown, murder me Vorster
and Allende in Santiago
For a dance give me Christ Castro's
head since the Baptist died
of American bullets in Bolivia
Who said the work of man is not done.[29]

It is perhaps Pablo Neruda who best represents the kind of poet which Awoonor now seeks to become – one who is intensely national, yet able to take a global view of man's condition. It was his sojourn in Asia during the revolutionary 30s and 40s which helped to shape Neruda's vision. Awoonor's has been similarly shaped by exposure to the revolution in black expectations in the USA over the years of his stay there. This ability to interpret and exploit exile instead of making it merely a theme of complaint is what links the two poets, and Awoonor recognizes that link in the book's other memorial poem, 'For Pablo Neruda':

Your legs were there hombre
When Ugarte with his cohorts
slit the throat of Salvador Allende
in the name of American liberty

and you had to die.
Where are those liberating secrets
of Machu Picchu, tellurian man
and of the earth, your earth?
Where is viejo corazon, olvidado?

I await the secrets
I am part of you, hombre
part of the octopus of this undying liberty.[30]

That closing line may stand as representative of what is new in the themes and language of this volume. Awoonor's long-standing obsession with his watermaid and the sort of resolution she promises is glimpsed only once in the whole collection, in the long concluding poem 'The Wayfarer Comes Home' which invites a recapitulation of the themes he left behind in the Ghana of the middle sixties:

... once I thought I saw you
on the horizon in Texas or Louisiana
between Corpus Christi and Baton Rouge,
another time in a crowded train
between Tokyo and Hiroshima.
But you were another spirit
of another time and place
You were the tired salmon
after the torrent time of the river
But like the spirit
and the fish
You swam on upon your journey.
You remain the visible flame of youth
the interstices between birth and dying. . . .[31]

This poem, written in prison in September 1977, is like a reverie over Awoonor's whole career. Appropriately, it draws much of its imagery from tradition and from the landscapes and seascape of Anlo country. Although one of the finest things Awoonor has done, it is not really typical of the prison poems which form the second half of *The House by the Sea*. The majority of these accept, like much prison poetry, the narrow limits of what is offered by daily experience, but make it the material for an exploration more searching and profound than is likely when we are bombarded by all the sensations of a free-ranging existence. They are generally brief and epigrammatic, showing some influence from Oriental poetry, and making particular acknowledgement to Mao tse Tung:

Who are we here
but timekeepers in the house by the sea,
watching for the dawning sounds
the mildest inflection in the announcer's voice
We clutch our hopes like pebbles

scoured by infants
with eyes on the northern shore
as we trail behind the gulls
Only we do not see the beach
nor the shore.[32]

The irony here is that the poet's homecoming, so long projected, has
brought him within the sound but not the sight of his beloved
Atlantic. The sense of a suspension in time is well evoked (for the
prisoner the world stands still, not just his own dark corner of it),
but incarceration in Ussher Fort Prison might equally well have
called forth reflections on the circularity of time, which men outside
believe to be progressive. For this same fort has seen the victims of
colonial conquest in the nineteenth century; of the fight for independence in the twentieth; then of successive Ghanaian rulers, from
Kwame Nkrumah to Jerry Rawlings. Perhaps this more historical
irony is glanced at in another poem:

but there is stillness here
which is crammed full of bits
of history executioners heroes condemned men
on such a day
who would dare think of dying?[33]

The effect of the volume as a whole is one of concentration, a
rigorous selection of effect. Whereas in *Ride me, Memory* the
experience of America was generally enjoyed, here it is used. Its use
is to refine the mind towards the meaning of return. That return,
when it comes, proves to be one of confinement and the menace of
death, rather than one of freedom and opportunity. The effect can
only be a still greater concentration of effort and effect. The long
threnodies and slashing satires of Awoonor's earlier styles are left
behind. What remains is an impression of poetry which circles around
stillness.

Awoonor's talents as a satirist are also evident in one of the two
short plays which he contributed to a collection edited by Cosmo
Pieterse. 'Ancestral Power' is a brief dialogue between two villagers,
one of whom is simply a feed for the colourful boaster Akoto. The

latter claims that lightning has struck the household of his quarrelling wife's family, but it seems more probable that he has set fire to it:

I called my great grandfather Agorsor seven times by name. I said to him, 'If the fault lies with me punish me; if it lies with my enemies and your enemies, fire your gun.' Like it was from nowhere, a sharp report from an unexpected thunder rent the sky three times in the east, three times in the west, and once, only once, over Asiyo. That one had the sound of a royal gun at a funeral, and it lit and smashed in echoes. Then I knew my ancestor had spoken.[34]

The appearance of a police squad to arrest this ancestrally minded disputant puts an abrupt end to all his vaunting. Structurally, this little play is no more than a sketch, but it stands out by virtue of its humour and observation. The other play in the same collection, 'Lament' is a dramatization of Awoonor's poem in memory of Christopher Okigbo. Passages from that lament, spoken by a girl's voice, are alternated with passages from 'I Heard a Bird Cry' and certain other dirges, spoken by a young man and a very old one. The play was performed in this manner at its first production in the USA, with Kofi Awoonor as the old man. Since both the poems which compose the bulk of the text were originally written for dramatic recitation, their presentation in this form should prove highly effective. It brings out their unity of mood and difference of emphasis; for 'Lament of the Silent Sister' is specifically addressed to the death of one beloved friend and fellow-poet; whereas 'I Heard a Bird Cry' is more concerned with the human condition and appeals to Awoonor's countrymen to renew themselves at the founts of their own culture. But this matches precisely the range of concern found in the traditional dirge itself. The beautiful lines which use sexual imagery to evoke the challenge presented to the imagination by Okigbo's heroic death are even more effective in this setting, where the sister's lament alternates with those of the other voices:

GIRL   Into the bright evening I rushed
    Crying 'I have found him, I have found him'.
    He stood there rustling in the wind;
    The desire to go was written large upon his forehead.
    I was not ready for his coming,
    I was not ready for his loneliness,
    For his sad solitude against the rustling wind.
    I was not ready for his entrance
    Into my fields and the shores of my river;

The entrance of raffia was closed,
Closed against his lonely solitude.

YOUNG MAN   The gourd went to the river
And never returned, what will the young ones do?[35]

In 1975 Awoonor established a prominent place for himself among African literary critics with the publication of *The Breast of the Earth*, an ambitious survey of the history, culture and literature of Africa south of the Sahara. The most valuable and original parts of the book are those dealing with literature, and in particular with the relationship between oral literature and the work of certain modern poets who work in a conscious relationship to oral tradition. Chapter 7, entitled 'Oral Literature' is one of the most valuable contributions yet made by an African scholar, since it is informed by passion and practice, as well as knowledge. Even today, much of the discussion of poetry in African languages barely transcends the narrow world of linguistic conferences and their proceedings. It does not infringe upon the kind of audience for which the poetry was originally intended, nor upon the general reader who must now to some extent replace that audience. Awoonor's main precursor in discussing the aesthetics and emotional impact of oral poetry was Ulli Beier, whose anthologies of Yoruba and other African poetry vastly expanded the materials available for general readership. Awoonor's volume of translations and originals from the three Ewe poets Akpalu, Dunyo and Ekpe will perform a similar function. The chapter here referred to extends the discussion from Ewe poetic practice into Yoruba, Akan and Zulu. As a poet and critic, Awoonor has contributions of his own to make, even where his examples have already been discussed by specialists like Professor J. H. Nketia and Mazisi Kunene. Particularly important is his illustration of the role which the individuality of the poet plays, even in the development of a tradition which is communally possessed and publicly celebrated. Although his examples here are Ewe, the point is surely of general application:

Even though their work has full meaning only within the all-embracing scope of folk tradition, the individual genius and talent of the poets come into full play, contradicting the notion that performers are generally following rigidly laid down patterns in their art. . . . The dirge tradition . . . owes its development to the work of Vinoko Akpalu . . . Akpalu's dirge pattern is not very rigid; yet it utilizes certain recurrent forms which reveal a structural regularity.[36]

Equally important is Awoonor's discussion of his own poetic practice in the later chapter entitled 'Samples of English-speaking African Poetry', a rather clumsy description of what is in fact a thorough and acute analysis of several complete poems by Kunene, Okigbo and himself; though I find him unduly severe on Okigbo's *Siren Limits*. Of his own work, Awoonor writes:

Some of my earliest poetry was an attempt to take over from the dirge a series of segments or individual lines around which to create longer pieces that still express a close thematic and structural affinity with the original. . . . The translations from which I worked at the earlier period were unpolished and retain a crudity which reflects not only an incomplete grasp of the English language, but perhaps an effective rending [*sic*] of typically Ewe idioms into English.[37]

It is perfectly true that Awoonor's work down to and including *Rediscovery* contains occasional clumsinesses or unexpected inversions, but these, like many of Hardy's, tend to grow upon the ear with familiarity, by virtue of a certain rugged strength. An example would be these lines from 'Songs of Sorrow', which Awoonor goes on to discuss:

The affairs of this world are like the chameleon faeces
Into which I have stepped
When I clean it cannot go.[38]

The meaning of the third line is, I think, clear, and the original strength of the image seems to benefit from this literal translation of it.

Turning to his more ambitious 'I Heard a Bird Cry', Awoonor writes:

In 346 lines, I tried to capture a total mood of the Ewe lament, its stock images, its flow and direction, its ability to digress into other areas expressing, say, humor, and above all its persistent preoccupation with the human condition. . . . But the realization of this poem (it was written for both radio and stage performance) lies in the use to which the Ewe dirge music is put, serving as background to the voice. The poem . . . was first composed in Ewe and then translated into English. It contains snatches of oral verse as I knew it, but its power, I believe, rests in the way in which what may on the surface appear as fragmented pieces are united by thematic flow and by linguistic variability.[39]

The book contains many other passages of value, but it is marred by careless proof-reading, which extends even to some of the poems quoted (for example, Kunene's 'We count a million' comes out as 'We count missions'). There is also the problem, inescapable in surveys of this kind, that Awoonor is not as much at home with African history, art, music and language as he is on his own chosen territory. His section on art is both sketchy and often inaccurate, as when he describes the Nok terracottas as being 'about three thousand years old', which is one thousand years too much, or when he speaks of the classical Ife heads, remarkable for their formal purity and somewhat idealized naturalism, as being 'elaborate'. Rich as it is in overall insight, *The Breast of the Earth* might have been a better book with a narrower focus.

Despite the range of his achievements, it is safe to say that Awoonor's reputation is safest as a poet, where it rests not only on the development he has shown over the past twenty years but on the unique relationship he has established with his native poetic tradition. This has points of resemblance with what has been achieved elsewhere by Okot p'Bitek and Mazisi Kunene, but Awoonor's dirges owe their distinction to the sombre melodic qualities with which he instils the English language. The best pages of his criticism are those which are filled with the urgency of his own poetic practice.

Thiong'o

Born 1938 at Limuru in the Gikuyu Highlands. Ngugi's school days at Kikuyu High School coincided with the Mau-Mau War of Resistance which raged in the vicinity from 1952 to 1958. From there, Ngugi moved to Makerere Collage in Uganda, where he wrote his first two novels and many stories whilst an undergraduate in English. After a brief spell of journalism in Nairobi, he went to Leeds University in 1965 to take an MA and has since pursued an academic career, which soon led to the Chairmanship of Literature at Nairobi University. Since *A Grain of Wheat* appeared in 1967, Ngugi has been increasingly militant and controversial as a writer, which led to his imprisonment without trial for twelve months in 1977–8. Ngugi's work since his return to Kenya has established him as one of Africa's most important and original novelists.

12 Towards Uhuru

Few African writers have achieved a development as rapid and drastic as that of Ngugi wa Thiong'o in the half-dozen years 1961–7. In some respects, this development can be compared with that of Sembène Ousmane during the previous decade. Both writers start off with central characters who bear the main burden of the action and of the expectations of the community; who are in some sense considered as 'redeemers' of their people. In both cases these romantic–individual redeemers fail, though the blame for their failure may seem to be attributed to the community (or elements within it), rather than to the falsity of such messianic hopes. Perhaps inevitably, these redemptive heroes bear a striking resemblance to the characters and circumstances of their authors: Sembène's being self-taught men who have spent long years out of Africa, but in humble employments which have not severed them from the common people; Ngugi's being bright young lads who have been singled out by their family or their clan for a special education and upbringing which will, supposedly, enable them to lead their people out of division and cultural confusion. Sembène's Diaw Falla and Oumar Faye have already an idea of communal action (expressed in Diaw's unionism and Oumar's farming projects). But Diaw's yearning for a literary prize (awarded anyway, by white 'metropolitan' judges), is at variance with his political ideals; whilst Oumar always bears too much the air of an external agent of regeneration. By contrast, Ngugi's early hero Njoroge in *Weep not, Child* (1964) seems single-minded in his devotion to self-improvement through an educational system devised and administered by the very authorities who have subjugated his people. He is not entirely to be blamed for this devotion, but education pursued in this passionate way would probably have resulted in his absorption into the new urban elite rather than into some collective redemption of his people. His own family, including his guerilla brother Boro, also connects Western education with liberation, although it was men like Dedan Kimathi and Stanley Mathenge, of little formal education, who were truly liberating the mentality of their people through struggle and resistance.

Ngugi does, of course, register the sense of failure and defeat which attacks Njoroge at the novel's end, but it was not until he wrote the essays on culture which appeared in *Homecoming* (1972) that he was able to analyse the causes of that failure. The young Makerere undergraduate of 1962 who wrote *Weep not, Child* was too close to the achievement of reaching university for that sort of analysis to be possible then.

Weep not, Child, however, was not Ngugi's first novel in composition or in the sequence of his historical vision of Kenya's twentieth-century experience, which runs: *The River Between* (1965), *Weep not, Child* (1964), *A Grain of Wheat* (1967) and *Petals of Blood* (1977). In considering his first two novels, it is rewarding to look also at some of the short stories which were likewise products of his undergraduate years at Makerere College and which appeared for the first time in local magazines such as *Penpoint*. Several of these stories were later collected in *Secret Lives* (1975). Many of the early stories show a preoccupation with one of the favourite themes of Ngugi's fiction, the relationship of mothers and children. Although the expectation of children, and especially of sons, may seem to dominate the horizon of African husbands, it actually lies at the very core of existence of their wives. In traditional society, men had other ways of establishing their worth, though the production of sons was a sort of guarantee that these achievements would not perish. To a woman, however, this was virtually the only criterion of success or failure offered her in life. It is Ngugi's compassion for women in these early stories which prepares us for their transformational role in his later fiction. In the story 'Mugumo' a barren wife runs off into the forest to flee the intolerable burden of her fate, though a moment of revelation at the foot of the sacred fig-tree shows her that she is in fact already pregnant. In 'And the Rain Came Down' a likewise barren wife wins some prestige in her husband's eyes by rescuing the child of another woman from death in a tropical downpour. 'Gone With the Drought' tells of an old woman, despised and ridiculed in the village, whose sons have all been starved to death in the successive droughts which ravaged Gikuyuland and whose husband has died at a beer-drinking party, leaving her alone to be consumed by a sorrow as agonizing as the pangs of starvation itself. What all these relatively simple and underdeveloped stories have in common is an ability to enter completely into the tragic plight of a childless woman in a society which accords her no other avenue for her energies and abilities than those of raising a family. This empathy, unusual in a young writer eager to express his own situation, provides a counterpoint to Ngugi's identification with the romanticized heroes of his early novels: Waiyaki in *The River Between* and Njoroge in *Weep not, Child.* Ngugi's maturity as novelist, signalled in the publication of *A Grain of Wheat,* is partly the harmonizing of his romantic-individualism and its attendant search for messianic heroes, with the realism and compassion evident in his stories.

To find an example of the former, it is necessary to look no farther than the early pages of *The River Between,* where Ngugi describes his hero in these terms:

Waiyaki looked at the ground and felt small. Then he turned to the group and let his eyes fall on them. His eyes were large and rather liquid; sad and contemplative. But whenever he looked at someone, they seemed to burn bright. A light came from them, a light that appeared to pierce your body, seeing something beyond you, into your heart. Not a man knew what language the eyes spoke. Only, if the boy gazed at you, you had to obey.[1]

The context of passages such as these is a plot which may be expressed simply as the development of Waiyaki's messianic mission and its eventual failure. For the two opposed ridges of Kameno and Makuyu are nothing less than a microcosm of the whole situation in the Gikuyu* Highlands in the years 1910 to 1945. Any success in uniting them and harnessing their energies towards a single objective would have signified the cultural and political liberation of the people throughout the Highlands; the very people whose confidence and unity had been most undermined by expropriation, intensive missionary activity, white settlement, and the forcing of the menfolk towards wage employment in the cities or the settled areas.

Although Waiyaki is certainly not a portrait of the young Jomo Kenyatta, no one can read the novel without being aware of the parallels. For the prophecy of the famous seer Mugo wa Kibiru that 'salvation shall come from the hills' was commonly applied in the 1930s and 40s to Kenyatta, who became the subject of innumerable songs, hymns and invocations. Likewise, the highly educated Kenyatta, who had begun life as a boy at the Church of Scotland

*I have followed the example of Ngugi in shifting from the more common spelling 'Kikuyu' to this more correct form.

Mission in Gikuyu, was a moving force in the rejection of that Church's preaching against circumcision and in the setting up of the Gikuyu Independent Schools, complete with their own Teacher Training College at Githunguri. The work of the Kenya African Union, in the period 1946 to 1952 leading up to the Mau-Mau Insurrection, was specifically an attempt to unify pagan and Christian, traditionally-educated and mission-educated, in a single movement towards liberation. That attempt failed when the militancy of Mau-Mau drove most of the Christians into the colonial camp.

In addition, it must be remembered that during most of Ngugi's early years at Makerere College (1959–62) Kenyatta was a still untried political force who had been out of circulation for almost ten years, and who had become invested with the mantle of prophet and liberator of his people. Whatever the final judgement on Kenyatta's years of power from 1963 to 1978, years which saw Ngugi himself in deepening political alienation and finally in jail, we must remember that he was the focus of millenarian hopes both before and after his trial in 1952. *Facing Mount Kenya* (1938, reissued 1961), which had argued so passionately for the original integrity of Gikuyu culture and custom, had helped to form the consciousness of a whole generation of Kenyan students. The restrictions imposed by the colonial authorities on the entire people lumped together as the KEM Gikuyu, Embu and Meru) had only served to heighten their political consciousness in comparison with other students, and to deepen their identification with what Kenyatta and the KAU had stood for.

Waiyaki, then, is not Kenyatta; but Ngugi was certainly influenced in drawing his hero by the atmosphere of a time which still looked towards Kenyatta as a figure of messianic import. The British Governor who dubbed Kenyatta 'the leader to darkness and death' had precisely reversed the estimation he held in the minds of his people as the leader *out* of the darkness of subjugation and deprivation. The fundamental difference between Waiyaki and the Kenyatta model, however, is the former's total neglect of the political dimension of the struggle for liberation. Only at the last moment does Waiyaki recognize that his shibboleth of 'education' is not enough. As he tells Kinuthia on the eve of his own death:

I had not seen that the new awareness wanted expression at a political level. Education for an oppressed people is not all.[2]

The trouble lies deeper than this, however. Waiyaki never realizes that Western education, even when separated from the direct influence of the missions, cannot possibly serve the unity and purity of the tribe, which is his other declared objective. Such an education, in Kenya as elsewhere, stirs in the young a hunger for new styles of life which only the cities can satisfy. Malinovsky's anthropology seminars may have helped to inspire Kenyatta with a love and reverence for the ways of his people, but this is not commonly the effect of a few years of village schooling. As Ngugi himself later remarked:

Education was not an adequate answer to the hungry soul of the African masses because it emphasized the same Christian values that had refused to condemn (in fact helped) the exploitation of the African body and mind by the European colonizer.[3]

Waiyaki's ideas are in fact deeply imbued with Christian values, and the whole book resounds with biblical allusions. Witness his obsessive search for 'reconciliation', which totally ignores the impossibility of reconciling those who utterly reject tribal belief and custom with those who seek, with equal fanaticism, to uphold them. On what basis could such a reconciliation be effected? As the book ends, the time is near when the Christian adherents will join the ranks of the Home Guard to fight alongside the white man for the preservation of his rule. Later they will grow fat on lands confiscated from the forest fighters and transferred to them by a grateful government. Likewise, the bright boys from the secondary schools will show no enthusiasm for the forests. They will continue their studies outside Kenya and return, safely, to eat the best jobs vacated by the whites at the time of independence. Those who flocked to the forests and fought devotedly for years, in hunger and exposure, were predominantly young men of little or no education. For the schoolroom not only implants alien or urban values, but cultivates self-advancement and individualism at the expense of solidarity. Waiyaki is a chronic example of such individualism because, although he claims that he wants only to serve the tribe, he in fact wants to lead it in directions chosen by himself. He confides in no one and thus finds himself ever more isolated on both ridges. His desire to marry the Christian girl Nyambura is the climacteric of this romantic individualism.

If the historical Kenyatta is one of the models for the fictional Waiyaki, an even more important one is Christ. It is not enough to have a messiah; the book must offer us a martyred one as well. The inflation of Waiyaki's role reaches new heights as his involvement with Nyambura deepens:

Nyambura knew then that she could never be saved by Christ; that Christ who died could only be meaningful if Waiyaki was there for her to touch, for her to feel and to talk to. She could only be saved through Waiyaki. Waiyaki then was her Saviour, her black Messiah, the promised one who would come and lead her into the light.[4]

From here it is but a short step to the even more inflated notion of Waiyaki and Nyambura as sacrificial victims, though it is hard to see what their sacrifice can achieve, for Kameno and Makuyu (and with them all the Gikuyu Highlands) are by this time on a collision course. More blood must flow before there can be peace in the land:

She was kneeling down in a praying posture. He was fascinated. A kind of holy light seemed to emanate from her body. The place would for ever remain sacred to him. . . . When Waiyaki realized she was praying he was moved. It was very strange and as he watched he experienced a frightening sensation, as if he and she were together standing on an altar ready for sacrifice.[5]

Although specifically accused of treachery to his age-grade Waiyaki really dies* for his confusions and contradictions rather than for any specific offence, but he could plead posthumously that the fault was partly his father's. For the old man, just like Ezeulu in *Arrow of God*, does not understand that the white man's alleged 'wisdom' is not some detachable commodity which his son can snatch away from him unscathed; it is part and parcel of a certain view of the world, a certain scale of values, which tend subtly to adhere to that wisdom, like burrs on a golden fleece. When Chege tells his young son Waiyaki:

'Arise. Heed the prophecy. Go to the Mission place. Learn all the wisdom and all the secrets of the white man. But do not follow his vices. Be true to your people and the ancient rites.'[6]

he is giving him a more or less impossible assignment. Ngugi does register that impossibility, but his identification with the hero prevented him analysing it adequately. While the schoolchildren sing:

Father if you had many cattle and sheep
I would ask for a spear and shield,
But now –
I do not want a spear
I do not want a shield
I want the shield and spear of learning[7]

*His death at the end of the novel, though not described, is clearly implied.

others are already sharpening their weapons, convinced that it is through resistance and resistance alone that freedom will be found.

What, then, is the quality which best survives in this book, marred as it is by sentimentality and romantic inflation? It is, surely, the lyricism with which the landscape of the ridges is evoked in the opening pages, or when Waiyaki and his father gaze down upon it from the sacred hill. If Ngugi had allowed more scope to his descriptive skill and less to the confused thoughts of his hero and heroine, he would have produced a far stronger novel. Consider, for example, the classical simplicity of this passage at the end of Chapter 4:

The ridges were all flat below his small feet. To the east, the sun had already risen. It could now be seen clearly, a huge red ball of smouldering colours. Strands of yellowish-red thinned outwards from the glowing centre, diffusing into the thick grey that joined the land to the clouds. Far beyond, its tip hanging in the grey clouds, was Kerinyaga. Its snow-capped top glimmering slightly, revealing the seat of Murungu.[8]

Behind this passage there surely lies a vivid memory of the author's own youth, when perhaps he glimpsed the possibility of unity in a tribe which was already disintegrating and losing its sense of any common direction. But the direction chosen by his hero fell short of liberating either him or the people. Ngugi's second novel (though the first published) also offers us a young hero with a single-minded and uncritical passion for education, of the kind then available in Kenya. Like Waiyaki, Njoroge is encouraged in this passion by his own family, who seem to see in it a token of their own advancement, though its actual effect may well be to alienate the boy from home, clan and *riika*.

Whereas *The River Between* skips quickly over Waiyaki's schooling in order to concentrate on the image of the teacher, the black messiah from the hills, *Weep not, Child* is a novel of childhood. It is able to draw more directly on Ngugi's own biography, as his secondary schooling was conducted in the very midst of Kenya's war of independence, in a fenced and guarded compound at Gikuyu. Njoroge's dilemma, with brothers and relatives in the forest, whilst others have thrown in their lot with the white authorities, was Ngugi's own during those terrible years 1952 to 1958. The location of the novel is also recognizable as Limuru, the author's own birthplace. Limuru is close to Nairobi and on the edge of one of the areas of white settlement, whilst *The River Between* is set in the vaguely defined 'country of the ridges'. The opening pages of *Weep not, Child* actually refer to Waiyaki and his mission of pre-war days:

Once in the country of the ridges where the hills and the ridges lie together
like lions, a man rose. People thought he was the man who had been sent
to drive away the white man. But he was killed by wicked people because
he said people should stand together. . . .[9]

Finally, Njoroge's education, like Ngugi's, is throughout conducted
in missionary schools, and not in the Independent Schools with which
Waiyaki is associated.

At the very start of the novel, Njoroge exposes to the reader
(though not to his mother) his consuming thirst for education and
his association of this with self-advancement and wealth. He begins
his schooling with no lofty sense of a tribal mission or a prophecy to
be fulfilled:

'You won't bring shame to me by one day refusing to attend school?'
   '*O mother, I'll never bring shame to you. Just let me get there, just let me.*'
The vision of his childhood again opened before him. For a time he con-
templated the vision. He lived in it alone. It was just there, for himself; a
bright future. . . . Aloud he said, 'I like school.'[10]

A little later he reflects:

'. . . . you know, I think Jacobo is as rich as Mr Howlands because he got
education.'[11]

We are now in the short but decisive period between the end of the
Second World War in 1945 and the full outbreak of Kenya's own
War of Independence in 1952. In Burma, many black soldiers had
fought in the front line. They had learnt something of military
tactics, jungle warfare and weapon-handling, which could be joined
to what they knew of traditional African fighting methods. Some of
those who returned were mutilated or mad; others were bitter and
disillusioned, looking for a way to hit back at a colonial system
which had exploited and then rejected them. Njoroge's elder brother
Boro is one of these. Inured to battle and embittered by the death
of his brother Mwangi in the war, Boro does not really find his
vocation until the outbreak of violence enables him to become a
guerilla leader. But Ngugi somewhat falsifies Boro's character by
making him a simple instrument of vengeance. As the only Forest
Fighter we see at close quarters, he might have been shown as having
more of an idea of what he is fighting for, beyond the gut-reaction of
revenge.

In this novel, Ngugi has a tragic scheme of more than adequate
scope. The destruction of Ngotho and his family, as well as the deter-

ioration of the ironically close relationship between Howlands and Ngotho into murderous violence, are in no sense melodramatic. Such fates must have overtaken many families and many relationships in those years. It is when he concentrates starkly upon these events that Ngugi is at his best, avoiding his youthful penchant for sentimental love-scenes and improbably high-flown dialogue. But the Ngugi who wrote *Weep not, Child* in 1961–2 was a Christian humanist, not the militant socialist of later years. His hero is still incomplete without that reaching after a girl from 'the other side' which to him symbolizes reconciliation, but to the reader may suggest something more like social climbing. And once embarked on his love theme, Ngugi can lurch into writing as banal as this:

She wanted to sink in his arms and feel a man's strength around her weak body.[12]

Perhaps the average Gikuyu girl is a bit too tough for the taste of this aspiring hero. Njoroge would also be incomplete without that sense of a biblical destiny which overtakes him later in his school career and convinces him that after all it is not only self-improvement and wealth that he wants. In the midst of one of the encounters with the girl Mwihaki, he too is suddenly absorbed in messianic hopes:

For a time Njoroge forgot Mwihaki; he was lost in speculations about his vital role in the country. He remembered David rescuing a whole country from the curse of Goliath. . . . If the Gikuyu people had sinned, then he might be sent to them by God.[13]

The problem with Njoroge is that he is too imbued with missionary ideas to be able to distinguish whether the chief enemy is some theological sin or the colonialism and racism which are devastating his country and killing his people. The chief irony of the book, to which Ngugi gradually draws our attention, is that Njoroge's escapism and educational zeal blind him to the fact that his family is being destroyed. While he deludes himself with hopes of helping them in a brighter tomorrow, they are perishing in the here and now. Only the brutal eruption of the security police into his enclosed school-world awakens him, too late, to reality. And from a too glib optimism he then plunges into suicidal despair, reflecting that he is 'all alone in the world' at the very moment when his anxious and loving mothers are searching everywhere for him. Ngugi's writing is at its finest in these last few pages, where romantic individualism is finally cast aside.

The saddest character in the book is Ngotho, the confident husband and respected father who has been sustained through the years by his belief in the prophecy that the white man will leave the stolen land at last. Everything conspires to destroy that confidence, that respect and that belief. He does not survive to see even the qualified fulfilment of the prophecy brought by official Independence in the 1960s, when many white farms passed, not to their original occupiers, but to the new African bourgeoisie. Had Ngotho lived, he might well have found himself tending the tea-plants for Mr Howland's black successor. It is this knowledge which makes the sacrifices of the Mau-Mau period all the sadder today. A whole generation discovered its manhood in resistance, only to be cast aside by those who snatched power behind their backs. And this sleight of hand was presided over by the very man whose name had sustained them in battle and detention. Nor was the trend of political assassinations to ease off with the collapse of white power.

These are the bitter truths which begin to show their backs above the surface at the end of *Weep not, Child*, but which emerge fully into the light in Ngugi's third and perhaps finest novel, *A Grain of Wheat*. The young man, still under thirty, who wrote this book had travelled far in both political and literary sophistication since the Makerere days. For a few years he had put fiction aside, to concentrate first on journalism and then on his literary studies at Leeds. The two years in England seem to have embittered him personally; they certainly deepened his art and clarified his political beliefs. The distinction of *A Grain of Wheat* announces itself quite quickly. Ngugi has now moved away from the unilinear plots and identification with his heroes which characterized his early fiction. The new novel offers us no single hero, and is indeed critical of the whole popular cult of heroes, which always oversimplifies both motive and achievement. The novel therefore offers a complex surface which holds the reader at a certain distance and warns him to suspend judgement on its characters until more is known about them. This approach is entirely different from that of presenting us in the opening pages with an idealized protagonist whose adventures we are then invited to follow. Ngugi's wider reading is as evident in the structure and technique of this novel as is the political education he won for himself in the West. The novel opens a few days before Kenya's independence celebrations in December 1963. But it is uneasiness, not celebration, which prevails in the opening pages of the book, as we follow Mugo from his sleepless bed; through his disturbing encounter with Githua, who suddenly cries out 'the Emergency destroyed us'; to the night visit by a delegation from the Party which reduces him to panic and incoherence. No sooner do we leave the terrified Mugo to follow the departing delegation than we are involved in Gikonyo's restlessness, fear and numbed domestic unhappiness. The focus then shifts to the recently returned Forest Fighters, Lt Koinandu and General R. They too seem jumpy and insecure, uncertain of their status in the new Kenya for which they fought. Their search for the betrayer of Kihika years before is truly an irrelevance; the betrayal is going on all around them at that very moment, as those who stayed in the wings during the struggle step forward to occupy the seats of power.

By this time we perceive that the Emergency has in effect destroyed the old life and personality for all of them. A man does not return from six years of beating and interrogation in the desert unchanged; nor does one who has spent these same years in virtual isolation in the forest, unable to communicate with his loved ones without endangering them. Equally changed is a man like Karanja, who has choked his youthful idealism and comradeship to throw in his lot with the white man, confident that the latter will never surrender power. Lastly, the ridges themselves have changed. The confiscation of land from the fighters and detainees has enriched the collaborators and left them masters of a situation which they never envisaged; a situation where the trappings of power are being transferred to Africans, and where many settlers are selling up their farms and leaving Kenya. The scattered homesteads of the old ridges have gone and the enforced 'villagization' has come to stay. Those villages which lie close to the city are already beginning to take on an urban look, as Gikonyo discovers shortly after his release from detention, as he wanders down to the old Rung'ei Market:

The Indian shops had been moved into a new centre; the tall buildings were made of stones; electric lights and tarmac streets made the place appear as a slice of the big city. . . . He went on and came to the African shops in Rung'ei; they were all closed; tall grass and wild bush clambered around the walls of the rusty buildings and covered the ground that was once the market-place. Most of the buildings had battered walls with large gaping holes, smashed and splintered doors that stared at him – ruins that gave only hints of an earlier civilization. At the door of one building, Gikonyo picked up a broken plank; the fading letters on it, capitals, had lost their legs and hands; but after careful scrutiny he made out the word HOTEL . . . Gikonyo rushed out, afraid of the building, of ghost-ridden Rung'ei, and did not stop running until he entered the fields.[14]

As the novel progresses, we begin to realize that all this insecurity and fear are related not only to the uncertainties of the present but to certain events of the past which haunt and dominate the lives of the characters. With the exception of the martyred Kihika, whose record is closed by death, everyone has had thoughts or actions, secret from others, of which he is ashamed. Gikonyo is followed everywhere by the sound of the footsteps which led him to confession and early release; his wife Mumbi finds her love suffocated by guilt and the continual reminder of another man's child at her breast; Mugo lives in constant fear of exposure yet ironically enjoys the reputation of the local hero. Even Koinandu, who wears the mantle of the newly amnestied Freedom Fighter, is soon identified as the man who once delivered Dr Lynd into the hands of the rapists.

The real sources of the unease which fills New Thabai are uncovered for us in the long flashback which begins on page 78 and fills the whole centre of the novel. This structural device is extremely well handled by Ngugi, for it stems quite naturally from Gikonyo's resolve to unburden himself to the taciturn Mugo, and that resolve stems equally naturally from the condition of mind we have already discovered in him. But Ngugi wisely gives us only occasional snatches of Gikonyo's actual words, which serve as reminders that the 'present' of the novel is Mugo's hut on the eve of independence. The narrative and descriptive passages of the flashback, however, are all presented through the memory and consciousness of Gikonyo, as he painfully reconstructs the past. These include an incident at Yala detention camp which serves as a warning to the reader that the images we build of others may have little to do with reality. Gatu has been the popular clown and hero of the camp, yet he suddenly reveals to Gikonyo that he is a disappointed and embittered man whose old life was empty:

As soon as he had finished his story, Gatu stood up and walked away from Gikonyo. 'Weak, weak like any of us', Gikonyo murmured inside, filled with pity. Gatu had seemed so sure, so secure, so able to laugh at himself and others. Then Gikonyo's pity changed into hatred, so strong that he couldn't understand it. The two avoided one another for the rest of the day as if they were and knew they were, involved in common guilt.

Gikonyo never saw Gatu again. For, on the following day, the well-known oath administrator and spirit of the camp was found hanging against a wall of his own cell. Gloom fell on Yala. They never discussed him. . . . His name, he who had taken godhead into his hands and ended his life, was never mentioned in Yala detention camp.[15]

If Gikonyo cannot understand his sudden hatred of Gatu, perhaps we can. By revealing his own weakness, Gatu, who has represented to his fellow detainees the very soul of laughing resistance, has only exposed their weakness. Soon after this episode, Gikonyo goes through a crisis of despair which leads to his own confession of the oath. His yearning for Mumbi and home has undermined his resolve, yet he returns before his fellows to a Thabai which is utterly changed, and to Mumbi who seems so.

The first flashback, giving us glimpses of the early life of Gikonyo, Mumbi, Karanja and Kihika, is followed immediately by Mugo's visit to the teashop, which revives his life-long fantasy of himself as a kind of Moses sent to redeem someone or something (note how Ngugi has by this time devalued these messianic beliefs), culminating in his dream of all his Yala companions, and even the dreaded Thompson, yelling out 'Mugo save us'. This dream-cry seems to break in upon reality, as more and more members of the Thabai community make claims upon Mugo, either as a recipient of their complaints and confessions or as the surviving hero who will speak for Kihika and all those who died. Wherever he goes, these voices haunt him. On the way to his shamba, the crippled Githua has accosted him. Soon afterwards, he feels the impulse to enter the house of the old woman, mother of the slain Gitogo. On his return home, he is importuned by the Party delegation. Then Gikonyo burdens him with the story of his betrayal of the oath and his unhappy return to Mumbi. In the circumstances it is hardly surprising that Mugo's Mosaic fantasies are revived and that he sees himself, in particular, as the one who is sent to help the most wretched sufferers from the Emergency, such as Githua and the old woman. Only later do we learn that Githua is a charlatan and that the old woman consistently mistakes Mugo for the spirit of her dead son.

The pattern of confession has been established and it is now Mumbi's turn to unburden herself to the taciturn Mugo. She tells him what she has never, in four years, been able to tell her husband. The observation of human frailty is here as sharp as in the Gatu episode, for Mumbi finally yielded to Karanja in the very moment when he told her of her husband's impending release. His insistence that Gikonyo would never return was never enough to win her, but his bearing of the news that the lost one had begun the painful journey back through 'the pipeline' makes her weak with joy and mistaken gratitude.

Mugo, the supreme recipient of confessions, certainly doesn't invite them. His normal reaction to any human approach is to cry, 'What do you want of me?' It must be the visible smoulderings of his intense inner life, a life which in truth leaves him no time or interest for others, which makes him both a popular hero and a receiver of confidences. Even Kihika, in the extremity of his danger, has bestowed on Mugo a rare measure of confidence. Yet Mugo hates claims of this kind, which seem to make demands on his separateness and freedom to pursue his own way. His hatred of Kihika is as old as the moment of their youth (p. 19) when the young hot-head's eye met his and he felt his whole security threatened by the summons in that look. This first impulse of hatred was felt in that same Rung'ei Market where Kihika was later hanged.

And finally it is Mugo's turn to confess, when Mumbi visits him in the privacy of his hut to make one last appeal for him to lead the Uhuru celebrations. But Mugo's confession lacks the coherence of Gikonyo's or Mumbi's; it does not press for utterance, but is wrung out of him by his desperation and distress:

'Imagine all your life cannot sleep – so many fingers touching your flesh – eyes always watching in dark places – in corners – in the streets – in the fields – sleeping, waking, no rest – ah! Those eyes – cannot you for a minute, one minute, leave a man alone – I mean – let a man eat, drink, work – all of you, Kihika, Gikonyo – the old woman – that general – who sent you tonight? Who? Aah! Those eyes again – we shall see who is stronger – now – '[16]

Mugo's inpulse in extremity is to murder whatever oppresses him. He first felt this impulse with his drunken aunt; he felt it again (as we later learn) when Kihika not only sheltered in his hut but called on him to join the struggle; he feels it in the moment of confessing this deed to Mumbi and, for the last time, when he visits the old woman and kills, not with violence, but with joy. Thus we perceive that his betrayal of Kihika was no aberration, but the inevitable consequence of his wretched childhood and haunted character.

Mumbi is now in possession of Mugo's secret, but she also sees herself as the only agent who can possibly reconcile all those who are unable to shake off the afflictions of the past. Her care for Karanja's son is a token of her own ability to do so. As Kihika's sister, Gikonyo's wife, the mother of Karanja's child and the confessor of Mugo, she sees her way clearly – perhaps the only one of the characters who can. She must save Karanja and she must guard Mugo's secret. Events overtake her, but her imminent reconciliation with Gikonyo at the book's end is at least something retrieved from the wreckage of the past.

The device of the race on Uhuru Day is a brilliant one for drawing all these threads together. Mugo's public confession, like his earlier protection of the beaten Wambuku and his endurance in the camps, proves that he is better as well as worse than the run of his fellows. Through his confession and his death he may, it is to be hoped, purge the guilt which is shared to some extent by all the characters.

A Grain of Wheat is the work of a declared socialist, yet it is still a deeply religious novel. Ngugi's socialism is evident in his condemnation of the society which will emerge from the Uhuru of 1963, a society already delineated in the MP who boycotts the Rung'ei ceremonies and filches the farm which was destined for local, co-operative ownership. His religious concern, though no longer dominant, is evident in the way that all his characters are brought to a spiritual crisis, are forced to confront their own failures and their own weakness. Henceforth they must live with what they are, and not with what they have seemed in the eyes of others.

The mastery of construction in this book is matched by Ngugi's far deeper insight into human behaviour. Even the brutal Thompson emerges as a kind of frustrated idealist. An earlier sketch of his character and his relationship with his wife can be found in the short story 'Good-bye Africa',[17] but Thompson's course through East African history is far more carefully plotted here, and Margery's affair with the drunken Dr van Dyke is far less predictable than the somewhat cliché-ridden involvement of the earlier woman with her shamba-boy. The language of *A Grain of Wheat* also breaks away from the sometimes excessive brevity of Ngugi's earlier, more lyrical style, evident in a passage like the following from *The River Between*:

And Waiyaki was pleased to see her. He had not set eyes on her since that night. And there she now stood, quiet and rather reserved. She did not appear as she had in the moonlight. But he could see that she was beautiful. He approached her hesitantly, his heart beating. She smiled.[18]

We may compare this with the way Karanja's premonitory vision at Rung'ei station is described:

Karanja was frightened by this absolute cessation of all motion and noise and he looked about him to confirm the truth of what he saw. But nothing had stopped. Everybody was running away as if he feared the ground beneath his feet would collapse. They ran in every direction; men trampled on women; mothers forgot their children; the lame and weak were abandoned on the platform. . . . Karanja braced himself for the struggle, the fight to live. I must clear out of this place, he told himself, without moving.[19]

In the limpid language of the first passage, everything is what it seems to the lovesick Waiyaki, and the reader is encouraged to accept it as such. In the second passage, this simple version of reality dissolves (as it often does in *A Grain of Wheat*) and gives place to writing which shows us simultaneously what is happening inside the characters and, objectively, outside them. Such writing discourages us from making hasty judgements or identifications. We must see the whole before we can truly see the parts.

Ngugi's new style also makes much more copious use of Gikuyu words and phrases, often without translation. He frequently addresses the reader as a fellow Kenyan, with sentences which begin with phrases like 'Do you remember when such-and-such-happened?' Songs also become a rich and indispensable part of the novel's texture.

A Grain of Wheat is a tragic novel which bears the burden of Kenya's suffering and hope in those years, culminating in the question-mark of Uhuru. Will the new order truly be such, truly break and remake the social and economic system created by white and Asian colonialism? By the time Ngugi wrote the novel, he knew the answer to those questions, but he restrains that knowledge (except in the epigraph) and shows us only what his characters could *then* know. Hence the novel is able to end on a note of measured hope. Gikonyo's reconciliation with Mumbi may stand as a symbol of that between those who suffered in detention and those who suffered at home. The bearing of a new child will give substance to that bond. But if the wounds can heal, the scars remain. The prevailing tone of the book remains sorrowful and grave, nowhere more so than in the beautiful songs which Ngugi translates for us:

And he jumped into the trench,
The words he told the soldier pierced my heart like a spear;
You will not beat the woman, he said,
You will not beat a pregnant woman, he told the soldier.
Work stood still in the trench
The earth too was silent,
When they took him away
Tears, red as blood, trickled down my face.[20]

There has been much speculation about Ngugi's possible debt to Conrad's *Under Western Eyes*, which concerns a hero, Razumov, somewhat similar to Mugo, whose concentration on lifting himself from poverty and obscurity makes him bitterly resent any claims upon him by causes or individuals. Like Mugo, too, his aloofness is mistaken by revolutionary colleagues as evidence of his austers dedication to the cause. Razumov, too, is visited by the young revolutionary hero Haldin immediately after a daring assassination; and Haldin, who scarcely knows him, expresses the same faith in his taciturn, unwilling host as Kihika does. The martyred Haldin, betrayed to the police by Razumov, is survived by a romantically minded sister who believes that Razumov was his greatest friend. So Razumov, wearing this borrowed mantle, is sent by the Tsarist police to penetrate the *émigré* revolutionary circles and is not unmasked until the very end of the book. The reader, however, knows his real character from the first.

So far, the resemblances are too strong to be purely coincidental. But Conrad's book is a rather cold, though brilliant affair. His deep dislike of revolutionary politics, especially of the *émigré* variety, still does not enable him to make Razumov anything but a thoroughly unpleasant young man. His egotism is no foil to the generous enthusiasm and courage of Haldin or his sister, even if we now believe them to have been mistaken. There is none of Ngugi's warmth, deep compassion and political conviction. *Under Western Eyes* is a kind of intellectual thriller, which lacks the tragic sweep or complexity of Conrad's own *Nostromo*, for example. What Ngugi has contributed to *A Grain of Wheat* is incomparably more important than what he has probably taken from Conrad. If the theme of betrayal in the two novels bears a certain resemblance, the structure of Ngugi's, with its pattern of confessions and recapitulations as the whole society moves towards Uhuru, is entirely different. There is thus no call to regard the comparison as some deep insult to African literature. A good novelist learns from the masters, as well as from his own experience with the pen.

The progression from *A Grain of Wheat* to *Petals of Blood* is precisely along the line of complexity in structure and depth in time which Ngugi had already explored in the earlier book. In the prefatory note to *Homecoming*, Ngugi had declared his faith:

Literature does not grow or develop in a vacuum; it is given impetus, shape, direction and even area of concern by social, political and economic forces in a particular society. The relationship between creative literature and these other forces cannot be ignored, especially in Africa, where modern literature has grown against the gory background of European imperialism and its changing manifestations: slavery, colonialism and neo-colonialism.[21]

The historicism implicit in this statement makes Ngugi intent on showing that process of change in the whole texture of society during the course of his novel. But just as George Eliot achieves this in *Middlemarch* whilst scarcely stirring beyond the boundaries of one small provincial town, Ngugi does the same by making the remote village of Ilmorog into a mirror through which we see what is afoot in the whole theatre of modern Kenya. Again, as in the preceding novel, we have an integrated structure which does not reveal itself in entirety until the book is finished. Ngugi has borrowed from the detective thriller in building this structure. The first pages of the novel show the arrest of its four principal characters in connection with an unsolved crime, the burning to death of the African directors of the local brewery. The story then jumps back to the first arrival of Munira, the puritanical headmaster, in Ilmorog, some twelve years before. It retells his first encounters with the other three protagonists: the storekeeper Abdulla, the mysterious 'free woman' Wanja and the young teacher Karega.

The unravelling of what exactly happened on the night of the fire, which takes the form of a remorseless interrogation of Munira by the detective in charge of the case, also exposes the entangled threads of relationship between the four characters, and sets this against the changes which these twelve years have wrought in the life of Ilmorog. From a dusty village centre for nomadic pastoralists and local peasantry, the place has gradually changed into an industrial town, adjoining the new Trans-Africa Highway. But, significantly, its major industry is a partly foreign-owned brewery making an adulterated beer, which has driven out the local brew for which Ilmorog was once famous. The changes in its life have done little to enrich its old inhabitants, but much to advance the new 'comprador' capitalists from Nairobi. Abdulla has been ruined along with his liquor business, whereas Wanja's one chance of real happiness as Karega's wife has been destroyed by Munira's jealousy, and she has ended up as a fashionable 'Madam' catering for the sexual needs of the new bourgeoisie.

The detective thus unravels for us far more than the story of a crime. He shows us the changing anatomy of Kenya in the twelve years following Uhuru. The hopes of 1963 for a meaningful liberation of the people on which *A Grain of Wheat* made a muted close, have not been realized. The idealism which once brought Munira to Ilmorog has turned sour; Wanja's search for freedom and happiness outside the Highlands has brought her neither; Karega's radicalism has been driven towards open revolt by a society whose structures cannot accommodate it; lastly, the old Mau-Mau warrior Abdulla, already crippled in the fight for freedom, has now been ruined as well. It is the sleek, prosperous directors, for whom Ilmorog means a Country Club hideout away from their wives in Nairobi, who represent the New Kenya for which these four have striven in vain. We learn, too, how the lives of these four refugees from the Limuru area have repeatedly and disastrously crossed with those of the three dead directors, who hail from the same region. It has been the role of Chui, Kimeria and Mzigo to frustrate or turn aside every true initiative, every life-assertion, of which the four protagonists were variously capable.

Although the basic structure here is similar to that of *A Grain of Wheat*, the new novel is much grander, more gradual and more complex in the unfolding of everything which has intervened between Munira's first arrival in Ilmorog and the murder of the three directors twelve years later. This is because we do not get a few big set-pieces of confession between the characters, like those of Gikonyo, Mumbi and Mugo, but numerous confessional scenes where they fill in one or two missing details or episodes. Not until the last page is the grand design complete. And by that time we have understood the formation and development of the four protagonists, right back to their grandparents' generation. We have seen the complex of motives, declared and undeclared, which first drove them to Ilmorog and which drove them to return again and again.

Through Nyakinyua, who becomes in a sense the mother of the whole community, we are linked also with the origins of Ilmorog itself and with its semi-legendary founder Ndemi. For Ndemi was the first cultivator in a community of nomadic herdsmen. His Ilmorog was a flourishing centre of farming and trade until the military conquest by the invading whites, which left a thousand braves on the battlefield. Thenceforth trade and development flowed elsewhere, while Ilmorog was left to decline through one drought after another. Nyakinyua is thus given a deeper dimension in African history than would be justified by strictly naturalistic standards; both she and the elusive seer Mugo extend into the mists of antiquity, linking us with the whole perspective of pre-colonial Africa. Nyakinyua's death and Mugo's disappearance symbolize the irrevocable end of Old Ilmorog. This device can be compared with the legendary air which surrounds the early years of Mor-Zamba and Abena in Beti's *Remember Ruben*.

The novel is organized in <u>four big movements, which</u> correspond with major <u>changes</u> in the characters of the protagonists. The first movement, <u>Walking</u>, shows us the first arrival of Munira as headmaster of the <s>village</s> school. Abdulla is already installed as keeper of the local store and bar, where he is soon joined by Nyakinyua's grand-daughter Wanja. Last to come is the young Karega who, like Munira in the earlier generation, has been dismissed from Siriana High School after a strike. This common experience places Karega almost in the situation of a son towards Munira, but his first visit lasts only a few hours and ends as mysteriously as it began.

At this point Abdulla has exposed almost nothing of his past or of his heroic potentiality. Wanja too has kept quiet about her search for a child and a relationship to replace her one-night involvements as a bar-girl, but her choice of Munira as a lover is doomed to failure, because he is a man in flight from the challenge of life and the failure of his own marriage:

There was . . . something soft and subdued and beautiful about Ilmorog ridge between the hour of the sun's death and the hour of darkness. . . . Standing anywhere on the ridge one could catch sight of the sun delicately resting on the tip of the distant hills which marked the far end of the grazing plains. Then suddenly the sun would slip behind the hills, blazing out a coppery hue with arrows of fire shot in every direction. Soon after, darkness and mystery would descend on the plains and hills. . . . Munira relished twilight as a prelude to that awesome shadow. He looked forward to the unwilled immersion into darkness. He would then be part of everything: the plants, animals, people, huts, without consciously choosing the links. To choose involved effort, decision, preference of one possibility, and this could be painful. He had chosen not to choose, a freedom he daily celebrated, walking between his house, Abdulla's place and of course Wanja's house.[22]

But Wanja and Karega, having entirely failed to find in Ilmorog what they are looking for, have already returned to the Highlands whence they came (for Wanja, although of Ilmorog origin, was not raised there). Munira goes to Limuru, lured into the obscene ritual of an oath to protect the property of the few Gikuyu 'haves' from 'the envy of other tribes'. His disgust at this betrayal completes his alienation from his wife and his father. Wanja and Karega have also recently met experiences full of terror and the fear of annihilation. <u>The three journey back to Ilmorog together, sharing an old bicycle</u>:

They returned to Ilmorog, this time driven neither by idealism nor the search for a personal cure but by an overriding necessity for escape.[23]

But they find the village sunk more than ever in drought, poverty and neglect. There can be no escape here, unless something can be done to save the community. The same trio, strengthened by the addition of Abdulla, his donkey-cart and a few 'genuine' Ilmorogians like Nyakinyua, are soon on their way south again, in search of help from the new powers of the land.

This journey of redemption, which forms the second movement of the novel, 'Towards Bethlehem', is deliberately invested with an epic atmosphere. Abdulla now emerges as a figure of valour and skill, the reincarnation of Kenya's ancient warriors, whilst Nyakinyua becomes the bard and storyteller of the group. The events of the journey to the city take on a fabulous character even while they occur, and soon afterwards retreat into legend; they become part of Ilmorog's heroic tradition. But the arrival in Nairobi, after so much sacrifice and endurance, sparks off a series of melodramatic encounters with figures of corruption and evil, such as the canting priest Jerrod Brown and Wanja's former seducer Kimeria. Is it a necessary part of the developing epic tradition in African fiction that it must erect cardboard 'baddies' who are never anything but bad? Is this not in conflict with the compassion and understanding with which the 'good' are handled in the same fiction, which depicts their blunders, weaknesses and false choices of direction? The same tendency to construct highly predictable figures of evil, helpless to change their fate because it is their very nature, can be found in other epic novels, such as Armah's *Two Thousand Seasons*. But it is avoided in Sembène's major novels and in Beti's *Remember Ruben*, where Joseph, for example, is depicted in a way which exposes everything that Beti admires in him, yet is not ultimately anything but a parasite on colonial enterprise. If it is a concern of such fiction to show us how ordinary people can change and grow under the challenge of extraordinary circumstances, then the difference between those who change positively, and those who don't, cannot be the difference between chalk and cheese. The defence for such a treatment may be that formulated by Soyinka for *Two Thousand Seasons*; that

The secular vision in African creative writing is particularly aggressive wherever it combines the recreation of a pre-colonial African world-view with eliciting its transposable elements into a modern potential.[24]

Soyinka's description of Armah's vision as 'secular and humane' is perhaps even more applicable to *Petals of Blood*. But what is objected to in the Nairobi encounters with Kimeria, Jerrod Brown or Wanja's

American businessman is a certain melodramatic quality, more appropriate to a James Bond movie than to a fiction which is, on the whole, realistic in texture, though epic in scale.

There is, in any event, no redemption for Ilmorog to be found in Nairobi, though the lawyer does provide a gleam of light and the sort of intellectual challenge that Karega needs for his own development. Empty of hope, the little party returns to skies still empty of rain. All seems lost, and yet their effort has somehow changed the direction of Ilmorog's fate. As we move into the third section, 'To Be Born', the rains begin to fall, an excellent harvest is gathered and a new age-grade is initiated amidst a revival of all the ancient songs and dances. Furthermore, Nyakinyua brews the ritual drink Theng'eta, which was long ago banned by the whites and has been almost forgotten. The scenes of its gradual fermentation, against the mounting excitement of the circumcision ceremonies, produce the most sustained lyrical writing in the book, culminating in the splendid exchange of ribaldry between Nyakinyua and Njuguma. Then comes the tasting of the brew itself. Under its influence, all the main characters reveal long stretches of their hidden lives. But in the narrow spirit of Munira, still unable to shake off his father's Calvinism, these sessions produce a crisis of jealousy rather than the wished-for purgation. For, amidst these scenes of renewed life and hope, Wanja and Karega have discovered one another. Wanja glimpses at last the prospect of fulfilling her life as woman rather than, as she puts it, her life as 'cunt'. But Munira is unable to endure the knowledge that Karega has been the lover of both Wanja and of his dead sister Mukami; he arranges Karega's dismissal and this single blow at Ilmorog's new harmony and fruition seems to presage, if it does not precipitate, the blasting of that renewal. A plane falls out of the sky, killing Abdulla's 'other leg' and, with it, the links with the heroic journey to the city. The long arm of Nairobi's bourgeoisie is reaching out, and Old Ilmorog begins its gradual death in the grip of the new town spawned by capitalism, loans and 'improvement'. The last words of 'To be Born' are ominous:

the biggest talking point was not so much the plane, or the crowds of visitors, or the sudden boost in the sales of food and drinks – but the death of Abdulla's donkey, the sole victim of the plane crash, and the departure of Karega from Ilmorog.[25]

For it is important to recognize that the rise of New Ilmorog, which fills the fourth movement of the novel, is not a continuation but a denial of the resurrection just achieved. It is not based in the efforts and renewed culture of the people themselves, working in alliance with nature, but in the machinations of distant businessmen who seek to create wealth for themselves out of Ilmorog's poverty. The peasantry are soon dispossessed, or gradually ruined by loans they cannot repay. Even the brief prosperity of Wanja and Abdulla in their bar and night-club is sick at the root, since it is based on the brewing of Theng'eta as a routine soporific, rather than the ritual drink of sacred occasions. Truly, Abdulla's donkey is not the only victim of the plane crash, for the plane was the herald of the new men who soon put Ilmorog and its people into their pockets. The death of Nyakinyua, already threatened with eviction from her ancestral land by banks and mortgage companies, is the death of Old Ilmorog itself. Its living link with the ancestors has been snapped. Hence it is not really a reversal of fate when Wanja's brewing rights are taken away in favour of the new brewery owned by foreign and city interests, and she turns all her despised talents into a new career as a brothel-keeper; whilst Abdulla lapses into querulous poverty. It is a logical consequence of all that happened to Ilmorog's hopes when Munira cycled to Ruwa'ini and the plane fell from the sky.

But if Munira is partly the author of Ilmorog's ruin, it is he who finally emerges as the hero-figure of the quartet. Wanja and Abdulla have already 'peaked' in their development, whilst Karega's fulfilment lies in a future of radical political action. Munira, who has been looking all his life for the Devil in everything, has finally located it in Wanja's corruption and her threat to Karega's virtue. It does not finally matter that he is mistaken in thinking Karega in any danger from that quarter; for the first time in his life he acts, decisively and alone, and thus ceases forever to be a spectator. He, who seemed to have least motive, is the author of the fire. It is true that his crisis coincides with a rather similar one in the lives of the others: Abdulla has irrevocably decided to kill Kimeria that very night; Wanja has already struck him down before the flames engulf him; and Karega has decided to damn the consequences of an all-out fight with the directors of the brewery. Still it is Munira, whose consciousness has dominated the entire narrative (since much of it is told through his recollections in the police cell), whose act eclipses them all and finally places him at the centre of attention. It is there that the mysterious girl of the final pages finds him with her message of hope. Twelve years earlier, he reacted with typical fear and insecurity when a pupil, finding a beautiful flower (was it Theng'eta?), cried out 'petals of blood! petals of blood!' At the end, he climbs calmly up Ilmorog Hill to watch these same petals, the flames of his desire, consume his enemies.

In this majestic novel, whose complexity demands a careful and perhaps double reading, Ngugi has used all his resources to link the art of fiction with the traditional arts of his people. The texture of the book is full of song, story and saga. Everything is seen at a certain distance, for although we are kept guessing to the end, we still perceive more than the actors individually can. We see an emerging pattern, while they often see only a confusion of events. Occasional bigotry sinks into insignificance against the scale of imaginative achievement here. It is possible that Ngugi's last two novels form the most impressive and original achievement yet in African fiction.

The Kenyan authorities put a brave face upon the publication of *Petals of Blood*, even giving it an official blessing. But Ngugi went on to write a play in Gikuyu about the struggle of the workers at the Bata shoe factory in Limuru, scene of many a bloody strike right back to colonial days. It was this attempt to bring his vision home to the hearts of the people which seems to have precipitated his arrest and his twelve months of solitary confinement. Like Soyinka and Sembène, Ngugi does not merely profess commitment; he is prepared to live it with all its consequences.

The first steps towards that Gikuyu play were taken the year before with the publication and triumphal performance of *The Trial of Dedan Kimathi*. Written jointly with Micere Mugo, this play was performed to packed houses in Nairobi before being sent to Lagos as one of Kenya's official entries for Festac 1977. The play does not attempt to reproduce the actual trial of Kimathi in 1956, which was a sorry and cursory affair, inflicted on a wounded man who had effectively been condemned to death even before he was betrayed and captured. It is not a 'courtroom drama', but a series of imaginary scenes which present, in the Brechtian manner of epic theatre, a series of trials upon Kimathi's courage and will. Shaw Henderson, the police officer who hunted him down with the aid of informers, alternatively cajoles and threatens Kimathi, wanting him to write 'surrender' letters to the other leaders, including Stanley Mathenge, who are still at large. The sleek black businessmen assure him that 'the struggle is over', since they are now in a position to buy up white houses and plantations in the formerly reserved Highlands. And, in a flashback to his last forest hideout, some of his own followers are detected in secret negotiations with the enemy. These last include his younger and only surviving brother Wambararia. Their mother has already gone mad in her terror of seeing Kimathi preside over the execution of his own brother. Here the play strikes its only false note, for the authors seem to endorse the views of the Woman, that there are only 'brothers in the struggle' and that kinship should count for nothing now:

WOMAN What is this superstition about
    Kindred blood even when it
    turns sour and treacherous
    to our long cherished cause?
    My clansman, my kinsman,
    My brother, my sister.
    If these are of my house
    Let them honour
    the oath of unity
    Let them uphold
    the struggle for liberation.[26]

This may be correct revolutionary rhetoric, but it is bad politics and loathsome to humanity. It is too reminiscent of those Nazi and Stalinist incitements of schoolchildren to betray their own parents for insufficient party zeal. Kimathi was a good enough leader to know that some traditional African pieties were necessary to the struggle, and of these none is more sacred than the life of a blood brother. Most readers will feel that Kimathi's decision for mercy is the right one, even if it finally leads to his betrayal. To have decided otherwise would have weakened the cause by destroying its conscience and turning its leader into a fearful, remorseless figure.

As usual with plays in the epic tradition, characters are presented as types rather than as individuals. They are spokesmen for particular attitudes and thus lack the subtleties and contradictions of ordinary mortals, which Ngugi has developed so well in characters like Mugo and Karanja. But these limitations are demanded by the sort of graphic and immediately graspable drama the authors are aiming at. That they succeeded seems to be borne out by the theatre critic who reported 'a degree of audience participation and appreciation one seldom sees in Nairobi – culminating in many of the audience joining in the final triumphant dance down the central aisle and spilling out into the street'.[27]

Like Sembène Ousmane, Ngugi seems to have decided that the novel has peculiar weaknesses as well as peculiar strengths. These must be compensated by the use of theatre or film, and that choice in turn leads almost inevitably to the use of a language which can unite a rural African audience in the way that English or French never can. Already in *The Trial of Dedan Kimathi* the songs are entirely in Gikuyu. The stage is set for Ngugi's next experiment with a fully Gikuyu text, presented to an up-country audience in Limuru. Significantly, it was this experiment which led to his most serious confrontation with authority. But the news of a new novel in the press assures us that, again like Sembène, Ngugi does not see this change of course as involving the abandonment of fiction, to which they have both brought such distinction.

References

Introduction

1 Eustace Palmer, *Introduction to the African Novel* (London: Heinemann, 1972), especially introduction.
2 Stanley Macebuh, 'African aesthetics in traditional African art', *Okike*, no. 5 (June 1974), pp. 13–24.
3 Isidore Okpewho, 'The aesthetics of old African art', *Okike*, no. 8 (July 1975), pp. 38–55.
4 Tony Bennett, *Formalism and Marxism* (London: Methuen, 1979), especially Chapter 2.
5 See Louis Althusser, *For Marx* (Harmondsworth: Allen Lane, 1969).
6 Pierre Macherey, *Theory of Literary Production* (London: Routledge and Kegan Paul, 1978).
7 Terry Eagleton, *Criticism and Ideology* (London: New Left Books, 1976).
8 Charles Larson, *The Emergence of African Fiction* (Indiana University Press, 1971).
9 Frobenius, *Liberté I* (Paris: Les Editions du Seuil, 1964), p. 83.
10 Okpewho, 'The aesthetics of old African art', p. 44.

1 Léopold Sédar Senghor: Assimilation or Negritude

1 L. S. Senghor, *Poèmes* (Paris: Editions du Seuil, 1973), p. 50. This is a collection of all Senghor's poems, first published as *Chants d'Ombre*.
2 Bernard Dadié, *Climbié* (Paris: Senghers, 1956).
3 Senghor, 'Joal', in *Poèmes*, pp. 13–14.
4 Senghor, 'Que m'accompagne Koras et Balafong', in ibid., pp. 34–5.
5 Senghor, 'Totem', in ibid., p. 22.
6 Senghor, 'Lettre à un Poète', in ibid., pp. 9–10.
7 Senghor, 'Nuit de Sine', in ibid., p. 12.
8 J. Reed and C. Wake (eds.), *Senghor: Prose and Poetry* (London: Oxford University Press, 1956), p. 6.
9 Abiola Irele (ed.), *Selected Poems of L. S. Senghor* (Cambridge University Press, 1977), Introduction, p. 36.

10   Claudel, 'Ballade', in Anthony Hartley (ed.), *The Penguin Book of French Verse* vol. 4 (Harmondsworth: Penguin, 1959), p. 40.
11   Senghor, 'Chant de Printemps', in *Poèmes*, p. 83.
12   Senghor, 'In Memoriam', in ibid., p. 7.
13   Senghor, 'A l'Appel de la Race de Saba', in ibid., pp. 56–7.
14   Wole Soyinka, *Myth, Literature and the African World* (Cambridge University Press, 1976), pp. xi–xii.
15   Senghor, 'Que m'accompagne Koras et Balafong', in *Poèmes*, p. 29.
16   L. G. Damas, 'Etcetera', in *Pigments* (first published and banned, 1937; reissued, Paris: Présence Africaine, 1956).
17   Senghor, 'Prière de Paix', in *Poèmes*, p. 93.
18   Senghor, *Chant pour Naëtt* (Paris: Editions du Seuil, 1949).
19   Senghor, 'New York', in *Poèmes*, pp. 113–15.
20   Senghor, 'Pour Khalam', in ibid., pp. 146–7.
21   Senghor, 'L'Absente', in ibid., p. 111.
22   Senghor, 'Elégie de Minuit', in ibid., p. 198.
23   Senghor, 'Que Fais-tu?' in ibid., pp. 220–1.
24   ibid., pp. 153–66.
25   Senghor, 'Assassinats', in ibid., p. 75.
26   Christopher Okigbo, in D. Duerden and C. Pieterse (ed.), *African Writers Talking* (London: Heinemann, 1972).

2   Ezekiel Mphahlele: The Urban Outcast

1   Ezekiel Mphahlele, *The African Image* (London: Faber & Faber, 1962 edition), p. 53.
2   Ezekiel Mphahlele, *Down Second Avenue* (London: Faber and Faber, 1959), p. 11.
3   Peter Abrahams, *Tell Freedom* (London: Faber & Faber, 1954), pp. 44–5.
4   Ezekiel Mphahlele, *Down Second Avenue*, pp. 44–5.
5   ibid., p. 184.
6   ibid., pp. 187–8.
7   Bloke Modisane, 'Why I ran Away', *New Statesman*, 19 Dec., 1959, pp. 874–5.
8   Mphahlele, *Down Second Avenue*, pp. 157–9.
9   ibid., p. 220.
10   ibid., pp. 164–5.
11   Ezekiel Mphahlele, 'Man Must Live', in *In Corner B* (Nairobi: East African Publishing House, 1967), pp. 31 and 36.
12   Bernth Lindfors, 'A preliminary checklist of English short fiction by non-Europeans in South Africa', *African Studies Bulletin*, vol. xii, no. 3 (December 1969).
13   Ezekiel Mphahlele, 'He and the Cat', in *The Living and Dead* (Ibadan: special publication of *Black Orpheus*, 1961), p. 66.
14   Mphahlele, 'The Living and Dead', in ibid., p. 14.

15 ibid., pp. 16–17
16 'Grieg on a Stolen Piano', in *In Corner B*, pp. 47–8.
17 ibid., p. 47.
18 Mphahlele, 'Mrs Plum', in *In Corner B*, p. 184.
19 ibid., p. 164.
20 ibid., pp. 191–2.
21 Ezekiel Mphahlele, *The Wanderers* (London: Macmillan, 1971), p. 11.
22 ibid., pp. 301–2.
23 ibid., pp. 90–1.
24 ibid., p. 24.
25 ibid., pp. 65–6.
26 Ezekiel Mphahlele, 'The Blacks', in *The African Image* (1974 edition) and 'Voices in the Whirlwind', in the collection of the same title (New York: Macmillan, 1972).
27 Mphahlele, *Voices in the Whirlwind*, p. 77.
28 ibid., pp. 15–16.
29 Mphahlele, *The African Image*, p. 43.

3 Sembène Ousmane: The Primacy of Change

1 Sembène Ousmane, *Le Docker Noir* (Paris: Nouvelles Editions Debresse, 1956), pp. 17–18.
2 Sembène Ousmane, *O Pays, Mon Beau Peuple!* (Paris: Amiot Dumont, 1957), pp. 57–9.
3 ibid., pp. 233–4.
4 Sembène Ousmane, *Les Bouts de Bois de Dieu* (Paris: Le Livre Contemporain, 1960), pp. 309–10.
5 ibid., p. 291.
6 ibid., pp. 61–2.
7 Sembène Ousmane, *L'Harmattan* (Paris: Présence Africaine, 1964), pp. 295–6.
8 Sembène Ousmane, *Vehi-Ciosane*, in *Le Mandat* (Paris: Présence Africaine, 1966), pp. 108–9.
9 Sembène Ousmane, *Xala* (Paris: Présence Africaine, 1973), p. 138.

4 Camara Laye: The Aesthetic Vision

1 David Diop, 'Africa', in Moore and Beier (eds.), *Modern Poetry from Africa* (Harmondsworth: Penguin, 1963), p. 63.
2 Camara Laye, *The African Child* (James Kirkup, trans.) previously published as *The Dark Child* (London: Fontana, 1959), p. 11.
3 ibid., pp. 45–7.
4 ibid., p. 54.
5 Ahmadou Kourouma, *Les Soleils des Indépendances* (Montreal: Presse Univérsitaire, 1968).
6 Camara Laye, *The African Child*, pp. 155–6.

7 Camara Laye, (James Kirkup, trans.) *The Radiance of the King* (London: Collins, 1956), pp. 11–13.

8 ibid., pp. 14–15.

9 ibid., pp. 19–22.

10 ibid., p. 102.

11 ibid., p. 235.

12 D. T. Niane, *Sundiata: An Epic of Old Mali* (London: Longman, 1965), especially pp. 4–21.

13 Wole Soyinka, 'Ideology and the social vision', in Soyinka, *Myth, Literature and the African World* (Cambridge University Press, 1976), pp. 121–6.

14 See Dorothy Blair, *African Literature in French* (Cambridge University Press, 1972), p. 274.

15 Alioum Fantouré, *Le Cercle des Tropiques* (Paris: Présence Africaine, 1972).

16 Camara Laye, *Dramouss* (Paris: Plon, 1966), pp. 185–6.

17 Camara Laye, 'The Eyes of the Statue' in *Black Orpheus*, no. 5 (Ibadan, 1959).

18 Kourouma, *Les Soleils des Indépendances*, pp. 143–4.

19 Camara Laye, *Dramouss*, pp. 201–4.

20 ibid., pp. 224–5.

21 ibid., p. 227.

22 ibid., p. 231.

23 Jack Goody (ed.), *The Myth of the Bagre* (Oxford University Press, 1972).

24 Camara Laye, *Dramouss*, p. 187.

5   Alex La Guma: Through Suffering to Resistance

1 Alex La Guma, 'Slipper Satin', in *Black Orpheus*, no. 8 (Ibadan, 1960).

2 Alex La Guma, *A Walk in the Night* (Ibadan: Mbari, 1962), p. 47.

3 ibid., p. 9.

4 ibid., pp. 89–90.

5 Alex La Guma, 'At the Portagees' in *Black Orpheus*, no. 11 (Ibadan, 1961), p. 18.

6 Alex La Guma, *And a Threefold Cord* (Berlin: Seven Seas, 1964), pp. 29–30.

7 ibid., p. 22.

8 ibid., p. 83.

9 ibid., p. 120.

10 Alex La Guma, 'Tattoo-Marks and Nails,' in *Black Orpheus*, no. 14 (Ibadan, 1964), p. 48.

11 Alex La Guma, *The Stone Country* (Berlin: Seven Seas, 1967; re-issued London: Heinemann, 1974), p. 67.

12 ibid., pp. 14–15.
13 ibid., p. 154.
14 Alex La Guma, *In the Fog of the Season's End* (London: Heinemann, 1972), pp. 160–1.
15 ibid., p. 150.
16 Alex La Guma, *Time of the Butcherbird* (London: Heinemann, 1979), p. 61.
17 ibid., pp. 118–19.
18 ibid., p. 1.

6 Chinua Achebe: Unless Tomorrow

1 Chinua Achebe, *Things Fall Apart* (London: Heinemann, 1958), p. 26.
2 ibid., p. 59.
3 ibid., p. 182.
4 ibid., p. 21.
5 Chinua Achebe, *No Longer at Ease* (London: Heinemann, 1960), p. 39.
6 ibid., pp. 53–4.
7 ibid., p. 138.
8 *Things Fall Apart*, p. 7.
9 ibid., p. 11.
10 *No Longer at Ease*, p. 54.
11 ibid., p. 32.
12 Chinua Achebe, *Arrow of God* (London: Heinemann, 1964), pp. 3–4.
13 ibid., p. 162.
14 ibid., pp. 162–3.
15 ibid., p. 198.
16 ibid., p. 256.
17 ibid., p. 217.
18 ibid., p. 138.
19 Christopher Okigbo, 'Elegy for Alto', in *Labyrinths* (London: Heinemann, 1971), p. 71.
20 Chinua Achebe, *A Man of the People* (London: Heinemann, 1966), pp. 161–2.
21 ibid., p. 65.
22 ibid., p. 146.
23 Chinua Achebe, 'Girls at War', in *Girls at War and other Stories* (London: Heinemann, 1972, 1977), pp. 108–9.
24 'Vengeful Creditor', in ibid., p. 54.
25 'Civil Peace', in ibid., p. 87.
26 Chinua Achebe, 'First Shot', in *Beware, Soul Brother* (London: Heinemann, 1972), p. 11.
27 'Love Song', in ibid., p. 25.

28   Chinua Achebe, 'Colonialist Criticism', in *Morning Yet on Creation Day* (London: Heinemann, 1975), p. 9.

7   Tchicaya U Tam'si: The Uprooted Tree

1   Tchicaya U Tam'si, 'Jadis', in *Le Mauvais Sang, suivi de Feu de Brousse et A Triche-Coeur* (Paris: P. J. Oswald), p. 29.
2   U Tam'si, 'Entendu dans le Vent', in ibid., p. 34.
3   U Tam'si, 'Le signe du Mauvais Sang', in ibid., pp. 46–7.
4   U Tam'si, 'Le Mal', in ibid., p. 31.
5   U Tam'si, 'Le Gros Sang', in ibid., p. 43.
6   U Tam'si, 'A Travers Temps et Fleuve' in ibid., p. 51.
7   U Tam'si, 'Presénce', in ibid., pp. 69–70.
8   R. F. Thompson, *African Arts in Motion* (University of California Press, 1975), pp. 14–16.
9   Tchicaya U Tam'si, 'The Scorner', in G. Moore (trans.) *Selected Poems of Tchicaya U Tam'si* (London: Heinemann, 1970), p. 72.
10   U Tam'si, 'Low Watermark', in ibid., p. 6.
11   ibid., p. 8.
12   U Tam'si, 'Equinocxiale', in ibid., p. 21.
13   U Tam'si, 'The Hearse', in ibid., pp. 28–30.
14   U Tam'si, 'Strange Agony', in ibid., pp. 15–16.
15   U Tam'si, 'The Scorner', in ibid., p. 74.
16   U Tam'si, 'The Dead', in ibid., p. 44.
17   ibid., p. 49.
18   ibid., p. 50.
19   Wole Soyinka, 'Harvest of Hate', in *Idanre* (London: Eyre Methuen, 1967), p. 50.
20   Tchicaya U Tam'si, 'The Belly', in *Selected Poems*, pp. 128–9.
21   Tchicaya U Tam'si, 'Chant pour pleurer un Combattant', in *Le Ventre* (Paris: Présence Africaine, 1964), p. 30.
22   Tchicaya U Tam'si, 'The Bodies and the Benefits', in ibid., p. 131.
23   Tchicaya U Tam'si, 'The Belly Remains', in *Selected Poems*, p. 133.
24   U Tam'si, 'Strange Agony' in ibid., p. 20.
25   Tchicaya U Tam'si, 'The Toltec Serpent' in *L'Arc Musical* (Paris: P. J. Oswald, 1970).
26   Tchicaya U Tam'si, 'The Salute', in *Selected Poems*, p. 138.
27   L. S. Senghor, in his preface to the first edition of *Epitomé* (Tunis: P. J. Oswald, 1962).
28   Tchicaya U Tam'si, 'The Promenade', in *Selected Poems*, p. 106.
29   U Tam'si, 'Rapt' in ibid., p. 140.
30   U Tam'si, 'Pourquoi donc dieu est-il Mort', in *L'Arc Musical*, p. 112.
31   Okot p'Bitek, *The Horn of my Love* (London: Heinemann, 1974).
32   Kofi Awoonor (trans.), *Guardians of the Sacred Word: Ewe Poetry* (New York: Nok Publications, 1974), p. 33.

33 Tchicaya U Tam'si, 'Legacy', in *Selected Poems*.
34 Tchicaya U Tam'si, 'La Fênetre', in *La Veste d'Intérieur* (Paris: Nubia, 1977).
35 Tchicaya U Tam'si, 'Notes de Vielle', in ibid., p. 108.
36 Tchicaya U Tam'si, *Le Zulu, suivi de Vwène le Fondateur* (Paris: Nubia, 1977), pp. 28–9.
37 ibid., p. 130.
38 ibid., pp. 111–12.

8 Okot p'Bitek: The Horn of the Grasslands

1 Okot p'Bitek, *Song of Lawino* (Nairobi: East African Publishing House, 1966), p. 14.
2 ibid., p. 22.
3 ibid., p. 44.
4 Nairobi; Eagle Press, 1953.
5 *Lawino*, p. 44.
6 ibid., p. 207.
7 Okot p'Bitek, *The Horn of my Love* (London: Heinemann, 1974), p. 48
8 G. A. Heron, *The Poetry of Okot p'Bitek* (London: Heinemann, 1976), esp. pp. 33–45.
9 Okot p'Bitek, *Wer pa Lawino* (Nairobi: East African Publishing House, 1969).
10 *Lawino*, p. 44.
11 ibid., p. 196.
12 ibid., p. 168.
13 ibid., p. 208.
14 ibid., p. 216.
15 Okot p'Bitek, *Song of Ocol* (Nairobi: East African Publishing House, 1970), pp. 21–2.
16 ibid., p. 41.
17 ibid., pp. 49–50.
18 ibid., p. 48.
19 ibid., pp. 52–3.
20 ibid., p. 86.
21 Heron, p. 19.
22 Okot p'Bitek, 'Song of Prisoner', in *Two Songs* (Nairobi: East African Publishing House, 1971), p. 11.
23 ibid., p. 15.
24 ibid., pp. 92–3.
25 ibid., pp. 102–4.
26 ibid., pp. 117–18.
27 ibid., p. 116.
28 ibid., p. 25.

29   ibid., p. 59.
30   Okot p'Bitek, 'Song of Malaya', in *Two Songs*, p. 147.
31   ibid., p. 142.
32   ibid., p. 166.
33   ibid., p. 184.

9   Mongo Beti: From Satire to Epic

1   Eza Boto, *Ville Cruelle* (Paris: Editions Africaines, 1954), p. 21.
2   ibid., p. 178.
3   Mongo Beti, *Le Pauvre Christ de Bomba* (Paris: Laffont, 1956); Gerald Moore (trans.) (London: Heinemann, 1971), pp. 8–9.
4   ibid., p. 19.
5   ibid., p. 152–3.
6   Mongo Beti, *Mission Terminée* (Paris: Buchet/Chastel, 1957); Peter Green (trans.), *Mission to Kala* (London: Muller, 1958; Heinemann, 1964), pp. 21–3.
7   ibid., pp. 150–1.
8   ibid., pp. 181–3.
9   ibid., pl 180.
10   Mongo Beti, *Le Roi Miraculé* (Paris: Buchet/Chastel, 1958), pp. 29–31.
11   ibid., pp. 127–8.
12   Mongo Beti, *Remember Ruben* (Paris: Editions 10/18, 1974), p. 37.
13   ibid., pp. 127–8.
14   Dorothy Blair, *African Literature in French* (Cambridge University Press, 1972).
15   Mongo Beti, *Main Basse sur le Cameroun* (Paris: Petite Collection Maspero, 1977).
16   Mongo Beti, *Perpétue* (Paris: Buchet/Chastel, 1974), p. 271.

10   Wole Soyinka: Across the Primeval Gulf

1   Biodun Jeyifo, *The Positive Review*, no. 1, Ibadan, 1978, p. 15.
2   Wole Soyinka, *Collected Plays* (London: Oxford University Press, 1973), vol. 1, p. 71.
3   ibid., pp. 166–7.
4   Wole Soyinka, *Madmen and Specialists* (London: Eyre Methuen, 1971), p. 55.
5   Wole Soyinka, *Death and the King's Horseman* (London: Eyre Methuen, 1975), p. 68.
6   ibid., p. 21.
7   ibid., p. 23.
8   ibid., p. 62.
9   ibid., p. 75.

10 ibid., pp. 69–70.
11 ibid., p. 76.
12 Wole Soyinka, *Season of Anomy* (London: Rex Collings, 1973), p. 11.
13 ibid., p. 20.
14 Peter Morton-Williams, 'The Yoruba Kingdom of Oyo' in *West African Kingdoms in the Nineteenth Century*, ed. Forde and Kaberry (Oxford University Press, 1967), p. 51.
15 *Season of Anomy*, pp. 97–8.
16 ibid., pp. 5–6.
17 ibid., p. 27.
18 'Ujamaa', *A Shuttle in the Crypt* (London: Rex Collings/Eyre Methuen, 1972), p. 80.
19 ibid., 'O Roots', pp. 3–4.
20 ibid., p. 3.
21 *Collected Plays I*, p. 265.
22 ibid., p. 292.
23 Wole Soyinka, *Ogun Abibiman* (London: Rex Collings, 1976).
24 Wole Soyinka, *The Man Died* (London: Rex Collings, 1971).
25 Wole Soyinka, *A Shuttle in the Crypt*, p. 65.

11 Kofi Awoonor: The Neglected Gods

1 Kofi Awoonor, 'The Consummation', in *Rediscovery* (Ibadan: Mbari Publications, 1964), p. 27.
2 Kofi Awoonor, *This Earth, my Brother* (New York: Doubleday, 1971), p. 226.
3 Kofi Awoonor, 'The Sea Eats the Land at Home', in *Modern Poetry from Africa*, Moore and Beier (eds.), (London: Penguin, 1968 edition), p. 101 (first published in the Ghanaian review *Okyeame* 1 in 1961).
4 Kofi Awoonor, 'The Nim Trees in the Cemetery', in *Rediscovery*, p. 8.
5 Samuel Beckett, *Waiting for Godot* (London: Faber paperbacks, 1965), p. 89.
6 Kofi Awoonor, 'Salvation', *Night of my Blood*, (New York: Doubleday, 1971), p. 38.
7 Kofi Awoonor (trans.), Ewe dirge by Akpalu, in *Guardians of the Sacred Word: Ewe Poetry* (New York: Nok Publications, 1974), p. 33.
8 First published in *African Arts* (Los Angeles: Autumn 1967) vol. 1, no. 1, p. 50.
9 Kofi Awoonor, 'A Dirge', in *Night of my Blood*, p. 63.
10 Kofi Awoonor, 'I Heard a Bird Cry', in ibid., pp. 46–7.
11 Kofi Awoonor, *Modern Poetry from Africa*, pp. 98–100 (also first published in *Okyeame* 1, 1961).
12 Kofi Awoonor, 'The Years Behind', in *Rediscovery*, p. 24.
13 Kofi Awoonor, 'I Heard a Bird Cry', in *Night of my Blood*, pp. 46–7.

14   Kofi Awoonor, 'The Return', in *Rediscovery*, p. 34.
15   *Guardians of the Sacred Word*, p. 32.
16   *This Earth, my Brother*, pp. 36–7.
17   ibid., p. 37.
18   ibid., p. 173.
19   ibid., p. 119.
20   ibid., p. 18.
21   Ayi Kwei Armah, *Fragments* (Boston: Houghton Mifflin, 1970), p. 2.
22   Kofi Awoonor, 'Comes the Voyager at Last', *Okike*, no. 7, (April 1975), p. 4.
23   Kofi Awoonor, 'America', in *Ride me, Memory*, (New York: Greenfield Review Press, 1973), p. 9.
24   'Harlem on a Winter Night', in ibid., p. 12.
25   'To my Uncle Jonathan', in ibid., p. 22.
26   *Guardians of the Sacred Word*, p. 83.
27   'Long Island Sketches', in *Ride me, Memory*, p. 18.
28   Kofi Awoonor, *The House by the Sea* (New York: Greenfield Review Press, 1978), p. 26.
29   ibid., pp. 27–8.
30   ibid., p. 6.
31   ibid., pp. 65–6.
32   ibid., p. 54.
33   ibid., p. 52.
34   Kofi Awoonor, 'Ancestral Power', in C. Pieterse (ed.), *Short African Plays* (London: Heinemann, 1972), p. 7.
35   ibid., pp. 123–4.
36   Kofi Awoonor, *The Breast of the Earth: a Survey of the History, Culture and Literature of Africa South of the Sahara* (New York: Anchor/Doubleday, 1975), p. 116.
37   ibid., p. 202.
38   ibid., pp. 202–8 for Awoonor's detailed discussion of this poem.
39   ibid., pp. 209–10.

12   Ngugi wa Thiong'o: Towards Uhuru

1   Ngugi wa Thiong'o, *The River Between* (London: Heinemann, 1965), p. 12.
2   ibid., p. 160.
3   Ngugi wa Thiong'o, 'Church, Culture and Politics' in *Homecoming* (London: Heinemann, 1972), p. 32.
4   Ngugi wa Thiong'o, *The River Between*, p. 117.
5   ibid., p. 119.
6   ibid., p. 24.
7   ibid., p. 107.
8   ibid., p. 19.

9 Ngugi wa Thiong'o, *Weep not, Child* (London: Heinemann, 1964), p. 30.
10 ibid., p. 3.
11 ibid., p. 4.
12 ibid., p. 150.
13 ibid., p. 107.
14 Ngugi wa Thiong'o, *A Grain of Wheat* (London: Heinemann, 1967), p. 135.
15 ibid., p. 127.
16 ibid., pp. 210–11.
17 Ngugi wa Thiong'o, first published in *Secret Lives* (London: Heinemann, 1975).
18 Ngugi wa Thiong'o, *The River Between*, p. 102.
19 Ngugi wa Thiong'o, *A Grain of Wheat*, pp. 108–9.
20 ibid., p. 204.
21 Ngugi wa Thiong'o, author's note in *Homecoming*, p. xv.
22 Ngugi wa Thiong'o, *Petals of Blood* (London: Heinemann, 1977), p. 71.
23 ibid., p. 106.
24 Wole Soyinka, *Myth, Literature and the African World* (Cambridge University Press, 1976), p. 115.
25 Ngugi wa Thiong'o, *Petals of Blood*, p. 259.
26 Ngugi wa Thiong'o and Micere Mugo, *The Trial of Dedan Kimathi* (London: Heinemann 1976), p. 74.
27 Critic of *The Sunday Nation*, quoted on the back cover of the play.

Bibliography

Achebe, Chinua

Novels
Things fall Apart, London: Heinemann, 1958
No Longer at Ease, London: Heinemann, 1960
Arrow of God, London: Heinemann, 1964
A Man of the People, London: Heinemann, 1966

Short stories
Girls at War and Other Stories, London: Heinemann, 1972, 1977

Poetry
Beware, Soul Brother, London: Heinemann, 1972

Criticism
Morning yet on Creation Day, London: Heinemann, 1975

Editing and translation
Founding editor of the review *Okike* from 1971 onwards
Don't Let Him Die: Poems in Memory of Christopher Okigbo, co-edited
    with Dubem Okafor, Enugu: Fourth Dimension, 1978

Amadi, Elechi

Novels
The Concubine, London: Heinemann, 1966
The Great Ponds, London: Heinemann, 1969
The Slave, London: Heinemann, 1978

Memoir
Sunset in Biafra, London: Heinemann, 1973

Drama
Isiburu, London: Heinemann, 1965

Pepper Soup and *The Road to Ibadan*, Ibadan: Onibonoje Publishers, 1977
The Dancer of Johannesburg, Ibadan: Onibonoje Publishers, 1978

Armah, Ayi Kwei

Novels
The Beautiful Ones are not yet Born, Boston: Houghton Mifflin, 1968
Fragments, Boston: Houghton Mifflin, 1970
Why are we so Blest?, New York: Doubleday, 1972
Two Thousand Seasons, Nairobi: East African Publishing House, 1973
The Healers, Nairobi: East African Publishing House, 1978

Awoonor, Kofi (Formerly Awoonor Williams, George)

Novels
This Earth, my Brother, New York: Doubleday, 1971
'Comes the voyage at last' (extract), *Okike* 7, 1975

Poetry
Rediscovery, Ibadan: Mbari, 1964
Night of my Blood, New York: Doubleday, 1971
Ride me, Memory, New York: Greenfield Review Press, 1973
The House by the Sea, New York: Greenfield Review Press, 1978

Criticism
*The Breast of the Earth: A Survey of the History, Culture and Literature of
    Africa South of the Sahara*, New York: Anchor/Doubleday, 1975

Plays
'Ancestral Power' & 'Lament', *Short African Plays*, Cosmo Pieterse (ed.),
London: Heinemann, 1972

Editing and translation
Guardians of the Sacred Word: Ewe Poetry, New York: Nok Publications,
    1974
Messages: Poems from Ghana, with Adali Mortty (eds.), London: Heine-
    mann, 1971

Beti, Mongo (Also Boto, Eza)

Novels
Ville Cruelle, Paris: Editions Africaines, 1954
Le Pauvre Christ de Bomba, Paris: Laffont, 1956
    English translation: *The Poor Christ of Bomba*, London: Heinemann,
    1971

Mission Terminée, Paris: Buchet/Chastel, 1957
  English translation: *Mission to Kala*, London: Muller 1958, Heinemann 1964
Le Roi Miraculé, Paris: Buchet/Chastel, 1958
  English translation: *King Lazarus*, London: Muller 1960, Heinemann 1970
Remember Ruben, Paris: Union Générale d'Editions 10/18, 1974
  English translation: *Remember Ruben*, London: Heinemann and Ibadan: New Horn, 1980
Perpétue, Paris: Buchet/Chastel, 1974
  English translation: *Perpétue and the Habit of Unhappiness*, London: Heinemann, 1978
La Ruine Presque Cocasse d'un Polichinelle (serialized in *Peuples Noirs, Peuples Africains* from no. 1, Mars-Avril 1978, onwards), Paris: Editions des Peuples Noirs, 1979

Short stories
'Sans Haine et Sans Amour', *Présence Africaine*, 14, 1953

Memoir
Main Basse sur le Cameroun, Paris: Petite Collection Maspero, 1977

Editing and translation
Founding director of the review *Peuples Noirs, Peuples Africains* from 1978 onwards

Brecht, Bertolt

Brecht on Theatre: *The Development of an Aesthetic*, John Willett (ed. & trans.), London: Eyre/Methuen, 1978
The Messingkauf Dialogues, John Willett (trans.), London: Eyre/Methuen 1965, 1977

Clark, J. P.

Poetry
Poems, Ibadan: Mbari, 1962
A Reed in the Tide, London: Longman, 1965
Casualties, London: Longman, 1970

Plays
Song of a Goat, Ibadan: Mbari, 1961
Three Plays, London: Oxford University Press, 1964
Ozidi, London: Oxford University Press, 1966

Memoir
America, their America, London: Deutsch 1964, Heinemann 1968

Criticism
The Example of Shakespeare, London: Longman, 1970

Editing and translation
The Ozidi Saga, edited and translated from the Ijo of Okabou Ojobolo,
    Ibadan: Ibadan University Press and Oxford University Press, 1977.
    Co-editor of the review *Black Orpheus* from 1967 onwards

Dadié, David

Novel
Climbié, Paris: Seghers, 1956
    English translation: *Climbié*, London: Heinemann, 1971

Damas, Léon

Poetry
Pigments, first published by GLM 1937 and destroyed. Reissued, Paris:
Présence Africaine, 1956

Dathorne, O. R.
The Black Mind, Minneapolis: Minnesota University Press, 1974

Diop, David

Poetry
Coups de Pilon, Paris: Présence Africaine, 1956
    English translation: *Hammer Blows and Other Writings*, London:
    Heinemann, 1973

Eagleton, Terry

Marxism and Literary Criticism, London: Methuen, 1976
Criticism and Ideology, London: New Left Books, 1976.

Fall, Malick

Novel
La Plaie, Paris: Albin Michel, 1967
    English translation: *The Wound*, London: Heinemann, 1973

Poetry
Reliefs, Paris: *Présence Africaine*

Fantouré, Alioum

Novel
Le Cercle des Tropiques, Paris: Présence Africaine, 1972

Farah, Nuruddin

Novels
From a Crooked Rib, London: Heinemann, 1970
A Naked Needle, London: Heinemann, 1976

Hussein, Ebrahim

Drama
Kinjeketile, Dar es Salaam: Oxford University Press, 1970

Jahn, Janheinz

Muntu: *An Outline of Neo-African Culture,* London: Faber & Faber, 1961
A History of Neo-African Literature, London: Faber & Faber, 1968

Kane, Hamidou

Novel
Aventure Ambiqüe, Paris: Julliard, 1962
    English translation: *Ambiguous Adventure,* New York: Collier/Macmillan, 1969

Kourouma, Ahmadou

Novel
Les Soleils des Indépendances, Montreal: Presse Univérsitaire, 1968; new
    copy Paris: Editions du Seuil, 1973

La Guma, Alex

Novels and short novels
A Walk in the Night, Ibadan: Mbari, 1962, London: Heinemann, 1967
And a Threefold Cord, Berlin: Seven Seas, 1964
The Stone Country, Berlin: Seven Seas, 1967
In the Fog of the Season's End, London: Heinemann, 1972
Time of the Butcherbird, London: Heinemann, 1979

Short stories
'A glass of wine', *Black Orpheus* 7, 1960
'Slipper satin', *Black Orpheus* 8, 1960
'At the Portagees', *Black Orpheus* 11, 1961
'Tattoo marks and nails', *Black Orpheus* 14, 1964
'Coffee for the road', *Modern African Stories*, Komey & Mphahlele (eds.), London: Faber & Faber, 1964
'Blankets': *African Writing Today*, Mphahlele (ed.), London: Penguin, 1967
'Out of darkness' and 'Nocturne', *Quartet*, Rive (ed.), London: Heinemann, 1963

Larson, Charles

The Emergence of African Fiction, Bloomington: Indiana University Press, 1971

Laye, Camara

Novels and Autobiography
L'Enfant Noir, Paris: Plon, 1953
    English translation: *The African Child*, London: Collins, 1955
Le Regard du Roi, Paris: Plon, 1954
    English translation: *The Radiance of the King*, London: Collins, 1956
Dramouss, Paris: Plon, 1966
    English translation: *A Dream of Africa*, London: Collins, 1968

Short stories
'The eyes of the statue', *Black Orpheus* 5, 1959

Lord, Albert B.

The Singer of Tales, New York: Athenaeum, 1965

Macebuh, Stanley

'African aesthetics in traditional African art', *Okike* 5, 1974

Modisane, Bloke

Autobiography
Blame me on History, London: Thames & Hudson, 1963

Essays
'Why I ran away', *New Statesman*, 19 Dec., 1959, pp. 874–5

Mphahlele, Ezekiel

Novels and autobiography
Down Second Avenue, London: Faber & Faber, 1959
The Wanderers, New York and London: Macmillan, 1971

Short stories
Man Must Live, Cape Town: African Bookman, 1947
The Living and Dead, Ibadan: Ministry of Education, 1961
In Corner B, Nairobi: East African Publishing House, 1967

Criticism
The African Image, London: Faber & Faber, 1962, 1974
Voices in the Whirlwind, New York: Hill and Wang, 1972 and London:
  Macmillan, 1973

Editing and Translation
Modern African Stories, Komey & Mphahlele (eds.), London: Faber &
  Faber, 1964
African Writing Today, London: Penguin, 1967

Ngugi, wa Thiong'o (Formerly Ngugi, James)

Novels
Weep not, Child, London: Heinemann, 1964
The River Between, London: Heinemann, 1965
A Grain of Wheat, London: Heinemann, 1967
Petals of Blood, London, Heinemann, 1977

Short stories
Secret Lives, London: Heinemann, 1975

Drama
The Black Hermit, London: Heinemann, 1968
The Trial of Dedan Kimathi, with Micere Mugo, London: Heinemann,
  1976

Criticism
Homecoming, London: Heinemann, 1972

Okigbo, Christopher

Poetry
Labyrinths: followed by Path of Thunder: London: Heinemann, 1971

Okpewho, Isidore

Novels
The Victims, London: Longman, 1970
The Last Duty, London: Longman, 1976

Criticism
'Africa and the epic', *Okike* 11, 1976
The Epic in Africa, New York: Columbia University Press, 1979
'The aesthetics of old African art', *Okike*, vol. 8, 1975

Omotoso, Kole

Novels
The Edifice, London: Heinemann, 1971
The Combat, London: Heinemann, 1972
Sacrifice, Ibadan: Onibonoje, 1974
Fella's Choice, Benin City: Ethiope, 1974
The Scales, Ibadan: Onibonoje, 1976

Drama
The Curse, Ibadan: New Horn, 1976
Shadows in the Horizon, Ibadan: Sketch Publishers, 1977

Criticism
The Form of the African Novel, Akure: Fagbamigbe, 1979.

Osofisan, Femi

Novels
Kolera Kolej, Ibadan: New Horn, 1975

Drama
The Chattering and the Song, Ibadan: New Horn, 1976, Ibadan University
    Press, 1977
Who's Afraid of Solarin?, Calabar: Scholar Press, 1978

Ousmane, Sembène

Novels and short novels
Le Docker Noir, Paris: Nouvelles Editions Debresse, 1956
O Pays, mon Beau Peuple!, Paris: Amiot-Dumont, 1957
Les Bouts de Bois de Dieu, Paris: Amiot-Dumont, 1960
    English translation: *God's Bits of Wood*, London: Heinemann, 1970

L'Harmattan: vol. 1: Référendum, Paris: Présence Africaine, 1964
Le Mandat suive de Vehi-Ciosane, Paris: Présence Africaine, 1966
   English translation: *The Money Order and White Genesis*, London:
   Heinemann, 1972
Xala, Paris: Présence Africaine, 1973
   English translation: *Xala*, London: Heinemann, 1976

Short stories
Voltaïques, Paris: Présence Africaine, 1962
   English translation: *Tribal Scars*, London: Heinemann, 1974

Films (dates approximate)
Borom-Sarratt (1967); *La Noire de–*(1962); *Mandabi* (1968); *Emitai* (1972);
   Xala (1974); *Ceddu* (1976)

Oyono, Ferdinand

Novels
Une Vie de Boy, Paris: Julliard, 1956
   English translation: *Houseboy*, London: Heinemann, 1966
Le Vieux Nègre et la Médaille, Paris: Julliard, 1956
   English translation: *The Old Man and the Medal*, London: Heinemann,
   1967
Chemin d'Europe, Paris: Julliard, 1960
Le Pandémonium, Paris: Julliard, 1971

Palmer, Eustace

Introduction to the African Novel, London: Heinemann, 1972

p'Bitek, Okot

Novels
Laktar Miyo Kinyero Lui Lobo (in Lwo), Nairobi: Eagle Press, 1953

Poetry
Song of Lawino, Nairobi: East African Publishing House, 1966
Wer pa Lawino (in Lwo), Nairobi: East African Publishing House, 1969
Song of Ocol, Nairobi: East African Publishing House, 1970
Two Songs ('Song of Prisoner' & 'Song of Malaya'), Nairobi: East African
   Publishing House, 1971

Scholarship
African Religions in Western Scholarship, Nairobi: East African Publishing
   House, 1970

Editing and translation
The Horn of my Love (Lwo poetry), London: Heinemann, 1974
Hare and Hornbill (Lwo folktales), London: Heinemann, 1978

Senghor, Léopold Sédar

Poetry
Poèmes, Paris: Editions du Seuil, 1964, 1972
  (includes *Chants d'Ombre* (1945), *Hosties Noires* (1948), *Ethiopiques*
  (1956), *Nocturnes* (1961) and *Lettres de l'Hivernage* (1972)
  English translations of many poems can be found in *Modern Poetry from
  Africa*, Moore and Beir (eds.), London: Penguin, 1963, 1968. *Senghor:
  Prose and Poetry*, Reed and Wake, London: Heinemann, 1965.
  Nocturnes, Reed and Wake, London: Heinemann, 1969. *Selected Poems
  of L. S. Senghor*, Reed and Wake, London: Oxford University Press,
  1964

Criticism
Liberté 1: Négritude et Humanisme, Paris: Editions du Seuil, 1964

Editing and Translation
Anthologie de la Nouvelle Poésie Nègre et Malgache, Paris: Presse Univérsitaire, 1948.

Soyinka, Wole

Novels
The Interpreters, London: Deutsch, 1965
Season of Anomy, London: Rex Collings, 1973

Poetry
Idanre and Other Poems, London: Methuen, 1967
A Shuttle in the Crypt, London: Collings and Eyre Methuen, 1972
Ogun Obibiman, London: Rex Collings, 1976

Drama
Collected Plays I, London: Oxford Universtiy Press, 1973 (includes *A
  Dance of the Forests, The Swamp Dwellers, The Strong Breed, The Road,
  The Bacchae of Euripides*)
Collected Plays II, London: Oxford University Press, 1975 (includes *The
  Lion and the Jewel, Kongi's Harvest, The Trials of Brother Jero, Madmen
  and Specialists*)
Camwood on the Leaves, London: Eyre Methuen, 1973
The Jero Plays, London: Eyre Methuen, 1973 (includes *The Trials of*

Brother Jero and *Jero's Metamorphosis*)
Death and the King's Horseman, London: Eyre Methuen, 1975

Criticism
Myth, Literature and the African World, London: Cambridge University
   Press, 1976

Editing and Translation
The Forest of a Thousand Daemons (from the Yoruba of D. O. Fagunwa),
   London: Nelson, 1968
Poems of Black Africa (ed.), London: Heinemann, 1975
   Also edited the review *Transition* (later *Chindaba*), 1973–6

Tutuola, Amos

Novels
The Palm-Wine Drinkard, London: Faber & Faber, 1952
My Life in the Bush of Ghosts, London: Faber & Faber, 1954
Simbi and the Satyr of the Dark Jungle, London: Faber & Faber, 1955
The Brave African Huntress, London: Faber & Faber, 1958
Feather Woman of the Jungle, London: Faber & Faber, 1962
Ajaiyi and his Inherited Poverty, London: Faber & Faber, 1967

U Tam'si, Tchicaya

Poetry
Le Mauvais Sang, suivi de Feu de Brousse et A Triche-Coeur, Paris: P. J.
   Oswald, Honfleur, 1970
L'Arc Musical précédé d'Epitomé, P. J. Oswald, Honfleur, 1970
Le Ventre, Paris: Présence Africaine, 1964
   English translation: *Brushfire*, Ibadan: Mbari, 1964
La Veste d'Intérieur suivi de Notes de Veille, Paris: Nubia, 1977
Selected Poems of Tchicaya U Tam'si, London: Heinemann, 1970

Drama
Le Zulu suivi de Vivène le Fondateur, Paris: Nubia, 1977

Editing and translation
Trésor Africain, Paris: Seghers, 1968 (a collection of African tales)

Suggested further reading

Journals and periodicals

African Literature Today, Eldred Durosimi Jones (ed.) (London: Heinemann). Appears more or less annually, devoting each issue to a special critical topic (for example no. 5, *The Novel in Africa*, no. 6, *Poetry in Africa*).

Black Orpheus, founding editor Ulli Beier 1957–67, thereafter occasionally edited by J. P. Clark and Abiola Irele to 1976, when it appears to have ceased publication. Formerly published in Ibadan, first by Ministry of Education, then by Mbari, latterly by Longman. Played a crucial role in the fifties and sixties publishing poetry, fiction and criticism of high quality from all over the Black World.

Chin'daba (formerly *Transition*), founding editor Rajat Neogy 1961–72, then Wole Soyinka 1973–6. Appears to have ceased publication after moving its base successively from Kampala to Accra and then to Ile-Ife. Always a journal of general ideas and debate, as well as literature, but has published much work of importance over the years.

The Classic (now *The New Classic*), edited successively by Nat Nakasa, Barney Simon & Sipho Sepamla (Johannesburg: New Classic Publications). Played a leading role in making known the poetry and fiction of a new generation of South African writers. Has had checkered career since its foundation in 1965, but appears to be indestructible.

The Conch, founding editor S. O. Anozie, Buffalo (Conch Magazine Limited). The chief voice of structuralist criticism in African literature. Appears irregularly.

Journal of Commonwealth Literature, founding editor Arthur Ravenscroft (Leeds: Heinemann and University of Leeds). A journal of criticism and bibliography which has appeared regularly since 1965. With wide focus, hence only partly concerned with African Literature, but an important channel for critical writing.

Okike: An African Journal of New Writing, founding editor Chinua Achebe (Nsukka: Okike Magazine Limited). Founded in 1971, has maintained a high standard of creative and critical contributions, especially in poetry. Thrice yearly.

Peuples Noirs, Peuples Africains, founding editor Mongo Beti (Paris: SARL). Founded in 1978 and has appeared bi-monthly with great regularity. Has become the leading Francophone voice in radical criticism and political commentary, as well as publishing new fiction by Beti.

Positive Review: A Review of Society and Culture in Black Africa, edited collectively at University of Ife. Seems likely to become the Anglophone equivalent of Beti's journal above in its generally Marxist orientation. Publishes fiction, poetry, art and criticism. Founded 1978 and appears roughly twice yearly.

Présence Africaine, founding editor Alioune Diop (Paris: Présence Africaine). Veteran among African literary and intellectual journals. Founded 1947 and published thrice yearly in both French and English editions. Indispensable for its record of African writing and criticism over three decades.

Research in African Literatures, founding editor Bernth Lindfors, Austin, Texas University Press. Does not publish creative work or reviews of it. Concentrates on critical articles, research reports, bibliographical items and conference reports. A useful academic tool, appearing twice yearly since 1970.

Sheffield Papers on African Literature, Christopher Heywood (ed.) (Sheffield: The University and African Educational Trust) .The first number of this periodical, which appeared in 1976, contained critical articles of high quality and originality.

Critical studies by one hand (in English)

The following should be consulted in addition to those listed in the Bibliography.

Armstrong, Robert Plant *The Affecting Presence: An Essay in Humanistic Anthropology*, Urbana: University of Illinois Press, 1971
Cartey, Wilfred, *Whispers from a Continent*, London: Heinemann, 1969
Cook, David, *African Literature: A Critical View*, London: Longman, 1977
Duerden, Dennis, *African Art and Literature: The Invisible Present*, London: Heinemann, 1975

Gakwandi, Shatto Arthur, *The Novel and Contemporary Experience in Africa*, London: Heinemann, 1977

Griffiths, Gareth, *A Double Exile: African and Caribbean Writing between Two Cultures*, London: Marion Boyars, 1978

Kesteloot, Lilyan, *African Writers in French: A Literary History of Negritude* (trans. from the French), Philadelphia: Temple University Press, 1974

Laurence, Margaret, *Long Drums and Cannons: Nigerian Dramatists and Novelists 1952–66*, London: Macmillan, 1968

Moore, Gerald, *The Chosen Tongue: English Writing in the Tropical World*, London: Longman, 1969

Obiechina, Emmanuel, *Tradition and Society in the West African Novel*, London: Cambridge University Press, 1975

Roscoe, Adrian, *Mother is Gold: A Study in West African Literature*, London: Cambridge University Press, 1971

— *Uhuru's Fire: African Literature East and South*, London: Cambridge University Press, 1977

Sartre, Jean-Paul, *Black Orpheus* (trans. from the French), Paris: Présence Africaine, 1963. This is a reproduction of Sartre's famous introduction to Senghor's 1948 anthology of Black Poetry

Tucker, Martin, *Africa in Modern Literature: A Survey of Contemporary Writing in English*, New York: Ungar, 1967

Udoeyop, J. N., *Three Nigerian Poets: A Critical Study of the Poetry of Soyinka, Clark and Okigbo*, Ibadan: University Press, 1973

Wauthier, Claude, *The Literature and Thought of Modern Africa* (trans. from the French), London: Pall Mall, 1967

Collections of critical articles by several hands (in English)

Heywood, Christopher (ed.), *Perspectives on African Literature*, London: Heinemann, 1971

— *Aspects of South African Literature*, London: Heinemann, 1976

King, Bruce and Ogungbesan, Kolewole (eds.), *A Celebration of Black and African Writing*, Zaria: Ahmadu Bello University Press, 1975

Lindfors, Bernth, and Schild, Ulla, (eds.), *Neo-African Literature and Culture: Essays in Memory of Janheinz Jahn*, Mainz: B. Heymann, 1976

Moore, Gerald (ed.), *African Literature and the Universities*, Ibadan: University Press, 1965

Ogunba, Oyin and Irele, Abiola (eds.), *Theatre In Africa*, Ibadan: University Press, 1978

Smith, Rowland (ed.), *Exile and Tradition: Studies in African and Caribbean Literature*, London: Longman, 1976

Wästberg, Per (ed.), *The Writer in Modern Africa* (Proceedings of African Scandinavian Writers' Conference, Stockholm 1967), New York: Africana Publishing Corporation, 1969

Wright, Edgar (ed.), *The Critical Evaluation of African Literature*, London: Heinemann, 1973

Interviews with writers or collections of their essays

Duerden, Dennis & Pieterse, Cosmos (ed.), *African Writers Talking: A Collection of Interviews* (Various), London: Heinemann, 1972

Killam, G. D. (ed.), *African Writers on African Writing* (Interviews with or essays by, Achebe, Aidoo, Clark, Gordimer, Kane, Mazrui, Mezu, Nkosi, Uculi, Okara, Rubadiri, Ousmane, Socé, U Tam'si, Laye, Diop Birago and Abdou Anta Ka), London: Heinemann, 1973

Lindfors, Bernth (ed.), *Palaver: Interviews with Five African Writers in Texas* (Achebe, Awoonor, Brutus, Clark & Mphahlele), Austin: Texas University Press, 1972

Morrel, Karen L. (ed.), *In Person: Achebe, Awoonor & Soyinka*, Austin: Texas University Press, 1975

Bibliographies

The following will be found the most useful and comprehensive:

Herdeck, Donald E., *African Authors, vol. 1: 1300–1973*, Washington DC: Black Orpheus Press, 1973

Jahn, Janheinz, *A Bibliography of Neo-African Literature from Africa, America and the Caribbean*, London: Deutsch, 1965
Who's Who in African Literature?, Tubingen: Horst Erdmann, 1972
— (with Dressler, C. P.), *Bibliography of Creative African Writing*, Nendeln: Kraus-Thomson, 1971

Zell, Hans and Silver, Helene, *Readers' Guide to African Literature*, London: Heinemann, 1972

South African poetry

For an idea of recent developments in South African poetry to which attention was drawn in the Introduction, the reader might consult:

Gordimer, Nadine, *The Black Interpreters: on African Writing*, Johannesburg: Spro-Cas/Ravan, 1973

Matthews, James, *Cry Rage*, Johannesburg: Spro-Cas Publications, 1972

Mtshali, Oswald Mbuyiseni, *Sounds of a Cowhide Drum*, Johannesburg: Renoster Books, 1971, London: Oxford University Press, 1972

Pieterse, Cosmo, *Seven South African Poets*, London: Heinemann, 1971

Royston, Robert (ed.), *Black Poets in South Africa*, London: Heinemann, 1974

Sepamla, Sipho, *The Soweto I Love*, London: Rex Collings, Cape Town: David Philip, 1977

Serote, Mongane Wally, *Yakhal'inkoma: Poems*, Johannesburg: Renoster, 1972
— *Tsetlo*, Johannesburg: Donker, 1974
— *No Baby must Weep*, Johannesburg: Donker, 1975

Acknowledgements

Special acknowledgement is due to the following authors and publishers for permission to reprint copyright material:

Extracts from *The Wanderers* by Ezekiel Mphalele, reprinted by permission of Macmillan, London and Basingstoke

Extracts from *The Selected Poems of Tchicaya U Tam'si,* reprinted by permission of A. D. Peters Ltd

Extract from *Collected Plays 1* by Wole Soyinka, reprinted by permission of Oxford University Press

Extracts from *This Earth my Brother* and *The Breast of the Earth* by Kofi Awoonor, reprinted by permission of Harold Ober Associates. (Copyright as given by Doubleday)

Index

'A Travers Temps et Fleuve', 152
A Triche-Coeur, 149, 153, 155–7,
  162, 311
Abrahams, Peter, 44, 48, 59
'Absente, L'', 34
'abstract', 14–15
abuse, songs of, 252–3
Achebe, Chinua, 7, 11, 41, 122–45,
  301, 314, 316
Acoli: language, 173–5, 178;
  people, 147
African Arts in Motion, 154
African Child, The, see Enfant Noir
African Image, The, 40, 42, 52,
  63–5
*African Literature and the
  Universities*, 63
African Literature Today, 313
'Africanity', 23–4, 29–30, 36, 86;
  see also negritude
Ahmed the Turk, 113–14
Akpalu, 166, 258
Al-Hadj Umar, 19–20
allegory, 247–9
Althusser, Louis, 12
Amadi, Elechi, 10, 141, 301
America, *see* 'New York'; United
  States
'Amour de la Rue Sablonneuse,
  Un', 79
ancestors *see* dead
'Ancestral Power', 256–7, 302
'And a Threefold Cord', 106,
  110–13, 116, 305

'And the Rain Came Down', 204
Anglophone writers, 9, 148; *see
  also* Achebe; Amadi; Armah;
  Awoonor; Clark; Farah; La
  Guma; Modisane; Mphahlele;
  Ngugi; Okigbo; Okpewho;
  Omotoso; Osofisan; Soyinka
Anlos people, 238, 255
apartheid, resistance to, 105–6;
  see also Bantu Education; La
  Guma; Mphahlele
Arc Musical, L', 159, 163–6, 311
Armah, Ayi Kwei, 10, 180, 228,
  249–51, 283, 302
Arrow of God, 127, 131–7, 140,
  268, 301
'As the Manatees go to Drink at
  the Source', 36
assassination, 118; *see also*
  violence
'Assassination', 37
assimilation, 17–38, 42–3
'At the Portagees', 110, 305
autobiography, *see Blame me on
  History; Down Second Avenue;
  Enfant Noir; Wanderers; Weep
  not, Child*
Awoonor, Kofi, 8, 10, 147, 166,
  178, 236–60, 302, 316

Bacchae, The, 233–4, 310
Balandier, Georges, 30
'Ballade', 26
Banjo, 70

Bantu Education Act, 43, 48–9,
    51; *see also* education
'Barber of Bariga, The', 57
*Beautyful Ones are not yet Born,
    The*, 180, 250, 302
'been-to', 96, 180, 225; *see also*
    exile
Beier, Ulli, 63, 107, 258, 313
Bennett, Tony, 12
Beti, Mongo, 7, 75, 192–215;
    attitudes, 14, 41, 85, 234; and
    journal, 314; studies of, 11;
    works of, 302–3
'Beware Soul Brother', 143, 301
Biafra, *see* war, Nigerian
Birago, Diop, 148, 159, 316
birth, 156; *see also* mother
birth-cord ritual, 237
Biyidi-Awala, Alexandre *see* Beti
'Black-African Civilization', 30
Black Label, 23
Black Orpheus, 63, 107, 305, 313,
    315
Black Zionism, 48
blackness *see* negritude
Blair, Prof. D., 98, 102
Blaxall, Dr Arthur, 48
Bognini, Joseph, 148
Borom Sarratt, 79–80
Bouts de Bois de Dieu, Les, 68,
    72–6, 309
Brathwaite, Edward, 188
Brazzaville Conference, 19
Breast of the Earth, The, 236,
    258–60, 302
Brecht, Bertold, 12, 303
Bunuel, 81

Cahier, 23
Cameroun, 192, 209; *see also* Beti
Camille, Roussan, 24
Ceddu, 83, 309
Cercle des Tropiques, Le, 98, 304
Cerina, Lacwaa, 173
Césaire, Aimé, 22–4, 151

'Chaka', 167–8, 234
change, primacy of, 69–83
'Chant de Printemps', 26–8
Chants d'Ombre, 16, 25, 28, 309
Chants pour Naëtt, 32, 35
chants *see* songs
Chardin, Teilharde de, 30
'*Chi* in Igbo Cosmology', 144
'Chike's Schooldays', 140
childhood, 33, 124, 157, 269; *see
    also* autobiography
children, 264–5; *see also* mother
Chin'daba see Transition
Christ, references to, 152–3, 155,
    158, 161, 165, 267–8; *see also*
    religion
'Civil Peace', 140, 142
'Civilization Negro-Africaine, La',
    30
Clark, John Pepper, 7, 47, 148,
    303–4, 313, 316
Classic, The (New), 313
Climbié, 19, 304
colonialism, 31, 85–6, 89, 279; *see
    also* war
'Colonialist Criticism', 144
colour symbolism, 250
Comes the Voyager at Last, 250–2
Communism, 104–6; *see also*
    Marxism
Conch, The, 313
Congo, 146–69
Congo, Le, 146, 157
Conrad, 278–9
'Corbillard, Le', 157
'Coups de Pilon', 10, 304
'Creatures, The', 113
criticism, literary, 8–12, 52, 63–5,
    144–5, 258–9, 301–11 *passim*,
    313–16
Criticism and Ideology, 12

Dadié, Bernard, 19, 304
Dakar Conference, 64
Damas, Léon, 22–4, 31, 304

Dance of the Forests, A, 218–19, 310

dancing, 154–5, 172, 174, 179, 185–7; *see also* music

Dark Child see Enfant Noir

Dathorne, Ronald, 8, 304

dead, communion with, 28–9, 33

death: ceremonies, 240–6, 249–50; Christian, 239; imagery, 154–64; *see also* dirge; elegy; suicide

Death and the King's Horseman, 218, 221–7, 310

Defoe, Daniel, 123

Delafosse, Maurice, 30

Devoir de Violence, Le, 144

dialogue *see* speech

Diola language, 82

Diop, Alioune, 20, 314

Diop, David, 9, 22, 24, 85, 148, 304

Dipoko, Mbella, 148

'Dirge, A', 241

dirges, 240–5; *see also* death

Docker Noir, Le, 68, 70–1, 79, 309

Down Second Avenue, 40–7, 52–3, 60, 65, 306

drama, 146, 167–9, 226–7, 233, 256–7, 286–8, 301–11 *passim*; *see also* films

dramatists *see* Amadi; Awoonor; Clark; Hussein; Omofoso; Osofisan; Soyinka; U Tamsi

Dramouss, 97–8, 102–3, 306

Dream of Africa see Dramouss

dreams, 95, 99–102; *see also* symbolism

Drum magazine, 40, 49–50, 52, 60–1

Duerden, Dennis, 314, 316

Dyali, *see* griot

Eagleton, Terry, 12, 304

'Easter Dawn', 239, 242

Eboue, Ginette, 35

education: abroad, 87–90, 193; and alienation, 237–8; boarding, 48, 51; French, 19–23, 30, 148–9, 192, 194; and liberation, 263–70; *see also* Bantu

Egudu, Romanus, 147

Ekpe, 253, 258

Ekwensi, Cyprian, 14, 123

'Elégie de Minuit', 35

elegy, 252, 257; *see also* death

Emitai, 79, 83, 234, 309

Enfant Noir, L', 84, 87–90, 237, 306

English speaking writers *see* Anglophone

epic novels, 86, 95, 205, 210–15

Epic of Sundiata, The, 95

Epitomé, 153–4, 157–9, 162–7, 311

'Equinoxiale', 156–7

essays *see* criticism

estrangement, 88, 237–8

Ethiopiques, 28, 32, 34, 309

'Etiage', 155–6

Ewe: people, 147, 178, 238, 254; poetry, 240–5, 253, 258–9

exile, 98; in Asia, 254; in Britain, 104, 151–2; in France, 22–3, 28, 30, 148–9, 158–9, 161–5, 192, 194; in Guinea, 89–90; in Kenya, 187; in Nigeria, 51–2, 65; in reserve, 43–4; in Senegal, 84, 88, 98, 103; from South Africa, 51; in USA, 51, 65, 251–2, 256; *see also* 'been-to'

exoticism, 36

'Eyes of the Statue, The', 99, 101

Facing Mount Kenya, 266–9

Fagunwa, 14

Fall, Malick, 9, 304

Fantoure, Alioum, 98, 304

Farah, Nuruddin, 8, 305

fate, 54, 79, 110, 114

father image, 149–50

Feu de Brousse, 149–55, 162, 165, 311
films, 79–83, 309–10; *see also* drama
'First Shot', 143
Fodeba, Keita, 98
'For Pablo Nemda', 254–5
Formalism and Marxism, 12
Fragments, 228, 249–50, 302
France: and Beti, 192, 194; Laye in, 89–90; Ousmane in, 69–71; and Senegal, 18–21; and Senghor, 16–17, 21, 28–31, 37; and U Tam'si, 148–9, 158–65; *see also* education exile
Francophone writers, 9, 148; *see also* Beti; Dadié; Damas; Diop; Fantouré; Kane; Kourouma; Laye; Oyono; Sembène; Senghor; U Tam'si
French language, 20, 25–7, 148; *see also* Francophone
Frobenius, 13
Fugard, Athol, 119
Fula language, 20
'Funeral Flamenco', 161
future, 227–31

Garvey, Marcus, 48
Ghana, 247–9; *see also* Awoonor
Gikuyu language, 278, 286, 288
Girls at War, 140–2, 301
'Glass of Wine, A', 107, 110, 305
God's Bits of Wood see Bouts de Bois
gods and man, 221
Golding, William, 115
'Gone with the Drought', 264
'Good-bye Africa', 277
Grain of Wheat, A, 76, 262–5, 272–81
Green, Peter, 202
Griaule, Marcel, 30
'Grieg on a Stolen Piano', 57–8, 110

griot (poet-musician), 20, 26, 36, 79, 84, 103, 163
'Gros Sang, Le', 151
Guadaloupe, 24
Guèye, Lamine, 20
Guiana, 22, 24
Guinea, Upper, 77–8, 98; *see also* Laye

Hardy, Thomas, 128
Hare and Hornbill, 175, 309
Harmattan, L', 72, 77–8, 82–3, 309
'He and the Cat', 53–4, 57
heat, 113–14
Heavensgate, 237
history and myths, 217–35
Homecoming, 145, 264, 279
Horn of my Love, The, 175, 309
Hosties Noirs, 16, 29–32, 309
House by the Sea, The, 253–5, 302
Hussein, Ebrahim, 8, 305

'I Heard a Bird Cry', 243, 257, 259
Idanre, 159, 310
identification, 96
Ife people, 14
Igbo: language, 130–1; people, 124–36, 140, 144, 147
imagery, 32–3, 36, 151–62, 174–7, 188; *see also* lyricism; myths; symbolism
immediacy, 87–8
In Corner B, 52–3, 57–9, 307
'In Memoriam', 28–9
In the Fog of the Season's End, 106–7, 115–18, 305
independence, 77–8, 98; *see also* war
individualism, 267
Inheritors, The, 115
Interpreters, The, 137, 219, 310
interviews with writers, 316
Irele, Abiola, 26, 313
isolation, 22–3, 154, 166; *see also* exile

Ivory Coast, 19

Jahn, Janheinz, 8, 26, 305, 316
Jeyifo, Biodun, 217, 235
Joachim, Paulin, 148
Johannesburg Star, The, 53
Johnston, Rev. Samuel, 224
Journal of Commonwealth Literature, 313
journals, 313–14; in Cameroun, 209; in Congo, 82, 146, 148; in France, 192, 194, 213, 303, 314; in Ghana, 216, 222, 236, 313; in Kenya, 264; in Nigeria, 107, 167, 250, 305, 313; at Nsukka, 122, 143, 250, 314; radical, 106; in South Africa, 40, 49–50, 52–3, 60–1, 313; in Uganda, 216, 222, 313

Kaddu, 82, 148
Kafka, 94, 97
Kamerun! Kamerun!, 148
Kane, Hamidon, 9, 305, 316
Kenya, 262–88
Kenyatta, Jomo, 265–7
Kibiru, Mugo wa, 265
Kimathi, Dedan, 264
King Lazarus see Roi
Kirkup, James, 90
Kourama, Ahmadou, 9, 89, 99, 305
Kunene, Mazisi, 147, 178, 258–60

La Guma, Alex, 59, 63, 104–20, 305–6
Ladipo, Duro, 225
Lak Tar Kinyero Wi Lobo, 173, 308
lament *see* dirge
'Lament of the Silent Sister', 257, 302
landscape imagery, 152–8, 255
Lango language, 173

'Language and the Destiny of Man', 144
languages: Acoli, 173–5, 178; Diola, 82; Fula, 20; Gikuyu, 278, 286, 288; Lango, 173; Lwo, 171, 175–7, 187; Manding, 20; Wolof, 20, 69, 82–3; Zulu, 178; *see also* Anglophone; Francophone; speech
Larson, Charles, 11, 306
Laye, Camara, 7, 42, 44, 84–103, 124, 237, 306, 316
'Legs', 166
Leslie, Omolara, 235
'Letter to a Poet', 23–4
'Lettres de l'Hivernage', 35–6, 309
Liberté I, 16
Lindfors, Prof. Bernth, 53, 314–16
Lion and the Jewel, The, 221, 310
Living and Dead, The, 52–7, 63, 110, 307
'Longest Journey, The', 242
Lord, Albert, 306
loss, sense of, 148–50, 155; *see also* exile
'Love Song', 143
Lumumba, Patrice, 157, 161
Lwo language, 171, 175–7, 187
lyricism, 269, 284; *see also* imagery

Macebuh, Stanley, 11, 306
Mackay, Claude, 70
Madmen and Specialists, 219–21, 310
magazines *see* journals
Main Basse sur le Cameroun, 194, 213
'Mal, Le', 150
Malinke civilization, 95, 102–3
Man Died, The, 235
Man Must Live, 40, 52–3, 57
Man of the People, A, 122, 136–40, 144–5, 301

Mandat, Le, 76, 79–80, 309
Manding language, 20
Mao tse Tung, 231, 255–6
'March, Kind Comrade, Abreast Him', 244
'Marriage is a Private Affair', 140
Martinique *see* Césaire
Marxism, 11–12, 15, 304, 314; *see also* Communism; Ousmane; politicia
'Master of Doornvlei, The', 55, 57
Mathenge, Stanley, 264
Matip, Benjamin, 193
Matshikiza, Todd, 49
Maurras, Charles, 30
Mauvais Sang, Le, 146–51, 167, 311
metaphors, extended, 188
Mission Terminée (Mission to Kala), 201–5, 210–11, 302
missionaries *see* religion
Modisane, Bloke, 49–50, 306
Money Order, The, see Mandat
moon imagery, 156
Morning Yet on Creation Day, 144, 301
Morton-Williams, Peter, 229
mother, importance of, 73, 148–50, 155–7, 184, 264, 270–1; *see also* children; woman
'Mother and Child', 143
Motsisi, Casey, 49
Mphahlele, Ezekiel, 40–66, 110, 306–7, 316
'Mrs Plum', 58–9, 63
'Mugumo', 264
music, 154–5, 172–5, 178–81, 185–7, 278, 288
Mwindo Epic, The, 86
My Life in the Bush of Ghosts, 10, 311
Myth of the Bagre, The, 86, 102
Myth, Literature and the African World, 144, 217
myths, 217–35

Naipaul, V. S., 144
nature *see* landscape
negritude, 17–38, 64; *see also* Africanity
Neo-African culture, 305
Neruda, Pablo, 254
Neto, Agostinho, 17
New Age, 106
'New York', 32–3, 37
Ngugi wa, *see* Thiong'o
Niger, Paul, 24
Nigeria, 10, 122–45 *passim*, 222; *see also* Soyinka; war
Night of my Blood, 236, 241–4, 252, 302
'Night Rain', 47
'Nim Trees in the Cemetery, The', 239, 243
Nketia, Prof. J., 258
Nkosi, Lewis, 49, 316
Nkrumah, Kwame, 244, 247, 256
No Longer at Ease, 127–31, 140–1, 301
Nocturnes, 34–6, 309–10
nomads, 181–2
'Notes de Veille', 167, 311
'Novelist as Teacher, The', 144
novelists *see* Achebe; Amadi; Armah; Awoonor; Beti; Dadié; Fantouré; Kourouna; La Guma; Laye; Okpewho; Omotoso; Osofisan; Ousmane; Oyono; Soyinka; Tutuola
novels: first English, 123; lack of, 59–60
'Nuit de Sine', 25, 37
numbers and divination, 246–50
Nxumalo, Harry, 49, 61
Nyerere, Julius, 232
Nyobe, Ruben um, 193

O Pays, Mon Beau Peuple!, 72–3 82, 309
'O Roots!', 232
Oba Waja, 225

observation, 195, 197
Oculi, Okello, 147
Ogun Abibiman, 234, 310
Okara, Gabriel, 148, 316
Okigbo, Christopher, 7, 38, 136, 148, 237, 259, 307; elegy for, 252, 257–8
Okike, 122, 143, 250, 301, 314
Okpewho, Isidore, 11, 13–14, 307–8
Okyeame, 236
Omotoso, Kole, 7, 218, 235, 308
Opera Wonyosi, 235
oral poetry, 258; *see also* Ewe
origins, 155, 237
Osofisan, Femi, 7, 218, 235, 308
Oswald, Pierre-Jean, 163
Ousmane, Sembène, 14, 64, 68–83, 85, 148, 234, 263, 309, 316
Oyono, Ferdinand, 7, 41, 193, 308

Palm-wine Drinkard, The, 10, 311
Palmer, Eustace, 11, 308
Pan-African Congress, 17
'Paris in the Snow', 37
parody, 220
past, 209
'Path of Thunder', 136
Pauvre Christ de Bomba, Le, 192, 197–201, 205, 209, 211, 302
p'Bitek, Okot, 10–11, 147, 166, 170–90, 243, 260, 308–9
Penpoint, 264
People are Living There, 119
People of the City, 123
periodicals, *see* journals
Perpétue, 210–15, 303
Petals of Blood, 75, 264, 279–86
Peters, Lenrie, 148
Peuples Noirs, Peuples Africains, 192, 194, 213, 303, 314
Pieterse, Cosmo, 256, 316
plagiarism, 97
poetry, 316
poets: categorized, 147–8; traditional, 178; *see also*

Achebe; Awoonor; Clark; Okigbo; p'Bitek; Senghor; Soyinka; U Tam'si
politician, writer as, 16–17, 20, 35–7, 104–7; *see also* Communism; Marxism
Poor Christ of Bomba see Pauvre
Positive Review, 314
'Pour Khalam', 34
'Pourquoi donc dieu est-il mort?', 165
'Prayer for Peace', 31–2
'Présence', 152–4
Présence Africaine, 192, 314
prison: Awoonor in, 236, 253, 256; in fiction, 113–15, 183–7; Ngugi in, 266, 286; p'Bitek in, 183–7
prophecy, 95
prostitution, 188–90
psychosis, African, 180–3
punctuation, lack of, 47

'Que M'accompagne Koras et Balafong', 30

racism, 41–62 *passim*, 105–20 *passim*, 164–5
Radiance of the King see Regard du Roi
rain symbolism, 11–12
ranking, 229
'realism', 12–14
reconciliation theme, 17, 32, 267
redeemer theme, 263, 265, 271–2, 283–5
Rediscovery, 239, 242–3, 259, 302
Reed, J., 25–6, 37
Regard du Roi, Le, 84, 90–7, 306
religion, Christian, 165, 197–201, 206–9, 226–9, 267, 271; *see also* Christ
Remember Ruben, 75, 205, 210–15, 234, 281, 283, 303
Research in African Literature, 314
reserve, tribal, 43–5

'Return, The', 242
'Return of the Prodigal Son, The', 17
return to Africa, 72–3
Revue Camerounaise, La, 209
rhyme, 151, 173–4, 188
rhythm, 34, 151, 173–4
Ride me, Memory, 252, 256, 302
Rimbaud, Arthur, 149–51
ritual, 228
River Between, The, 132–3, 264–5, 269, 277
river imagery, 153
Road, The, 219–21, 310
Roi Miraculé, Le, 201, 205–9, 211, 303
romanticism, 73, 265, 267
Roumain, Jacques, 24
Ruine Frescue Cocasse d'un Polichinelle, La, 213

sacrifice, 268
sadism, 200, 214
salvation, 239; *see also* redeemer
'Salvation', 239–40, 243
Samory, 20, 103
Sampson, Anthony, 49
'Sans Haine et Sans Amour', 192
Sartre, Jean-Paul, 16, 315
satire, 137, 197, 252, 256
sea images, 238
Season of Anomy, 219, 221, 227–33, 310
Secret Lives, 264
self-irony, 159
Senegal, 10, 18–20; *see also* Diop, David; Ousmane; Senghor
Senghor, Léopold Sédar, 16–38, 148, 159, 164, 167; attitudes, 12–13, 42–3; and Ousmane, 69; studies of, 11; works of, 309–10
Senghor: Prose and Poetry, 25, 310
sexuality, 94–6, 102, 157, 200, 257–8
Sheffield Papers on African Literature, 314
Shuttle in the Crypt, A, 232, 310
'Signe du Mauvais Sang, Le', *see Mauvais Sang*
Siren Limits, 259
Slave, The, 141, 301
'Slipper Satin', 107, 305
Smuts, Jan, 48, 105
Soleils des Indépendences, Les, 89, 95, 99–102, 305
Song of Lawino, 170–9, 187, 309
'Song of Malaya', 188–90, 309
Song of Ocol, 179–83, 309
'Song of Prisoner', 183–90, 309
'Song of War', 242
songs, 173–5, 178–81, 278, 288; *see also* chants
'Songs of Abuse', 252–3
'Songs of Sorrow', 242, 259
South Africa *see* journals; La Guma; Mphahlele
Soyinka, Wole, 7, 10, 137, 216–35; essays of, 144, 283; interviewed, 316; on Laye, 97; imagery of, 159, 162; on 'self-apprehension', 29, 86; studies of, 11; works of, 310
speech, written: appropriate, 221; Nigerian, 131–2, 138; poetic, 230; South African, 59, 61–3, 110; unrealistic, 60–1
Stone Country, The, 113–15, 117, 305
Strong Breed, The, 219, 310
Sudan, Western, 20, 86
suicide, 222–6; *see also* death
'Suitcase, The', 54–5
Surrealism, 151
symbolism, 44, 75, 90–7, 102, 249–50; *see also* dreams; imagery

Tati-Loutard, Jean-Baptiste, 148
'Tattoo-Marks and Nails', 113, 305

teaching, 48–9, 192; *see also* education

Tell Freedom, 44

Theory of Literary Production, 12

Things Fall Apart, 122–33, 301

Thiong'o, Ngugi wa, 11, 75–6, 132–3, 145, 262–88, 307

This Earth, my Brother, 237–8, 244–9, 302

Thompson, Robert Farris, 154

Three Plays, 216, 303

Threefold Cord see And a

Tirolien, Guy, 24

Time of the Butcherbird, 118–20, 305

torture, 116

'Totem', 23

totems, 101

train image, 75–6

Transition, 216, 222, 313

translation, 23, 90, 175–6

treason trial, 115–18

Trial of Dedan Kimathi, The, 286–8

Trials of Brother Jero, The, 221, 310

Tutuola, Amos, 10, 14, 123, 311

Two Songs, 183–90, 309

Two Thousand Seasons, 283, 302

U Tam'si, Tchicaya, 10, 146–69, 237, 311, 316

Uganda *see* p'Bitek

Uhuru, 277, 280

'Uncle Jonathan', 252–3

United States, 41–2, 254; *see also* exile; 'New York'

'universalism', 144

urban life, 41–66, 108–11, 189, 195; *see also* Ville

Vehi-Ciosane, 72, 76, 78–9, 82, 309

'Vengeful Creditor', 140, 142

Ventre, Le, 159–63, 165, 311

'Ventre Reste, Le', 162–3

Veste d'Interieur, La, 165–7, 311

Ville Cruelle, 192, 194–7, 205, 302

violence, 116, 118, 200, 214, 251

Voices in the Whirlwind, 52

Voltaïque, 79

Vwène le Fondateur, 167

Wake, C., 25–6, 37

Walk in the Night, A, 59, 104–11, 305

Wanderers, The, 51–2, 59–63, 306

war: colonial, 31; in Congo, 153–4, 157–61; Kenyan Independence, 270–3; Nigerian Civil, 122, 136, 140–3, 159, 216; Second World, 31

'Wayfarer Comes Home, The', 255

'We have Found a New Land', 242

'Weaver Bird, The', 242

Weep not, Child, 263–5, 269–72

'We'll Have Dinner at Eight', 54–5

Wer pa Lawino, 170–8, 309

whale image, 245

'What Song Shall We Sing?', 242, 244

White Genesis see Vehi-Ciosane

whiteness, obsession with, 180

Why I Ran Away, 50

Wild Conquest, 44–5

Wolof language, 20, 69, 82–3

woman: compassion for, 264–5; as iconoclast, 77–8; new, 75, 78–9, 81; role of, 73–4, 180–1; *see also* mother

Wonodi, Okogbule, 147

Xala, 72, 76, 79–83, 309

Yambo, 144

'Years Behind, The', 242–3

Yeats, 124, 224–6

Yondo, E., 148

Yoruba people, 140, 221, 226–33, 258

Zulu, Le, 167–9, 311

Zulu people, 147, 178